MW00474489

THE GRIFT

The **Downward Spiral** *of* **Black Republicans** *from the* **Party** *of* **Lincoln** *to the* **Cult** *of* **Trump**

CLAY CANE

 sourcebooks

ONE STREET BOOKS

Copyright © 2024 by Clay Cane
Cover and internal design © 2024 by Sourcebooks
Cover design by Pete Garceau
Cover images © Bakai/Getty Images
Internal design by Tara Jaggers/Sourcebooks

This publication is designed to provide accurate and authoritative information in regard to the subject matter covered. It is sold with the understanding that the publisher is not engaged in rendering legal, accounting, or other professional service. If legal advice or other expert assistance is required, the services of a competent professional person should be sought. —*From a Declaration of Principles Jointly Adopted by a Committee of the American Bar Association and a Committee of Publishers and Associations*

Published by Sourcebooks in association with One Street Books
P.O. Box 4410, Naperville, Illinois 60567-4410
(630) 961-3900
sourcebooks.com
onestreetbooks.com

Cataloging-in-Publication Data is on file with the Library of Congress.

Printed and bound in the United States of America.
MA 10 9 8 7 6 5 4 3 2 1

Contents

INTRODUCTION

"Every minority and every people has its share of opportunists, traitors, freeloaders, and escapists."

—Dr. Martin Luther King Jr.[1]

WHAT IS THE GRIFT? A GRIFTER, TECHNICALLY, IS A CON ARTIST or a scammer. In other words, a hustler or a sellout. I define grifters as opportunists who shape-shift for personal gain to achieve proximity to power. Yes, there are grifters of every background in all political parties, but the Black Republican grift is on an insidious rise.

In the days after the Civil War, being a Black Republican meant something vastly different than today. The pillars of Black Republicanism were a balanced critique of both political parties, civil rights for all Americans, reinventing an economy based on exploitation, and, most importantly, building thriving Black communities. Contrary to today's historical mythmaking, President Abraham Lincoln and the Republican Party weren't steadfast supporters of Black Americans. It was visionaries like Frederick Douglass, a formerly enslaved person, who disrupted the Grand Old Party (GOP) to achieve important victories for Black citizens.

Over time, the relentlessness of white supremacy and early prototypes of grifters unwound those victories. Political parties shifted. Once the party of enslavers, the Democratic Party became the home of progressive reforms, and the Republican Party embraced bigotry. All the while, the Black Republican grift deepened, growing more sinister. Today, a pernicious strain of Black Republicans has seized influence by disregarding the interests of Black voters for their advancement. The evolution of Black Republicans from the party of Lincoln to the cult of Trump and their journey through emancipation, Reconstruction, segregation, integration, and to today are the subject of this book.

Is every Black Republican created equal? No, and not all Black Republicans are grifters. Colin Powell, a four-star U.S. Army general, spoke the truth about racism in the GOP, even when it hurt his political career. Many of the Black Republicans during President Richard Nixon's era were sincerely invested in positive change for Black communities and denounced white Republicans when promises weren't kept. Others are more complicated, and their trajectories are unique. Like Madam Secretary Condoleezza Rice, an accomplished scholar and former provost at Stanford University, who, like Powell, led American foreign policy at the highest level. But arguably, Rice contributed to the downward spiral of Black Republicanism by being an apologist for the GOP.

This is not to say Black people do not hold conservative views, regardless of their political party. While I may use *conservative* and *Republican* interchangeably, I have no intention of settling the debate over what it means to be a conservative. Many argue that although Powell was a Republican, he was not a true conservative. Others will say his temperament may not be typical of a hardline conservative; when it came to the issues of the 1990s—like opposing President Bill Clinton lifting the ban on gay people in the military or leading the first war against Iraq—he was most definitely conservative.

Even so, this is *not* a book about Black voters. I am not examining Black voters who own guns, express concerns about immigration policies, or have grown exhausted with Democrats. They are not grifters motivated by maintaining a congressional seat or lining their pockets. Furthermore, you can vote Democratic and still be conservative.

Throughout my career, I've had personal encounters with grifters. When my SiriusXM radio show launched in November 2017, my first guest was a Black Republican. I had hoped to engage with someone on the opposite side of the aisle. I had never heard of this person before the Trump era. Starting in 2015, he earned a reputation as a consistent defender of Trump on cable news and for going viral on social media. It didn't take long before I realized attempting a rational conversation was futile. He argued Trump was not racist and insisted that his tax bill would benefit the middle class. On social issues like same-sex marriage, he remarked, "Sanctity of marriage is rooted in the Bible." In fact, according to him, the LGBTQ community had no place in the church whatsoever. "If you want to change that," he asserted, "don't be a part of that faith."

He was a sincere Republican and had a record of working with the GOP, but I wasn't convinced he believed his Trump talking points. He appeared to be reading from a script. Over the course of the interview, I was obviously talking to a fact-averse border wall, built by Trump but originally constructed over decades of Republicanism. There was no nuance or logic, but my guest had found a profitable, grifting lane and basked in Twitter mentions from the forty-fifth president. It was clear to me he was happy with the space he secured on cable news and that producers were elated to return the favor by giving him airtime because he was a Black man willing to defend Trump. He was exactly what Republicans and a subset of news media craved. It was a gimmick that worked (for a few years at least) and briefly made him a star in the clickbait world of punditry.

My second guest was an openly gay, Black combat veteran. He couldn't be more different from the first guest. We were long-time acquaintances and mutually supported each other's projects over the years. Before coming on my SiriusXM show, he had recently appeared on CNN, blasting the Trump administration for attempting to ban transgender troops. On my airwaves, we engaged in the same discussion; he said about the administration, "They are coming for the trans people now; they could come for any of us next."

He also called out how veterans are represented as "always white, always male."

After the interview, we sat down for lunch and traded horror stories about our various gigs. He was all over the media game for years, including a brief stint on reality television, but his career never took off. He congratulated me for landing a radio program at SiriusXM. In media, especially in 2017, there was only room for a few Black voices. *How are you different from your Black colleagues who have similar talking points? What makes you special?* were questions I and so many others heard from white and Black higher-ups.

A few months later, he sent me a text message saying he wanted to return to SiriusXM to break some news. I was curious how he could "break news," considering he wasn't well known enough for anyone to care about breaking news from him. He revealed he intended to "come out" as a conservative. I was scratching my head.

This was a Black gay man who handcuffed himself to the White House gate over the military's "don't ask, don't tell" policy, which banned troops from serving their country as openly gay. Later that year, when President Barack Obama repealed "don't ask, don't tell," he talked about the joy he experienced shaking Obama's hand.

This was a Black gay man who was just on my show a few months before, condemning the Trump administration over their treatment of transgender soldiers. For all the years I had known him, I was unaware he supported Republican policies.

Via text, I asked why he was coming out as a conservative. He replied, in a message I still have, "You have to understand from a consumer's perspective it's far more interesting hearing different points of view and not just people agreeing with each other all the time in an echo chamber."

I declined to bring him on the show. I didn't want any part of his coming out. "If you are doing it for that reason and it's not one thousand percent real," I told him, "then it will backfire." I had no desire to participate in a verbal battle on air with someone I had known for years who was, in my opinion, now willing to transmogrify his beliefs in the hopes of appealing to a "consumer's perspective."

As someone who has worked in broadcasting and politics for years, I saw how he rationalized his decision. The road to success or stability for Black journalists, commentators, and politicians is much longer if you are progressive. I've witnessed downtrodden colleagues pitch the idea of a miraculous conversion to Republicanism, hoping their careers would soar, especially financially. Regardless of your credentials or degrees, after years of scrambling to find a foothold in politics or media, the temptation to sell one's soul is real—but there is a price to be paid for grifting. You must be willing to dishonor your community regardless of facts and history. Grifting is a betrayal; some people become political superstars like South Carolina senator Tim Scott. Others, like former Trump sympathizer Omarosa Manigault Newman, go on the apology tour or become a lying laughingstock like former NFL player Herschel Walker, an unsuccessful candidate for the U.S. Senate in Georgia.

By May 2018, my former friend managed to have his coming out written up in a tabloid. His Twitter followers skyrocketed, he became a frequent guest on Fox News, and he was considered a prominent voice among Black Trump supporters. With his transformation complete, I predict he will eventually run for political office and GOP wallets will open up for his grift.

I have since seen him and others labeled with slurs like "Uncle Tom" or claims that they are no longer Black. While we are no longer friends, he did not cease to be Black. It's important to stress that Black Republicans should not be demonized as "coons," "Uncle Toms," or "Oreos," all language that I reject. Being a Republican does not erase Black identity. Denying their Blackness dismisses and simplifies the threat. I prefer, taking a cue from legendary author Zora Neale Hurston, all my skin folk ain't my kinfolk.[2]

In Black communities, terms like "house Negroes" or having a "plantation mentality" are used to label people who are considered sellouts. It is important to explore the historical background of these terms and why they should not be used to describe someone on either side of the political aisle.

During chattel slavery, when enslaved people were plotting a revolt, the prevailing fear wasn't just that the white enslaver would discover their plan; it was that another enslaved person would betray them. These fears had a strong basis in reality. In Richmond, Virginia, Gabriel Prosser was planning an uprising in an area where Black people outnumbered whites. After months of preparation, Prosser hoped to end slavery in the commonwealth by leading hundreds of armed, enslaved people to take control of the Virginia State Armory and the Virginia State Capitol. The day the revolt was to take place, August 30, 1800, two enslaved people told their white master—and it was all over. Prosser, his two brothers, and over twenty others were hanged. The reward for the two enslaved people who told their master? They were gifted freedom.[3] Twenty-six Black people were killed and countless others probably tortured for two Black men to be granted their freedom.[4]

Denmark Vesey, a free Black man in Charleston, South Carolina, was inspired by the Haitian Revolution, which resulted in Haiti becoming the first Black sovereign nation in 1804. In 1822, after over a year of strategizing with enslaved and free Black people, the plan was to attack the Charleston Meeting Street Arsenal, retrieve the weapons, and sail a boat to Haiti.[5] The uprising was foiled after two enslaved people, George Wilson and Joe LaRoche, warned their master. Wilson "professed loyalty to his master and enjoyed an unimpeachable reputation among Blacks and whites."[6]

An unimpeachable reputation…

These betrayals are behind the accusations of "plantation mentality" or "house Negro"—the willingness to trade "an unimpeachable reputation" for the lives and freedoms of people who look like you.

It's central that we do not lose track of the context that shaped these decisions. The enslaved people who sold out Denmark Vesey and Gabriel Prosser lived in a state of fear. They were controlled and weakened by a system that prevented them from seeing a future. That's why I nix the notion that Black Republicans have a "slave mentality." To explain away current Black Republican grifters as merely having a slave mentality minimizes their conscious and corrosive schemes for power. They are *not* trapped in a system of slavery. The fact that they are free to choose to act in ways that elevate themselves over the needs of the rest of their community is what makes them so vile—*not* enslaved.

These terms have a parallel on the other side of the aisle. Black Republicans often spat "Democratic plantation" to flip the accusation back onto their opponents. This is equally disgusting. The language is not only wildly racist but perverts the history of enslaved people in the United States.

I am not calling for every Black person to think alike or to vote Democratic, especially in local elections. Nor do I believe Democrats are above critique. The Democratic Party is not free of racist policies or supporters, considering conservatism is evidenced in the ideological makeup of both major political parties. That said, as of January 2023, over fifty-three Black men and women serve in the House of Representatives, forty-nine as Democrats. There is little to no diversity in the Republican Party. Currently, there isn't one Black Republican woman, and only four Black Republican men (Burgess Owens of Utah, Byron Donalds of Florida, John James of Michigan, and Wesley Hunt of Texas) are in the House of Representatives. The one and only Black Republican woman to hold a seat in the House is Mia Love of Utah. She was voted out in 2018.[7] In the U.S. Senate, Tim Scott of South Carolina is the only Black Republican and only the third Black Republican in the Senate's history.

The Black Republicans of today—regardless of how much the

GOP selectively references Frederick Douglass—are not what I call Douglass Republicans, leaders who placed Black interests at the forefront, which required building and being held accountable within Black communities. The Black Republicans of today do not foster coalitions in Black communities. Their building, whether in the Senate, the House of Representatives, or the media, is for the support of white conservatives, especially the white men who are power players in the GOP. As you will learn in this book, those who attempted to organize alliances with Black communities suffered political consequences.

Another distinction is that the original Black Republicans fought for and supported policies that were race-conscious or race-specific. Today's Black Republicans call for race-neutral or color-blind legislation; those who don't quickly lose power. There is no space for Black people who strive to advance Black interests in the GOP. As Black Republican and former Oklahoma representative J. C. Watts said once he was no longer in office, "Republicans, conservatives, I think the issue on the right is that they do not allow an African American to be Republican, conservative, and Black. They say you've got to be one or the other. And I think it's very difficult for African Americans to say, 'You expect me to denounce the experiences that I've had.'"[8]

The folks willing to denounce those experiences and take the grift as far as it goes stand to join the most influential and high-profile people in government or media. As Frederick Douglass remarked about Isaiah Montgomery, a trailblazing grifter who voted against Black suffrage in 1890, others will be "dazzled by the fame" and "probably imitate his bad example."[9] Frederick Douglass was prophesying. There is celebrity, money, reward, and, for some, considerable power for those willing to exploit their own. While modern-day Black Republican grifters aren't primarily to blame for the party's demise or for white supremacy in politics, nor are they stronger than white anti-Blackness, they are enablers. Anyone upholding white supremacy is dangerous, especially if they reach a level of power.

Justice Clarence Thomas is one of the most powerful Black men in the country, a frightening thought for anyone concerned about voting rights, affirmative action, fair housing, criminal justice, the right to privacy, and other issues that affect marginalized communities. His ascension is astounding, and his rulings on the court have been downright treacherous. This Black man on the Supreme Court, who replaced Thurgood Marshall, cemented his legacy as one of the most anti–civil rights justices on the nation's highest court.

South Carolina senator Tim Scott, currently the only Black Republican in the U.S. Senate, is a case study in the opportunism of the grift. He will call on his Blackness for leverage but otherwise opposes issues important to most Black communities: voting rights,[10] health care,[11] the George Floyd Justice in Policing Act, and even the commission on the January 6 insurrection.[12] Yet his "unimpeachable reputation" will keep him in office.

In 2021, Winsome Sears stayed the course from grifting to real power. With her only meaningful political experience being two years in the Virginia House of Delegates, nearly twenty years ago, she became the first Black woman elected lieutenant governor of Virginia. Her winning campaign? She posed with an AR-15–style rifle in a campaign ad[13] and ranted that critical race theory teaches "as soon as we see a white person, they are racist."[14] She spread this erroneous claim without regard for the broader impact on public school education and teachers' safety. Not only was she applauded for daring "to leave the plantation of ideology," but she won the election.[15]

Black Republican grifters are on the rise. While some, like YouTube stars, failed actors, and narcissistic rappers, can be dismissed as attention-seeking clowns, others are charting a path to becoming the next protégé of a high-ranking senator or a future Republican president, all under the lie that they are "freethinkers."

Truthfully, Black voters are not as wedded to Democrats as pundits argue, especially considering the largest voting bloc is the nonvoter. The Republican Party refuses to do the necessary work to gain Black voters—if you presume Republican leaders care about Black voters. Instead, the party leaders bargain on remixed forms of the Southern strategy. The architects of the Southern strategy, mainly Barry Goldwater and Richard Nixon, relied on white politicians appealing to their constituents' irrational racism. Who knew that in 2024, not only white politicians but also Black politicians would be vehicles for Southern strategy tactics? Like voter-suppression denier Senator Tim Scott[16] or Herschel Walker, who said before Congress that reparations are "outside the teaching of Jesus Christ."[17] These anti-Black talking points have an epic history. Today's Republican Party is the cult of Trump but also the party that welcomed racism long before Trump rose to political prominence.

Compared to the Black Republicans of today, Black Democrats do markedly different work. Thankfully, this is not the Democratic Party of my father's generation; these are post-Obama Democrats. Lisa Blunt Rochester of Delaware, Ilhan Omar of Minnesota, Ayanna Pressley of Massachusetts, Jamaal Bowman of New York, and Cori Bush of Missouri are just a few who actively push for legislation that will lift all communities while keeping an eye on the nuances of Black issues. They would make revolutionary Black political figures like Frederick Douglass proud.

The history of Black Republicans has been forgotten and mangled by conservative pundits, Black and white, who rant, "Black people used to be Republicans!" In fact, the legacy of Black Republicanism, in the spirit of Douglass, has been distorted for decades by, as Dr. Martin Luther King Jr. said, "opportunists, traitors, freeloaders, and escapists."[18] I would add grifters.

Again, not all Black Republicans are identical. Massachusetts senator Edward William Brooke III, the third Black U.S. senator from 1967 to 1979, has nothing in common with Senator Tim Scott.[19] Former Oklahoma congressman J. C. Watts, who served from 1995 to 2003,[20] cannot be compared to Florida congressman Byron Donalds. The latter advocated overturning the 2020 election,[21] which would have disenfranchised millions of Black voters. There has been a tragic de-evolution of Black Republicans.

The grifters, among other things, provide cover for a political party with anti-Blackness as a policy point. Black people can indeed be anti-Black. Although operating differently from whites who are anti-Black, anyone who holds the water for white supremacy is dangerous. If GOP politics were only a debate about tax cuts, big government, and how robust social safety nets should be, that would be a separate issue—but that's not where Republicanism is today. This is the party that worships in the cult of Trump. Is Trump a cult figure? Two survivors from the 1978 Jonestown massacre under People's Temple leader Jim Jones told me so three months after the January 6, 2021, insurrection.

In April 2021, Jonestown survivor Yulanda Williams said on

my SiriusXM radio show, "He [Donald Trump] is an impulsive liar, just like Jim Jones. He's a control freak, just like Jim Jones." She added, "His [Jim Jones's] spirit was right inside of Donald Trump." Another survivor Leslie Wagner-Wilson, who lost her mother and brother in Jonestown, said, "What if there were social media in the time of People's Temple? How much damage could Jim Jones have done?" Wagner-Wilson hypothesized if Jim Jones ordered his people to storm the U.S. Capitol, they would have followed his orders, explaining, "That's how dedicated and loyal they were to Jim Jones, the same as Trump supporters."[22]

Yet there's a crucial difference. The followers of Jim Jones were victims and vulnerable people who were brainwashed. While Trump is a cult figure, his followers are not brainwashed. They are willing participants, whether part of an insurrection or not, who condoned his behavior with a powerful tool—their vote. In Trump, they found their dear leader who spoke their language, a pattern that the GOP created over decades.

Williams and Wagner-Wilson pointed out a similar one-liner from Trump and Jones. In July 2020, Trump famously insisted, "I've done more for Black people than anyone."[23] Williams recalled, "When he said that, I said, 'Jim Jones, that's what he said to us!'"

Characteristically, the Trump cult also makes grandiose claims. Like another former NFL player, Jack Brewer, who said at the White House during Black History Month in 2022 that Trump was "the first Black president." Brewer suddenly became a Republican in the Trump era. By August 2020, the short-time Republican was speaking at the Republican National Convention, days after he was charged with insider trading by the U.S. Securities and Exchange Commission.[24]

Black people in high places supporting white supremacy

place our democracy in peril. As Ed Kilgore wrote for *New York Magazine*, "The more Black Republicans embrace the same candidates and causes as white racists, the more they become not just acceptable but even preferable to other GOP candidates."[25]

For example, in 2020, Mark Robinson was campaigning to become the first Black lieutenant governor of North Carolina. The former factory worker had gone viral on conservative media outlets for calling former First Lady Michelle Obama "anti-American" and stating that Black Democratic voters were "slaves." He also attacked Black moviegoers for supporting the 2018 movie *Black Panther*. According to him, the character was created "by an agnostic Jew and put to film by [a] satanic Marxist."[26] Nonetheless, in the GOP primary, he was the only Black man in the race and won by a landslide.

In November 2020, Robinson won the general election against Democrat Yvonne Holley, a Black woman and a four-term state representative for Raleigh's District 38, with 51 percent of the vote. An April 2022 survey revealed only 5 percent of Black registered voters approved of his performance.[27] His support among Republicans has only increased after antiabortion rhetoric, his "fight" against critical race theory, and the assertion that there is no systemic racism.[28] This toxic formula gives Robinson a shot at being governor of North Carolina, and others are following his lead at all levels of government.

Black Republican grifters appeal to this constituency within the GOP, who are eager to feel reassured they're not racist. Anyone who challenges their position, especially other Black people, is labeled "the real racist" for attacking "independent thought."

There is also planning within the GOP to grab Black male voters. Steve Bannon, a former senior counselor to Trump who supported overturning the 2020 election, said at an event for Pennsylvania Republicans in November 2021, "African-American males are also another central part of our coalition, and you wait, we're gonna get 50 percent of that vote in 2022…and once we do that…[we] can govern for 100 years."[29] Fifty percent is implausible, but garnering just 25 percent of Black men in 2024 could reshape the electoral college. Black Republicans are another hope to bait Black men. Many of them are debasing themselves on YouTube, hoping to be discovered and become the next Candace Owens.

Black people are not a monolith, but we must all be a monolith against white supremacy. With impending elections, there are political hacks savagely fighting for material gain as the country is tiptoeing closer to a dictatorship. Black voters, whether they were majority Republican in the 1800s or overwhelmingly Democratic today, are the moral voice of the electorate. Black voters have rescued this democracy many times, but today the fight isn't to save democracy; it's to save humanity. There are bad-faith actors solely fighting for brutal individualism and a power grab. If this were the 1800s, I'd be a Republican. It's 2024, and I vote Democratic— but my loyalty isn't to a party; I back the party that defends the most vulnerable and attempts to right past wrongs. The words and actions of today's Black Republican grifters suggest their aim is the opposite. There is a cruelty to conspiring with the enemy to politically hurt your own. They cannot be ignored as harmless buffoons, especially when only one political party embraces and finances liars even when their con is front-page news. They must be called out. In these trying times with an unscrupulous Republican Party, silence is complicity. In the pages ahead, their jaw-dropping scandals, bombastic rhetoric, and histories of dastardly deeds will be examined. Studying these figures and the descent of Black Republicanism allows us to expose the grift and emancipate our future. To quote Ida B. Wells, "The way to right wrongs is to turn the light of truth upon them."[30]

CHAPTER 1

DOUGLASS

"He was preeminently the white man's President, entirely devoted to the welfare of white men."

—Frederick Douglass on President Abraham Lincoln[1]

THE FIRST REPUBLICAN PRESIDENT, ABRAHAM LINCOLN, IS considered one of the greatest presidents in American history.[2] Scholars have built careers analyzing the legacy of the so-called Great Emancipator.[3] The GOP often reminisces about returning to the good old days of the party of Lincoln.[4] One of the most beloved Republicans in history, General Colin Powell, said in 1995, "I believe I can help the party of Lincoln move once again close to the spirit of Lincoln."[5]

Lincoln is valorized as a great beacon of freedom, but let's be clear: Abraham Lincoln was not an abolitionist. He was a stone-cold politician. Without the Black Republicans of the time, Black people may not have seen freedom in 1865. As Chicago pastor Reverend Otis Moss III said, "Lincoln had a position, but [Frederick] Douglass had the power."[7]

To unearth the spirit of righteous, American political

activism—Black or white—for change, look not to Lincoln but to Frederick Douglass. Oft ignored in the annals of history are Douglass Republicans, the Black Republicans of the era, forcefully steering the sixteenth president into emancipation. Learning the origins of Black Republicanism is the first step in understanding the current state of the party. Douglass, who laid the groundwork for Black political thought, and other Black leaders who fought to end slavery represented an enduring vision of upward mobility. This platform included federal and race-conscious measures that enforced voting rights, fair wages, equal access to education, protection from white violence, and the economic rights of formerly enslaved people.

Douglass—the most well-known Black Republican of his era[8]—is the blueprint of Black Republicanism that the current GOP debases. Douglass was born to a white father and an enslaved Black mother, later becoming an abolitionist, orator, newspaper publisher, and author. Today's Republicans would call him a radical, communist, and anti-American, similar to what he heard from Democrats and some Republicans during his time. Amid constant death threats and living under a white terror that few of us could imagine, Douglass lampooned Lincoln when necessary and demanded equality. No amount of proximity to power was worth the price of his soul. If Frederick Douglass could be so courageous in the nineteenth century, it is despicable that today's Republicans—Black and white—refuse to acknowledge the present danger of the majority of the Republican Party, which has been clear since the early days of the Southern strategy. When Powell or any other Republican calls for a return to the party of Lincoln, the genuine aspiration should be the party of Douglass. Douglass was the liberator; he was the emancipator.

Any bit of freedom Black people have achieved is always due to Black lives being on the front lines. It's never been because presidents or delusional politicians suddenly had a come-to-Black-Jesus moment. For Black folks in the 1860s, their war wasn't Democratic, Republican, or partisan politics; all parties had been swords in the souls of their communities. Their fight for freedom centered around strategic decisions that enabled them to battle for their right to exist. Frederick Douglass and Black Republicans were the first progressives, a title that many of today's ahistorical Black Republicans forget or willfully ignore.

Abraham Lincoln and Frederick Douglass's history is nuanced. Douglass is often quoted for affirming comments about Lincoln, but much of their complicated history is ignored, minimizing the ways Douglass held Lincoln's feet to the fire. Above all else, Douglass understood that Lincoln was "preeminently the white man's President, entirely devoted to the welfare of white men."[9]

As an Illinois congressman, Lincoln supported and enforced the horrific Fugitive Slave Act, which became law on September 18, 1850. The law empowered U.S. marshals, deputies, and white citizens to capture enslaved people who escaped. The legislation was so heinous that federal officials could go into free states, capture formerly enslaved people, and place them back in bondage.[10] One of the many inhumane parts of the law was that people who were deemed runaway "slaves," many of whom were wrongfully charged with the "crime" of seeking freedom, were denied a trial by jury. As a result, countless free Black people—those who had never been enslaved—were kidnapped and accused of being runaways.[11] Without a trial, they had no way to prove they were free, in many ways making slavery a federal and national policy.

Supporting the Fugitive Slave Act is unforgivable, and

Honest Abe would make it clear, in his own words, that he was a white supremacist. In 1858, in one of the seven debates against incumbent Stephen Douglas for the Illinois U.S. Senate seat, he famously said, "I am not, nor ever have been, in favor of bringing about in any way the social and political equality of the white and black races, that I am not nor ever have been in favor of making voters or jurors of negroes, nor of qualifying them to hold office, nor to intermarry with white people; and I will say in addition to this that there is a physical difference between the white and black races which I believe will forever forbid the two races living together on terms of social and political equality. And inasmuch as they cannot so live, while they do remain together there must be the position of superior and inferior." Here is where Lincoln proudly declares he is a white supremacist: "I as much as any other man am in favor of having the superior position assigned to the white race."[12]

In future debates, Stephen Douglas would accuse Lincoln of flip-flopping on racial equality, but that same year, Lincoln also claimed he supported "gradual emancipation," meaning people in bondage should not get total freedom for at least one hundred years. In the America Lincoln imagined, Black folks would have their first taste of freedom at some point in the 1950s.[13]

Lincoln would lose the Illinois Senate seat, which was elected by the state legislature. However, he was elected president in 1860.

Many Black Americans recognized the truth about Lincoln and were not happy with his victory. The weekly *Anglo-African* was one of the most popular Black newspapers at the time, founded by abolitionist brothers Thomas Hamilton and Robert Hamilton. In a March 1860 issue, Thomas Hamilton wrote, "We have no hope from either [of the] political parties. We must rely on ourselves, the righteousness of our cause, and the advance of just sentiments among the great masses of the...people."[14]

On the other hand, white abolitionist Oliver Johnson wrote, "It seems utterly preposterous to deny that Lincoln's election will indicate growth in the right direction."[15] While this was prophetic because slavery would end under his administration, Lincoln needed to be muscled in that direction; it was not by his own volition.

Lincoln's priority was not liberating enslaved Black people. In his first inaugural address, in 1861, he promised slave states full enforcement of the Fugitive Slave Act,[16] which was his attempt to prevent the march toward a civil war. Even though Lincoln upheld one of the most pro-white supremacist laws the country had ever seen,[17] white southerners were not satisfied. Lincoln's inability to satiate the white southern elite's demand for a wholesale embrace of slavery is coupled with the fact that he issued the flaccid Emancipation Proclamation.

After the attack and ultimate fall of Fort Sumter in April 1861, which sparked the Civil War,[18] Lincoln called on men to serve in the Union Army.[19] Thousands heeded the call, including many Black men inspired to fight for freedom.[20] Adhering to the racist demands to keep the army white, Lincoln refused to let Black men serve in the Civil War,[21] until it became clear that he could not win the war without the manpower of Black soldiers.[22]

Black people knew that their freedom could only be won on the battlefield. The *Anglo-African* stated, "We are concerned in this fight and our fate hangs upon its issues. The South must be subjugated, or we shall be enslaved. In aiding the federal government in whatever way we can, we are aiding to secure our own liberty; for this war can end only in the subjugation of the North or the South."[23]

Yet despite the availability of Black soldiers, Lincoln and his allies were reluctant. Secretary of War Simon Cameron wrote in 1861, "This Department has no intention at the present to call into the service of the government any colored soldiers."[24] Many white soldiers lost their limbs and lives in the name of stubborn loyalty to white supremacy.

Some Black people who had escaped the South hoping to enlist were sent back to their owners. Many Union generals gleefully returned enslaved people and even allowed enslavers to cross behind Union lines to retrieve their "property." Other Union commanders had a bit of humanity and considered the enslaved people they came upon as "contraband." While they were not "freed," they weren't returned to their owners but were allowed to work for the Union.[25] By 1861, Douglass was so outraged by the president's handling of slavery that he called Lincoln the most powerful slave catcher in the country, according to historian David Blight.[26]

Even when Lincoln's generals attempted to do what was morally and strategically right, Lincoln refused. When Union general David Hunter, who once employed Harriet Tubman as a spy and army scout, issued a proclamation under martial law for slavery to be abolished in South Carolina, Florida, and Georgia, the alleged Great Emancipator revoked the order.

On May 9, 1862, Lincoln wrote, "I, Abraham Lincoln, president of the United States, proclaim and declare, that the government of the United States had no knowledge, information, or belief of an intention on the part of General Hunter to issue such a proclamation; nor has it yet, any authentic information that the document is genuine. And further, that neither General Hunter, nor any other commander, or person, has been authorized by the Government of the United States, to make proclamations declaring the slaves of any State free; and that the supposed proclamation, now in question, whether genuine or false, is altogether void, so far as respects such declaration."[27]

Frederick Douglass was incensed. He is quoted in *Battle Cry of Freedom* as saying, "To fight against slaveholders without fighting against slavery, is but a half-hearted business and paralyses the hands engaged in it... Fire must be met with water... War for the destruction of liberty must be met with war for the destruction of slavery."[28]

Lincoln had another vision in mind: "compensated emancipation," which meant enslavers would receive reparations in the form of cash[29]—yes, reparations to *slave owners*—after which enslaved people would be deported to the Caribbean, Latin America, and parts of West Africa.[30] He hoped if border states freed enslaved people, it would be an easier path to gradually end slavery. Republicans in 1862, with the support of Lincoln, voted to provide money to "any state which may adopt gradual abolishment of slavery." They hoped to prevent border states, like Missouri, Kentucky, Delaware, and Maryland, from joining the Confederacy.[31] The plan was a failure, and senators from border states refused.[32] Compensated emancipation was rejected by whites who wanted to maintain their power.

The turning point came after Lincoln realized his allegiance to maintaining a pure-white military might lose him the war. Secretary of the Navy Gideon Welles said Lincoln told him that "it was a military necessity absolutely essential for the salvation of the Union, that we must free the slaves or be ourselves subdued. The slaves [are] undeniably an element of strength to those who [have] their service, and we must decide whether that element should be with us or against us."[33] Lincoln finally admitted he needed Black people to win the war, but he wouldn't move just yet.

After a month of debate and compromise, on July 17, 1862, Congress passed the Second Confiscation Act, which would name Confederates as traitors, allow the permanent seizure of rebels' property, and, most importantly, in the bill's ninth section, free all enslaved people of rebels.[34] It was crucial legislation for Black people and well-needed punishment for treasonists, but according to historian Lerone Bennett Jr., Lincoln was flip-flopping on emancipation throughout July 1862.[35] Lincoln threaten to veto the Second Confiscation Act because he believed permanent property confiscation violated the Constitution. Ohio senator Benjamin Wade, a longtime abolitionist, warned if Lincoln vetoed the bill, "It will be the saddest announcement that ever went out of the Capitol." Around this time, Adam S. Hill, Washington correspondent for the *New York Tribune*, reportedly told his managing editor that General James S. Wadworth said the president was opposed to emancipation. Hill said, "He [Wadworth] says that the President is not with us; has no Anti-slavery instincts. He never heard him speak of Anti-slavery men, otherwise than as 'radicals,' 'abolitionists,' and of the 'nigger question,' he frequently speaks."[36]

After changes to the Second Confiscation Act were made to give more leeway to forgive Confederates, on July 25, 1862, Lincoln declared the Second Confiscation Act would be the law of the land in sixty days, but the enforcements were limited. Black Republicans and white abolitionists were increasingly outraged over Lincoln's slow-moving pace on the urgency of ending slavery and appearing to show leniency for Confederates. That same month, Frederick Douglass wrote, "Abraham Lincoln is no more fit for the place he holds than was [the previous president] James

Buchanan, and the latter was no more miserable tool of traitors and rebels than the former is allowing himself to be."[37]

Horace Greeley, founder and editor of the *New York Tribune*, scribed a biting piece, specifically addressing the Second Confiscation Act: "We think you are strangely and disastrously remiss in the discharge of your official and imperative duty with regard to the emancipating provisions of the new Confiscation Act. Those provisions were designed to fight Slavery with Liberty. They prescribe that men loyal to the Union, and willing to shed their blood in her behalf, shall no longer be held, with the Nations consent, in bondage to persistent, malignant traitors, who for twenty years have been plotting and for sixteen months have been fighting to divide and destroy our country. Why these traitors should be treated with tenderness by you, to the prejudice of the dearest rights of loyal men, we cannot conceive."[38]

The answer was simple: Lincoln's priority was his white man's America. As the president wrote in a letter to Greeley, "My paramount object in this struggle is to save the Union, and is not either to save or to destroy slavery. If I could save the Union without freeing any slave I would do it, and if I could save it by freeing all the slaves I would do it; and if I could save it by freeing some and leaving others alone, I would also do that. What I do about slavery and the colored race, I do because I believe it helps to save the Union; and what I forbear, I forbear because I do not believe it would help to save the Union."[39]

The Second Confiscation Act never went into effect. Less than two months later, the day before the Second Confiscation Act was to become law, Lincoln signed the Preliminary Emancipation Proclamation,[40] which delayed what would have been the actual emancipation Congress had already authorized in July.

For Lincoln, an idea to save the Union was to continue to push colonization—deporting Black people to areas unknown to them with little resources. While this was a mainstream idea for most white politicians at the time, in 1862, Lincoln foolishly attempted to recruit Douglass to support colonization, which he refused. The plan was unpopular with Black communities as well. In August 1862, a group of Black Philadelphians wrote to Lincoln, "Many of us, in Pennsylvania, have our own houses and other property, amounting, in the aggregate, to millions of dollars. Shall we sacrifice this, leave our homes, forsake our birth-place, and flee to a strange land, to appease the anger and prejudice of the traitors now in arms against the Government?"[41]

A few months before, in April 1862, an experiment in colonization was launched.[42] Since slavery was now abolished in Washington, DC, Congress awarded area enslavers up to $300 for each enslaved person they no longer owned.[43] More than 450 Black Americans were sent to an island near Haiti. Many died from disease and starvation. Among those who survived, mutiny, infighting, and corruption ensued. In the end, 350 enslaved people returned to the United States.[44] A "Petition of the Colored Citizens" of Queens County, New York, in September 1862 offered a different idea—abolish slavery and allow Black people to "colonize" the South: "Why not declare slavery abolished, and favor our peaceful colonization in the rebel States, or some portion of them?" The petition stated Lincoln "only served the cause of our enemies" and colonization was "a mistaken policy."[45]

Regardless, Lincoln maintained his vision of "exporting" Black people until the end of his life. By July 1864, policies to deport Black people were no more. However, despite loyal Lincoln scholars who argue he gave up his dream of colonization,

Lincoln's vision of exporting Black people after slavery ended is evidenced until the last month of his life. In April 1865, General Benjamin Butler quoted Lincoln as saying, "But what shall we do with the negroes after they are free? I can hardly believe that the South and North can live in peace, unless we get rid of the Negroes." He then expressed concerns about Black people who are "armed and disciplined"[46] returning to the South as free people. Black soldiers fighting in the Civil War could empower them more than Lincoln wanted, especially if the war was won. Thankfully, Lincoln had no choice; it was let Black men fight or lose his war.

Lincoln finally give in to the looming possibility of the North losing the Civil War and allowed Black men to fight. On January 1, 1863, he issued the Emancipation Proclamation.[47] Here is where it gets complicated. One of the biggest lies told in American history is that the Emancipation Proclamation freed enslaved people, which it certainly did not. Some scholars claim it freed no enslaved people, which is closer to the truth but not exactly accurate. These theories and the whitewashing of Lincoln are brilliantly deconstructed in Lerone Bennett Jr.'s *Forced into Glory: Abraham Lincoln's White Dream*.[48] After his book was published in 2007, Bennett was attacked by critics and scholars—loyalty to Lincoln can be as delusional as loyalty to Trump.

The Emancipation Proclamation freed enslaved people in small pockets of the South, like parts of South Carolina.[49] Historian Eric Foner claimed up to seventy thousand people were initially freed, but the exact number is unknown.[50] To put this number in context, there were approximately four million Black people in slavery.[51] Seventy thousand out of four million is a tiny percentage—far from total emancipation.

Furthermore, freeing people in parts of South Carolina or another state does not mean they were free outside that area. Newly "freed" Black citizens could have easily been captured and put back in slavery if they traveled outside the area or the state where they were "free." Emancipation could not exist locally; if 99 percent of enslaved people were not freed, then no one was free. To say otherwise would be a stretch to cleanse Lincoln's record. The Emancipation Proclamation only applied in states that were in rebellion and over which Lincoln had no control. In border states, like Missouri, Kentucky, Delaware, and Maryland, where Lincoln had jurisdiction to free enslaved people, the Great Emancipator did not.[52]

That said, the Emancipation Proclamation is a crucial document in American history not because of "freedom" but because it was a step to a Northern victory and made slavery a central issue in the war. The Emancipation Proclamation was a war document that allowed Black men to serve and enslaved people in the South to escape to fight for the Union. While the narrative is "Lincoln freed the slaves," as Reverend Al Sharpton has said, "The slaves freed Lincoln."[53]

Frederick Douglass was jubilant about the Emancipation Proclamation, but terror was to come for Black men serving in the war.[54] Douglass set about actively recruiting soldiers, including his two sons, for the Union Army.[55] However, he was horrified to learn Black soldiers in the army were being abused by white soldiers and not adequately compensated. Many Black Union soldiers were kidnapped by the Confederate troops, tortured, and sold into slavery. The White House was silent.

For the first time, Douglass met with Lincoln at the White House in August 1863 to protest the treatment of soldiers. By all accounts, the two had a civil discussion, and Lincoln showed a modicum of respect to Douglass. He later wrote that he demanded equal pay for Black soldiers and better protection from the Confederate troops, calling on the Union to handle their Confederate prisoners the same as the Confederate troops treated their Black soldiers: "If Jefferson Davis should shoot or hang colored soldiers in cold blood, the United States government should retaliate in kind and degree without delay upon Confederate prisoners in its hands." Davis was a former Mississippi senator and president of the Confederate States.

Lincoln made no promises to protect Black soldiers, but Douglass did not walk away completely dismayed: "Though I was not entirely satisfied with his views, I was so well satisfied with the man and with the educating tendency of the conflict that I determined to go on with the recruiting."[56]

Historians love to highlight this meeting,[57] but it goes too far to use this conversation to frame Lincoln as the Liberator. Lincoln had previously met with Black pastors and insisted they support Black people being deported out of the country, which they refused to do.[58] Just because Lincoln didn't hurl the n-word at Douglass or order him to be swinging from a tree does not mean he had "evolved" to the point that he wasn't a white supremacist. Showing basic humanity to one Black man while thousands are fighting for your country and you are aware they are suffering due to white soldiers is little cause for admiration.

While Douglass would visit the White House again[59] after the initial meeting, he recognized that Lincoln would be little help to Black Americans, which was clear after the Fort Pillow Massacre.

April 12, 1864, was one of the most violent and sinister days for Black men in the Civil War. Known as the Fort Pillow Massacre, in Henning, Tennessee, over two hundred Black soldiers were

brutally slaughtered by Confederates led by General Nathan
Bedford Forrest, a well-known trader of enslaved people and the
first grand wizard in the Ku Klux Klan. After being overpowered
by the Confederates, Black men tried to escape to a river but were
shot to death in the water, nailed to exploding barrels, and burned
alive. A naval officer wrote in his account to the *New York Times*, "I
feel personally interested in the retaliation which our Government
may deal out to the rebels, when the fact of the merciless butchery
is fully established... I found many of the dead lying close along
by the water's edge, where they had evidently sought safety; they
could not offer any resistance from the places where they were, in
holes and cavilles along the banks. Most of them had two wounds.
I saw several colored soldiers of the Sixth United States Artillery,
with their eyes punched out with bayonets; many of them were
shot twice and bayonetted also."[60] The naval officer and Black
leaders called on the Lincoln administration to retaliate. What
did Lincoln do? Outside of a few speeches, absolutely nothing.

The following month, repulsed by Lincoln and his disregard
of the horrors Black soldiers endured, Frederick Douglass and several hundred Republicans formed the Radical Democracy Party.
By May 1864, a week before the Republican convention, General
John C. Frémont, who freed enslaved people owned by Missouri
rebels in 1861 (later revoked by Lincoln's White House), became
the Radical Democracy Party's presidential candidate to challenge
Lincoln in the upcoming election.[61]

A week later, at the Republican convention (called the National
Union Convention) in Baltimore, the GOP delivered a blow by
replacing Lincoln's first-term, antislavery Vice President Hannibal
Hamlin of Maine with a southern Democrat named Andrew
Johnson. The military governor of Tennessee was a fiery racist[62]

who opposed secession from the Union but was a Confederate sympathizer.[63] Vice President Hamlin—often accused of having "Black blood"—did not know he was to be replaced until he arrived at the Republican convention. Lincoln was reportedly spreading the word that he wanted Hamlin dropped. Longtime journalist Jules Witcover described the replacement as a "secret move" by Lincoln. The decision to make a southern Democrat the second man in charge would shift history. When Lincoln was assassinated, Johnson, who was drunk at the March 1865 inaugural ceremony, would become president and annihilate Reconstruction.[64]

If, after Lincoln's assassination, the country had had President Hannibal Hamlin, it's conceivable Reconstruction would have been a long-term success. Nonetheless, Lincoln was a politician first. He did not honestly care about the betterment of Black people. Lincoln relied on Andrew Johnson to deliver racist votes from the southern states that were not under the Confederacy—it was the Southern strategy before the Southern strategy existed.

The truth is Lincoln didn't need Andrew Johnson to up the ante for white supremacy. His sympathetic treatment of violent Confederate leaders was evident. In July 1864, Congress, planning for the country's future after the war ended, passed the Wade-Davis Bill, their Reconstruction plan. The mission was to ensure that former Confederate leaders could not reclaim control over the South once the war ended. The bill required 51 percent of eligible white voters in Confederate states to take loyalty oaths and recognize the "permanent freedom" of enslaved people in order to rejoin the Union. The legislation also required white men in the state to accept an "ironclad oath" to the Union and denounce the Confederacy; if not, they could not vote or participate in constitutional conventions. Most importantly, the bill permanently disenfranchised Confederates who held political office or were high-ranking officers, meaning they would never be able to vote. Sounds like a solid plan, considering the blood that was shed due to the Confederacy launching a war. The Republicans knew what was ahead: even after losing the war, Confederate leaders would attempt to regain their power, which had to be preempted. Although the bill passed through Congress, Lincoln, whose chief concern was the reunification of the country, pocket vetoed the bill. Members of Congress, like Pennsylvania representative Thaddeus Stevens, were disgusted. The so-called Great Liberator's plan was for only a measly 10 percent of white men to take the loyalty oath, opening the pathway for the Confederacy under a different name to take over in the South. While the failure of Reconstruction is blamed on President Andrew Johnson, who would assume office after Lincoln was assassinated, Lincoln set in motion the floundering of Reconstruction with his Confederate sympathizer philosophy.[65]

Black soldiers were not fairly compensated and were murdered by Confederates, and now the president vetoed the Wade-Davis Bill. An infuriated Douglass wrote, "The President has virtually laid down this as the rule of his statesmen: Do evil by choice, right from necessity. You will see that he does not sign the bill adopted by Congress, restricting the organization of State Governments only to those States where there is a loyal majority. His plan is to organize such Governments where there is one-tenth of the people loyal!—an entire contradiction of the constitutional idea of the Republican Government."[66]

Imagine Douglass's courage, as a formerly enslaved person and the most well-known Black man alive, whose life was constantly at risk, demanding that the sixteenth president of the United States be held accountable. This is what every Black Republican should aim for today—to address the racism in your party, even if it comes from the top.

Given Lincoln's willingness to go easy on whites who committed treason, the Radical Democracy Party hoped to deny him reelection. The calculus changed when the Democrats nominated General George B. McClellan from New Jersey, who was both proslavery and against "negro equality."[67]

The fear of McClellan winning the presidential election was chilling. By September 1864, General Frémont dropped out of the race,[68] fearing he would split the Republican vote and give the win to the Democrats. In a letter to the *New York Times*, Frémont blasted Lincoln. "I consider that his Administration has been politically, militarily, and financially, a failure, and that its necessary continuance is a cause of regret for the country." He observed that "the pressure of his party will, we may hope, force him" to end slavery. At the same time, he recognized the political stakes. Frémont wrote, "I believe I am consistent with my antecedents in withdrawing [from the presidential race], not to aid in the triumphs of Mr. Lincoln, but to do my part toward preventing the election of the Democratic candidate."[69]

Although Frederick Douglass initially opposed Lincoln for a second term, he ultimately did what many of us do today. When the other option is a demonic, politically violent beast from white supremacist hell, you make the pragmatic decision. Some things never change.

Douglass was also influenced by another meeting with Lincoln at the White House in August 1864, this time at the president's request. Lincoln urgently requested that Douglass travel to Washington, DC, because he feared losing the election. Upon arriving in DC, Douglass was famously picked up in a presidential carriage and taken to the White House. The two-hour meeting was a watershed moment for Douglass's perception of Lincoln. The president told Douglass he wanted to craft a plan so thousands of enslaved people in rebel states could escape to the north. With their help, the North would be victorious in the Civil War or, if he lost reelection, at least thousands of Black people would be free.

It is unclear whether Lincoln was playing the conniving politician to get Douglass on his side or if he was sincerely concerned with freeing as many enslaved people as possible. The plan never happened, but according to author John Stauffer, Douglass said that he had not recognized how much Lincoln despised slavery until that August 1864 meeting.[70]

Perhaps—or perhaps he simply recognized that Lincoln was considerably better than the alternative. In a letter to abolitionist William Lloyd Garrison dated September 17, 1864, Douglass wrote, "I, like many other radical men, freely criticized, in private and in public, the actions and utterances of Mr. Lincoln, and withheld my support. That possibility is now no longer conceivable; it is now plain that this country is to be governed or misgoverned during the next four years, either by the Republican Party represented in the person of Abraham Lincoln, or by the (miscalled) Democratic Party, represented by George B. McClellan."[71]

The danger was apparent during the campaign. Democratic presidential nominee General George B. McClellan launched what David Goldfield, author of *America Aflame: How the Civil War Created a Nation*, called "probably the most racist presidential campaign in American history."[72] McClellan's campaign ads were political cartoons that stoked fears of interracial sex with a fictional "Miscegenation Ball at the Headquarters of the Lincoln Central Campaign Club."[73] One pamphlet referred to Lincoln as "Abraham Africanus the First" and declared that the first commandment of the Republican Party was "Thou shalt have no other God but the negro."[74]

Proslavery newspapers began circulating a scandalous rumor that Lincoln had a plan to wipe out whiteness with an administration of endless interracial sex. The word *miscegenation* was coined for the anti-Lincoln "Miscegenation" pamphlet—the critical-race-theory scare tactic of the time.[75]

You might ask, why did Democrats attack Lincoln if he was a white supremacist? Both things can be true. By 1864, Lincoln and many white men were certainly white supremacists but knew to save the Union, slavery must be abolished, resulting in the loss of millions of dollars in free labor for the South. Lincoln never respected Black people as citizens who built the country, but he loved the Union,[76] making him a threat to enslavers. On the other side, the Democrats of the 1860s were the predecessors of today's Republicans in that they were willing to sacrifice humanity to maintain a death grip on political power.

Despite the efforts of the Democrats, Abraham Lincoln became the first president to win a second term since Andrew Jackson in 1832.

As for the Civil War, there are several reasons why the North was ultimately victorious. In addition to General Ulysses S. Grant's military strategy,[77] the tide turned when Black Americans could join the Union Army in 1863. The sacrifice of 180,000 Black men who fought for the Union Army[78] and the nearly 40,000 who died[79] is downplayed as a significant factor that led the Union to victory. The Union would not have won the Civil War without Black soldiers—period.

On April 9, 1865, Confederate general Robert E. Lee surrendered to Grant, signaling the war was coming to an end.[80] Two days later, Lincoln gave his final public speech,[81] which some scholars interpret as a signal of Lincoln "evolving" on racial equality.[82]

When speaking of Reconstruction in Louisiana, Lincoln claimed he would "prefer" the right to vote be given to "very intelligent" Black men or Black soldiers who served in the Civil War.[83] He is given a round of retroactive applause for the "very intelligent" line—which means very stupid white men could vote. There were white men with power who undoubtedly believed in Black suffrage, known as the Radical Republicans, a progressive but small group of lawmakers in Congress, including U.S. representative from Pennsylvania Thaddeus Stevens,[84] Massachusetts U.S. senator Charles Sumner,[85] and Ohio governor Salmon P. Chase,[86] just to name a few. It's simply not enough to say, "Lincoln was a man of his time." Vague quotes Lincoln made in his final years do not erase his continuation of an unnecessary hell by delaying emancipation and vetoing the Wade-Davis Bill or the tricky logic of advocating to deport millions of Black Americans.

Lincoln's extra-soft support of "very intelligent" Black men voting was enough for one white terrorist, John Wilkes Booth. The actor and Confederate spy fatally shot President Abraham Lincoln on April 14, 1865. The president died the next day.[87]

On December 9, 1865, the Thirteenth Amendment, which barely passed through Congress and was supported by Lincoln before his death, went into effect. Black people were technically free from slavery.

After Lincoln's death, Frederick Douglass praised the sixteenth president of the United States. He wrote, "Abraham Lincoln, while unsurpassed in his devotion to the welfare of the white race, was also in a sense hitherto without example, emphatically the Black man's President: the first to show any respect to their rights as men."[88]

Yet at the unveiling of the Freedmen's Monument in Lincoln Park, Washington, DC, in 1876, Douglass had a more nuanced critique of Lincoln. "He was preeminently the white man's President, entirely devoted to the welfare of white men... He was ready to execute all the supposed guarantees of the United States Constitution in favor of the slave system anywhere inside the slave states. He was willing to pursue, recapture, and send back the fugitive slave to his master, and to suppress a slave rising for liberty, though his guilty master were already in arms against the Government... You [white citizens] are the children of Abraham Lincoln. We are at best only his stepchildren; children by adoption, children by forces of circumstances and necessity."[89]

By 1880, Douglass wrote about Lincoln, "A great man: Tender of heart, strong of nerve, of boundless patience and broadest sympathies, with no motive apart from his country." He also called Lincoln "one of the noblest, wisest and best men I ever knew."[90]

Maybe it was his age, the horrors of the fall of Reconstruction, or the reign of white terrorism that made Douglass think differently about President Abraham Lincoln. The party of Lincoln betrayed Black people time and again. Only when they were about to lose the country did they allow Black soldiers to win their war, a war Frederick Douglass superbly called the slaveholders' rebellion.[91]

Again, it's not the spirit of Lincoln that anyone, especially Black Republicans, should aspire to; it's the spirit of Frederick Douglass, a formerly enslaved person who boldly exposed the president of the United States in the 1860s and centered the freedom of Black people. Douglass witnessed the weaknesses in Lincoln's character, but he would also grasp the treachery to come from the earliest grifters in the aftermath of the Civil War.

CHAPTER 2

RECONSTRUCTION

"The longer we procrastinate to apply the proper remedies the more chronic becomes the malady that we seek to heal."

—Former Mississippi U.S. senator Hiram Rhodes Revels[1]

RECONSTRUCTION PAVED THE WAY FOR AMERICA'S FIRST Black elected officials, who I call Douglass Republicans. The policy positions associated with present-day Republicans—an eagerness to disenfranchise voters, a worship for states' rights, and the steadfast refusal to address bigotry in their party—came about due to white opposition to progress. Alexander K. Davis, a lawyer who became the first Black lieutenant governor of Mississippi, Charles Caldwell, a state senator for Mississippi, Robert Smalls, a Civil War hero who represented South Carolina in the House of Representatives, and many more were political revolutionaries who saw a world where white and Black functioned together. Reconstruction was supposed to bring a new day for the United States, establishing life for formerly enslaved people who were now citizens. Federal laws were put in place to transition the nation from an enslaved economy, restructuring wealth and power to benefit the average citizen and, idealistically, reconstitute the country, especially the South.

The Confederate surrender in 1865 marked the Civil War coming to an end. However, partly due to a flawed Reconstruction plan, life did not miraculously change for Black people in the South. Slavery may have been abolished on paper, but white terror continued. Whites assaulted and killed Black Americans in plain sight for refusing to obey white rule.[2] From 1865 to 1868, approximately four hundred Blacks were killed by whites in Texas.[3] The New Orleans slaughter in July 1866 resulted in thirty-four Black people and three white allies being murdered.[4] In Pine Bluff, Arkansas, in 1866, a white mob burned down a Black settlement and lynched twenty-four Black people, including children.[5] White terrorist attacks on free Black citizens were commonplace.

Federal intervention was slow, thanks to the Republican Party's decision to elevate a southern Democrat to the vice presidency. When Lincoln was assassinated, Andrew Johnson became president. A southerner who did not support secession, Johnson had opposed slavery but not for humanitarian reasons. He believed rich men owning enslaved people was oppressive toward poor white men.[6] Johnson, who grew up in poverty, despised the "plantation elite" but saw no connection between the exploitation of poor whites and enslaved Black people by wealthy whites. If anything, he believed Black communities with even a pinch of equality would threaten the livelihood of poor whites.[7] Johnson chose to maintain the white supremacy culture of the antebellum South, minus chattel slavery.[8] However, President Andrew Johnson was far from the only one to blame for the fall of Reconstruction.

While Abraham Lincoln had been weak on slavery, his deficient ten percent Reconstruction plan to forgive former Confederates if a small number agreed slavery was abolished was also troubling. Clearly, these racist white men were angry they lost the war and would not treat Black people as equals. It is unknown if Lincoln would have supported Black men holding political power in the South, but considering Lincoln pocket vetoed the Wade-Davis Bill and his ten percent Reconstruction plan, which Johnson mainly followed, I would argue Lincoln would not approve of Black men as political leaders. Lincoln made it clear his priority was Confederate states rejoining the Union, and he believed whites were superior.

That said, Lincoln's administration crafted federal policies with innovative potential. Contemporary Republicans often claim to believe in small government and advocate returning to the party of Lincoln, but Lincoln believed in the power of big government federal policy, which would be a form of welfare and socialism for whites. In 1861, Lincoln passed the Revenue Act, our first national taxation,[9] helping to fund the Union Army that would fight the Civil War.[10] The Homestead Act of 1862 allowed citizens to become landowners.[11] (This mainly benefited poor whites but gave a small number of formerly enslaved people access to land; however, the act robbed land from Native Americans.) The Land-Grant College Act of 1862 afforded poor whites, not just the upper class, the ability to receive education specializing in "agriculture and the mechanic arts"[12] and would open the door for historically Black colleges and universities (HBCUs) like Alcorn State University and Tuskegee University. Additionally, the Lincoln administration passed the Pacific Railroad Act of 1862,[13] creating the country's transcontinental railroad. These are just a few of the crucial federal acts the Lincoln administration put into law. However, it's important to note that Lincoln's Reconstruction plan to forgive former Confederates would reinstall their power in the South. Therefore, Reconstruction was doomed from the start.

President Andrew Johnson quickly set about crippling the Freedmen's Bureau, which assisted formerly enslaved people after the war, and softening punishments against insurrectionists who had attacked the United States during the Civil War. Months after Lincoln's assassination, Johnson, who claimed to despise the "planter elite," was handing out thousands of pardons to wealthy Confederates as long as a personal request was made to him, turning his back on poor whites. Following much of Lincoln's ten percent plan, he was handing the South back to the enemy.[14] Despite pushback from the Radical Republicans, Johnson allowed southern leaders to rebuild new, all-white governments. Johnson also ordered land promised to Black people to be given back to the treasonists.[15]

With the racists rapidly returning to political office under Johnson, state and local officials instituted Black codes. These laws criminalized homelessness and forbade Black people from owning weapons, testifying against whites, meeting after dark, or traveling without a pass. Offenders were punished with long prison sentences.[16] Once convicted of these "crimes," Black prisoners were forced to work for free, returning to slavery. Southern politicians, many who were former Confederates with all their power restored, also created barriers that prevented newly freed Black people from starting businesses or buying land. Instead, most Black Americans were forced to sign exploitative sharecropping contracts that ensnared them in a cycle of debt.[17]

Not shockingly, many white Republicans were opposed to slavery but were also opposed to Black Americans having full equality, especially the right to vote. Radical Republicans in Congress advocated for equality beyond slavery, but just as had been the case during the fight to end slavery, the driving force behind a meaningful Reconstruction of the South consisted of Black leaders, organizers, and everyday people.

In 1865 and 1866, Black people held freedmen's conventions throughout the South.[18] Black communities gathered from North Carolina to Mississippi[19] to agree on a strategy for life after slavery. They settled on a platform that included establishing schools, protesting Black codes, and collaborating with whites, believing cooperation was required for peace. The freedmen's conventions were shaping a "Black agenda" before that term existed.

The conventions were not a call for a separate Black nation; they presented precise, reasonable demands for equality and equity. As Sidney Andrews, a journalist who covered the freedmen's conventions, wrote about a North Carolina convention, "I do not see how they could have presented their claims with more dignity, with a more just appreciation of the state of affairs, or in a manner which should appeal more forcibly either to the reason or the sentiment of those whom they address."[20]

An unknown man at a Georgia convention is quoted as saying, "We ask not for a Black man's governor, nor a white man's governor but for a people's Governor, who shall impartially protect the rights of all, and faithfully sustain the Union."[21]

Those who attended the conventions appeared to share a sense of optimism that Black folks and whites could coexist. Delegate James Walker Hood, who was once captured, sold into slavery, and escaped, said at the 1865 North Carolina Freedmen's Convention, "Let us keep constantly in mind that this State is our home, and that the white people are our neighbors and many of them are our friends. We and the white people have to live here together. Some people talk of emigration for the black race, some of expatriation, and some of colonization. I regard this as all nonsense. We have been living together for a hundred years or more, and we have got to live together still; and the best way is to harmonize our feelings as much as possible, and to treat all men respectfully."[22]

Although Hood could not have seen the Jim Crow future, his optimism verged on naivete. He added, "If we respect ourselves we shall be respected." Sadly, in the long term, Hood, who founded the historically Black college Zion Wesley Institute (later renamed Livingstone College), was wrong.[23] Self-respect would not be enough to save Black lives.

In the short term, due partly to the pressure of the freedmen's conventions, Congress reasserted control over Reconstruction against President Johnson. They passed the Civil Rights Act of 1866, declaring all persons born in the United States—except for Native Americans—to be citizens "without distinction of race or color, or previous condition of slavery or involuntary servitude."[24] It was the nation's first civil rights law, allowing Black people to enforce contracts, testify in court, and file lawsuits.

President Andrew Johnson griped that granting Black people full recognition as citizens would diminish the rights of white people. He whined, "In all our history, in all our experience as a people living under Federal and State law, no such system as that contemplated by the details of this bill has ever before been pro-posed or adopted. They establish for the security of the colored race safeguards which go indefinitely beyond any that the General Government has ever provided for the white race. In fact, the dis-tinction of race and color is by the bill made to operate in favor of the colored against the white race."[25] As early as 1866, presaging today's GOP, President Johnson was protesting about "reverse racism."

The Radical Republicans continued to use federal power against the former Confederacy over the following year. In March 1867, Republicans passed the First Reconstruction Act,[26] which placed U.S. Army troops throughout the South to protect Black people from white terrorists.[27] The Reconstruction Act ensured all adult males could vote[28] unless they once supported the Confederacy.

Given white resistance to Black rights, Republicans were concerned that the Civil Rights Act of 1866 could easily be overturned. They took a gigantic step further and, with a large majority of Republicans in Congress, passed the Fourteenth Amendment, guaranteeing citizenship to every person born in the United States—also known as birthright citizenship.[29] The amendment enshrined in the Constitution "equal protection under the laws" and guaranteed that formerly enslaved people would receive full citizenship. The amendment threatened representation in Congress if states refused Black men the right to vote—a tool that has never been enforced. President Andrew Johnson panned the Fourteenth Amendment[30] but had no power to stop it due to Republican control over the House and Senate.

The path was set in place to elect and appoint Black officials. Black men responded to the constitutional guarantee of citizenship by registering to vote in massive numbers. In 1868, approximately 80 percent of Black men were registered, electing Black men to political office in record numbers and making Ulysses S. Grant the eighteenth president of the United States.[31] As abolitionist William Lloyd Garrison beautifully described, it was a "wonderful, quiet, sudden transformation of four millions of human beings from the auction block to the ballot-box."[32] With President Andrew Johnson leaving office (Democrats nominated New

York governor Horatio Seymour over Johnson, who was formally impeached in February 1868, at the 1868 Democratic National Convention), Grant, a war hero for the Union who Black soldiers fought for across the South, was believed to be a friend of formerly enslaved people.

By 1870, a Republican Congress passed the Fifteenth Amendment, which explicitly stated a person could not be denied the vote because of race. Not only did the Fifteenth Amendment help Black men in the South, but it also granted Black men the right to vote in the North.[33] Only eight states in the North allowed Black men to vote before the Fifteenth Amendment.[34]

Women were not granted the right to vote with the Fifteenth Amendment, leading some white suffragists and abolitionists to show their racist colors.[35] In reality, the Fifteenth Amendment would not have passed through Congress if women had been included. Activist Susan B. Anthony was so outraged that she famously ranted at the American Equal Rights Association annual meeting in 1869, "I will cut off this right arm of mine before I will ever work or demand the ballot for the Negro and not the woman."[36]

Frederick Douglass was also in attendance and hastened to remind them that there was a difference. He said, "When women, because they are women, are hunted down through the cities of New York and New Orleans; when they are dragged from their houses and hung upon lamp-posts; when their children are torn from their arms, and their brains dashed out upon the pavement; when they are objects of insult and outrage at every turn; when they are in danger of having their homes burnt down over their heads; when their children are not allowed to enter schools; then they will have an urgency to obtain the ballot equal to our own."[37]

Susan B. Anthony responded by questioning Black people's intelligence. "If you will not give the whole loaf of suffrage to the entire people, give it to the most intelligent first. If intelligence, justice, and morality are to have precedence in the Government, let the question of woman be brought up first and that of the negro last."[38] The irony of saying this in front of someone as formidably intelligent as Frederick Douglass was clearly lost on her. She then headed South to warn other whites about the danger of Black men voting before white women.

Much has been written about Douglass's comments on women's suffrage. He supported women voting, but he disagreed with the juxtaposition of Black men. It is important to remember that white women were also complicit in slavery. The book *They Were Her Property* by Stephanie Jones-Rogers lays this out brilliantly. Frederick Douglass was born in slavery, escaped at twenty years old,[39] and was nearly killed several times as he traveled the country to speak as a Black abolitionist.[40] Though white women may not have been his priority regarding voting rights, I doubt that Douglass believed he was superior to white women. Susan B. Anthony, however, had little doubt that she was superior to Black men.

It was Sojourner Truth who perfectly summed up the dangers of fighting for Black men's rights without fighting for Black women. In 1867, she said, "There is a great stir about colored men getting their rights, but not a word about the colored women; and if colored men get their rights, and colored women not theirs, the colored men will be masters over the women, and it will be just as bad as it was before."[41]

Even with the Fourteenth and Fifteenth Amendments, the rights of Black men to vote were fragile. The Ku Klux Klan was born to undermine the Black vote during this time.[42] Klan members and sympathizers would spread hateful propaganda about Black leaders in the South, depicting them as lazy animals who obsessed over white women. It would prove to be a successful effort to cultivate an environment ripe for acts of widespread racial terrorism.

Douglass Republicans fought back. They worked collectively to create self-sufficient Black communities while still keenly aware of white fragility. Black elected officials crafted crucial policies at every level of state government from secretary of state to superintendent of education and lieutenant governor. The first Black man in the U.S. Senate was Republican Hiram Rhodes Revels.[43] Born free in Fayetteville, North Carolina, Revels was a well-traveled minister with a passion for public education. During slavery, he preached all over the country, from Indiana to Illinois, Kansas to Missouri, to bring religion to enslaved people.[44]

He would eventually settle in Galesburg, Illinois, to study religion at Knox College. Revels founded a Black school in St. Louis[45] and numerous churches throughout the South.[46]

By 1868, Revels moved to Natchez, Mississippi, as a minister of the African Methodist Episcopal Church,[47] and his political career was born. That same year, former Union general and Mississippi governor Adelbert Ames (governor from 1868 to 1870 and again from 1874 to 1876) selected Revels to serve on the Natchez Board of Aldermen. Revels would eventually join Mississippi's state senate.[48]

In January 1870, Mississippi had to fill both U.S. Senate seats. At the time, U.S. senators were elected by the state legislature rather than the voters. (This would change with the ratification of the Seventeenth Amendment in 1913.)[49] One short-term Senate seat remained to be filled, and Black leaders demanded that a

Black man be sent to the U.S. Senate in return for the loyalty Black Mississippians had shown to the Republican Party. At that time, the Mississippi state legislature included over thirty Black members.[50] They voted to seat Hiram Revels in the Senate

Officially electing Revels as a U.S. senator for Mississippi would not be easy. On February 23, 1870, the same day President Ulysses S. Grant readmitted Mississippi into the Union, Revels was in Washington, DC, ready to be sworn in, when Senate Democrats blocked his seating.[51]

The fight to seat a Black elected official was a constant during Reconstruction, most famously with Pinckney Benton Stewart Pinchback, who pushed through a civil rights bill in Louisiana and a measure to legalize interracial marriage in the state.[52] In 1872, he was nearly elected to be the U.S. senator from Louisiana before his election was contested. Although Pinchback, a former riverboat gambler who was once described by W. E. B. Du Bois as a "congenial white man, with but a few drops of Negro blood,"[53] never served as Senator, he did make history by holding the office of acting governor of Louisiana from December 9, 1872, to January 13, 1873—a little over a month.

As for Revels, racist Democrats constructed many excuses not to seat him. The most appalling was that Revels, forty-two at the time, was ineligible because he had not met the Senate requirement of being a citizen for nine years. They argued he had only been a citizen for two years due to the Fourteenth Amendment in 1868. Southern Democrats attempted to use the 1857 *Dred Scott* decision, which asserted Black people were not citizens, as their legal argument.[54] Obviously, *Dred Scott* was nullified with the Fourteenth Amendment.[55]

The southern Democrats were still fighting for the last

vestiges of the Confederacy. Mississippi's Senate seats had a symbolic power, one having previously been held by Jefferson Davis, the president of the Confederacy.[56] The partisan media of the time jumped on the story. The *New York World*, a popular Democratic and proslavery newspaper, arguably the Fox News of the 1870s, described Revels as "a lineal descendant of an orangutan" and with "hands resembling claws."[57]

Republicans did not take the insult lying down. Nevada senator James Nye famously railed against the Democrats, "[Jefferson Davis] went out to establish a government whose cornerstone should be the oppression and perpetual enslavement of a race because their skin differed in color from his. Sir, what a magnificent spectacle of retributive justice is witnessed here today! In the place of that proud, defiant man, who marched out to trample under foot the Constitution and the laws of the country he had sworn to support, comes back one of that humble race whom he would have enslaved forever to take and occupy his seat upon this floor."[58]

In the end, the southern Democrats failed. Two days later, the Senate voted for Revels with the Republicans in the majority.

Charles Redmond Douglass, Frederick Douglass's son, who was twenty-five years old, was present in the Senate Gallery on February 25, 1870, to witness the event. He wrote in a letter to his father, dated February 26, "Yesterday was one of the greatest days to me, in the history of this country. I was present and listened to the dying groans of the last of the Democracy, it was on the occasion of administering the oath to H. R. Revels as U.S. Senator. The Democrats fought hard, but were met on all sides with unanswerable arguments on behalf of justice and right."[59]

John R. Lynch, who served as Speaker of the Mississippi House of Representatives and represented Mississippi in the House, wrote about Revels in his iconic book *The Facts of Reconstruction*, "He had never voted, had never attended a political meeting, and of course, had never made a political speech. But he was a colored man, and presumed to be a Republican, and believed to be a man of ability and considerably above the average in point of intelligence."[60]

Revels, described by Lerone Bennett Jr. in 1967's *Black Power U.S.A.: The Human Side of Reconstruction, 1867–1877* as "a timid, cautious and conventional black man,"[61] would serve less than a year in office. He fought against racial segregation in schools and transportation and proved a fierce advocate for public education.[62] Less than a month after being sworn in as senator, he became the first Black American to give a speech on the U.S. Senate floor in March 1870. The Georgia General Assembly had wrongfully expelled approximately thirty Black state legislators from their seats even after they were voted in by the citizens of Georgia. Revels raised his voice in opposition.

He demanded the Black state legislators be seated and gave a compelling speech that remains relevant today as Congress stalls. "Delay is perilous at best," Revels stated before the Senate, "for it is as true in legislation as in physic, that the longer we procrastinate to apply the proper remedies the more chronic becomes the malady that we seek to heal." He courageously called out the all-white U.S. Senate, many of whom who were afraid that the "Negros" would take over, reminding them, "The people of the North owe to the colored race a deep obligation."[63]

As one can imagine, being the first Black man in the U.S. Senate in 1870, his hands were politically tied for much of his brief term. The only known measure he submitted that became law was to restore civil and political rights to former Confederate Army officer Arthur E. Reynolds. It was not unusual for some

Black leaders in Mississippi to embrace former Confederates, considering they were forced to coexist with the treasonists. Lynch wrote there "were several thousand Republicans both white and colored—but chiefly colored—who were opposed" to a clause that would disenfranchise those who supported the Confederacy.[64] Soon after, Mississippi's governor from 1870 to 1871, James L. Alcorn, a former member of the Whig Party who served in the Confederate Army and arguably only became a Republican to obtain power, appointed Reynolds to a judgeship.[65] Regardless of his support for a former Confederate, Revels's dedication to public education is beyond reproach. He served on the education committee, and in 1870, Mississippi launched statewide public education. According to Mississippi native and researcher GeColby Youngblood, in 1871, Revels wrote what would become the higher education policy in Mississippi.[66]

Revels was profiting from being the first Black U.S. senator. The summer while he was in office, he earned thousands of dollars speaking all over the country. By October 1, he garnered $3,000, a considerable amount for 1870, which he used to buy a plantation, according to historian Eric Foner.[67] After Revels left office in March 1871, he continued to work in education and became the first president of Alcorn University, now called Alcorn State University, which was named after Mississippi governor James L. Alcorn. A former Confederate, Alcorn believed in basic rights for Black people but insisted whites should hold all major political power.

Here is where Revels's story gets complicated. Numerous scholars state that Revels supported "white Democrats" who overthrew the "Republican-controlled state government" in 1875.[68] The Mississippi election of 1875 was a bloody nightmare for Black communities and another indication of how Republicans were turning on Black people. In what was deemed the Mississippi Plan, white terrorists were determined to regain control over the Magnolia State, regardless of the over 50 percent Black majority population.[69] A Mississippi newspaper famously read, "Mississippi is a white man's country, and by the eternal God we'll rule it."[70]

White terrorists began flooding Vicksburg, Mississippi, in the summer of 1874. In December, a white mob killed countless Black people; the exact number of deaths is unknown but could be in the hundreds. Black citizens were protesting the removal of Peter Crosby, their legally elected Black sheriff who was also responsible for collecting taxes.[71] Whites in Vicksburg were incensed a Black man would bear the responsibility of collecting taxes and demanded that Crosby resign. He refused but was nonetheless forced out by armed white men. According to historian Philip Dray, the historical record is unclear but there were reports that Governor Adelbert Ames responded to the attack in Vicksburg by saying if Black people are "not willing to fight to maintain that freedom, they are unworthy it."[72] If this is true, Ames, a Republican, abandoned the Black people of Mississippi who got him elected. He had to have known Blacks in Vicksburg were outnumbered by whites—some who had traveled from out of state to kill Black people. A congressional investigation called the attack a "simple massacre, unutterably disgraceful."[73]

A disturbing article from the *New York Times* blamed Crosby for the actions of the white terrorists, claiming the "Negro government" was "obnoxious to them." The paper accused "ignorant Black men" of committing crimes and praised "lawyers, doctors, and even ministers" for participating in the massacre. The writer, only known as H.C., stated that the whites were "desperate and bloodthirsty. They must have known the ignorant negroes were misguided and misled."[74]

Governor Ames was not completely passive in the aftermath of the Vicksburg attack. Ames requested that President Grant send federal troops to Vicksburg, which he did in July and December 1874. Peter Crosby was also reinstated by January 1875. However, the southern Democrats were relentless in their campaign of political violence. In September 1875, over fifty Black people were killed in Clinton, Mississippi, at a political rally that was supposed to be peaceful until whites started screaming at speakers and began shooting. The violence continued for days. Ames again called for federal intervention, writing to Grant's attorney general that he was "powerless to protect" Black Mississippians. The response from Grant's attorney general? "The whole public are tired of these annual autumnal outbreaks in the South and the great majority are ready now to condemn any interference on the part of the Government."[75] So much for Grant's "Let us have peace" campaign slogan.

The next month, one of the Black Republicans who barely escaped with his life during the Clinton massacre, state Senator Charles Caldwell, was assassinated. He was shot to death on the street, and his brother was murdered the same day.[76] In February 1876, southern Democrats voted to impeach Alexander Kelso Davis, the first Black lieutenant governor of Mississippi, and he resigned. Governor Adelbert Ames stepped down in March 1876. The Mississippi Plan was a white supremacist success. Democrat John Marshall Stone became governor and would terrorize Black Mississippians for three terms.

During the same period, Hiram Revels was calling out the leader of the GOP. In November 1875, two months after Grant refused to send troops to Clinton, Mississippi, Revels wrote to the president, "My people are naturally Republicans and always will be, but as they grow older in freedom so do they in wisdom. A great portion of them have learned that they were being used as mere tools."

Revels closed with, "If the state administration had adhered to Republican principles, advanced patriotic measures, appointed only honest and competent men to office, and sought to restore confidence between the races, bloodshed would have been unknown, peace would have prevailed, federal interference been unthought of; harmony, friendship, and mutual confidence would have taken the place of the bayonet."[77]

In March 1876, Revels gave testimony to a Senate investigating committee that has spurred much historical debate. Revels is accused of stating that he was unaware of widespread violence toward Black voters in his state. If true, this would be jaw-dropping considering the well-known terrorism of the Mississippi Plan. When reading the court records, Delaware senator Thomas Bayard, who voted against Revels serving in the U.S. Senate in 1870, asked Revels a series of questions. Revels said he did not know of violence in an area called Marshall County. "In Marshall County, I am satisfied that the canvass was characterized by order and quiet." Bayard demanded that Revels be more specific, and he responded, "Well, I do not know that I could safely go much beyond what I have already said."

Bayard later asked, "Do you know any acts of intimidation or violence of your own knowledge in the State?"

Revels answered, "No, sir; I do not; I have no present knowledge of anything of the kind."

In Revels's final words, he stated that since the election of 1875 in Mississippi, "So far as I know, there has been peace and quiet everywhere."[78]

Was Revels lying about white terror in Mississippi? Was he only commenting on what he saw with his own two eyes, or was he intimidated by a hostile prosecutor who voted against him being a U.S. senator six years before? Was he measuring his words in the hopes of being reinstated president of Alcorn University? In 1874, Revels was no longer president of Alcorn University, although it is unclear why he left. Historian Lerone Bennett Jr. claimed it was due to a feud with Republican governor Ames "over some trifling political issue."[79] Mississippi historian George A. Sewell claimed Revels supported Democrats in 1875 and "his accommodating posture paid off. In 1876, Governor Stone reappointed him to the presidency of Alcorn."[80] By July 1876, four months after Revels's testimony, he was once again president of Alcorn University.

Lawrence Otis Graham, author of a seminal book on Blanche Bruce, the second Black U.S. senator from Mississippi, claimed Revels "lost Black support with his moderate stands."[81] Historian and Vicksburg, Mississippi, native Julius E. Thompson wrote that Revels "betrayed his people by joining the ranks of their arch enemy, the Southern Democrats—for personal gain (his salary as president of Alcorn University)." Thompson also wrote, "His life serves as an example of the road which Black leaders should never take; if, in the final analysis Black people are to realize political, social and economic justice in America."[82] Bennett wrote in his 1967 book on Reconstruction that Revels supported "Klan-oriented Democrats. In public statements and public letters, Revels supported the Democrats and expressed the opinion that Democratic rule was best for his people."[83] Through all my extensive research, I could not find direct quotes from Revels that he supported the murderous Democrats in Mississippi. If he did, Revels was most certainly a grifter. If not, his legacy has been wrongfully mangled. We will never know.

There were other Douglass Republicans who clearly were not supportive of any movement to overthrow the gains of Reconstruction, including Robert Smalls, who became a war hero during the Civil War and served as a member of the U.S. House of Representatives from South Carolina's Seventh District; Joseph Rainey of South Carolina, the first Black member of the House of Representatives; and Aaron Bradley, a ferocious force in Georgia politics who famously critiqued white Republicans and passive Black leaders.[84]

There was also British-born Robert B. Elliott. He moved to the United States in 1867 and began studying law the next year in South Carolina. As a lawyer and a Republican, he served in many roles, including as a member of the South Carolina House of Representatives from 1871 to 1875. Elliott advocated for Black political power and biracial coalitions. He supported reinstituting political rights to former Confederates, but with some exceptions. He also worked on a measure to disempower the Ku Klux Klan.[85] In 1870, after the Klan murdered thirteen Black men accused of killing a white man in Union Courthouse, South Carolina, Elliott created legislation to enfeeble the hate group and was successful.

In an April 1870 speech, Elliott addressed the racist media of the time that was demonizing the Black victims of the KKK. "It is custom, sir, of Democratic [newspapers] to stigmatize the negroes of the South as being in a semi-barbarous condition; but pray tell me, who is the barbarian here, the murderer or the victim? I fling back in the teeth of those who make it this most false and foul aspersion upon the negro of the southern States."[87] Elliott became so popular that in 1872, he was reelected to the South Carolina House of Representatives with a whopping 93 percent of the vote.[87]

In January 1874, Elliott was a fighter for the Civil Rights Act of 1875,[88] which prohibited discrimination in public places and on public transportation. He delivered another incredible speech in the House of Representatives, saying in part, "In that dire extremity the members of the race which I have the honor in part to represent—the race which pleads for justice at your hands today, forgetful of their inhuman and brutalizing servitude at the South, their degradation and ostracism at the North—flew willingly and gallantly to the support of the national Government. Their sufferings, assistance, privations, and trials in the swamps and in the rice-fields, their valor on the land and on the sea, is a part of the ever-glorious record which makes up the history of a nation preserved, and might, should I urge the claim, incline you to respect and guarantee their rights and privileges as citizens of our common Republic."[89]

The country would have only one more Black U.S. senator during Reconstruction with Blanche Bruce, seated in 1875,[90] who represented Mississippi as a Republican until 1881. Born enslaved in 1841 Virginia, Bruce and his family worked on several plantations, including in Mississippi, and were often "rented" out to plantations. Bruce escaped slavery during the Civil War, and once slavery was abolished, he attended Oberlin College. In 1869, he arrived in Mississippi with only seventy-five cents. Like many Black Americans, Bruce heard about Reconstruction and the rise of Black communities all over the South. Governor James Alcorn took notice of Bruce and appointed to him to several government roles, and he was soon elected as sheriff of Bolivar County.[91]

Bruce was on the rise to the upper class. He was able to buy land, but life on Bruce's plantation had challenges. According to the seminal book on Blanche Bruce, *The Senator and the Socialite: The True Story of America's First Black Dynasty* by Lawrence Otis Graham, Black sharecroppers working on the Bruce plantation lived in "flimsy wooden shacks" and suffered in oppressive conditions.[92] Meanwhile, Blanche Bruce's wealth was growing, and by 1872, he cofounded Floreyville, Mississippi,[93] further increasing his status.

Bruce was creating close ties with the political elite at the time, including President Ulysses Grant.[94] Bruce also aligned himself with Governor Adelbert Ames, who was continuing to feud with James L. Alcorn, now the former Mississippi governor.[95] Bruce had his eyes set on the Mississippi U.S. Senate seat.

In 1874, the state legislature of Mississippi (again, at the time, the Senate was not elected by the people but by the state legislature) elected Blanche Bruce to the U.S. Senate. However, this was toward the end of the Reconstruction era, and times were quickly changing. Areas with once high Black voter turnout now saw turnout decline due to threats from white terrorists.[96] Nonetheless, once he arrived in Washington, DC, in March 1875, Bruce took his seat.[97] He was now the only Black man and the first formerly enslaved person in the U.S. Senate.

By March 1876, Bruce mounted an aggressive campaign to convene a Senate investigation into the violence of the Mississippi 1875 election. He demanded desegregation of the army, chaired the Senate select committee to investigate the Freedman's Savings and Trust Company, and proposed legislation to give unclaimed money from Black Civil War soldiers to Black colleges. Bruce also advocated against the Chinese Exclusion Act and argued for better treatment of Native Americans. Most of his proposed legislation

would flounder. Neither Revels nor Bruce was successful in pass-
ing much legislation in the deeply racist U.S. Senate of the time.
Instead, Black Republicans elected on a state level, often times in
biracial conventions, were mainstays in Black areas, empowering
renter and sharecropper rights, shaping fair tax policies, and outlining new state constitutions[98]—wildly different from the perfor-
mances of the Black Republicans of today.

Even with all Bruce's efforts, back in Mississippi, there were
rumblings that Bruce was ineffective in the U.S. Senate and
becoming removed from the Black community, especially as
his profile grew in high society. This chatter only worsened in
1877 when he voted to seat a former Confederate and defense
attorney for Klansmen, Lucius Quintus Cincinnatus Lamar, as a
Mississippi senator. Lamar benefited from the Mississippi Plan
that disempowered countless Black elected officials, but Bruce
supported Lamar, who replaced Republican James Alcorn, without uttering a word of objection.[99] The following year, Bruce
married a privileged Black socialite named Josephine Willson.
Blanche Bruce was already a political star, nearly as famous as
Frederick Douglass in his time, and the senator's every move
was documented by Black media. Their wedding was the first
wedding of a Black couple featured in the *New York Times*.[100]
Given Bruce's growing wealth, which included two homes in
Washington, DC, Black people in Mississippi were increasingly
unsure about where his allegiance lay. As Lawrence Otis Graham
said, Bruce "lived outside of the Black world."[101] With Mississippi
continuing to rage with violence and the right to vote vanishing,
a wealthy Black senator featured in the *New York Times* was not
representative of what Black Mississippians needed.

Congressman John R. Lynch prodded Bruce to imagine what

might become of him if he continued to immerse himself in the DC elite. Lynch wrote a letter to his colleague, which read in part, "I see the *Tribune* says that a U.S. Senator from Mississippi is actually afraid to come home. Have you seen that article? What will your Bolivar County Democratic Friends think of that?"[102] Lynch was not above critique either. After he married Ella Somerville, a wealthy light-skinned woman, and supposedly held a segregated wedding, hosting separate gatherings for whites and another for their Black friends, the *Washington Bee*, a popular Black newspaper, wrote about the Mississippi congressman, "Mr. Lynch has, we don't believe, elevated himself in the estimation of the colored people by his marriage to a young lady who is so prejudiced against people of color." The *Washington Bee* also accused Somerville's sister of being upset "because she married a nigger."[103]

With Bruce, Lynch, and even Revels, the Black elite, while small in number, were emerging, outlining class divisions that would become an ongoing issue for Black politicians and the communities they served for decades to come. Political power gave them access to social status and wealth. Bruce and Lynch were both born enslaved. Revels was a freeman but was not privileged. No one knows what these men said at their kitchen tables, without the surveillance of white eyes and ears, but publicly they certainly made questionable moves, particularly believing restoring rights to former Confederates would bring peace to the South. Even so, for one of the first times in history, there were Black southerners in elite social circles, and the immediacy of a better life could have been dangerously tempting while their constituents suffered.

In the end, Senator Blanche Bruce only served one term. He

didn't run for reelection, seeing the racist southern writing on the wall, and left the Senate in 1881.[104] He watched Black political power shrink, but Blanche Bruce remained one of the most well-known Black men in the country. He sat on the board of trustees at Howard University and continued work in politics. In 1898, Bruce died sixteen days after his fifty-eighth birthday from diabetes complications. It would take over 80 years for the next Black U.S. senator to be elected and more than 130 years for a Black U.S. senator to hold office in the South.

Throughout the 1870s, white violence permeated every corner of the South. While federal troops continued to be stationed in the interest of maintaining order, it was clear the white supremacists and the Ku Klux Klan were gaining power as terror made visiting the voting booth increasingly perilous. Former Republican state legislatures became Democratic state legislatures,[105] and white Republicans in the North were growing weary of the "Negro problem."[106] Vile propaganda and misinformation flooded newspapers nationwide, saying that the Black elected officials were incompetent and causing chaos. True to the example of Abraham Lincoln, northern white Republicans were ultimately more concerned about the Union collapsing than the livelihood of Black people.

After the Panic of 1873, a massive financial crisis,[107] and corruption in President Ulysses Grant's administration,[108] Democrats took control of the House of Representatives[109] for the first time since 1860. The year 1876 marked one hundred years since the signing of the Declaration of Independence. With President Grant's term ending, Republican Rutherford Hayes ran against Democrat Samuel J. Tilden.[110] The contested election had 82 percent voter turnout, the highest in American history.[111] Turnout may have been higher, but the Black voter numbers are unknown, and it's safe to assume white southerners suppressed the Black vote. Tilden won the popular vote with 51 percent, and Hayes earned 48 percent, but the electoral college had other plans.

Both political parties claimed to be the winner of three southern states: Florida, South Carolina, and Louisiana.[112] To this day, we have no idea who officially won those states. If the Black vote hadn't been suppressed, it is certainly possible Hayes would have been victorious without debate.[113] Instead, a constitutional crisis ensued, and what would become known as the Compromise of 1877 would be another assault on Black southerners.

The compromise was an agreement between the political parties that allowed Republican Rutherford Hayes to win the presidency with the condition that federal troops would leave the South, returning complete control to southern Democrats, many of whom were former Confederates. Republicans agreed, turning their backs on Black men, women, and children. Reconstruction had vanished, along with all its gains.

One can only imagine the trauma Black citizens endured seeing the party that they fought for in the Civil War sell them up the soon-to-be Jim Crow river.

Henry Adams, a Black leader and Louisianian, said, "The whole South—every state in the South—had got into the hands of the very men that held us as slaves."[114] Most importantly, the Compromise of 1877 illustrated the threat of the Black electorate, which was growing. If Black men were voting for other Black men, where did that leave a white elected official—Democrat or Republican? Eventually, white men would no longer be the mouthpiece for Black citizens; whites needed Blacks to not gain too much independence to maintain their political power. The betrayal of Black people in 1877 was to maintain white supremacy in both political parties.

Frederick Douglass had already seen the betrayal of the Republican Party coming two years before. During his 1875 July 4th speech, Douglass prophetically stated, "If war among the whites brought peace and liberty to the Blacks what will peace among the whites bring?"[115]

As he did with President Lincoln, Douglass addressed the cowardice of the Republican Party. "The signs of the times, are not all in our favor," he said. "There are even in the Republican Party, indications of a disposition to get rid of us. Men are seeking new allies and smiling in faces upon which they never smiled before since the war. A disposition is seen to shake off the Negro and accept the old master's class."[116]

Most prophetic of all, Douglass pointed to fissures within the Black community. "One of the most unpleasant features of the situation for us is in ourselves," he said. "We are a divided people, and have no men among us, I fear, whose counsel will be headed in the right direction. It has been our misfortune to be educated by two hundred years of slavery to respect white men and despise ourselves."[117]

Douglass's critique of the Republicans was borne out to be true. In the horrific years to come, the Black Republican grift would fully bloom, and Douglass Republicans would nearly become extinct.

CHAPTER 3

MONTGOMERY AND WASHINGTON

"It were well that such a man had never been born, much less have been elected to represent the Negroes of Mississippi."

—The Cleveland Gazette on Isaiah Montgomery[1]

IN MARCH 1877, REPUBLICAN RUTHERFORD B. HAYES BECAME the nineteen president of the United States. The hell that followed was the seeds of Jim Crow beginning to sprout with Democrats and Republicans enabling more white terror. As agreed on in the Compromise of 1877, federal troops abandoned the South. Democrats tightened their hold on the former Confederacy. Reconstruction, a time designed to repair the nation after war, was a closed chapter. It wasn't only slavery that led to Black America starting from behind the rest of the nation; it was the Democratic and Republican failure of Reconstruction.

When the topic of slavery comes up, many of today's Republicans say it's time to "move on." As Winsome Sears, Virginia's first Black female lieutenant governor who is also Jamaican American, stated, "How long are we going to go back there?"[2]

Let's say Black people somehow dismissed hundreds of years

of rape, family separation, denial of formal education, uncom-
pensated manual labor, and being stripped of cultural ties to the
African continent—also racial inequality, systemic oppression, and
grim statistics that have barely budged since the 1960s.[3] Racism
would still exist, by no fault of Black Americans. The onus goes on
whites of all economic backgrounds who fell for racist and classist
gaslighting.

How different would Black communities be if we still had
thriving majority-Black business districts and neighborhoods
that hadn't been destroyed like those in Memphis, Tennessee
(1866) or York County, South Carolina (1871)?[4] In May 2021, the
Associated Press reported that Tulsa, Oklahoma, had not recov-
ered one hundred years after the violent race massacre in 1921.
Reverend Robert Turner, the pastor of Vernon African Methodist
Episcopal Church there, told the outlet, "What happened in Tulsa
wasn't just unique to Tulsa. This happened all over the country. It
was just that Tulsa was the largest. It damaged our community.
And we haven't rebounded since. I think it's past time that justice
be done to atone for that."[5]

Yes, slavery is America's greatest sin, but the gutting of
Reconstruction reforms is America's greatest failure.

When Republicans compromised away the protections of
Reconstruction, the last shreds of federal protection were tossed
aside, and white racists were free to suppress Black political power
and siphon off Black wealth and land. Deprived of a federal government willing to back up the rights of Black people to vote,
within ten years of the Compromise of 1877, Black Republicans
who were elected during Reconstruction lost reelection or were
pushed out of office.[6]

South Carolina attorney general Robert B. Elliott, who had

given the iconic speech in 1874 in support of the Civil Rights Act of 1875, was forced out of office in May 1877. Although he remained in politics, sadly, Elliott passed away on August 9, 1884, at only forty-one years old and died in poverty.[7] Joseph Rainey, representing South Carolina's First District, was voted out by 1879.[8] Jeremiah Haralson, who represented Alabama's First District, lost to a white Democrat in 1877[9]—questionable, considering the district had a large Black population. Haralson ran again in 1878 but lost. Mississippi senator Blanche Bruce was out of the Senate by 1881. By 1887, the last Black man elected to Congress before the Compromise of 1877—Robert Smalls, representing South Carolina's Seventh District—was voted out of office.

It wasn't enough to remove Black people from office; white supremacists sought to bar them from public life. October 15, 1883, is considered one of the most "barbarous" moments in American history. On that day, in an 8–1 decision, the Supreme Court deemed the 1875 Civil Rights Act unconstitutional. This law, which had given Black Americans the right to equal access to public accommodations and prohibited racial discrimination by individuals or private businesses, was nullified by a racist Supreme Court.[10]

There was one dissenting opinion. Justice John Marshall Harlan, who once owned enslaved people, wrote, "Scarcely a day passes without our seeing in this court-room citizens of the white and black races sitting side by side watching the progress of our business. It would never occur to anyone that the presence of a colored citizen in a court-house or court-room was an invasion of the social rights of white persons who may frequent such places."[11]

Black communities across the country were horrified. Bishop Henry McNeal Turner, the first Black chaplain in the United States Colored Troops during the Civil War, condemned the decision: "The world has never witnessed such barbarous laws entailed upon a free people as have grown out of the decision of the United States Supreme Court, issued October 15, 1883."[12] In a speech that same year, Frederick Douglass said, "This decision has inflicted a heavy calamity upon the seven millions of the colored people of this country, and left them naked and defenseless against the action of a malignant, vulgar and pitiless prejudice."[13]

The ruling created a domino effect. By 1890, southern states, starting with Mississippi, were holding constitutional conventions to erode the rights of Black men to vote.[14] One Black man, Isaiah Montgomery, the only Black delegate in Mississippi,[15] participated. While complicated, Montgomery was a grifter, to be sure—participating in a shocking clause that would wreak havoc all over the South. He would also lend his support to another, even more successful grifter named Booker T. Washington. The story of these men who perfected the Black Republican grift starts decades earlier on a Mississippi plantation.

Montgomery, born May 21, 1847, and his father, Benjamin Thornton Montgomery, were formerly enslaved on the Hurricane Plantation,[16] which held 350 humans in bondage near Vicksburg, Mississippi.[17] Their enslaver, Joseph E. Davis, was the older brother of Jefferson Davis, the president of the Confederate States of America. Benjamin was a "manager" and bookkeeper on the Hurricane Plantation, and his son Isaiah was a "house slave."

As a child, Isaiah learned how to read and write, which was illegal, and he had access to the Davis's library.

When the Civil War came, Joseph Davis left the Hurricane Plantation, leaving Benjamin in charge. Eventually, Benjamin and the rest of the Montgomerys fled for Union-occupied territory.

After the war, the family returned to Mississippi with other formerly enslaved people and began farming on the land where they were once enslaved. By the end of the Civil War, the land had gained an enormous profit, all under Black supervision. Then-General Ulysses S. Grant deemed the area "negro paradise" and sought to have the land leased to free Black people.[18]

Several Black Republican leaders came out of the Hurricane Plantation. The speaker of Mississippi's House of Representatives and one of the first Black Americans to hold office in the state, Israel Shadd, was one.[19] Albert Johnson, who served in Mississippi's legislature and constitutional convention, was another.[20]

After the war, due to President Andrew Johnson's push to restore property to white supremacists in Southern states, the land was returned to Joseph Davis. But he did something unheard of. In desperate need of money, Davis sold the land to Benjamin Montgomery. By 1867, Benjamin and his son Isaiah had earned enough wealth to buy not only the Hurricane Plantation but a neighboring plantation called Brierfield. The family was on the rise, and that same year, Isaiah Montgomery took public office as justice of the peace in Davis Bend, Mississippi.[21]

By 1877, however, the Montgomerys were struggling to keep their plantation afloat. Benjamin Montgomery had died, and Isaiah used the farming and business skills he had learned from his father to reestablish new land.

In 1887, Isaiah and his cousin Benjamin Green founded Mound Bayou in northwest Mississippi. Mound Bayou was an all-Black, thirty-thousand-acre, prosperous piece of land cultivated by hundreds of Black farmers.[22] What's more, Mound Bayou somehow avoided a white terrorist attack, unlike many other thriving Black areas in the South.

Isaiah Montgomery not only had influence in ownership of the land but also found fame with a new level of treachery.

In August 1890, Mississippi held a state constitutional convention, the first of many throughout the South, aimed at disenfranchising Black men. The plan was to suppress Black votes without explicitly saying, "Black men cannot vote," which would violate the Constitution. Despite the coded language, Solomon Saladin Calhoon, the Mississippi convention's president and a white county judge, made the intentions clear: "Let's tell the truth if it bursts the bottom of the universe. We came here to exclude the Negro. Nothing short of this will answer." At the convention, a new state constitution was created that included an "understanding clause," which meant a voter must be able to read and understand every part of the state constitution or they could not vote. Their tactics included a poll tax and literary tests.[23]

There were 134 delegates: 130 were Democrats, one was a member of an independent party, another a white Republican conservative, and former Republican governor James Alcorn—identified as a "conservative." All three of them supported disenfranchising Black men, a vile move from Alcorn, considering he claimed to support civil rights for Black people and Alcorn University, a land-grant college for Black people, was named after him. Last, there was Isaiah Montgomery, only labeled as a Republican. Montgomery, a formerly enslaved person who reaped the benefits of Reconstruction, served as the sole Black delegate at the convention and cast a vote to disenfranchise his own people.[24]

Casting a vote in silence, similar to how Bruce and Revels in the U.S. Senate quietly voted to restore rights to former Confederates, would have been perplexing enough. But Montgomery went a step further and delivered a disgraceful speech—published in the *New*

York World—that could have come straight from the mouth of a white supremacist: "The work of this Convention in order to be successful, must restrict the franchise by prescribing such qualification for voters as would reduce the negro vote considerably below the white vote of the State; and such restrictions, of course, to be fairly applied and only affecting the colored voters to a greater or lesser extent because of their inferior development in the line of civilization."

He went on, "In the Convention and in the committee room I have taken an active interest in every practical movement to purify the ballot and lift it to a higher standard in the estimation of the people, at the same time conscious of the fact that the reforms under consideration would result in placing the voters of my race largely in the minority."

We can only speculate what might have motivated Montgomery to so publicly back white supremacy. Perhaps it was a strategy to keep Mound Bayou safe from white violence. Even so, it is hard to imagine that this goal required Montgomery to willingly call for striking "down the rights and liberties of 123,000 freemen" who looked like him.

He rounded out the speech by saying, "It is a fearful sacrifice laid upon the burning altar of liberty. Many of these men I know personally; their hearts are true as steel. Many are soldiers who have stood amid the smoke of battle on bloody fields in defense of the flag which every American probably hails as the ensign of freedom and his talisman of protection and all civilized lands... I wish to say to my people, may we have not taken away your high privilege, but only lifted it to a higher plane and exalted the station of the great American birthright. I wish to tell them that the sacrifice has been made to restore confidence, the great missing link between the two races; to restore honesty and purity to the ballot box and to confer for the great boon of political liberty upon the Commonwealth of Mississippi."[25]

Montgomery's words substantiate the notion that he had cut a self-serving bargain with Mississippi's white elite. Two weeks after Montgomery's vote, he reportedly stated, "It was the best that could be done. We had to take the best that we could get."[26]

Apart from his nakedly bigoted speech, Montgomery's position made no sense. He created Mound Bayou because of the political power Black citizens gained during Reconstruction— power he helped strip away. Montgomery's success, if you want to call it that, wasn't the result of his individual initiative but came as part of a collective effort of Douglass Republicans. His traitorous act is one of the first examples of the nefariousness of Black capitalism that figures like Booker T. Washington would later come to admire. Montgomery took things even further. He didn't argue, as Booker T. Washington might have, that Black people should slow down and prioritize economic development over civic participation. He essentially said that Black people are too stupid to vote so let's appease white supremacists.

Black media and leaders loudly disagreed. In October 1890, the *Cleveland Gazette* called Montgomery's speech "a disgrace to the race and our civilization. It were well that such a man had never been born, much less have been elected to represent the Negroes of Mississippi… A few more Montgomerys and we will be mortally wounded in our house."[27] Lawyer and civil rights leader Thomas McCants Stewart said Montgomery would "make it possible for the judges of election to enfranchise every illiterate white man and to disenfranchise every illiterate Black man."[28] Journalist Ida B. Wells "criticized him [Montgomery] severely" in her newspaper

Free State, stating, "Montgomery should never have acquiesced." Montgomery traveled to Memphis for a meeting with Wells to "explain his position." Wells wrote in her autobiography, "Although we never agreed that his course had been the right one, we became the best of friends, and he helped to increase the circulation of the paper wonderfully by sending me all through the Delta."[29]

On October 21, 1890, at Bethel Literary and Historical Association in the Metropolitan AME Church in Washington, DC, Frederick Douglass delivered his own fiery verdict on Isaiah Montgomery. "He has virtually said to the nation: 'You have done wrong in giving us this great liberty. You should give us back a part of our bondage,'" Douglass said. "He has surrendered a part of his rights to an enemy who will make this surrender a reason for demanding all of his rights. He has conducted his people to a depth from which they will be invited to a lower deep, for if he can rightfully surrender a part of his heritage from the National Government at the bidding of his oppressors, he may surrender the whole. The people with whom he makes this deal are restrained in dealing with the rights of colored men by no sense of modesty or moderation in their demands. They want all that is to be had and will take all that they can get. Their real sentiment is that no Negro shall or ought to have the right to vote."

Douglass relented only insofar as he suggested Montgomery may have been too ignorant to know what he had done. "Yet I have no denunciation for the man Montgomery. He is not a conscious traitor though his act is treason: treason to the cause of the colored people, not only of his own State, but of the United States. I wish the consequences of his act could be confined to Mississippi alone, but I fear this cannot be. Other colored men in other States, dazzled by the fame obtained by Mr. Montgomery through the

Democratic press, will probably imitate his bad example."[30] For Douglass to say that Montgomery was "not a conscious traitor" is charitable—but "dazzled by the fame" is an instructive phrase for understanding what Montgomery had in common with the grifters of today. As to "imitate his bad example," Southern states would follow Mississippi's example and strike down the right to vote for Black men state by state.

Montgomery was praised by white supremacist media for years. The *New York World* wrote about Montgomery "the man is an orator of whom any race should be proud." The *Washington Post* raved Montgomery "has shown so much intelligence in the Mississippi constitutional convention." He even earned praise from former President Grover Cleveland.[31]

The praise, over 130 years ago, mirrors the adulation current Black Republicans receive from right-wing media today when they proclaim they left the "Democratic plantation,"[32] rail against "critical race theory,"[33] rant that the first Black president divided America,[34] or wrongly make welfare a Black issue.[35]

It's unknown if Montgomery had a secret deal with the white Mississippi delegates and, in return, Mound Bayou would be protected. What is known is that he personally prospered in the years that followed. In 1902, Montgomery stepped down as mayor of Mound Bayou, and with the help of Booker T. Washington, President Theodore Roosevelt made him the receiver of public funds in Jackson, Mississippi. Approximately a year later, Montgomery was accused of personally pocketing $5,000 of government money. Booker T. Washington demanded that Montgomery resign. Nevertheless, Montgomery was a Mississippi delegate for the Republican National Convention the following year.[36]

In the wake of the convention, Mound Bayou thrived. It was celebrated in the media for being segregated and prosperous—within white rule. However, Mound Bayou's economy eventually disintegrated, partly due to a lack of capital and the town's bank being overextended.[37]

Having retired from the mayor's office, Montgomery remained a presence in Mound Bayou. According to the book *Black Leaders of the Nineteenth Century*, while Montgomery in his later years was "comfortably established as the patriarch in a twenty-one-room red brick mansion which dominated the village scene," he would admit that "the dominant spirit of the South will be satisfied with nothing less than a retrogression of the Negro back towards serfdom and slavery."[38]

Isaiah Montgomery died in 1924 and was eulogized by a member of the Mississippi House of Representatives, Walter Sillers Sr., a proud racist who praised the Ku Klux Klan and helped to abolish Reconstruction in the state. Sillers said at Montgomery's funeral that he was "one of the greatest of his race, a man known throughout this great nation as one of the most thoughtful and helpful leaders of his people."[39] Though a white supremacist exalted him even in death, a northern missionary said Montgomery was "more hated by Negroes" than any other Black man in the state.[40] Such is the legacy a grifter receives for betraying Black interests for vested interests.

Montgomery was an outlier among the few Black elected figures during this era. There were several Black Republicans in the House of Representatives during the mid to late 1800s. Henry P. Cheatham represented North Carolina's Second District from March 4, 1889, to 1893.[41] John Mercer Langston served in Virginia's Fourth District, the first Black person elected to Congress in the state,[42] and Thomas E. Miller, who was white-passing, served in South Carolina's Seventh District from September 1890 to March 1891, only six months.[43] George W. Murray served in South Carolina's Seventh District from 1893 to 1895 and the state's First District from June 1896 to March 1897.[44] George Henry White represented North Carolina's Second District from 1897 to 1901.[45]

Unlike Montgomery, these Douglass Republicans advocated for Black farmers and teachers and helped to establish HBCUs. However, whites thwarted them as the right to vote for Black men across the South rapidly slipped further away with each state constitutional convention.

With the vote increasingly out of reach, Douglass Republicans being pushed out of office, and Jim Crow segregation hardening across the South, the prospects for Black prosperity looked increasingly grim. The door was open for a new Black leader—and he couldn't have been more different from Frederick Douglass.

Seven months after Frederick Douglass died, Booker T. Washington, who was already well known in Black circles as president of Tuskegee Institute (later Tuskegee University), would become one of the most famous Black men in the country after delivering his Atlanta Compromise speech, also known as the Atlanta Exposition speech, of 1895. Washington would outrage many Black citizens, though white elites and media were overjoyed.

On September 18, 1895, before a predominately white audience at the Cotton States and International Exposition in Atlanta, Georgia, for which Isaiah Montgomery was one of the Black commissioners,[46] thirty-nine-year-old Washington said that Black people should accept being second-class citizens. He called on Blacks in the South to limit themselves to industrial skill and not push for social equality. He blamed the failure of Reconstruction on the "ignorant and inexperienced" and declared, "It is at the bottom of life we must begin, and not at the top."[47] While some may call this strategy and a speech to bring the races together, it was a stab to the countless Black people during Reconstruction who paved the way for his success, including as president of Tuskegee. To think that Black people somehow began "at the top" after the Civil War is a noxious narrative. There is no shame in industrial skill, but how effective is that skill if there is no political power, which many towns across the South saw as their homes and businesses weren't burned to the ground? Was Washington a man of his times, or did he know if he said what southern whites wanted to hear, he would rise? Maybe the latter. Washington became a sensation and was showered with love by the white press.

Charleston, South Carolina's *News and Courier* called Washington "one of the great men of the South" and wrote this wildly racist line: "His skin is colored, but his head is sound and his heart is in the right place."[48] The *Atlanta Constitution* praised Washington as a "sensible and progressive Negro educator."[49]

The *Tuskegeean* declared Washington was "the new Negro leader."[50]

Black media and leaders wasted little time blasting Booker T. Washington. Bishop Henry McNeal Turner, who was close to Frederick Douglass, said Black people "will have to live a long time to undo the harm he has done to our race."[51] The *Atlanta Advocate* labeled Washington "Prof. Bad Taste" and wrote with tons of sarcasm, "Prof. B.T., or Bad Taste Wash made a speech… The white press style Prof. Bad Taste the new Negro but if there is anything in him except the most servile type of the old Negro we fail to find it any of his last acts. So let the race labor and pray that no more new Negroes such as Prof. Bad Taste Washington will bob up."[52]

The movement against Washington persisted. In 1896, John Hope, president of Atlanta University who would eventually become the first Black president of Morehouse College, said about Washington, "I regard it as cowardly and dishonest for any of our colored men to tell white people or colored people that we are not struggling for equality. If money, education, and honesty will not bring to me as much privilege, as much equality as they bring to any American citizens, then they are to me a curse, and not a blessing."[53] W. E. B. Du Bois, having earned a PhD from Harvard, certainly did not believe that Black people should be confined to trades and joined a group of anti-Bookerites led by activist and writer William Monroe Trotter.[54]

Nonetheless, the Atlanta Compromise speech of 1895 was like hitting the lottery for Washington. The white elites were so enraptured by Washington that a year later, Harvard University gave him an honorary degree,[55] and he lectured across the country. If there were Fox News in 1901, Booker T. Washington would have landed a primetime cable news show. In the words Frederick Douglass used to describe Isaiah Montgomery in 1890, Washington had been "dazzled by the fame."

By 1901, Washington had published his iconic autobiography *Up from Slavery*. One of the most outrageous parts of the pull-yourself-up-by-your-slavery-boot-straps memoir was that Washington expressed sympathy for the white enslaver who raped his mother, writing, "He was just another unfortunate victim of the institution."[56]

Although Washington was not an elected official, he accrued considerable power. He served as an adviser to Presidents William

McKinley, William Howard Taft, and Theodore Roosevelt. Telling Black people to be subservient made Washington rich, powerful, and famous. Donations from wealthy whites poured in for Tuskegee University, including, in 1903, $450,000 from Scottish American philanthropist Andrew Carnegie. Additionally, Carnegie gifted Washington with a whopping $150,000 for his personal use. Washington's three children attended all-white boarding schools and prep schools. Portia Washington, his daughter, was a student at Wellesley College and Bradford Academy, white institutions that were very different from industrial education.[57]

Ida B. Wells basically called Washington a grifter, lambasting him for "telling chicken-stealing stories on his own people in order to amuse his audiences and get money for Tuskegee."[58]

Was Booker T. Washington a grifter? He profited from excusing racism and insisted that Black people were at their best as second-class citizens. By insisting that Black people stay poor, uneducated, and docile, he was able to become a wealthy man, pointedly disregarding his own advice. That self-serving hypocrisy defined him as a grifter for his era.

While some Black people agreed with Washington, many pushed back. On July 30, 1903, Washington appeared at a National Negro Business League meeting in Boston. A near riot broke out after William Monroe Trotter, Granville Martin, Bernard Charles, and others heckled Washington from the crowd as he spoke at a podium. Trotter was a figure of some prominence as editor of the *Boston Guardian*. A week before Washington arrived, he had written, "In view of the fact that you are understood to be unwilling to insist upon the Negro having every right (both civil and political) would it not be calamity at this juncture to make you our leader... Don't you know you would help the race more by exposing the new form of slavery just outside the gates of Tuskegee than by preaching submission? Are the rope and the torch all that the race is to get under your leadership?"[59]

Nearly two thousand people were in attendance when chaos ensued at the Boston meeting. Trotter, Martin, and Charles were arrested, and Trotter's sister Maude reportedly stabbed a police officer with a hatpin. Trotter and Martin spent a month in jail, while Maude was fined and released.

Trotter had captured something vital about Washington. He realized that Washington's anti-Black rhetoric was all about Washington. He wanted to be the leader. He wanted to lead the line. Washington thought he alone could fix all the ills of Black people in America, while the white elite handsomely paid him to be their mouthpiece

The danger in Washington's rhetoric is that it was another nail in the coffin of disempowering Black elected officials in the South. The Atlanta Compromise speech was reported all over the country and represented nothing less than a gift to white supremacists. If an allegedly distinguished Black man like Booker T. Washington was arguing that Black men should submit to white political rule, then saying so wasn't "racist." If Booker T. Washington insisted that Black people should know their place and have zero political power, white supremacists seeking to preserve that powerlessness in law could take cover behind Washington's Blackness. Exactly eight months after Washington's Atlanta Compromise speech, *Plessy v. Ferguson* solidified Jim Crow and the lie of "separate but equal."

Yes, Washington was fighting to uplift Black businesses with the National Negro Business League,[60] and he spoke out against lynchings,[61] secretly donated to civil rights cases, and did not want to return to chattel slavery. If Washington were ever an elected official, I doubt (though I could be wrong) that he would have voted to disenfranchise Black men like Isaiah Montgomery. Yet as W. E. B. Du Bois wrote in *The Souls of Black Folks* about Washington, "His doctrine has tended to make the whites, North and South, shift the burden of the Negro problem to the Negro's shoulders and stand aside as critical and rather pessimistic spectators; when in fact the burden belongs to the nation, and the hands of none of us are clean if we bend not our energies to righting these great wrongs."[62] Translation—do not blame an oppressed community for being oppressed; point the finger at the oppressor. Washington made Black people, who were only a few generations removed from slavery, the problem in a system they did not design or propagate.

Not surprisingly, Booker T. Washington would praise Isaiah Montgomery and Mound Bayou in the 1907 essay "A Town Owned by Negroes," writing, "In a certain sense, it may be said that the Mound Bayou town and colony have been a school in self-government for its colonists. They have had an opportunity there, such as Negro people have rarely had elsewhere, to learn the real meaning of political institutions and to prepare themselves for the duties of responsibility and citizenship."[63]

It's unclear if Washington knew of Montgomery's destructive past or if he didn't care.

Thankfully, others weren't willing to be an Isaiah Montgomery. When Representative George H. White, the final Black elected official from the nineteenth century, left Congress in March 1901, he delivered a rousing speech, reminding his racist white colleagues of the success Black Republicans had since Reconstruction.

White said, "We have reduced the illiteracy of the race at least 45 percent. We have written and published near 500 books. We have nearly 300 newspapers, three of which are dailies. We have now in practice over 2,000 lawyers, and a corresponding number of doctors. We have accumulated over $12,000,000 worth of school property and about $40,000,000 worth of church property. We have about 140,000 farms and homes, valued at in the neighborhood of $750,000,000, and personal property valued at about $170,000,000."

White added, "We have done it in the face of lynching, burning at the stake, with the humiliation of 'Jim Crow' laws, the disfranchisement of our male citizens, slander and degradation of our women, with the factories closed against us."

He closed with, "This, Mr. Chairman, is perhaps the negroes' temporary farewell to the American Congress but let me say, Phoenix-like he will rise up someday and come again."[64]

It would take twenty-eight years for the next Black man to be in Congress.

The Republican Party was losing its ironclad grip on Black voters. There were numerous and blatant betrayals of a community that helped to empower two of the most important presidents in American history: Lincoln and Grant. A new dawn was coming, and not only would Black voters not be welcomed in the GOP, but they would be disinvited and eventually exiled from the party of Lincoln.

CHAPTER 4

ROBINSON, BROOKE, AND NIXON CAPITALISM

"A vote against me is a vote against Stokely Carmichael."

—*Edward Brooke during his 1966 Senate campaign*[1]

BLACK AMERICANS REMAINED LOYAL TO THE REPUBLICAN Party for decades. The sea change came with Democratic president Franklin D. Roosevelt and the New Deal.

Americans responded to the Great Depression by voting out Republican president Herbert Hoover and delivering the White House and both houses of Congress to Franklin D. Roosevelt and the Democratic Party in 1933. Upon taking office, Roosevelt launched the New Deal, a series of financial reforms and social safety nets that would reinvent America: the federal Social Security Act of 1935, the Public Works Administration, the Federal Emergency Relief Administration, the National Youth Administration, and more.

The New Deal was rife with discrimination. Programs were tailored to exclude Black Americans whenever possible.[2] The Social Security Act purposely did not include agriculture and domestic workers—60 percent of Black Americans held jobs in those fields at the time.[3] The New Deal's housing programs helped to enforce segregated neighborhoods. Democrats may have taken up a "big government" approach to solving an economic crisis, but they still were Democrats, a party rooted in the Jim Crow South. Roosevelt believed that if programs assisted Black communities, he'd lose the southern Democrats or Dixiecrats, and his New Deal would flounder in Congress.[4] It was a political scenario not so different from President Andrew Johnson's push to gut Reconstruction. Johnson and Roosevelt didn't want whites to "pay" for formerly enslaved and Black people to succeed, a ludicrous notion.

Nonetheless, whether Roosevelt liked it or not, some programs inadvertently helped Black communities, particularly strengthening labor unions, which would empower the Brotherhood of Sleeping Car Porters, led by A. Philip Randolph.[5] This economic boost resulted in over 70 percent of Black people voting for Roosevelt's second term.[6] A November 1936 front-page headline from the *New York Amsterdam News* read, "Big Negro Vote Backs F.D.R. as New Deal Sweeps Nation." The article pointed out Black Democrats, especially locally, were being elected across the country in Philadelphia, St. Louis, New York City, Chicago, and more: "Both the national and local Democratic parties have given Negro leaders opportunities to become integrated into their cities... In all of these cities Negroes helped to shape the policy of the Democratic party; and by so doing they have reached political heights no Negro Republicans have ever attained."[7]

Republicans were proving themselves to be increasingly difficult partners with Black America. The first Black Republican of the twentieth century elected to Congress was Oscar Stanton De Priest, who dealt with hell from his Republican colleagues. Even when the GOP elected a Black Republican, he couldn't get acceptance and support within his party.

De Priest was born in Florence, Alabama, to parents who were formerly enslaved. He moved to Chicago in the late 1880s during the great migration of Black people moving from the South to the North. He began a career in Chicago politics, working with grassroots Black organizations that were leveraging political power due to the rising number of Black residents in the city. De Priest made history as Chicago's first Black alderman, but his election to Illinois's First District in 1929 was no easy battle.[8]

During the 1928 primaries, the Republican incumbent died of a heart attack. Similar to how Black people in Mississippi during Reconstruction insisted on a Black U.S. senator, Black people in Illinois's First District demanded the choice to vote for a Black man to represent them in the House of Representatives. Five ward committeemen chose Oscar Stanton De Priest, which caused a political war. Weeks before the November election, De Priest was indicted and arrested on voter fraud and other bogus charges. According to the *Negro History Bulletin*, the *Chicago Defender* described the attack on De Priest as the "white political machine of the Republican party wanted De Priest to withdraw." De Priest was able to post bond and refused to exit the race. In the end, he beat a white Democrat, winning all the Black precincts and losing every white precinct.[9]

Unfortunately, Oscar De Priest's battles had only just begun. Under Republican president Herbert Hoover, De Priest's wife, Jessie, was invited by First Lady Lou Hoover to a tea for congressional wives at the White House.[10] The prospect of a Black woman attending the reception with white women at the White House caused an uproar. The Texas legislature passed a resolution to censure First Lady Lou Hoover, and the Mississippi legislature passed a measure for President Hoover to give "careful and thoughtful consideration to the necessity of the preservation of the racial integrity of the white race."[11]

The Hoovers responded by appeasing the racists. The First Lady ultimately held four separate receptions, so Jessie De Priest would attend the smallest reception consisting only of the white congressional wives who weren't in a tizzy with being in the same room as a Black woman.

Oscar Stanton De Priest held nothing back when addressing his racist colleagues. He told a newspaper, "I've been elected to Congress the same as any other member. I'm going to have the rights of every other congressman—no more and no less—if it's in the congressional barber shop or at a White House tea."[12]

Hoover took offense. In his memoirs, he defended his wife: "In giving the usual teas for Congressman's wives, Ms. Hoover insisted upon inviting the Negro's wife equally with the others. She was warned by some of her Congressional lady friends not to do it. The Negro Congressman did not particularly help matters by announcing to the press that his wife had received such an invitation. In consequence the southern press denounced this 'defiling' of the White House and southern reporters lined up to watch the colored lady come and go, hoping to witness the prophecy that some Congressman's wife would drop out. Mrs. Hoover had more sense than to give any such an occasion for affront to her guest or to the White House. Nor did she wish to offend ladies from the South... The speeches of the southern Senators and Congressmen, the editorials in the southern press and a denunciatory resolution by the Texas legislator wounded her deeply. Her tears, however, did not melt her indomitable determination."[13] The expectation, it seems, was that in exchange for being invited to the White House, a Black congressman and his wife had to stay mum about the racist backlash.

Facing constant death threats, De Priest racked up a long list of fights, but he didn't have many wins. He demanded pensions for formerly enslaved people "to give recognition and do justice to those who are now living who were emancipated by the Emancipation Proclamation issued by Abraham Lincoln in 1863." He attempted to desegregate a restaurant in the House of Representatives after one of his aides, who was Black, was denied service. De Priest also fought to pass an anti-lynching law, which never made it through Congress.[14]

For much of his time in Congress, he was a political star in the Black press. He spoke across the country at HBCUs, receiving an "enthusiastic ovation" at Tuskegee Institute, and traveled down South to support voting rights.[15] But dealing with constant battles from Democrats and Republicans in Congress, he would eventually face criticism in the Black media. In 1934, the *Atlanta Daily World* wrote he was "conspicuous by his silence on important questions. As a legislator, as a statesman, as a student of those things affecting the Negro's welfare, he has been a grand and glorious flop."[16] After three terms, De Priest lost his congressional seat to Democrat Arthur W. Mitchell. In 1935, Mitchell became the first Black man to serve as a Democrat in Congress. It would take fifty-six years for the GOP to elect another Black man to the House of Representatives. Mitchell's historic election and President Hoover's passiveness on civil rights were a signal that Black voters were shifting away from the GOP.

By the end of President Roosevelt's first term, the traditional linkage between Black voters and the Republican Party was continuing to erode. In spite of the racism built into the New Deal, Black Americans saw some positive change in their communities and responded by showing up at the voting booth. By 1948, Blacks were voting Democratic at 77 percent.[17]

For the next few decades, Black voters remained somewhat up for grabs. Democrats had not yet expelled the Dixiecrats; Black Republicans, though fewer in numbers than before, still remembered the legacies of the Civil War, Frederick Douglass, and Reconstruction. A chunk of Black voters were Republicans, maintaining around the 30 percent range for several presidential elections. It was possible to tactically identify as a Republican and try to push the party to take a better position on civil rights. However, a difficult path was ahead for a few notable figures—including baseball legend Jackie Robinson and politician Edward Brooke.

By the 1950s, the most famous Black Republican was Jackie Robinson,[18] the sports legend who integrated baseball.[19]

In late 1956, Robinson had retired from baseball but continued to use his status as a public figure and civil rights activist.[20] He met future President Richard Nixon in the early 1950s and developed a friendship. For the 1960 presidential election, Democratic Massachusetts senator John F. Kennedy was up against Vice President Richard Nixon. Robinson refused to endorse John F. Kennedy,[21] believing he was weak on civil rights. Kennedy had been called "a friend of the South" after breakfast with racist Alabama governor John Patterson,[22] alongside reports that Kennedy was meeting privately with other southern leaders, reassuring them he would not push for civil rights.[23] Also, as a senator from Massachusetts, Kennedy had cast a procedural vote against President Dwight Eisenhower's Civil Rights Act of 1957, despite supporting some sections. Robinson had ample reason to believe that Kennedy was no friend to Black people.

Losing the support of Robinson was politically costly, and Kennedy defended his controversial vote in a 1959 letter directly to Robinson. Along with recounting his civil rights record, he wrote, "You refer in your column to a vote to send the 1957 civil rights bill back to committee. This vote was largely a question of judgment and such staunch civil rights supporters as Senator Morse agreed with me that it would be the better procedure to have the bill sent to committee."[24]

The fact was Republicans did not have a stellar civil rights record either. President Dwight Eisenhower, with Nixon as vice president, had been a feeble champion for the rights of Black people, and Robinson was losing patience. Robinson wrote in a 1960 letter to Nixon, "I submit that Negroes have been patient for nigh onto a hundred years, and now our patience is rapidly wearing thin. In this last year of President Eisenhower's stay in the White House, is it too much to hope that he will finally take the reins firmly in his hands and give the nation some aggressive direction in the field of civil rights?" Eisenhower did no such thing.

Still, with the presidential election looming, Robinson favored the GOP. In December 1959, Robinson was quoted as saying, "If it should come to a choice between a weak and indecisive Democratic nominee and Vice President Nixon, I, for one, would enthusiastically support Nixon." He insisted that he still believed that, as president, Nixon would cultivate a civil rights platform that would "be his own and one with teeth."[25]

Kennedy struggled with Black voters during the Democratic primaries and tried again to win Robinson over. Kennedy reached out to the baseball legend who wrote a weekly column, which was extremely popular with Black audiences. Robinson turned down an invite from the Democratic National Committee to serve on the platform committee. However, Robinson did accept an invitation to meet with Kennedy just weeks before the Democratic National Convention in July 1960.

The meeting would become fodder for Robinson's newspaper column. He wrote that Kennedy admitted to "limited experience" with the Black community but asked for time to prove himself. Robinson came away with mixed feelings, though he remained open-minded. "Senator Kennedy is an impressive man who makes an impressive point," Robinson wrote. "While I still have reservations about his position, I believe he is sincere in admitting past misunderstandings and expressing his willingness to learn." He added a rightful dig. "Senator Kennedy is a little late in seeking to make himself clear, after 14 years in Congress. But if he is sincere, there is still time to catch up."[26]

Behind the scenes, their conversations were ice-cold. When Kennedy continued to inquire about what Robinson needed to support him, the sports icon interpreted that as the senator offering him money for public support. Robinson reportedly told Kennedy, "Look, Senator, I don't want any of your money. I'm just interested in helping the candidate who I think will be best for Black America." Kennedy kept pushing, insisting that he wanted an "end to all discrimination." Robinson asked for "evidence" and added, "Please don't consider me presumptuous but I would like to make one suggestion. While trying to impress anyone with your sincerity you must be able to look them squarely in the eye."[27]

Twenty days before the presidential election came a turning point. On the afternoon of October 19, 1960, Dr. Martin Luther King Jr. was jailed, along with fifty-one others, after refusing to leave their seats at downtown Atlanta department-store lunch counters.[28] King was quickly sentenced to four months at the Georgia State Prison in Reidsville.[29]

Jackie Robinson had been serving on Richard Nixon's presidential campaign and had already felt dismayed at the lack of Black outreach. Robinson reportedly begged Nixon to call Dr. King while behind bars. Nixon campaign aide William Safire said after a ten-minute meeting with Nixon, Robinson had "tears of frustration in his eyes."

Nixon, never the smartest politician, was concerned he might lose southern votes. Robinson told Safire, "He thinks calling Martin would be 'grandstanding.' Nixon doesn't deserve to win."[30] Eisenhower also declined to pardon King.

The Democratic nominee stepped in. After much convincing by key aides, John F. Kennedy called not only Dr. Martin Luther King Jr.'s wife, Coretta Scott King, who was pregnant then, but also phoned King's father. Kennedy said to Coretta Scott King on their ninety-second call, "This must be pretty hard on you, and I want to let you both know that I'm thinking about you and will do all I can to help."[31] True to his word, Kennedy had already phoned Georgia governor Ernest Vandiver and requested that King be released. King was a free man on October 27, 1960.

Just hours after leaving the state prison and at the airport headed home to his pregnant wife, King told reporters, "I understand from very reliable sources that Senator Kennedy served as a great force in making the release possible. For him to be that courageous shows that he is really acting upon principle and not expediency."[32]

Although King could not explicitly endorse Kennedy because he was the leader of the nonpartisan Southern Christian

Leadership Conference,[33] he did give a statement that came close to an endorsement: "I hold Senator Kennedy in very high esteem. I am convinced he will seek to exercise the power of his office to fully implement the civil rights plank of his party's platform."[34]

King dropped another bomb: he had heard nothing from Vice President Richard Nixon or any other Republican. King's father, an influential figure in the Black community with a popular radio show, publicly stated, "I had expected to vote against Senator Kennedy because of his religion. Now he can be my president, Catholic or whatever he is."[35]

The news spread quickly, particularly in Black media. Nixon was slammed. John Patterson, owner of the Harlem newspaper *Citizen-Call*, stated, "Mr. Nixon, in his refusal to comment or take a stand on the civil rights issue that Rev. King's arrest symbolized, merely extends the say-nothing, do-nothing rule-by-golf-club philosophy of President Eisenhower regarding this moral issue."[36]

In an extremely close election, Black Americans voted Democratic for Kennedy at 68 percent, seven points more than they had voted for Democrat Adlai Stevenson in 1956. Democrats were learning that Black voters could make a difference—but in return for their votes, they would need results.

By 1964, the Democratic party was delivering, often against the wishes of its long-standing white southern base. For the first two years of John F. Kennedy's presidency, Democrats controlled the Senate, House, and White House. Even so, Kennedy pushed for zero civil rights legislation during that time. It was only after Kennedy's assassination that President Lyndon B. Johnson was "forced into glory"[37] by activists who demanded the passage of the Civil Rights Act of 1964, which legally ended Jim Crow and secured Black Americans equal access to public accommodations. Johnson was a racist in his personal life, but he was held accountable, and the policies under his administration were transformative.[38]

At the same time, the Republican Party was mutating into something increasingly malevolent. Jackie Robinson said that the outcome of the 1960 election had left him "terribly disappointed," but he already saw the white supremacy writings on the wall. In 1964, he served in the cabinet of New York governor Nelson Rockefeller[39] and campaigned for Rockefeller to become the Republican candidate over Arizona senator Barry Goldwater.[40] Goldwater opposed the Civil Rights Act of 1964 and was the architect of the Southern strategy, a Republican plan to play on racial resentment and white fears to gain voters in the South.[41] Falling out of love with the GOP, Robinson fought back against Goldwater's takeover, writing in 1963, "The danger of the Republican Party being taken over by the lily-white-ist conservatives is more serious than many people realize."[42]

Even though Republicans were losing the Black vote in presidential elections, in areas like Louisville, Memphis, and Atlanta, there remained pockets of Black Americans still voting heavily Republican.[43] Black Republican leaders passed state civil rights acts even before the Civil Rights Act of 1964 was signed into law. Harry Cole, the first Black state senator in Maryland,[44] worked on the state's civil rights act. Hobson Reynolds was a Republican state legislator in Philadelphia[45] and the Grand Exalted Ruler of the Black Elks, a nonprofit organization that funded many elements of the civil rights movement.[46] Most famously, Reynolds helped to craft the fair employment law in the Keystone State.

Dr. T. R. M. Howard was a stone-cold Republican with a long history of advocacy in the GOP during the 1950s, especially in Mississippi. Howard was also an abortion provider in

1960s Chicago and fought for abortion access. He was arrested twice for performing abortions. Mamie Till-Mobley, Emmett Till's mother—who he advocated for—once said about Howard, "The man was dynamic. I just thought he was the greatest in the world."[47] These Black Republican leaders were progressives, Douglass Republicans, not conservative, which is why many Black and white Republicans today won't speak their names. Black Republicans didn't merely switch parties; they were pushed out of the GOP—and the 1960s marked the beginning of the purge.

In 1961, New York representative William Miller was the head of the Republican National Committee (RNC).[48] Under his tutelage, the Republican Party launched the draft Goldwater movement and Operation Dixie, a campaign to attract white Southern voters.[49] (This should not be confused with a very different Operation Dixie, in which teams of union organizers were sent to southern states starting in 1946 to organize textile workers. The operation failed and was shut down in 1953.)[50] To finance the Republicans' racist movement, Miller defunded the RNC's Minority Division, which ran the party's outreach to Black voters.

In attendance at the July 1964 Republican National Convention in Daly City, California, there was a legendary Black Republican leader from Memphis, Tennessee, named George W. Lee. Lee's history with the Memphis Republican Party included twenty years of advocacy for Black voices in the GOP, extensive success in electing Republicans, and attending six Republican conventions since 1952.[51]

That year, however, Lee was not a delegate, and he put up a fight. White Republicans were disenfranchising Black Republicans in Memphis through voter intimidation. An all-white delegation was sent to the Republican National Convention to represent Memphis, Tennessee. Lee attended the Republican National

Convention to air his grievances before the RNC's credentials committee. In a televised speech, he argued that white supremacists systemically pushed him out. The committee decided, "Any agreement or accommodation with Mr. Lee can result in no benefit to the Republican Party."

Jack Craddock, future chairman of the Memphis Republican Party, told the press that the Memphis Republican Party is now "a white Republican Party."[52]

George W. Lee said whites had been trying to push him out of the party for two decades, and finally "they did it with a rigged election."[53]

Memphis wasn't alone. For the first time in four decades, Georgia brought an all-white delegation to the Republican National Convention. John H. Britton wrote for *Jet* in 1964, "This year, the Negro GOP wheels in Georgia were stopped cold." Not to be outdone, another state in the Deep South booted Black Republicans from the GOP. As Britton wrote, "In Mississippi, once Negro GOP-ers' stronghold, white Republicans wrested control of the party, purged what few Negroes remained and refused to encourage further Negro memberships."[54] The Republicans actively disenfranchised their loyal voters.

In May 1964, Dr. King issued a stark warning about the GOP, telling Dan Rather on *Face the Nation* about the danger of the Republican Party becoming a white man's party, "I've talked with some Negro Republicans who are very concerned about this. I see trends and developments which will reveal that unless the liberals of the Republican Party play a much more decisive role in leadership positions, this will become a white man's party. And I think this will be tragic for that Republican Party as well as tragic for the nation."[55]

The 1964 Republican National Convention was a tragedy.

When Goldwater accepted the Republican presidential nomination, he famously said, "Extremism in the defense of liberty is no vice. Moderation in the pursuit of justice is no virtue." It was the GOP's proud embrace of white supremacy, declaring that white American values must be uplifted and protected no matter the extreme.[56] Southern delegates waved Confederate flags, and according to a July 1964 article from the *Pittsburgh Courier*, "a lily-white Southern delegation" named their headquarters Fort Sumter, where Confederates attacked, starting the Civil War.[57] Future senator Edward Brooke, who made history as the first Black attorney general of Massachusetts, was stopped from stepping on the convention floor. Black journalist Belva Davis and her news director were told, "What the hell are you niggers doing here? Get out of here, boy! You too, nigger bitch" and "I'm gonna kill your ass."[58] As Jackie Robinson wrote about the convention, "If I could couch in one single sentence the way I felt, watching this controlled steam-roller operation roll into high gear, I would put it this way, I would say that I now believe I know how it felt to be a Jew in Hitler's Germany."[59]

The Republican Party's message couldn't have been more apparent—we don't want Black people in our party. They succeeded.

Dr. Martin Luther King Jr.,[60] A. Philip Randolph,[61] Jackie Robinson, who organized a "Republicans for Lyndon B. Johnson" group,[62] and countless others joined forces to defeat Goldwater. He would lose to Lyndon B. Johnson. Black Americans voted Republican at only 6 percent, a 26 percent drop from 1960.[63] It was the lowest GOP share of the Black vote in history until the 2008 election of President Barack Obama, which resulted in only 4 percent of Black Americans voting Republican.[64]

Although Goldwater lost the presidential election, in the long term, he won the white supremacist game. Goldwater's conservatism, Operation Dixie, and pushing out Black voters were a winning formula for the GOP, then and now. In 2015, Kentucky senator Mitch McConnell said, "My party does really good with white people, and I'm proud of that."[65]

Disgusted with race-baiting and Republicans fighting for the white, racist vote, Robinson officially left the party of Lincoln in 1968 and endorsed Hubert Humphrey[66] against his erstwhile friend Richard Nixon. That same year, Robinson said, "The election of Nixon would be death to the Blacks."[67] Nixon was sworn into office on January 20, 1969.

There were still a few holdouts among Black Republicans, including Republican Edward William Brooke III. He had not been intimidated by what occurred at the 1964 Republican National Convention. To become the first Black man in the Senate in eighty-six years, he would have to define his lane in the Republican Party, and he would do so by taking aim at the Black Power movement.

Two years before Nixon was elected, in January 1967, Brooke became the United States senator from Massachusetts. He was the third Black American in history in the U.S. Senate and the first to be elected by the people. Brooke had previously run for a seat in the Massachusetts House of Representatives but lost. By 1963, he was the thirty-fifth attorney general of Massachusetts, making him the highest-ranking Black politician.[68]

In 1966, Brooke faced off in the race for a Senate seat against Massachusetts's former Democratic governor Endicott Peabody, who was a clear supporter of civil rights and famously opposed the death penalty when it was unpopular to do so.

This was the turbulent 1960s, and there were questions of whether Brooke could win a Senate seat as a Black man in a majority white state. Brooke swayed in the polls throughout his campaign, and race was a constant topic in the press, but his strategy was slick. Running in a state that was 95 percent white and majority Catholic, Brooke opted to use what author Leah Wright Rigueur called in *The Loneliness of the Black Republican* (the seminal book on Black Republicans during the Nixon area) "non-Negro politics" to make white constituents comfortable.[69] Originally called "Mr. Non-Negro Politics" by journalist Chuck Stone in 1968,[70] Brooke maintained a stance that differed starkly from Douglass Republicans who saw the ineffectiveness of race-neutral policies.

To draw a line in the "non-Negro politics" sand, Brooke denounced activist Stokely Carmichael, one of the most prominent voices of Black liberation, as his nemesis. Famous for coining the phrase "Black Power," Carmichael terrified white America and even some Black Americans. Brooke stoked that fear by setting Carmichael in the same category as Lester Maddox, Georgia's proudly racist governor, saying they were "extremists of Black power and white power."[71]

More than likely fearful of losing the white vote in Massachusetts due to civil rights protests, one of Brooke's 1966 election strategies was to assure white voters he wasn't Stokely Carmichael. As the *Boston Globe* wrote in October 1966, "Edward Brooke says, 'A vote against me is a vote against Stokely Carmichael.' That's how he will handle the white backlash question."[72]

Here, Brooke is making a clear indication of who he wasn't. The coded language is, "I am not *that* Black man." Brooke's "non-Negro politics" may have been why Barry Goldwater supported him. Brooke had not endorsed Goldwater during the 1964 presidential election, but Goldwater liked what he saw in Brooke. Goldwater wrote in a letter to Brooke during his Senate campaign,

"I believe your election to the U.S. Senate would be good for the country and for the party."[73]

Brooke showed that "Black Power" could become a weapon for conservatives and moderates—even Black moderates—in the same way that "defund the police" was blamed for any seat Democrats lost in 2020, from dogcatcher to the House of Representatives.

In an article for the *Harvard Crimson*, titled "Brooke Says Black Power's Failed, Makes Plea for Negro Moderation," Brooke was quoted giving a speech at the elite institution a month before the 1966 Senate election. He downplayed race and stated Black people in Watts and white men were equally "bitter" against Black businessmen. "The problem is more social and economic than racial, believe me. The Negro in Watts is just as bitter against the successful Negro businessman as the white man. They are people sitting on the side of the road rebelling against society."[74]

It might have helped him win his election, but it was a particularly ridiculous claim considering the 1965 Watts riot was sparked, like many others, by years of police violence.[75] This had nothing to do with Black businessmen.

Brooke, who grew up middle class and attended Howard University,[76] went so far as to blame failures of the civil rights movement on welfare. "In moving around the country, I've heard that people have been finding it more profitable not to work than to work. You can't get people to work for $125 a week because they're getting $87 in relief and, after taxes, they'd do better staying there. There ought to be programs which would give them an incentive to work."[77]

Brooke, ahead of his time, used an awful talking point to soften wage and job discrimination. The *Harvard Crimson* described the crowd of seven hundred applauding. Brooke knew his audience well. Downplaying race, dismissing uprisings, and shaming the poor, it was Brooke's very own Atlanta Compromise speech. In November 1966, Edward William Brooke III was elected and won with more than 1.2 million votes in Massachusetts.[78]

Similar to how Isaiah Montgomery and Booker T. Washington were praised by "mainstream" media, a February 1967 piece for *Time* glorified Brooke for not being like the *other Blacks*. The article managed to insult everyone from Dr. Martin Luther King Jr. to James Baldwin while honoring the new senator: "Brooke has never rallied his race to challenge segregation barriers with the inspirational fervor of a Martin Luther King. Unlike Thurgood Marshall, Roy Wilkins, or Philip Randolph, he has not been a standard-bearer in the civil rights movement. He has made none of the volatile public breakthroughs to equality of a Jackie Robinson or a James Meredith. He has triggered none of the frustrated fury of a Stokely Carmichael, written none of the rancorous tracts of a James Baldwin or a LeRoi Jones, drawn none of the huzzahs of a Louis Armstrong or a Joe Louis, a Willie Mays or a Rafer Johnson. He has never sought or wanted to be a symbol of negritude." Brooke told *Time*, "I do not intend to be a national leader of the Negro people... I intend to do my job as a senator from Massachusetts."[79]

The same story described Brooke as a "Capitol Hill tourist attraction." Brooke had crafted a path to power for Black Republicans in the civil rights era and discovered a viable way of garnering media attention.

This is the ongoing theme for Black Republicans who shape-shift around racial ideology for political gain—secure enough praise from the mainstream media for not being like the "other" Black people, and eventually, you are seated in power.

But in March 1966, before he went full throttle "non-Negro politics," Brooke offered insight into the Black community and the GOP. He published a book titled *The Challenge of Change: Crisis in Our Two-Party System* and directly critiqued Barry Goldwater's *The Conscience of a Conservative*. Brooke reprimanded the failure of the Republican Party in appealing to Black voters, writing, "Democrats have not won them so much as we have lost them. In fact, we all but exiled them."[80] It was a true statement and could be why the GOP rarely acknowledges him today.

Once he was seated as senator, Brooke was considered a liberal Republican. A champion for housing rights, Brooke cowrote, along with several Democrats, the 1968 Fair Housing Act.[81] In 1969, the "Brooke Amendment" lowered the rent for tenants in public housing.[82] Despite his campaign rhetoric, Brooke also supported affirmative action and a higher minimum wage, called for a Social Security increase, and was an advocate for voting rights. Brooke supported the Vietnam War before becoming senator, but within his first year in office, he called for negotiations.

Brooke still had strife with Black leaders; he refused to join an early version of the Congressional Black Caucus (CBC), which was officially founded in 1971. Brooke was a far cry from the grifters of today. He may have won votes by pandering to whites in his district, but he maintained an independent streak in office and governed like a progressive. He was unafraid of calling out the GOP's racism, which, again, might explain why the Republican Party blatantly ignores Brooke's legacy.

In January 1969, Richard Nixon was sworn in as the country's thirty-seventh president. According to journalist Chuck Stone, Nixon's winning strategy was ignoring Black voters, except when jabbering about Black capitalism and the "law and order"

narrative, which was pointed directly at Black communities to ease
the white southern base. Stone also claimed Brooke "had become
disenchanted with Nixon during the campaign because Nixon
wanted to use him as negro window dressing."[83] Despite Jackie
Robinson saying Nixon would be "death to the Blacks" and the
debacle of the 1964 draft Goldwater movement, the former vice
president managed to receive 15 percent of the Black vote.[84] Much
of this is credited to the backing of Black Republican leaders and
to Nixon's promises to invest in Black communities. Nixon, who
still pandered to white southerners, was promoting Black economic
development, but it often came with a dig about welfare. In April
1968, Nixon asserted on a CBS radio show, "For too long, white
America has sought to buy off the Negro—and to buy off its own
sense of guilt—with ever more programs of welfare."[85] Welfare is
not a Black issue; the majority of people who receive federal assistance are white.[86] Tricky Dick was hell-bent on trying to frame
the Democratic Party as the party of welfare and the Republican
Party as the party of hard work and success.

Nixon settled on the idea of "the bridge of Black success"
and entrepreneurship through Black capitalism. A 1968 ad in *Jet
Magazine* read, "A vote for Richard Nixon for President is a vote
for a man who wants Homer to have the chance to own his own
business. Richard Nixon believes strongly in Black capitalism.
Because Black capitalism is Black power in the best sense of the
word... It's the key to the Black man's fight for equality—for a
piece of the action."[87]

This strategy may have only garnered 15 percent of the Black
vote in 1968, but Nixon wasn't done with his effort to reclaim
the Black vote from the Democrats. He continued to draw on
the assistance of Black GOP leaders like Floyd McKissick, the

executive director of the Congress of Racial Equality (CORE) from 1963 to 1966,[88] Arthur Fletcher, the father of affirmative action, and Robert Brown, a former police officer who became Nixon's only Black special assistant. In 1970, Brown was described by the *New York Times* as having "little power" in the Nixon administration.[89] Brown was also a former Democrat with ties to Dr. Martin Luther King Jr. and worked on Robert F. Kennedy's presidential campaign; both were assassinated in 1968. Brown became a Republican due to the influence of Clarence Townes, a longtime Black Republican, according to Leah Wright Rigueur.[90]

Soon after Nixon was elected, there was talk of him creating a "Black Cabinet."[91] Senator Brooke was reportedly offered several positions but wanted to remain in the Senate. Fletcher, who worked on the Philadelphia Plan, which was the beginning of a federal affirmative action plan, a policy that began with President Lyndon B. Johnson to fight segregation in building construction,[92] was named assistant secretary of labor.[93] Eventually, James Farmer, longtime civil rights activist and cofounder of CORE, was named the assistant secretary in the Department of Health, Education and Welfare. By 1973, Dr. Gloria Toote was the assistant secretary of housing and urban development and would remain in the role during the Ford administration. Importantly, these cabinet jobs were prefaced by "assistant."

When Nixon introduced his new presidential cabinet, it was all-white. Nixon's "Black Cabinet" included leadership positions but none in his presidential cabinet. President Lyndon B. Johnson made history by appointing Robert C. Weaver as the first secretary of housing and urban development, the first Black man to serve in a presidential cabinet. Nixon was moving backward. Clarence Mitchell, the director of the Washington, DC, chapter of the NAACP, told *Time* in December 1968, "Johnson, a President from Texas, desegregated the Cabinet, while Nixon, a President from California, resegregated the Cabinet."[94] While "the bridge of Black success" painted dreams of aspirational capitalism, Nixon is still the man who helped to further the Southern strategy with the "silent majority" language and was chummy with segregationists like Strom Thurmond.[95] Nixon advocated for the white southerners who Democrats lost in the mid-1960s.[96]

While the Black middle class was already on the rise, there was some progress for Black businesses under the Nixon administration.[97] By early 1969, Nixon, who also supported affirmative action due to the tireless work of Arthur Fletcher and strengthened the policy with Executive Order 11478,[98] launched the Office of Minority Business Enterprise. Although the federal program didn't specifically focus on Black businesses, its goal was to establish "minority"-owned companies. Black businesses would grow under the program.[99] Funding for HBCUs also increased under the Nixon administration, thanks to the work of Robert Brown.[100]

Starting in the early 1960s, the Black middle class had grown. A June 1974 issue of *Time* published a cover story headlined "Middle-Class Blacks Making It in America." The cover featured a smiling Black family: mother, father, daughter, son, and a German shepherd. The article reported that in 1961, only 13 percent of Black Americans reached the middle class. By 1971, nearly 30 percent achieved middle-class status.[101] By 1972, Black Americans enrolled in college at double the rate of 1967, and from 1960 to 1971, the number of Black Americans in professional and technical jobs skyrocketed by 128 percent. This was the Booker T. Washington dream of the Black Republican elite—or at least it seemed to be.

The sin of Black capitalism is that it forgets the poor, trots out the lie of trickle-down economics, and sells the fantasy that if the middle to upper class grows, prosperity will spread down to the working poor.

A growing Black middle class did not translate into gains for those less fortunate. In 1972, the Black unemployment rate reached as high as 11.2 percent.[102] The *New York Times* wrote the following year that the Black poor had a "growing resentment directed at members of the expanding Black middle class who appear to the ghetto dweller to be too concerned with individual survival to take any risks for a resolution of the unfinished Black struggle."[103]

While the Black middle class may have been increasing, the number of Black working poor was also growing.

Roy Wilkins, the executive director of the NAACP from 1964 to 1977, said about Nixon's policies, "I can think of nothing more harmful to Black people than the substitution of the delusion of Black capitalism for the absolute necessity for federal programs to provide all Negroes with dignified employment, decent housing and superior schools."[104]

Black people saw upward mobility when the federal government protected their lives and invested in their communities.

What was accurate in the Nixon years and earlier eras of American history is as true today: the powers that be are only against government when it helps the poor, especially if those poor folks have melanin. It is a throwback to the mudsill theory, courtesy of former South Carolina senator and enslaver James Hammond: the rich need the lower class to serve the upper class.[105] The translation for Hammond was that the white elite needs Blacks—and sometimes poor whites—to serve them. In truth, we have a welfare government for the rich, whose wealth only increases with government subsidies, tax loopholes, and legacy affirmative action.

This is where Black Republicans fail, whether under Booker T. Washington, Nixon's Black Cabinet, or some of the bootstrap-ism of today from random rappers. Black capitalism is not the remedy for inequality. A handful of Black people who achieve wealth or open a Black-owned business do not lift a whole community. Jay-Z becoming a billionaire[106] does not give the working poor a living wage. Sure, Jay-Z can be as charitable as he wants, but how does that transform the life of someone who works six days a week for starvation wages? Black capitalism is not liberation and can result in deeper Black oppression.

Civil rights organizer Floyd McKissick thought he had found a way to channel Black capitalism into liberation in Soul City. First proposed by McKissick in 1969, the North Carolina town was supposed to be an area owned and created by Black people: Black businesses, banks, and schools. Not solely Black or a separatist nation—whites would be welcomed—but it was a shining example of Black capitalism. McKissick, a native of North Carolina who was close to Dr. Martin Luther King Jr., was so invested in Soul City becoming a success that he changed his affiliation from Democratic to Republican and endorsed Richard Nixon.[107]

Nixon backed McKissick's vision, and Robert Brown, special assistant to Nixon, declared at the groundbreaking ceremony of Soul City in July 1972, "We are trying to break the cycles of poverty and they cannot be broken if we are held in bondage as the present welfare system has done and still does."[108]

But Soul City was held in bondage by the system of the Republican-controlled North Carolina government. When Republican Jesse Helms, who was against voting rights, affirmative action, and even an MLK holiday, was elected U.S. senator for North Carolina in 1973, the Black capitalism fantasy was doomed. Helms and McKissick were both Republicans, but Helms saw no kinship. Helms called for a federal audit of Soul City that prompted a series of negative stories in the Raleigh *News & Observer.* The investigation ultimately cleared Soul City and McKissick of wrongdoing,[109] but the federal government reneged on their agreement and shut Soul City down.

Before white Republicans destroyed Soul City, they dangled federal funding to lure McKissick into throwing his support to Nixon. McKissick took the bait and campaigned hard for Nixon in 1972. He spoke at a high-profile Nixon event that included jazz legend Lionel Hampton and Malcolm X's widow, Betty Shabazz. McKissick said it was time for the Black community to give up on the Democrats because "we continue sucking the sugar tits not even tasting milk."[110]

Hampton even performed a song titled "We Need Nixon."

Nixon relied heavily on Black star power. At the 1972 Republican National Convention, he enlisted one of the era's biggest superstars—Black or white—to make an appearance: Sammy Davis Jr. Davis's relationship with Nixon came under scrutiny, and he was accused of having "sold out." Nixon angrily denied the claim from the stage of the convention. "You aren't going to buy Sammy Davis Jr. by inviting him to the White House," Nixon said. "You are going to buy him by doing something for America, and that is what we are doing."[111] Davis, sitting on the stage with Nixon's daughter, got up from his seat and hugged Nixon.

If this was intended to fend off criticisms of Davis's support for the Republican Party, it failed. Davis was lampooned by Black media. A photo of the five-foot-six Davis hugging six-foot Nixon went "viral" by 1972 standards. Legendary journalist Carl Rowan, whose name was on Nixon's master list of political enemies, wrote, "The whole nation saw Sammy Davis Jr. like a hungry orphan, clutching President Nixon to his bosom at the Republican convention."[112]

The episode dramatically revealed the Nixon administration's focus on Black elites and its disinterest in appealing to the larger Black community. As Robert Jordan wrote for the *Bay State Banner*, a Black newspaper based in Boston, "With the general knowledge that Mr. Nixon has done so little for the nation's Black populace, it is discouraging, if not distressing, to see [Sammy Davis Jr.] and other well-known Blacks, including so-called militants, latch onto Mr. Nixon's coattails."[113]

What indeed drove these Black Nixon supporters was self-interest. In Jordan's words, "There are more than a few Blacks who feel the Blacks working for Mr. Nixon this year are doing it purely out of self-interest, that they really don't give a damn about the masses of Black people who have suffered under four years of Nixon politics."

Davis wasn't the only one. That same year, soul singer James Brown endorsed Nixon. Protesters made their feelings known at the Apollo Theater in Harlem, where one sign read, "James Brown, Nixon's Clown."[114] In response, Brown defended himself with, "I'm not selling out, I'm selling in." NFL player and rising movie star Jim Brown also endorsed Nixon that year and faced threats of boycotts.

Members of the CBC blamed Nixon, not the Black celebrities, for "blatant exploitation of the politically naive." Just weeks before the 1972 presidential election, Representative Louis Stokes of Ohio said, "Either the Black entertainers know about this record and don't care, or they are uninformed. In either case, they have turned their backs on their own people, and they deserve the strongest condemnation from Black Americans."[115]

Julian Bond, a Georgia state representative at the time, had a more biting critique of Nixon's Black supporters. Although he didn't say names, he called them "political prostitutes."[116] Decades later, there would be a new crop of celebrities, naively involving themselves in politics, willingly becoming tools for misinformation, all under the cheap veil that they cared about Black communities. In the end, they appeared to only care about themselves and their wallets.

Nixon won reelection in 1972, but those Black Republicans, Black capitalists, and Black celebrities who supported him got little in return for sacrificing their reputations. Black capitalist dreams like Soul City turned into nightmares, and Black Republicans commanded scarce power throughout the Nixon administration. Clarence Townes, a special assistant to the chairman of the RNC, was frustrated with his party and saw the racist writing on the wall two years before. He told the *New York Times* in 1970 that he was the committee's "house nigger."[117]

An unhappy Townes added, "We've abandoned all black programs in the committee. We don't want the black vote. We had a big conference of national Republican leaders recently and one of the seminars was The Black Vote. Almost nobody showed up— except maybe a handful of black Republicans, all over 45, all of them hand-picked by white folks, and they were all whiter than the whites that picked them."

Townes saw the direction that the Republican Party was taking. "As I see the black vote now, there's a total fear of what's called the Southern strategy. Blacks understand that their well-being is being sacrificed to political gain. There has to be some moral leadership from the President on the race question—and there just hasn't been any. To the blacks the President has placed the name of the Republican Party in greater darkness than it was under Goldwater."

In a haunting statement that every Black Republican elected official should read today, Townes added, "Why do I stay at the committee? I don't know. Maybe I'm afraid of catching hell when I go back to black country where I came from. It's a kind of pride, I guess. Maybe I can't admit to my kids and my friends that I've been wrong. Sure, there are some blacks with nice titles working for the Administration. Some of them are doing a lot for their people. But they've got no power. Politically, they ain't scratching nothing."[118]

Townes left the RNC shortly after the *New York Times* story. But he was correct; the GOP was diminishing Black Republicans. Jackie Robinson had it right when he warned that "the election of Nixon would be death to the Blacks." While it would be a slow death and Black communities fought back, Nixon readied the chamber.

In 1971, Nixon famously announced his war on drugs. Within years, the incarceration rates in Black communities would skyrocket. According to the Equal Justice Initiative, "the number of people incarcerated in American jails and prisons escalated from 300,000 to 2.3 million."[119]

Former Nixon domestic policy chief John Ehrlichman told *Harper's Bazaar* the disgraced president purposely waged war on the left and, specifically, Black people. "The Nixon campaign in 1968, and the Nixon White House after that, had two enemies: the antiwar left and black people."

He continued, "We knew we couldn't make it illegal to be either against the war or black, but by getting the public to associate the hippies with marijuana and blacks with heroin, and then criminalizing both heavily, we could disrupt those communities. We could arrest their leaders, raid their homes, break up their meetings, and vilify them night after night on the evening news. Did we know we were lying about the drugs? Of course we did."[120]

The hippies represented a lifestyle choice that eventually died off, but they could rely on their whiteness as cover. Black people didn't have that privilege.

During Nixon's second term, Senator Edward Brooke remained so beloved in the Republican Party that he was considered as a replacement for Vice President Spiro Agnew, who resigned in 1973.[121] But Brooke had become disillusioned with the Nixon administration. He opposed three of Nixon's Supreme Court appointees, which was rare for a sitting Republican senator. In late 1973, Brooke was the first Republican senator to demand that President Richard Nixon step down after the Watergate scandal. By August 1974, Nixon had resigned; the disgraced president wasn't a cult figure and quickly lost support in his own party, unlike Trump's enablers. Even Barry Goldwater told Nixon to resign.

Black Republicans continued to be valuable to the Republicans who followed. When Gerald Ford succeeded Nixon as president, he appointed William T. Coleman Jr. as transportation secretary, the first Black Republican to serve in a presidential cabinet. Coleman had a long history as a civil rights lawyer and had worked alongside Thurgood Marshall.

Appointing one Black man to a cabinet-level position did not translate into support from the Black community. Ford was passive on civil rights, even with Arthur Fletcher as the deputy assistant to the president for urban affairs attempting to push him. Though he fended off a primary challenge from future president Ronald Reagan, Ford lost reelection to Jimmy Carter in 1976.[122] That same year, months before his death, George W. Lee said the GOP "has not done very much in advancing the cause of Black people."[123] Seventeen percent of Black voters supported Ford. Still, enthusiasm was in decline, with voter turnout under 50 percent.[124]

Black Republicans struggled to find their ground as the political landscape shifted under their feet. In 1979, Senator Edward Brooke lost reelection in Massachusetts to Paul Tsongas, a white Democrat. Brooke's pro-choice stance hurt him among conservatives, and his finances were investigated while he was going through a divorce. There would not be another Black Republican in the U.S. Senate until thirty-four years later.

Regardless of his loyalty, back in 1964, Brooke knew what was ahead: "You can't say the Negro left the Republican Party; the Negro feels he was evicted from the Republican Party."[125]

The Nixon era officially killed Douglass Republicans. A new kind of Black Republican was emerging.

They would not follow the slick logic of Senator Edward Brooke, who certainly played "non-Negro politics" to get elected but, when in office, was a fighter for Black communities.

There would be no policies like affirmative action, founded by Arthur Fletcher and broadened under Nixon. The preoccupation with the middle class and Black capitalism was not even an agenda item.

The new Black Republican focused on rigid individualism, proximity to power, the lie of color-blind policies, and polishing the scheme of pathologizing Black people who didn't pull themselves up by their bootstraps. They focused on loyalty to a party that fully embraced Barry Goldwater's vision of leveraging white fears to win elections. The Black Republicans who would ascend in the Reagan era and beyond carved out their own grifting lane.

CHAPTER 5

REAGAN, PIERCE, AND THOMAS

"It is a high-tech lynching for uppity Blacks who in any way deign to think for themselves."

—Clarence Thomas[1]

THE 1980S: DISCO WAS SUPPOSEDLY DEAD, THE AIDS EPIDEMIC was about to devastate the country, and CNN debuted twenty-four-hour news. Suburbia was on the rise, and greed was good, especially with Republicans back in power. President Ronald Reagan took office in 1981, partly due to Jerry Falwell's Moral Majority, making Jimmy Carter a one-term president, and the GOP regained control of the U.S. Senate.

While today's pundits attempt to romanticize Reagan, he enacted dangerous, anti-Black, anti-poor, and anti-middle-class policies that still impact us today.[2] Similar to Nixon, Reagan promised Republicans that he would be the GOP president who would restore the party of Lincoln to its roots. In June 1981, a Black woman who was a Democrat turned Republican told the *Washington Post*, "The time of the Black elephant has come."[3] She couldn't have been more wrong.

It's stupefying how any Black Republican could believe Reagan was the great hope for Black people. This was a man who supported Barry Goldwater for president in 1964, called the Civil Rights Act of 1964 a "bad piece of legislation," and stormed out of a meeting with the National Negro Republican Assembly in 1966 when confronted on his record.[4] In 1976, legendary Black Republican George W. Lee warned the GOP that Reagan "represents the extreme ideas of conservatism."[5] From the beginning, it was clear that Reagan was an enemy to Black communities.

The former actor disturbingly launched his 1980 general election campaign with a speech on states' rights in Neshoba County, Mississippi,[6] miles away from where three civil rights activists, James Chaney, Andrew Goodman, and Michael Schwerner, were murdered in 1957.[7] Even though Ronald Reagan was far from a southerner, he was taking cues from leaders in the GOP, like the future chairman of the RNC, Lee Atwater, and was the Southern strategy on steroids. Atwater said in 1981, when "you can't say nigger," just run on the same policies and "Blacks get hurt worse than whites"—and that remains a strategy for winning as a Republican today.[8]

Reagan understood the assignment and armed himself with racist propaganda. In 1976, during Reagan's first run for president, his version of Trump's "We'll build a wall and Mexico will pay for it" was a story he would repeatedly return to about a "welfare queen." Reagan babbled on the campaign trail, "She has 80 names, 30 addresses, 12 Social Security cards and is collecting veterans' benefits on four nonexisting deceased husbands. And she's collecting Social Security on her cards. She's got Medicaid, getting food stamps, and she is collecting welfare under each of her names. Her tax-free cash income alone is over $150,000."[9]

Reagan knew his audience, and they ate the story up. The *New York Times* described a New Hampshire crowd in January 1976 as "angry" and said he "hit a nerve." "Welfare queen" was printed in newspapers, and he often referenced that "woman from Chicago."[10] Reagan would publicly say "welfare queen" at least twice,[11] referring to a woman named Linda Taylor in Chicago, Illinois. However, as the *New York Times* noted, "the problem is that the story does not quite check out."[12] Taylor was indicted on $8,865.67, not $150,000,[13] and she used four alias names, not eighty. Taylor served her time behind bars for the minor crime. (Linda Taylor's life is troubling and bizarre, outside of being found guilty of welfare fraud. Read Josh Levin's *The Queen: The Forgotten Life Behind an American Myth* for more details.) Regardless of the racially coded language, most people on Aid to Families with Dependent Children, the cash welfare program in Chicago at the time, were overwhelmingly non-Black—60 percent.[14]

The racially coded language was apparent. The alleged welfare queen, who may not have even been black, was plastered all over the news. She was photographed wearing a glamorous hat and a fur coat. Reagan deployed an old-school, racist political ploy—find a narrative and make it relatable to white voters so they can blame the dangerous "other." The invented welfare queen was now the villain ruining their lives and the economy. More specifically, the lazy Black woman was the scapegoat for wage discrimination,[15] overpriced health care,[16] a bloated military budget that was exasperated by the Vietnam War,[17] corrupt politicians,[18] and poorly funded public schools.

Even for Black people in apartheid South Africa, Reagan delved deep into his white supremacy bag of tricks. In 1981, Reagan expressed his clear support of the South African government because it was "a country that has stood by us in every war we've ever fought; a country that, strategically, is essential to the free world in its production of minerals."[19] In 1986, he famously vetoed a bill that placed economic sanctions on South Africa (Congress overruled Reagan's veto), and according to historian David Schmitz, Reagan saw the African National Congress, a political party in South Africa that fought against apartheid, "as a dangerous, pro-communist movement"—the same language used for leaders during the civil rights movement.[20] While some conservatives argue that Reagan gets a bad rap for his stance on apartheid, Nobel Prize winner Bishop Desmond Tutu said it best. While criticizing the Reagan administration's "constructive engagement toward the white government" in South Africa, he called their policy "immoral, evil and totally un-Christian."[21]

Reagan had little respect for Black African people across the continent. In 1971, during a conversation with Nixon, which was not public until 2019, Reagan, governor of California at the time, called African delegates to the United Nations "monkeys" and said, "They're still uncomfortable wearing shoes!" Nixon laughed.[22]

As for the hope that Reagan would have a diverse administration, Reagan, like Nixon, relegated Black people to subcabinet roles—except for one. The former governor of California included one Black person in his presidential cabinet. From 1981[23] to 1989,[24] Samuel Riley Pierce Jr. was the secretary of housing and urban development. But Reagan couldn't recognize the one and only melanated person in his presidential cabinet.

In June 1981, at a White House reception, the president greeted Pierce with, "Hello, Mr. Mayor."[25] Ronald Reagan mistook Pierce for a random Black mayor. Pierce was reportedly deeply embarrassed by the gaffe, especially as it was heavily reported in the press.[26] This was just the beginning of Pierce's embarrassment, which would taint his otherwise stellar record.

Pierce made history as a lawyer, becoming the first Black partner of a prominent New York firm in 1961. In the 1950s, he was an assistant U.S. attorney in New York and an assistant to the undersecretary of labor, and he served as counsel to the antitrust subcommittee of the House Judiciary Committee.[27] In 1961, Pierce was part of Dr. Martin Luther King Jr.'s legal team for the U.S. Supreme Court case *New York Times v. Sullivan*,[28] which established limitations on the use of defamation lawsuits. In 1964, Pierce cofounded the Freedom National Bank in Harlem, which shut down in 1990.[29]

Coretta Scott King, Dr. King's widow, wrote a letter to President Reagan urging him to consider Pierce for U.S. attorney general.[30] According to Pierce's own words, he aspired to be on the U.S. Supreme Court.[31] Still, it appeared Reagan did not want to give a Black man that much power. Secretary of housing and urban development is a role that would be a favorite for Black people in Republican administrations. As of 2020, out of the seven Black men and one Black woman who have been presidential cabinet members in Republican administrations, four have been secretary of housing and urban development.

By accepting the position, a role had to be played, and Pierce obliged. In many ways, Pierce was an old-school Republican, more along the lines of former Massachusetts senator Edward Brooke. His unnecessary loyalty to Reaganism ran deep. No one knows why Pierce, who never cut off ties with his law firm,[32] accepted the title of Department of Housing and Urban Development (HUD) secretary, especially since he was reportedly unhappy in the job. Arguably, he simply wanted to be in a presidential administration

and grifted, willing to pay the debt for power, knowing the insid-
iousness of Reagan.

The person he became in the Reagan administration was
unrecognizable from his civil rights history. In 1981, Pierce was
defending his boss, telling *People*, "There's a feeling in the black
community that the Reagan Administration is not a friend of blacks,
but the President is not saying, 'Forget them; let 'em die.' We're not
cutting back that far."[33]

They did cut back "that far," but not just in Black communities.

During Pierce's tenure, the budget authorizations for HUD were
slashed by an abhorrent 78 percent.[34] New housing construction was
gutted as homelessness skyrocketed, many of the homeless being
Vietnam veterans.[35] Reagan also cut annual spending on subsidized
housing programs by 20 percent.[36] There was the hell of Reagan's
tax plan, which raised taxes on the bottom 50 percent of Americans,
and by the end of the 1980s, Black Americans were the poorest they
had been in relation to whites since the 1950s.[37] By 1983, Black
unemployment was the highest in history at a tragic 21.2 percent.[38]
Black unemployment did not fall below 11 percent under Reagan.

Reagan also laid out a disturbing vision that churches should
bear the responsibility of helping the homeless, saying in 1981 that
the crisis would resolve itself if "every church and synagogue would
take in 10 welfare families."[39] Religious figures were unimpressed.
Reverend Paul Moore, New York City's Episcopal bishop, called
Reagan's plan "absolute balderdash" and added, "Housing the homeless and feeding the hungry is the responsibility of the public sector.
They should have a permanent policy whereby homeless persons
would have a place to live."[40]

In a 1984 interview on *Good Morning America*, Reagan cruelly
blamed the homeless spike on homeless people, saying, "People

who are sleeping on the grates…the homeless…are homeless, you might say, by choice."[41]

Loyal as he was to Reagan, Pierce's legacy was spoiled with political scandals and accusations of influence peddling. A 1989 *Washington Post* article described Pierce as "a private man thrust by white politicians into increasingly public roles" and said "he has climbed the ladder of success even while delegating the details to others." Pierce rarely granted interviews, and his nickname was "Silent Sam." His staff claimed he "came to work after 10 and left before 5, often watching television in his tenth-floor office rather than deal with bureaucratic conflict."[42]

Quiet incompetence appeared to be Pierce's plan. He was known to use Black Republican talking points from the Nixon administration, saying that Black people would return to the Republican Party if they only got an economic piece of the pie. That wasn't happening under Reagan, but Pierce was suspected of giving several pieces of the pie to his Republican colleagues. For all the talk about Black communities returning to the GOP with policy, his mismanagement at HUD was not a shining example.

In 1989, after an internal audit of HUD, a congressional committee alleged that under Pierce's leadership, an enormous amount of money was going to Republican consultants while $18 billion was being cut, which should have been for better housing in low-income communities. There was a five-year criminal investigation of Pierce. He reportedly didn't give his phone number to House investigators, and they were only allowed to communicate with him via a letter or if he called them. Pierce was never charged,[43] but former aides were incarcerated. When the investigation ended, he said in a statement, "My own conduct failed to set the proper standard."[44]

Pierce allegedly lined the pockets of wealthy Republicans; who knows if or how he profited as poor people suffered. Pierce debased himself for Reaganism. His 2000 obituary in the *Washington Post* referenced the financial scandal: "The investigation ended a career that had been marked by an almost unbroken string of successes."[45]

After Reagan's second term ended, President George H. W. Bush was elected in 1988. He made history in 1989 by appointing Dr. Louis Wade Sullivan as secretary of the U.S. Department of Health and Human Services, the first Black Republican in that role and the only Black American in his cabinet.

Sullivan brought ample experience to the job, having served as the founding dean of the Morehouse School of Medicine and worked to make the HBCU one of the most respected medical schools in the country. He grew up in rural Georgia, graduated from Morehouse College in 1954, and earned a medical degree from Boston University School of Medicine. While in the Bush administration, he built a diverse team, selecting the first Black commissioner of the Social Security Administration, Gwendolyn King, and the first Black acting administrator of the Health Care Financing Administration, William Toby Jr. He also appointed the first woman and the first Hispanic person as U.S. surgeon general, Antonia Novello.

Sullivan would also introduce a new food label, which allowed Americans to know what was in their food. He launched a minority male health and injury prevention initiative, which allocated $100 million in a three-year period.

However, due to the Republicans' obsession with big government in a woman's uterus, Sullivan nearly didn't get the job. "Anti-abortionists" protested the possible nomination after an interview with the *Atlanta Journal-Constitution* appeared to reveal that Sullivan was pro-choice. Even after conservative backlash, he declined "four opportunities to disavow" that he was pro-choice.[46]

In time, Sullivan gave in to the outcry. He eventually stated that he was against abortion, except in the case of incest or if the mother's life was at risk. This was enough for Republicans: according to a *Philadelphia Inquirer* article from late 1988, after a three-hour meeting with Bush, "anti-abortion activists and members of Congress said that they were convinced he opposes abortion and that they would support his nomination."[47] It remains unclear if Dr. Sullivan truly opposed abortion or if he calculated that saying so was necessary to be approved for the presidential cabinet.

It wasn't the only controversy to mark Sullivan's time in the Bush administration. In August 1990, a pending civil rights bill was stalled. Representative Pete Stark, a white Democrat from California, was on the House floor slamming the Bush's administration despicable record of poor access to health care in Black and brown communities. He aimed for the one Black man in Bush's cabinet, the secretary of the U.S. Department of Health and Human Services, and called Dr. Sullivan a "disgrace to his race." Stark believed Sullivan was pushing policies that were hurting Black and poor communities.

Sullivan said he was "deeply offended," and Republicans in the House were supposedly fuming.

Stark responded in the House chamber, which was not quite an apology: "I should not have brought into the discussion his race, because it obscures the fact that he is carrying on a bankrupt policy for an Administration who inadvertently has been impacting the poor and minorities in this country by denying them decent medical care, by turning away from job training programs that would help those who are mostly minorities... By discharging people from the military and refusing to provide them the extended benefits they need for unemployment, by denying poor women abortions…and I apologize for obscuring that."[48]

No white person should ever tell a Black person they are a "disgrace to their race." Just as Trump should have never said Jewish people who did not vote for him show "great disloyalty,"[49] and Biden should have never proclaimed, "You ain't Black,"[50] if you weren't his supporter. Stark was way too comfortable. At one point, he tried to join the CBC and was not accepted.

The bleeding liberalism of white Democrats like Stark may have backfired, but for all the GOP mortification over the "disgrace to his race" comments, two months later, in October 1990, Bush vetoed the Civil Rights Act of 1990.

Sullivan left the Bush administration in 1993, resuming his role as president of Morehouse School of Medicine, where he remained until 2002. Like William Coleman Jr., who became secretary of transportation under the Ford administration after a respectable career in service of civil rights, Sullivan's tenure in the Bush administration begs the question: does a Black public figure's willingness to serve in a Republican administration translate into an endorsement of Republicans' anti–civil rights policies? If the answer were ambiguous for Coleman and Sullivan, it would become more evident for a new wave of Black Republicans.

Pierce and Sullivan set the stage for other Black Republicans in the Reagan era, who were distinctly different from Jackie Robinson,[51] Arthur Fletcher, or Senator Edward Brooke. Pierce may have been a quiet grifter who was unhappy with his role in Reagan's administration. Sullivan's plan could have been to alter his public positions to gain access to power under Bush. However, Clarence Thomas was an anti-Black profiteer who would reinvent the formula of Black Republicanism more recklessly than Isaiah Montgomery[52] and with an impact more enduring than Booker T. Washington. The rise of Thomas is a watershed moment in the Black Republican grift. He is a man who attempted to obliterate the policies he benefited from to become one of the most powerful people in the country. Bishop Henry McNeal Turner said about Booker T. Washington in 1895, Black people will "have to live a long time to undo the harm he has done our race."[53] The same rings true for Supreme Court Justice Clarence Thomas.

Clarence Thomas was born in 1948 in Pin Point, Georgia, a town formerly enslaved people founded. He saw the horrors of Jim Crow firsthand and grew up in deep poverty.[54] His father left the family, and by the first grade, he was sent to live with his maternal grandfather, Myers Anderson. His grandfather, without formal education, managed to own a fuel-oil business,[55] allowing Thomas to attend Catholic schools. In his 2007 memoir, Thomas wrote his grandfather said, "Don't shame me, and don't shame the race." Although Thomas grew up in the Jim Crow South, he wrote about the sting of colorism from Black people. He said other children mocked him for being darker skinned. He was nicknamed "ABC," which meant "America's Blackest Child," a disgusting example of colorism that still plagues Black communities today.[56]

In 1980, Clarence Thomas had his big grifting break when he spoke at the Black Alternatives Conference, a two-day event of one hundred Black conservatives and other leaders in San Francisco. The conference was the brainchild of Thomas Sowell, economist and mentor to Clarence Thomas, and a Black Republican named Henry Lucas, who was close to Reagan and one of the first Black men to serve on the RNC.[57] The Reagan administration sponsored the conference.[58]

The star of this conference wasn't Brooke, Arthur Fletcher, or William T. Coleman Jr., credible Black Republicans who were in politics for decades. A young Clarence Thomas was the leading man and featured in a story by Juan Williams for the *Washington Post* titled "Black Conservatives, Center Stage." In the article, Thomas questioned "Black support for the minimum wage," complained about the access affirmative action granted him, and declared that he refused "to work on any issue directly related to Black people." Thomas was touting the color-blind narrative, which was hypocritical considering he and over one hundred others were attending a conference specifically for Black conservatives. Juan Williams wrote that at the Black Alternatives Conference, a "minority within a minority had finally found a home." The most telling part of the article is how then president-elect Ronald Reagan reacted. Williams wrote that the constant message at the conference was that Black people should not focus on "Black-only" issues "if they want to be thought of as more than Black free-loaders." Reagan's reaction? "That attitude has apparently impressed President-elect Reagan."[59] Less than a year later, Thomas was working for the Reagan administration.

There was an infamous moment for Thomas at the Black Alternatives Conference. Throughout Thomas's career, he has relied on his Black southern roots when convenient but shames others who aren't as successful as him—even his older sister.

At the conference, Thomas portrayed his sister, Emma Mae Martin, as a welfare queen,[60] a phrase popularized by President Ronald Reagan.

Martin, a mother of four, had briefly relied on public assistance after her husband left her. According to the *Los Angeles Times*, Thomas "aired his disgust" and lambasted his flesh and blood at the conference. "She gets mad when the mailman is late with her welfare check," Thomas said. "That's how dependent she is. What's worse is that now her kids feel entitled to the check, too. They have no motivation for doing better or getting out of that situation."[61]

The welfare tale was reportedly an exaggeration, and journalists began digging after Thomas was selected as Bush's pick for the Supreme Court. A 1991 *Chicago Tribune* headline read, "Thomas' Sister's Life Gives Lie to His Welfare Fable." Journalists discovered that Martin's ex-husband abandoned her and her four children in 1973. While Thomas was attending law school, his older sister worked two minimum-wage jobs in Georgia and was the caretaker for her elderly aunt, who had suffered a stroke. She was on welfare for approximately four years and was far from living the glamorous life. Martin was trying to survive on only $169 a month. By 1991, she worked for a hospital and was no longer on welfare. Martin stated that Thomas never criticized her need for assistance in person. Those words only came out when he spoke publicly. Clarence Page wrote for the *Chicago Tribune* in 1991, "There's a lesson in this, I suppose. A little scapegoating can take you a long way in politics, even when you use your own sister."[62]

In 2007, Emma Mae Martin said about her brother, "He's supposed to be a judge but you can't judge anybody unless you judge yourself. I've never judged anybody, but people judge me all the time."[63]

In July and August 2022, I briefly spoke to Clarence Thomas's sister, seventy-six at the time and working with children. When asked about Thomas, Martin said, "I don't have any opinion on what he does. I don't get into his politics. I don't follow his politics because what I think may be wrong. I don't even give an opinion on what he does."[64]

Martin also revealed she currently has no relationship with her brother.

Willing as Clarence Thomas was to publicly and incorrectly shame his sister, it was obvious that he would have few scruples when it came to strangers.

Before he became a Supreme Court justice, Thomas was a perfect example of affirmative action. Thomas admittedly was accepted to Yale University because of affirmative action.[65] In 1983, he was quoted as saying about affirmative action policies, "But for them, God only knows where I would be today. These laws and their proper application are all that stand between the first 17 years of my life and the second 17 years." A contradiction to his comments at the 1980 Black Alternatives Conference.

In 1981,[66] under President Ronald Reagan, Thomas became the assistant secretary of education for the Office for Civil Rights in the Department of Education.[67] Reagan then appointed him chairman of the Equal Employment Opportunity Commission (EEOC) in 1982,[68] where he stayed for eight years.[69] By 1987, as Thomas was rising in the ranks of the Reagan administration, he declared, "any race-conscious remedy is no good" when questioned about affirmative action.[70] For Thomas, it appears that those policies, which had benefited him, lost their efficacy after he made it into the highest echelons of government. Black Republicans, especially Thomas, who are against affirmative action but simultaneously push the "self-help" narrative are offensively contradictory. While white women are massive beneficiaries of affirmative action, from 1969 to 1988, Arthur Fletcher's policy put $18 billion into the hands of Black people.[71] Affirmative action resulted in better access to higher education, fair wages, and financial stability, all with "self-help."

In May 1987, Thomas took a stab at Justice Thurgood Marshall. Giving a speech for the bicentennial of the U.S. Constitution in Maui, Hawaii, Marshall critiqued the Constitution and its framers, specifically as related to slavery: "The focus of this celebration invites a complacent belief that the vision of those who debated and compromised in Philadelphia yielded the 'more perfect Union' it is said we now enjoy. I cannot accept this invitation, for I do not believe that the meaning of the Constitution was forever 'fixed' at the Philadelphia Convention. Nor do I find the wisdom, foresight, and sense of justice exhibited by the Framers particularly profound. To the contrary, the government they devised was defective from the start, requiring several amendments, a civil war, and momentous social transformation to attain the system of constitutional government, and its respect for the individual freedoms and human rights, we hold as fundamental today."[72]

By September, Thomas was slamming Marshall's speech. He wrote for the *San Diego Union-Tribune* that Marshall's words were "exasperating" and "incomprehensible."

"His indictment of the Founders alienates all Americans and not just Black Americans from their high and noble intention. Thus quite to the contrary of Martin Luther King Jr., Justice Marshall pits Blacks, along with women and all Americans other than defenders of the Confederacy, against the Founders."

Thomas continued, "Justice Marshall's understanding of Blacks and the Constitution stands in stark contrast to that of notable Americans, from Frederick Douglass and Abraham Lincoln to Martin Luther King."[73]

This anti-Thurgood Marshall speech might have been the performance Thomas needed to be rewarded with an appointment to the U.S. Supreme Court. Nathaniel R. Jones, former legal counsel for the NAACP, would describe Thomas's critique of Marshall as "auditioning."[74]

As the second Black man on the Supreme Court, Thomas was an affirmative action move. Thurgood Marshall, the first Black man appointed to the Supreme Court, retired in 1991. President George H. W. Bush knew he had to nominate a Black man. Bush attempted to convince the American people he was focused solely on qualifications, saying in July 1991, "I expressed my respect for the ground that Mr. Justice [Thurgood] Marshall plowed but I don't feel there should be a black seat on the Court or an ethnic seat on the Court."[75] When Thomas was asked about being chosen because he was Black, he responded with, "I think a lot worse things have been said. I disagree with that, but I'll have to live with it."[76]

At the same time, Bush argued that "Blacks" should be grateful for Thomas, saying in 1991, "Blacks ought to rejoice at his nomination."[77] They did not—and the reaction was decidedly negative even as it was happening. As William W. Sales Jr. wrote in 1991 about Bush's selection of Thomas, "It is the Supreme Court for the era of George Bush's New World Order... Black people will recognize that Judge Thomas is no more nor less than a political hack."[78]

Thomas was selected not only because he was Black but because Bush knew he was a staunch conservative, especially on civil rights.[79] Coined the anti-Thurgood Marshall,[80] Thomas had only served on the DC Circuit for sixteen months before his elevation to the highest court.[81]

How does that compare to other justices who made history? Justice Thurgood Marshall served as a judge of the U.S. Court of Appeals for the Second Circuit from 1961 to 1965 and argued several cases before the Supreme Court. Justice Sonia Sotomayor was a judge for the U.S. Court of Appeals for the Second Circuit for eleven years, from 1998 to 2009.[82]

Justice Ruth Bader Ginsburg served on the U.S. Court of Appeals for the DC Circuit from 1980 to 1993.[83]

Although Justice Elena Kagan was never a judge, she was a scholar with credentials that included being a law clerk for Thurgood Marshall, the deputy assistant to the president for domestic policy under the Clinton administration, and the dean of Harvard Law School from 2003 to 2009. She was also the solicitor general of the United States at the time of her nomination announcement. Kagan received a "well-qualified" rating by a unanimous vote from the American Bar Association.

Judge Ketanji Brown Jackson, the first Black woman and the third Black person on the U.S. Supreme Court, received a "well-qualified" rating by a unanimous vote from the American Bar Association. From 2013 to 2021, the former public defender was a district judge for the U.S. District Court for the District of Columbia. Even with additional experience, like her role as vice chair of the U.S. Sentencing Commission from 2010 to 2014 and being a Harvard Board of Overseers member, she was framed by Republicans as a pedophile sympathizer in one of the most disturbing confirmation hearings in history.

Merrick Garland was given a "well-qualified" rating but was infamously blocked by Republicans from being appointed to the Supreme Court, specifically by Senate majority leader Mitch McConnell.

Unanimous "well-qualified" ratings are not just limited to judges appointed by Democratic presidents. Justices Brett Kavanaugh, Neil Gorsuch, John G. Roberts Jr., Samuel A. Alito

Jr., Anthony M. Kennedy, and Antonin Scalia all received unanimous "well-qualified" ratings from the American Bar Association.

In August 1991, no one on the American Bar Association committee found Thomas "well-qualified" for the Supreme Court, and two members stated he was "unqualified." The *New York Times* reported, "It is highly unusual, if not unprecedented, for a nominee to be confirmed without a unanimous evaluation of at least 'qualified.'"[84]

The press was highly critical. In September 1991, journalist Anthony Lewis wrote in the *New York Times*, "He has never been in the private practice of law. He has never been a teacher, a scholar. He has never argued a case in an important court. He was the highly ideological chairman of a federal agency (EEOC), spending much of his time making 150 political speeches, and then a federal judge for one year."[85]

As for Thomas's time as the head of the EEOC, civil rights attorney William L. Taylor said in 1991, "While he was in federal government, he took a view of civil rights laws that was so narrow as to be ineffective. He refused to recognize the affirmative role of the government in protecting against discrimination." While he was head of the EEOC, thirteen thousand age discrimination claims lapsed. In 1988, according to the General Accounting Office, the investigative arm of Congress, regional EEOC offices were not wholly studying cases, and "41 percent to 82 percent of the cases closed by those offices, with no evidence of discrimination found, had not been fully investigated."[86]

The NAACP also accused Thomas of only focusing on "individual random acts of bigotry" and "ignoring systemic patterns of discrimination." Herbert Hill, the former labor director for the NAACP, wrote in a letter to Thomas in 1987, "Because you and other commissioners reject the idea that Title VII (of the Civil Rights Act of 1964) was meant to be an instrument of social change, you have transformed the EEOC into a claims adjustment bureau."[86]

Dr. John Hope Franklin wrote about Thomas for the *New York Times* in 1991 that he "has placed himself in the unseemly position of denying to others the very opportunities and the kind of assistance from public and private quarters that have placed him where he is today."[88]

Also in 1991, civil rights legend Rosa Parks warned the country about the danger of Thomas, writing, "His confirmation to the highest court in the land would not represent a step forward in the road to racial progress but a U-turn on that road… His statements on the *Brown v. Board of Education* case and even on the *Roe v. Wade* to me indicate that he wants to push the clock back… The Supreme Court now appears to be turning its back on the undeniable fact of discrimination and exclusion… I believe that Judge Thomas will accelerate that trend and that will be destructive for our nation."[89]

In 2022, Parks's words were haunting. *Roe v. Wade* was overturned, and Thomas wrote that the right to obtain contraception and same-sex marriage should be reconsidered.[90]

Thomas's radical ideology was exactly what President George H. W. Bush wanted. He was the gruesome opposite of Justice Thurgood Marshall. A Black man who opposed civil rights[91] was the political tool Bush needed. This was the only qualification—affirmative action with the expectation of doing the filthy work of the Republican Party. Thomas also appeared to have a mission, according to his friend Armstrong Williams in 1995: "He's going to change these race-based laws in this country, forever."[92]

Race-based laws to Thomas seem to mean any policies that sought to create an equal playing field to achieve the so-called American dream—policies that helped him climb out of the poverty of Georgia to make it to the U.S. Supreme Court.

Suppose Bush had sought to appoint a qualified, experienced Black Republican. In that case, he might easily have considered William T. Coleman Jr.[93] He served as a law clerk to Judge Herbert F. Goodrich of the U.S. Court of Appeals for the Third Circuit[94] and made history as the first Black American to be a Supreme Court law clerk, which was to Justice Felix Frankfurter in 1948. He was a protégé of Thurgood Marshall,[95] a Democrat, helping to write the legal briefs for *Brown v. Board of Education* in 1954. Additionally, Coleman was the fourth U.S. secretary of transportation under President Gerald Ford's administration.[96]

Coleman was no Clarence Thomas. He unapologetically called out the GOP during the 1980s.[97] In 1982, Coleman spoke before the U.S. Supreme Court against the Reagan administration. Reagan attempted to revoke an Internal Revenue Service policy that banned "racially discriminatory private schools from receiving federal tax benefits."[98] As a "friend of the court," Coleman stated, "Their argument is that because their racism is religiously based, they have a right to tax benefits denied to all others who cannot defend their policies on religious grounds. When fundamental public policy is violated, a defense of religious belief is not available."[99]

The high court sided with Coleman. This was not the escapist Black Republican who would meet President George H. W. Bush's quota.

At the same time, some hoped Thomas would not be a charlatan.

Arthur Fletcher, another Black Republican and the father of affirmative action, would eventually endorse Thomas for the Supreme Court. Despite Thomas being explicitly against the affirmative action policy, Fletcher said, "In his heart of hearts he knows how he got where he is" and that Thomas "has benefited from the dramatically improved opportunities environment created by the employment affirmative action enforcement movement and...has ridden it all the way to the top."[100]

Fletcher was wrong. By 1995, Thomas voted to limit affirmative action in a 5–4 decision. Fletcher told *Jet* magazine, "As far as I'm concerned...Justice Thomas, who is Black, is leaning over to try and think white."[101] Fletcher may have been correct. In 2007, *Baltimore Sun* writer Clarence Page described Thomas as expressing "an odd sort of pride" when he testified in the high court's budget hearing and said his clerks "happen to be all white males." Thomas added, "I don't have quotas."[102]

Some have attempted to make sense of Thomas's rulings on the court through his temporary embrace of Black nationalism. According to Thomas, when he was enrolled at the College of the Holy Cross in Massachusetts, he was an "angry Black man" and a "radical" who was inspired by author Richard Wright and revolutionaries like Malcolm X. During his years in college, he protested, supported the Black Panthers, and joined the Black Student Union.[103] By 2009, Thomas downplayed his role in the Black Student Union, telling Julian Bond he was only called to join the group because he could type and edit.[104]

The Black Student Union had an eleven-point manifesto, which included, "The Black man does not want or need the white woman. The Black man's history shows that the white woman is the cause of his failure to be the true Black man." Thomas opposed interracial unions and would publicly accost interracial couples.[105] All of this is quite ironic, considering Clarence Thomas married a white woman in 1987,[106] just three years after divorcing his Black wife of thirteen years.

The courtship of his current wife, Virginia Thomas, also known as Ginni, Republican activist and founder of conservative lobbying company Liberty Consulting,[107] is fascinating in its own right. A 1991 feature in the *Washington Post* revealed they married within a year of meeting. Virginia Thomas's family said they were "surprised" when they discovered she was marrying a Black man. Most people in her family didn't know Clarence Thomas was Black until the wedding. Virginia's aunt Opal also dropped this line to the *Washington Post*: "He treated her so well, all of his other qualities made up for his being Black."[108]

Was being Black something to "make up for" in Virginia Thomas's family?

Ginni Thomas has been immersed in the radical wing of the Republican Party for years. In 1995, she bragged about being partisan and political: "I've been on a mission for a long time. I wouldn't be in this town if I wasn't on a mission."[109] When Donald Trump became president, Ginni Thomas enjoyed unusual access, allegedly giving him reports on the most loyal White House staffers. A former senior Trump administration official told the *Daily Beast* in April 2022, "We all knew that within minutes after Ginni left her meeting with the president, he would start yelling about firing people for being disloyal. When Ginni Thomas showed up, you knew your day was wrecked."[110]

On the morning of January 6, 2021, she was cheering on Trump supporters via Facebook: "God bless each of you standing up or praying."

She also posted: "Love MAGA people!!!!"[111]

She admitted to attending the January 6 Stop the Steal Rally, the precursor to the January 6 insurrection, but claimed she left because it was "cold."

The *Washington Post* revealed that same month that Ginni was ranting on a private Listserv called Thomas Clerk World, which included former staff of her husband. Her pro-Trump gibbering caused a "rift" on the Listserv, which she later apologized for: "My passions and beliefs are likely shared with the bulk of you, but certainly not all. And sometimes the smallest matters can divide loved ones for too long. Let's pledge to not let politics divide THIS family, and learn to speak more gently and knowingly across the divide."[112]

A feature by Jane Mayer for the *New Yorker* stated that Ginni has "her own links" to people who participated in the January 6 insurrection.

Norman Eisen, a senior fellow at the Brookings Institution, told Mayer, "It is hard to understand how Justice Thomas can be impartial when hearing cases related to the upheaval on January 6th, in light of his wife's documented affiliation with January 6th instigators and Stop the Steal organizers. Justice Thomas should recuse himself, given his wife's interests in the outcome of these cases."[113]

In March 2022, the *Washington Post* reported that Ginni Thomas was texting Mark Meadows, Trump's chief of staff, in November 2020 about overturning the election. There was also a text message on January 10, 2021.[114]

Are the American people to believe she never discussed January 6 with her husband, the only justice who voted to seal the January 6 records?

In May 2022, reports of Ginni Thomas calling Arizona lawmakers to overturn the 2020 election results emerged. The same month, Clarence Thomas complained that the leaked *Roe v. Wade* draft opinion impacted the "trust" of the high court.[115] But what of the actions of his right-wing activist wife?

Ginni Thomas is a spouse of the senior member of the U.S. Supreme Court.[116] If Judge Sonia Sotomayor had a third cousin in the Bronx posting on social media about a Black Lives Matter rally where a police officer was harmed, Sotomayor would be under immediate investigation. Such is the double standard of politics in our times. (In my brief conversation with Emma Mae Martin, Thomas's sister, I asked her thoughts about her sister-in-law, considering she was in the news cycle. Martin let out a laugh and declined to comment.)[117]

Marrying a conservative white woman does not make Thomas a grifter, but it's worth noting, considering his much-discussed transformation from alleged Black nationalist to a hypocritical Republican.

Thomas claims he had a miraculous shift in 1970. In his own telling, after attending a protest in Boston, he returned to Holy Cross and prayed, "I just asked God to take hate out of my heart, and I just vowed that if he did I would never hate again."[118]

Thomas's whimsical transformation due to prayer makes for a good story. What appears more realistic is Thomas saw Black radicalism as too much of a sacrifice. He could not climb the pale ladder of power as a radical. There are no Black radicals in government. Instead, Clarence Thomas plotted to become the greatest grifter of them all.

In 1998, Thomas reflected on this "anger," blaming it on authors and musicians. "Perhaps my passion for Richard Wright novels was affecting me. Perhaps it was listening too intently to Nina Simone. Perhaps, like Bigger Thomas, I was being consumed by the circumstances in which I found myself, circumstances that I saw as responding only to race."[119] He continued, "Perhaps I was empowered by the anger and relieved that I could now strike back at the faceless oppressor. But why was I conceding my intellect and rather fighting much like a brute? This I could not answer, except to say that I was tired of being restrained."[120]

This is an ongoing narrative from Thomas. His anger made him a victim who blamed white people for everything and expected the government to take care of him; maybe that is why he shamed his sister.

Before he was officially appointed to the Supreme Court in 1991, Thomas bizarrely misinterpreted Malcolm X, a stunt many Black Republican grifters pull today. "I don't see how the civil-rights people today can claim Malcolm X as one of their own. Where does he say Black people should go begging the Labor Department for jobs? He was hell on integrationists. Where does he say you should sacrifice your institutions to be next to white people?"[121]

Thomas stated this as if he was a segregationist. He is arguably the biggest integrationist of them all. His white wife, affiliation with a Republican Party lacking Black representation, and a Yale degree partially owed to affirmative action all point to an identity crisis.[122] If Malcolm X were alive, age sixty-six in 1991, he would have given hell to Clarence Thomas. Malcolm probably would have used this line: "He identified himself with his master, more than his master identified with himself."[123]

It's also imperative to note that Malcolm X wasn't a segregationist but a separatist. In 1963, he stated, "We don't go for segregation. We go for separation. Separation is when you have your own. You control your own economy; you control your own politics."[124]

Black self-reliance was not unique to Malcolm X or the Nation of Islam. Ida B. Wells, Dr. Martin Luther King Jr., Bayard Rustin, Adam Clayton Powell, the innumerable Black Republican elected officials during Reconstruction, and nearly every Black leader in American history fought for Black self-sufficiency. From Frederick Douglass to Marcus Garvey to Malcolm X, they were aware of white terror even when Black folks achieved independence. Wilmington, North Carolina (1898), Tulsa, Oklahoma (1921), and Rosewood, Florida (1923), were prosperous Black areas obliterated by domestic terrorism. There was no escaping white supremacy that fed on the blood and bodies of Black people.

Thomas should know Black people are not waiting for good white folks to give them a handout. Fighting for justice in the courts, elections, housing, and health care is not begging for charity from white people; it's demanding equal access.

To try to grasp what makes Clarence Thomas tick, I spoke to Paul Butler, a professor at Georgetown University. He told me that, in fact, Thomas is not so unusual in some ways. He said that Thomas "is obsessed with race in the way that many Black conservatives are." However, he maintained Thomas's angst is with white liberals: "I think he is probably more angry at white progressives than Black progressives." Butler stated that Thomas is concerned about white liberals "meddling in the lives of Black people" with policies like affirmative action.[125]

I have endless criticisms of white liberals, but if Thomas's quarrel is with this group, he neglects how white conservatives have meddled in the lives of Black people with treacherous policies.

Butler also stated that Thomas's roots in Black nationalism are consistent in his legal thinking and writing. While it is true there is conservativism in Black nationalism, it is not the conservativism of Thomas. Would a man rooted in Black nationalism allegedly display a Confederate flag on his desk?

In 1991, Thomas was accused of displaying a Confederate flag on his desk sometime between 1975 and 1976 while he was the assistant attorney general of Missouri. Two people claimed they saw the flag but would later say they were unsure if it was the Confederate flag or the Georgia state flag, which included the Confederate emblem at the time. The flag's presence on his desk was summed up as a "quirky display of his individuality."[126]

Former Democratic representative William L. Clay called the display of the Confederate flag an "insensitive advertisement of Mr. Thomas's lack of respect for Black culture and values." Former senator John Danforth, Thomas's mentor and boss while he was the assistant attorney general of Missouri, slammed Clay and the CBC for "reckless attacks that have been made on Clarence Thomas, which have been based on misstatements of fact."

In 1991, it was unclear if Thomas displayed the Georgia flag or the Confederate flag on his desk. (The New York Times said Thomas's "recollection" of the flag "may have been fuzzy.")[127] In Thomas's 2007 memoir, he wrote that in 1976, he brought to the office "a miniature Georgia state flag—the same one that had been adopted in 1956, with the Confederate flag and the Georgia state seal displayed side by side." Thomas claimed he displayed the flag for a white coworker "to try to imagine how he would have felt growing up under a flag like that had he been Black."[128] It's unknown how his white coworker reacted to Thomas's strange lesson on racism.

Regardless of whether Thomas proudly propped the flag on his desk or brought the Confederate flag or the Georgia state flag for his white coworker to "imagine" racism, the question remains the same: Why would a Black man who endured the terror of Jim Crow and was allegedly inspired by Black nationalism display the Georgia state flag with a Confederate symbol? The fight to remove the Confederate emblem from the Georgia flag and other state flags has been ongoing for decades.[129] It's not far-fetched to argue Thomas's display of the Georgia state flag is an example of his "lack of respect for Black culture and values."[128]

As for Thomas's view of Black self-reliance, because Malcolm X and other Black nationalists inspired him fifty years ago, that might be the story line some accept. I do not, especially from a man who, as reported in 1995, listened to Rush Limbaugh as "one of his few mass-media sources" and officiated the radio host's third wedding.[131] Thomas's actions are glaringly inconsistent with Black nationalism, and the best example is Curtis Flowers.

Flowers is a Black man in Mississippi who had been tried six times for the same crime, a 1996 quadruple killing.[132] He said his constitutional rights were denied after Black people were consistently struck from the jury pool. District Attorney Doug Evans, who is white and had a documented history of striking Black jurors, convicted Flowers in 2010.[133] He was sentenced to death, and the Mississippi State Supreme Court repeatedly upheld the conviction. Flowers always maintained his innocence.

In June 2019, the U.S. Supreme Court overturned Flowers's murder conviction.[134] In his ruling, conservative Justice Brett Kavanaugh wrote, "In sum, the State's pattern of striking Black prospective jurors persisted from Flowers' first trial through Flowers' sixth trial. In the six trials combined, the State struck 41 of the 42 Black prospective jurors it could have struck. At the sixth trial, the State struck five of six. At the sixth trial, moreover, the State engaged in dramatically disparate questioning of Black and white prospective jurors. And it engaged in disparate treatment of Black and white prospective jurors, in particular by striking Black prospective juror Carolyn Wright."[135]

In response, Thomas appeared gleeful that prosecutors could bring a case against Mr. Flowers for the seventh time. Thomas wrote, "If [the Kavanaugh] opinion today has a redeeming quality, it is this: the State is perfectly free to convict Curtis Flowers again."[136]

One of the most powerful Black men in the country wrote this—and it is not Black nationalism, pro-Black, or self-reliance. It is classic Justice Clarence Thomas and arguably the most hateful ruling since 2013 when he argued Section 4 *and* Section 5 of the Voting Rights Act should be eliminated. Only Section 4 was struck down, which is the formula for who is covered by the preclearance provision. Section 5 defines preclearance and the process of securing it.[137] In light of the expansion of the conservative wing of the court, Thomas may get his wish to dismantle the rest of the Voting Rights Act soon enough. Malcolm X called for Black people to have political power in their communities. Justice Thomas supporting an end to the Voting Rights Act crushes political power in Black communities—and that is not Black nationalism.

In December 2019, Curtis Flowers was finally released from prison after twenty-three years. Despite Thomas's hateful wishes, Flowers wasn't tried for a seventh time, and Mississippi attorney general Lynn Fitch dropped all charges in September 2020.[138] Flowers said in a statement, "Today, I am finally free from the injustice that left me locked in a box for 23 years."[139]

In March 2021, Mississippi paid Flowers a measly $500,000 for over two decades of bondage.[140] In September 2021, he filed a federal civil rights lawsuit seeking damages from District Attorney Doug Evans and the police officers who wrongfully put him behind bars.[141]

Flowers also deserves an apology from Justice Thomas.

Despite weak qualifications, Clarence Thomas depended on powerful white men to move forward in life, getting a handout from affirmative action to ignoring sexual harassment claims. From his role on the Supreme Court to his second wife, who cheered on the rally that would mutate into the January 6 insurrection, Malcolm X would be disgusted by Clarence Thomas and his rise in the ranks of the white power structure.

Thomas is a textbook grifter who calls on race when it's to his benefit. There is no better example than his appointment to the Supreme Court.

In October 1991, Dr. Anita Hill was forced to testify before the Senate Judiciary Committee.[142] She alleged that then Supreme Court nominee Clarence Thomas had sexually harassed her.[143]

Hill sat before the country and revealed that while working as an attorney under Thomas at the EEOC, she was subjected to sexual advances from Thomas,[144] including lewd comments about his sexual prowess and the relay of detailed descriptions of pornographic movies.[145] She claimed there were references to a pornographic film star named "Long Dong Silver," and pubic hair was found on a Coca-Cola can.[146]

Hill was grilled by an all-white, all-male Senate Judiciary Committee with Senator Howell Heflin, a Democrat from Alabama, asking if she was a "scorned woman." But there were others who could have backed up her story.

Many people forget Angela Wright, Clarence Thomas's director of public affairs in 1984 when he was the chair of the EEOC. Wright wanted to testify against Thomas, which would corroborate Hill's story. Wright was subpoenaed and spent several days in an attorney's office in Washington, DC, waiting to be called to testify. Wright was told that "because of the lateness of the hour," she was never called, but her statement was put in the record.[147]

Clarence Thomas delivered his famous retort in a speech before the Senate Judiciary Committee: "From my standpoint as a Black American, as far as I'm concerned, it is a high-tech lynching for uppity Blacks who in any way deign to think for themselves, to do for themselves, to have different ideas, and it is a message that unless you kowtow to an old order, this is what will happen to you. You will be lynched, destroyed, caricatured by a committee of the U.S.—U.S. Senate, rather than hung from a tree."[148]

"High-tech lynching" was a grand grift for Thomas. There is no such thing as a high-tech lynching, but Thomas put the imaginary noose in the hands of "uppity Blacks." For the older white men on the Senate Judiciary Committee, who may have witnessed a few lynchings in their time, Thomas handed them the ability to become saviors, rescuing him from the savage, deranged Black people who didn't support him because he is a Republican. Most disgusting, Thomas blamed Dr. Anita Hill, a Black woman, for the "lynching" of a Black man. Thomas became the victim after years of whining that Black people victimize themselves.

In Thomas's mind, the victims were not Dr. Anita Hill, Angela Wright, Curtis Flowers, his sister Emma Mae Martin, and the Black people who would suffer at the hands of his power; the victim was *him*. After griping that Black people were sacrificing their "institutions to be next to white people," he was sacrificing his Pin Point, Georgia, soul with the help of elite white men who would crown him the Black king of the U.S. Supreme Court.

Thomas was confirmed to the U.S. Supreme Court with a 52–48 vote. Eleven Democrats voted for Thomas, one being Illinois senator Alan J. Dixon. Cook County Recorder of Deeds Carol Moseley-Braun was so disgusted by Dixon's support of Thomas that in 1992, she ran against him and became the first Black woman elected to the U.S. Senate. A key to her historic win was the high voter turnout in the Black areas of Chicago, where residents were probably just as repulsed by Dixon's support of Thomas.[149]

Justice Thomas represented a new class of Black conservatives, extraordinarily different from Black Republicans before the Reagan era. John Wilks, a Black Republican who served in the Nixon and Ford administrations in subcabinet roles, saw the grift early. In December 1991, two months after Thomas was appointed to the U.S. Supreme Court, Wilks said to the *New York Times*, "They merely say they're conservative, say they're opposed to affirmative action and are immediately picked up by a right-wing white sponsor, such as the Hoover Institution, Heritage Foundation, and American Enterprise Institute, groups not known for their sensitivity to Black issues. That's the main shortcoming of these new Black conservatives."[150]

Wilks saw the future. It's a diabolical formula we would see from Tim Scott, Daniel Cameron, Ben Carson, Herman Cain, Mia Love, and countless others. Today's grifters may be elevated by right-wing white sponsors and supported by cable networks like Fox News, but Justice Thomas is their ideological and tactical blueprint. Clarence Thomas perfected the grift, polished the talking points, and, unlike the Black Republicans before him, morphed himself into the victim of the angry Black mob who were simply outraged because he is the sanctified "independent thinker."

With his radical, right-wing activist wife by his side, Thomas lives and breathes Republicanism. The record shows he is a political cancer—when justices should be apolitical—and his ideology is metastasizing.

CHAPTER 6

FRANKS AND WATTS

"I think the issue on the right is that they do not allow an African American to be Republican, conservative, and Black. They say you've got to be one or the other."

—J. C. Watts[1]

FROM 1929 TO 2022, THERE HAVE ONLY BEEN NINE BLACK Republicans as voting members in the House of Representatives.[2] When Oscar Stanton De Priest lost reelection in 1934 in Illinois, it would take nearly sixty years for the next Black Republican representative to be elected. (Republican Melvin Herbert Evans was in the House for the U.S. Virgin Islands' at-large district from 1979 to 1981, but he was a delegate, a nonvoting member.) His name was Gary Franks, and he served in Connecticut's Fifth District from 1991 to 1997—but Gary Franks was no Oscar Stanton De Priest.[3] Representing Connecticut's Fifth District, which was overwhelmingly white at the time of his election,[4] Franks would make De Priest spin in his grave.

Franks was against affirmative action (the creation of a Black Republican named Arthur Fletcher), supported the nomination of Clarence Thomas to the Supreme Court, believed Roosevelt's New

Deal enslaved Black people,[5] blasted the 1995 Million Man March while comparing the Nation of Islam to the Ku Klux Klan,[6] and supported lifting sanctions against South Africa before apartheid had ended.[7]

As Franks was running for office, Congress nearly passed the Civil Rights Act of 1990, which would have made it less difficult for individuals in race or sex discrimination lawsuits to win. President George H. W. Bush vetoed the bill, arguing that if companies feared lawsuits, they might feel forced to maintain race or gender quotas. In October 1990, Benjamin Hooks, executive director of the NAACP at the time, called Bush's veto "a sharp and shocking disappointment" and said he was "at a loss" why the president described the Civil Rights Act of 1990 as a quota bill.[8]

Franks carried this bizarre logic even further—according to the *Washington Post,* his "opposition was based on his experience, his fear that companies might use a policy of forced quotas as an excuse to move out of communities." Franks said about the bill, "I question whether some Democrats truly want a civil rights bill or if they want a political issue."[9]

Franks's shenanigans didn't sit well with the CBC, where he was the first Republican voting member.[10] After he stood in opposition to redistricting that would benefit Black communities and voters, he was temporarily kicked out, and his access to strategy sessions was limited.[11]

While Franks did support the Civil Rights Act of 1991, his colleagues in Congress saw through his grift. In 1995, Representative Julian Dixon, a Democrat from Los Angeles, said about Franks, "My measure of him is that he does not have any following in the Black community. And he does give white Americans cover by virtue of the color of his skin. He makes them feel more comfortable in dismantling programs that I think are still well needed."[12]

When Gary Franks finally lost reelection to white Democrat James Maloney,[13] he went so far as to blame Black people for his loss, even though he represented a 90 percent white district.

"You probably didn't know that Jesse Jackson Jr. was in Waterbury recently bad-mouthing Gary Franks," Franks told the *Hartford Courant* in 1996. "You probably didn't know that Al Sharpton was in Danbury, telling church audiences not to vote for me, or that the Million Man March people were working, night and day, to spread lies, distortions and half-truths about my record. I made myself a target for a number of organizations."[14] To the contrary, the *Hartford Courant* claimed Franks's critics felt he was too "preoccupied with his newfound fame to tend to the nitty-gritty of constituent work."[15]

As recently as 2021, Franks was complaining about the CBC, which he described as "craziness." He also wrote it's "very obvious" the CBC doesn't have "all the answers on improving the lives of Black Americans."[16]

Franks's remarks are reflective of the post-Clarence Thomas crop of Black Republicans. These grifters have little in common with their colleagues across the aisle. Their strategy was to whitewash racism for the benefit of their constituencies, which are usually predominately white. That plan sometimes runs out of gas and requires a particular level of cleverness to survive, which we would see in J. C. Watts, the next Black Republican elected to the House of Representatives in 1995, representing Oklahoma's Fourth District.

Watts, a former college football star and minister, won in a predominately white district. He grew up in a home of Democrats, according to the *Washington Post*, but switched parties because he believed Democrats took the Black vote for granted.[17]

There's some truth to that, but the idea that the contemporary GOP would be any better is hard to swallow, considering the policy records of Nixon, Ford, Reagan, and Bush. Yes, some Democrats have taken Black votes for granted, but Republican leaders are pathologizing Black communities to win over white voters and pursuing policies few Black voters would support. From the Barry Goldwater days of Black people literally being evicted from the GOP to the violent racism Jackie Robinson saw at the 1964 Republican National Convention, this was the party of racism like the Democratic Party was the party of racism in the 1800s. By 1995, when Watts was elected, more than sixty Black Democrats either were or had been in the House of Representatives since the early 1930s. Watts was only the third voting Black Republican in the House of Representatives since the 1930s.[18]

While Watts claimed he switched parties because he thought Democrats took the Black vote for granted, his district did not include many Black voters. It's hard not to wonder: is it possible that Watts switched parties because he knew he could not win in Oklahoma's predominantly white Fourth District as a Black Democrat? Did Watts crave political power and realize that the shortest route was as a Black Republican?

Like Franks, Watts played into the same language popular with Republicans since Nixon and Reagan. While campaigning, he blamed the number of people on welfare as "cultural decay." He also ranted about depending on the government and "being a victim" and spoke out against affirmative action.[19]

In taking these views, Watts was the opposite of people who

looked like him, including Black conservatives. In 1995, conservative African Americans supported affirmative action at 79 percent, wanted cuts in military spending at 76 percent, and 81 percent called for more spending on public education. Watts, as a candidate, was not aligned with his own community.[20]

In an interview with the *Washington Post*, titled "J. C. Watts: No Excuses," he boasted that his parents never needed public assistance and called on Black voters to hold Democrats accountable: "Whenever a candidate comes asking for your vote, make them accountable. I don't believe that the Black community has done that with the Democratic leadership."[21] The irony of this is Watts, at this point, wasn't holding his party accountable for their horrific policies, especially against poor whites.

Nonetheless, Watts was elected and quickly considered the newest star in the GOP.

Taking a cue from Massachusetts senator Edward Brooke, who had said, "A vote for Brooke is a vote against Stokely Carmichael," Watts adopted the tactic of assuring white voters that he was not *that* kind of Black person. In 1997, Watts was chosen to deliver the Republican response to President Bill Clinton's State of the Union address.[22] In a feature for the *Washington Post*, published right before the address, Watts was quoted as calling Reverend Jesse Jackson and DC Mayor Marion Barry "race-hustling poverty pimps."[23] Watts also harkened back to the "plantation" rhetoric, saying Jackson and Berry "talk a lot about slavery, but they're perfectly happy to have just moved us to another plantation." Not very Christlike language from the minister.

Watts's rhetoric was that of a classic bootstrapper. His words weren't on the same level as a predecessor such as Isaiah Montgomery or a successor such as Senator Tim Scott or

Representative Byron Donalds, and certainly not like the offensive commentary of Trump-supporting personalities like Diamond and Silk. But just because his words weren't as ludicrous doesn't mean Black GOPers, like Watts, didn't pave the way for those who use exaggerated, malicious, and self-serving rants against Black people. Watts's language was a gateway drug for the full-blown high of today's right-wing Black commentators, who don't merely preach opposition to Democratic policies but malign ongoing civil rights activism, denigrate successful Black progressives, and try to broadly pin the nation's woes on trumped-up controversies such as critical race theory, "defund the police," and the semantics of systemic racism.

They push the narrative that they, and only they, are independent thinkers. The point isn't to persuade or convert more Black voters to their cause but to place themselves on a pedestal above Black voters who typically vote for Democrats and, like Montgomery, win the applause of powerful white interests.

Black media rebuked Watts, and so did Barry and Jackson. The initially acrimonious exchanges signaled what would be at least a partial upcoming conversion from Watts. While DC Mayor Barry had a complicated history and was not perfect, it was a misnomer to say or insinuate he was pimping out poverty. Barry's administration balanced the city's budget and reinvented downtown DC with investment in construction, and his most famous policy is the District Youths Employment Act of 1979, which guaranteed summer jobs to everyone from fourteen to twenty-one years old.[24] Barry responded to Watts, saying, "I worked all my life for poor people. He ought to apologize."[25]

Representative Jesse Jackson Jr., representing Illinois's Second District at the time,[26] ripped into Watts via a letter, which read in part, "If you were quoted accurately, I am deeply saddened and disappointed that you would, not only as a distinguished member of Congress but as a clergyman and minister of the Gospel, make such an uncivil, immature, ignorant, and insensitive statement about my father. I have always known you to be more mature, more enlightened and more generous of spirit than that."[27]

Watts attempted to backtrack. He said he didn't name specific people, only "Black leaders," insinuating the *Washington Post* misquoted him. The *Washington Post* stood by its reporting. Watts then complained that Representative Jackson released his letter to the media, making what should have been a private conversation public. Ultimately, Watts apologized and reportedly had a "very pleasant" conversation with Barry.[28]

But the slamming of Black Democrats had done its work. White Republicans loved this performance, and it only made Watts more of a political star. Watts's press secretary bragged they received so many supportive phone calls that the lines were busy.

Yes, Watts was grifting in his own way and shaming Black leaders with all the trite tropes, but he still surprised his white Republican colleagues by throwing a policy curveball. As much as Watts had previously denounced affirmative action, he stood up for the policy at a crucial moment. In 1998, as House Republicans were trying to demolish affirmative action, Watts joined Democratic representative John Lewis of Georgia in a "Dear Colleague" letter: "This is not the time to eliminate the one tool we have—imperfect though it may be—to help level the playing field for many minority youth."[29]

The year before, Watts debated on a 1997 bill that would have gutted affirmative action in federal contracting and hiring. The *Washington Post* said in the "closed meeting" with the House

Republicans, there was an "impassioned debate." In the end, the bill was tabled, and four Republicans joined with the Democrats. Representative John Linder of Georgia, chairman of the National Republican Congressional Committee, reportedly said, "It was his [J. C. Watts's] objection last fall that really convinced us to hold off on this and talk about it more."[30]

The years 1997 to 1998 appeared to be a wake-up call for Watts. He made what seemed to be an implicit jab at his party: "I work very hard not to have to play the role of the Black Republican, the Black conservative. Like it or not, people force me to play the role of the Black Republican." Maybe he realized Black Democrats were not his enemies.

By 2003, Watts sounded like a stone-cold progressive Democrat, saying, "Affirmative action isn't the problem. Lousy education for Black kids is the problem. Until you fix these schools don't talk to me about equal opportunity."[31]

Watts ended up at war with his party, specifically Representaive Tom DeLay, who represented Texas's Twenty-Second Congressional District from 1985 until 2006.[32] In November 1998, Watts was the fourth-ranking Republican in the House, and by the following year, according to journalist Jake Tapper, DeLay was "charging right for him."[33] Watts was accused of doing an unsatisfactory job as House Republican Conference chair. But was this about job performance or about being insufficiently in step with the GOP line—and insufficiently solicitous of the biases of white Republicans?

Watts told Jake Tapper that he was being blocked from doing his job. "I didn't get a staff and budget until the middle of March. And everybody was saying, 'Oh, he's gotten off to a rocky start,' but I didn't have the ability to do the job I was elected to do." Watts added, "There was, I am convinced, an orchestrated effort to cause me problems and to keep me from doing my job."[34]

When President Bush was sworn into office in 2001, Watts felt he wasn't getting the same respect as other members of House leadership. No one from the administration would return Watts's calls, even for issues in his district. By 2002, after being ignored by the administration despite being a longtime supporter, Watts refused to attend a House Republican Conference where President Bush was scheduled to speak. Not being allowed to do his job and feeling underappreciated by his party would be a similar fate for the first and only Black chair of the Republican Party, Michael Steele.

By 2003, Watts resigned, and Black Democrats were singing his praises. South Carolina representative James Clyburn said, "J. C. is someone who really has been quietly but very forcefully doing a lot of good." The late, great Representative John Lewis agreed, "He's not one of the old, traditional guys who go around slapping backs, the good ol' boys. That's not his style."[35] Civil rights legend Rosa Parks wrote him a letter, asking him not to resign. He was a different politician than he had been in 1995.

To be clear, Watts was and is absolutely a Republican. The American Conservative Union gave him a lifetime rating of 94 percent.[36] When he was out of office, he supported Bush's war in Iraq[37] and once described same-sex marriage as "decay."[38] However, Watts distinguished himself by refusing to kowtow to the GOP, at least after he got into office.

For years, Watts has been openly critical of how Republicans handled racial issues and never held back calling out the Trump administration.[39]

In August 2020, Watts said, "Republicans, conservatives, I think the issue on the right is that they do not allow an African American to be Republican, conservative, and Black. They say you've got to be one or the other. And I think it's very difficult for African-Americans to say, you expect me to denounce the experiences."[40]

It's an essential point from Watts, but another question is—when did Watts know Republicans wanted him to erase his Blackness? Did he ever participate in the racial erasure for political clout, and if so, what was his breaking point? In 2022, Watts endorsed Democrat Joy Hofmeister for governor of Oklahoma, saying, "I was a Republican then, and I'm a Republican now, and, friends, I'm voting for Joy Hofmeister."[41] Incumbent Governor Kevin Stitt won by over ten points.

I reached out to J. C. Watts's team for an interview, but his team declined.

Black Republicans like Watts may eventually reckon with the racism of their party, but the question remains: How were they blind to it? Did they sincerely believe the party wasn't what it showed itself to be, or did they convince themselves they were the great Black savior who would rescue the GOP from their racism? It's a question that could just as easily be asked of the Black Republicans to come, like General Colin Powell and Madam Secretary Condoleezza Rice.

CHAPTER 7

RICE, POWELL, AND BUSH

"Nobody needs to tell me how to be Black."

—Madam Secretary Condoleezza Rice[1]

IN 1992, THE GOP'S TWELVE-YEAR REIGN ENDED. PRESIDENT Bill Clinton was elected and would appoint a historic number of Black people to his presidential cabinet during two terms. He would also select more Black federal judges than any president in history at the time, the Black unemployment rate was nearly slashed in half, and the administration increased funding for HBCUs.

Still, Clinton's record with the Black community was far from perfect. The Violent Crime Control and Law Enforcement Act of 1994, also known as the 1994 Crime Reform Bill, solidified mass incarceration. (It's important to note that the Crime Reform Bill has its roots with Reagan and Nixon, who were the original "law and order" presidents.) As for the poor of any racial background, the most horrific policy was the Personal Responsibility and Work Opportunity Act of 1996, also known as the Welfare Reform Act, which kicked millions of people off public assistance without better access to jobs or higher wages. That said, considering Republicans, especially Black Republicans, so passionately despise welfare, one would think they would love President Clinton for this legislation.

The Republican Party was mobilizing for the next GOP take-over. Representative J. C. Watts was the most prominent Black Republican elected official in the 1990s. The National Rifle Association (NRA) was gaining massive political power, and white evangelicals were etching in stone their role in politics. The old-guard Republicans passed on their racist Operation Dixie tactics to a new generation of elected officials.

After the fiasco of the 2000 election, when the race was briefly called for Vice President Al Gore but was retracted due to a dispute over a little more than five hundred votes in Florida, George W. Bush eventually became the forty-third president of the United States. Unlike Trump and his "big lie" minions, Gore conceded.

It wasn't a good start for the Bush administration and the Black community. Bush had lost the Black vote by nine to one.[2] During the 2000 election, many Black voters in Florida believed their vote was suppressed,[3] especially after it was reported that more than 175,000 ballots were not counted in the Sunshine State, many in heavily Black areas.[4] Speaking of voter suppression, while Bush did sign the Voting Rights Act Reauthorization and Amendments Act of 2006, which he is often praised for, one of the most under-reported stories of his administration is his Department of Justice waging a political war on a Black man in Mississippi.

In 2005, Bush's Department of Justice filed a civil case against Ike Brown, accusing him of discriminating against white voters in Mississippi. For the first time in history, the Voting Rights Act of 1965 was used as a weapon against a Black citizen. Brown, in his early fifties at the time, had been registering people to vote since he was a teenager and was a "legend"[5] in Mississippi for turning out the Black vote in Noxubee County. He was the chairman of the Noxubee County Democratic Executive Committee, but his civic engagement resulted in him being accused of engaging "in racially motivated manipulation of the electoral process in Noxubee County to the detriment of white voters." According to Ko Bragg in *Scalawag Magazine*, in the mid-1960s, Noxubee County was 70 percent Black, and all the elected officials were white. By the early 2000s, "the racial demographics remained the same, but 93 percent of the elected officials were Black this time."[6]

Bush's DOJ was screaming racism with voter fraud accusations, which resonated with some of the county's white residents. In 2006, an unidentified white woman in Noxubee County was quoted as saying, "There's a lot of voting irregularities, but that's all I'm going to say."[7] Words that could easily come from one of Trump's "big lie" supporters in 2020.

The obsession over Brown was quite rich, considering Bush's DOJ hadn't filed a voting rights case for Black people since 2001.[8] In 2007, the court ruled against Brown, and he was banned from electoral work for four years.

In 2018, Brown said about the case, "They called it 'reverse voter rights…reverse discrimination.' Said I was discriminating against white folks." Brown was also accused of misusing the absentee ballot, to which he responded with, "The whole thing is they wanted to stop Black people from doing absentee ballots— that's what the whole trial was about… In Mississippi that's all they did [use absentee ballots]—white folks. When Black folks started doing it, it was a problem—it was fraud and everything else. As long as they were doing it, it was alright."[9]

While the Bush administration made history by twisting the Voting Right Act, Bush got more attention for having the first GOP administration with four Black members in a presidential cabinet. As most well know, Colin Powell and then Condoleezza Rice became secretary of state. Alphonso Jackson was appointed secretary of housing and urban development in 2004.[10] Rod Paige, the former superintendent of the Houston, Texas, public schools, became the first Black American secretary of education in 2001.[11]

Bush came into office keen on satisfying his key base, white evangelicals. While Rod Paige's appointment as the first Black secretary of education was historic, he became infamous for his involvement with Bush's ill-fated attempt to remake American education. Using the tagline the "soft bigotry of low expectations" as his vision and with No Child Left Behind (NCLB) as the policy, he appealed to hard-right Republicans.

In 2002, NCLB was signed into law and was supposed to remedy the racial achievement gap in public schools with federal dollars.[12] Much of the bill was "cut and pasted" from Clinton's Improving America's Schools Act of 1994, but Paige and Bush added their GOP twist with more insidious testing requirements.[13] The policy faced immediate pushback from teachers' unions, who saw the disaster of NCLB before it became law. The National Education Association, one of the largest labor unions at the time, and the American Federation of Teachers did not publicly support the legislation.[14] Although the Bush administration committed to improving schools,[15] there were accusations of not adequately funding the policy[16] and that NCLB's biased, one-size-fits-all statewide testing requirements left more children behind.[17]

Paige, who had a long history of working in education in Texas and was close to George H. W. Bush, got into hot water by making statements that sounded more like a white evangelical than someone sincerely concerned about improving education for all. In 2003, the *Baptist Press* quoted Paige as saying, "I would prefer to have a child in a school that has a strong appreciation for the values of the Christian community, where a child is taught to have a strong faith… The reason that Christian schools and Christian universities are growing is a result of a strong value system. In a religious environment the value system is set. That's not the case in a public school where there are so many different kids with different kinds of values."[18]

Paige's suggestion that the public schools' problem was the presence of "so many different kids with different kinds of values" set off alarm bells. There were immediate calls for Paige to resign. Barry W. Lynn, former executive director of Americans United for Separation of Church and State, wrote in a statement, "You do not appreciate religious diversity in America or the application of church-state separation to public schools. Since you are unable to endorse these important features of American life, I urge you to step down as secretary of education."[19]

Paige reportedly refused to resign or apologize. If anything, he stepped up his overheated rhetoric.[20] After back-and-forth with the unions, in February 2004, Paige outraged the National Education Association when he said it was like "a terrorist organization" because its members were pushing back against Bush's education policies. At least this time, Paige would apologize—comparing teachers to terrorists just a few years after 9/11 was beyond the pale—but the damage was done. Reg Weaver, who is Black and the former president of the National Education Association, said, "Secretary Paige's comments were pathetic and morally repugnant. They are no laughing matter." Terry McAuliffe, the Democratic national chairman, stated, "Secretary Paige and the Bush admin-istration have resorted to the most vile and disgusting form of hate speech, comparing those who teach America's children to terrorists."[21]

By the end of 2004, Paige resigned.[22] He had little to show for his time in the cabinet. The following year, the National Education Association and school districts from three states sued the Bush administration and accused the "government of short-changing schools by at least $27 billion."[23] In 2012, the *Washington Post* reported several letdowns of NCLB, like failing to increase academic performance, not narrowing achievement gaps, and damaging "educational quality and equity."[24]

In 2014, even Rod Paige admitted disappointment in edu-cation reform. "So far, most reform efforts have been about re-engineering the system. This is not an engineering problem; it's not about when, how, and where. Kids have to understand why it is important to do this."[25] The "why" behind Republican educa-tion reform had nothing to do with making a system that better served children. It appeared to be about disempowering teachers, attacking unions, and undermining public education altogether. Paige was willingly drafted into a campaign of attacking Black children and Black teachers for decades. Moreover, Bush's mantra of the "soft bigotry of low expectations" as he was gutting public schools was ironic, considering he was a C student who essentially received undeserved affirmative action due to his political family.[26]

In 2017, Paige's dedication to Republicanism continued, even in the Trump era. While the interim president of Jackson State University, he sympathized with Betsy DeVos, arguably the worst education secretary in history, who was appointed under Trump. "It was clear that she's kind of a target for the group that

I loosely refer to as the guardians of the status quo," Paige said about DeVos's confirmation hearing. He insisted public education "should be interested in positive change." He also criticized some of the questions to DeVos, which he felt were to "derail" rather than make judgments about her leadership.[27] At the disastrous confirmation hearing, DeVos made wildly bizarre comments all on her own—such as that guns should be allowed in a Wyoming school for protection "from potential grizzlies."[28]

Low expectations certainly appeared to be the HUD motto under Alphonso Jackson. In late 2003, Jackson, former president and chief executive officer of the Housing Authority of the City of Dallas[29] and a longtime friend of Justice Clarence Thomas,[30] became the acting secretary of housing and urban development.[31] By 2004, he was named the permanent secretary.[32] Jackson followed the tradition set by President Gerald Ford of Black Republicans being called to the cabinet to oversee HUD. Sadly, the position is tainted by scandal and mismanagement from Republicans and Democrats alike.

Jackson's term rapidly descended into a catastrophe when he suggested to a business group that he was weighing politics in awarding federal contracts. Speaking in Dallas in April 2006, Jackson told an anecdote about when he refused to give a "minority" contractor a contract. His reason? The contractor didn't support George W. Bush. "He didn't get the contract," Jackson said. "Why should I reward someone who doesn't like the president, so they can use funds to try to campaign against the president? Logic says they don't get the contract. That's the way I believe."[33] Adopting a political position in service of personal gain may have been how Jackson approached the world, but what he described was a crime. It is against federal law to refuse government contracts for political reasons.

Making things worse, Jackson attempted to backpedal by claiming he had made the whole story up. In a statement, Jackson said, "I deeply regret the anecdotal remarks I made at a recent Texas small-business forum and would like to reassure the public that all HUD contracts are awarded solely on a stringent merit-based process. During my tenure, no contract has ever been awarded, rejected, or rescinded due to the personal or political beliefs of the recipient."[34]

The public and press didn't buy it. In May 2004, a writer for *East Bay Times* wrote, "Either Jackson broke the law and then lied about it, or he lied that he had broken the law. Which of those actions makes him fit to be secretary of housing and urban development?"[35]

His comments sparked an investigation into whether Jackson had favored supporters of President Bush when awarding HUD contracts. His chief of staff told investigators that Jackson "personally intervened with contractors whom he did not like… These contractors had Democratic political affiliations." However, the report concluded Jackson "did not disclose any pattern or practice of issuing contracts based on political affiliation… There were some limited instances where political affiliation may have been a factor in contract issues involving Jackson," but there was "no evidence that a contract was canceled, rescinded, terminated or not issued as a result of the encounter between Secretary Jackson and the contractor."[36] In other words, Jackson was more of a liar than a criminal.

It wasn't the end of Jackson's troubles. Also in 2004, he made a clueless and classist comment that "poor is a state of mind, not a condition," which received backlash.[37] Another Republican trope to blame the working poor for starvation wages and high rent versus policies that are designed to keep people in poverty.

Scandal appeared to be a state of mind for Jackson. He was accused of giving deals to friends and loyalists in the Republican Party.[38] The FBI investigated a connection between Jackson and a friend who was allegedly paid $392,000 by HUD as a construction manager in New Orleans post-Hurricane Katrina.[39] The Philadelphia Housing Authority also sued Jackson for allegedly meddling with a land deal, and he was accused of moving thousands of dollars in government contracts to friends in the Virgin Islands.[40]

Alphonso Jackson always denied any wrongdoing, and the Justice Department declined to file charges,[41] but by March 2008, he could no longer escape the multiplying scandals. Jackson stepped down, facing demands for his resignation from Democrats like Connecticut senator Chris Dodd and Washington senator Patty Murray.[42]

His record at HUD was a tarnished one. He maintained that the Bush administration had "transformed public housing" during his tenure.[43] There was one major transformation: from 2004 through 2008, $1.8 billion was slashed from HUD programs.[44] Jackson had presided over a scandal-ridden agency that had worsened the state of public housing as the country descended into a housing crisis. In 2016, Jackson appeared to still be delusional about HUD and endorsed Ben Carson, who had zero housing experience, as Trump's pick for secretary of housing and urban development because "he's extremely compassionate and he really cares about the inner cities."[45]

The disasters of Paige and Jackson are due to the Bush administration's policies. They both claimed they worked for the people, but the results were the opposite. Theirs was a grift not as extreme and profitable as others ahead, but they certainly contributed to the downward spiral of Black Republicanism while undermining key institutions.

There was another kind of Black Republican during these years: Colin Powell, a four-star Army general who served in multiple administrations. He was seen as a potential presidential candidate by both parties,[46] until Powell came out as a Republican in November 1995. He stated he wanted to "help the party of Lincoln move once again close to the spirit of Lincoln."[47] In some ways, Powell's role in the GOP reflects the true colors of original Black Republicanism.

For many Black people, being a Republican in 1995 would be as illogical as being a Democrat in 1875. Neither party is impeccable, but just as the Democratic Party of 1875 was the party of white supremacists,[48] in 1995, the Republican Party was the party of racism.[49] Racist southerners gradually shifted to the GOP after President Lyndon B. Johnson signed the 1964 Civil Rights Act.[50] Arizona senator Barry Goldwater and disgraced President Richard Nixon perfected the Southern strategy[51] to win the white vote. President Ronald Reagan weaponized those racist political strategies by supporting apartheid in South Africa,[52] advocating for states' rights,[53] attempting a veto of the Civil Rights Restoration Act of 1987,[54] waging the coded war on drugs, and promoting many other policies that would annihilate Black communities across the country.[55]

President George H. W. Bush continued Reagan's legacy by bringing on Lee Atwater as his campaign manager for the 1988 presidential election. Despite outcry from several Black leaders, Bush vetoed the Civil Rights Act of 1990[56] and appointed Clarence Thomas, the anti-Thurgood Marshall, to the U.S. Supreme Court. Bush had won the 1988 election partly due to the infamous Willie Horton ad,[57] which used an image of a Black man convicted of rape and murder to claim that a weekend furlough program was dangerous. Bush rocketed in the polls, framing his opponent, Democrat Michael Dukakis, as weak on crime. Bush won the presidential election, and the Horton television commercial was a turning point in the campaign. Colin Powell would call the ad "racist," "cold political calculation," and a "political cheap shot." Even so, Powell said he never detected the "slightest trace of racial prejudice" in Bush or Reagan. Powell would serve as Bush's chairman of the Joint Chiefs of Staff.[58]

I have always wondered: How did Powell reconcile the abhorrent anti–civil rights agenda of the GOP when he joined the party in 1995? The child of Jamaican immigrants and a City College of New York graduate, Powell had to be cognizant of the party's bigotry. A 1995 article from the *Washington Post* claimed Powell told a friend about Reagan, "Reagan himself is color-blind, but he bears a responsibility for being blind to the impact of what his administration has not done for Black people."[59]

Powell's Republicanism could be compared to that of Arthur Fletcher, William Coleman, or Massachusetts senator Edward William Brooke.[60] These men did not shame Black folks for not sharing their political ideology and weren't afraid to call out their party. In a 1990 speech at the University of the District of Columbia during Black History Month, Powell made it clear his ascension to power did not erase his Blackness: "People say to me, gee, you were the first Black chairman of the Joint Chiefs of Staff, you were the first Black national security adviser of the president of the United States, so you had it made and obviously there is a meritocracy, in the Army anyway—you're not Black, you're not white, you're just green. And so all of this really doesn't matter anymore. You've made it. What I say to them is: Wrong! Wrong! I'm Black. I'm not green, I'm Black. I've been Black all my life. I've had to fight the prejudice that came my way all my life."[61]

Powell's language was refreshing, completely devoid of paternalizing Black people who weren't as successful as him. He would tell *Ebony*, "I have always tilted toward the Black media. I've made myself very accessible to the Black press and I do that as a way of just showing people, hey, look at that dude. He came out of the South Bronx. If he got out, why can't I?"[62]

For a time, Powell operated outside conventional partisan politics. Some regarded him as likely to become the first Black president of the United States—regardless of his party affiliation. When he joined the Reagan administration, his work was not necessarily an endorsement of Reagan's policies. Powell appeared committed to service above self-interest. After he came out as a Republican in November 1995, he paid lip service to the old line about the "party of Lincoln." It would only be a matter of time until Powell became exhausted with the GOP's racism. Like his predecessors, Powell learned he could not reform the Southern strategy party. The question remains: Colin Powell was disgusted by the GOP during the rise of Trump in 2016; where was his outrage decades before? Despite the revisionist history, policy-wise, the GOP in 2016 wasn't that different from the party in 1995.

Powell may have developed an affinity for the Republican Party throughout his lengthy military background, dating back to the 1950s. He was part of the Army Reserve Officers' Training Corps and an Army second lieutenant when he graduated from college in June 1958.[63] Powell served two combat tours in Vietnam and earned three medals.[64]

Vietnam would be the first stain on Powell's record, as he was criticized for participating in what has been described as a cover-up of the My Lai massacre.[65] On March 16, 1968, more than five hundred women and children from the village of My Lai, an area of south Vietnam, were murdered. There were horrific reports of mutilation and gang rape.[66] The public would not find out about the massacre until November 1969, and twenty-six American soldiers were charged.[67] Lieutenant William Calley Jr., a platoon leader, was the only person who was convicted. He was initially given a life sentence but served three and a half years under house arrest.[68]

Powell, an Army major in 1969,[69] was not tied to any wrongdoing on the ground. However, according to the *Washington Post*, "Gen. Powell received a written complaint from a young soldier accusing U.S. forces of brutality against civilians. The complaint did not refer specifically to My Lai, and Gen. Powell dismissed the allegation of widespread abuses after a cursory investigation. It took a letter from another soldier months later for the Army to open a formal inquiry and for the facts of the massacre to emerge."[70] Powell would eventually discuss his knowledge of what occurred in Vietnam. He blamed the fog of war. In Powell's 2010 book *My American Journey*, he wrote, "If a helo spotted a peasant in black pajamas who looked remotely suspicious, a possible MAM [Military Assistance Mission], the pilot would circle and fire in front of him. If he moved, his movement was judged evidence of hostile intent, and the next burst was not in front, but at him. Brutal? Maybe so. But an able battalion commander with whom I had served at Gelnhausen (West Germany), Lt. Col. Walter Pritchard, was killed by enemy sniper fire while observing MAMs from a helicopter. And Pritchard was only one of many.

The kill-or-be-killed nature of combat tends to dull fine percep-
tions of right and wrong."[71]

Writing years after the event, Powell finally seemed willing
to admit the massacre was a massacre. "My Lai was an appalling example of much that had gone wrong in Vietnam... The
involvement of so many unprepared officers and noncoms led to
breakdowns in morale, discipline, and professional judgment—
and to horrors like My Lai—as the troops became numb to what
appeared to be endless and mindless slaughter." Yet according to
at least one historian, Jeffrey J. Matthews, there may have been
another reason for Powell to participate in a cover-up. Matthews
noted that if Powell had challenged his superiors, it would have
"derailed his promising career."[72]

What does this mean for Powell's legacy in Vietnam? To
be fair, Powell was a career military man. No one could have
expected him to be removed from the tragedies of war. Sure
enough, Powell's promising career flourished within the GOP as
he served in military roles under the Reagan and Bush administrations. From 1989 to 1993, he made history as the first Black
person to be chairman of the Joint Chiefs of Staff. By 1996, there
were calls for him to run for president, but he refused, saying it
wouldn't be "the right thing for me at this time" and his wife was
against it.[73]

Powell had a vision for how the GOP might woo Black voters
away from the Democratic Party. According to the *New York
Times*, Powell believed because he was moderate on "positions
favoring gun control, abortion rights and affirmative [action] he
may have eased the party beyond its usual conservative rhetoric."[74]
He seemed to believe that the key to overcoming partisan differences was moderation on culture-war issues.

Powell was wrong. Though he was beloved on both sides of the political aisle,[75] it would take more than a moderate position by a single figure. One Black Republican with the soundness of history is not enough to convert Black voters. Moreover, Republicans in power wanted a Black leader to assure them they weren't racist. At the 2000 Republican National Convention in Philadelphia, Powell learned the hard way that Republicans weren't ready for him to speak the truth. He received a clear message from the GOP.

During a speech on the convention floor, Powell said, "We must understand the cynicism that exists in the Black community, the kind of cynicism that is created when, for example, some in our party miss no opportunity to roundly and loudly condemn affirmative action that helped a few thousand Black kids get an education, but you hardly hear a whimper when it's affirmative action for lobbyists who load our federal tax code with preferences for special interests. It doesn't work. It doesn't work. You can't make that case."[76]

Powell almost sounded like a democratic socialist, and sure enough, the four-star Army general was booed by delegates, according to journalist Andrea Mitchell.[77] This moment crystallizes Powell's relationship with the Republican Party. As Black Republicans had been arguing for decades, it would take meaningful policy changes, like Roosevelt's New Deal, which sparked the beginning of Black Americans going from Republican to Democrat[78]—regardless of Roosevelt's racism[79]—to entice Black voters to switch parties. The GOP was not willing to change policy. Nonetheless, Powell endorsed George W. Bush for president, and Bush won the electoral college, losing the popular vote.[80] In 2000, Bush only received 9 percent of the Black vote, the lowest since Reagan in 1980.[81] Powell signed up for his third Republican administration.

In January 2001, Powell became the sixty-fifth U.S. secretary of state and the first Black man to hold the position.[82]

Eight months later, on September 11, 2001, the country suffered the worst terrorist attack on American soil, which prompted an unnecessary war in Iraq—and Colin Powell found himself in the middle of an international scandal.

The war in Iraq is extremely complicated, but the simplest explanation for how it came about is that it was a matter of overreach by the Bush administration. The terrorist organization al-Qaeda, founded by Osama Bin Laden and predominately based in Afghanistan, was behind the 9/11 terrorist attacks. The U.S. declared war on Afghanistan—and then, after a few months, Iraq. Saddam Hussein, the fifth president of Iraq, was not involved with Bin Laden, Al-Qaeda, or the attacks. As for why the Bush administration wanted to go to war with Iraq, there are many theories, but the most popular was that the *next* terrorist attack on U.S. soil could be from Hussein. The administration allegedly believed there were "weapons of mass destruction" in Iraq. In fact, there weren't[83]—and some in the administration may have known better. The Bush administration worked closely with UK prime minister Tony Blair, settling on weapons of mass destruction as the reason to start a new war. The case would be presented before the United Nations.[84] This was when Powell stepped in.

On February 5, 2003, Powell, one of the most trusted people on the globe, famously spoke before the United Nations Security Council and claimed that there were weapons of mass destruction in Iraq. Powell held up a tiny vial, which was supposed to symbolize anthrax and the threat of biological warfare from Saddam

Hussein. Powell dramatically stated, "My colleagues, every statement I make today is backed up by sources, solid sources. These are not assertions. What we're giving you are facts and conclusions based on solid intelligence."[85]

While all politicians make mistakes, the United Nations speech was on a larger order. Powell cannot be blamed for Bush's warmongering decision, but he allowed himself to become a face of an unnecessary war. In March 2003, at the war's outset, when it was still incredibly popular with the American public overall, Gallup found that fewer than a third of Black Americans supported the war.[86]

Colin Powell resigned as secretary of state in 2004, letting Condoleezza Rice take the Bush reins of the State Department. Though he didn't forcefully rebuke the Bush administration, according to CNN, a senior State Department official characterized Powell's resignation by saying, "He was not asked to stay."[87]

His break with the Republican Party was coming. In 2008, he endorsed Illinois senator Barack Obama for president.[88]

Just sixteen days before the 2008 election, Powell said, "I firmly believe that at this point in America's history, we need a president that will not just continue, even with a new face and with the changes and with some maverick aspects, who will not just continue basically the policies that we have been following in recent years."

He continued, "We need a transformational figure, a president who is a generational change. That is why I'm supporting Barack Obama."[89] Rush Limbaugh and Pat Buchanan suggested Powell supported Obama because he is Black. Funny how Republicans never accuse other Republicans of endorsing each other simply because they are white.[90]

Powell supported a much younger, less experienced political

figure, not fellow Vietnam veteran Senator John McCain. This signaled a clash with the GOP's Iraq policy and his turn toward a more outspoken critique of the party's racialized politics. In 2013, years before Trump, Powell blasted Republican voter suppression laws in North Carolina and fake outrage over voter fraud. "What it really says to the minority voters is...'We really are sort of punishing you,'" he stated. "You can say what you like, but there is no voter fraud. How can it be widespread and undetected?"[91]

Powell would never endorse another Republican president. In 2012, he endorsed Obama for a second time over Mitt Romney. Like Limbaugh and Buchanan, future president Donald Trump implied in a dog-whistle tweet that Powell endorsed the forty-fourth president due to something other than his qualifications: "Obama is about to destroy the mililtary [sic] through the sequester. The Middle East is a mess. Yet Colin Powell still endorses him. Wonder why?"[92]

In 2016, Powell supported Hillary Clinton,[93] the third-ever female secretary of state.[94] After the horrors of Trump, he endorsed Joe Biden in 2020.[95]

In a June 2020 CNN interview, Powell called Trump "a liar" who had "drifted away" from the Constitution when the former president threatened to use active-duty military on protesters.[96] After the January 6 insurrection, when domestic terrorists ransacked the U.S. Capitol, assaulted police, and threatened to kill elected officials, Powell officially left the Republican Party after nearly twenty-six years.[97]

Why did it take a full-on insurrection to finally convince Powell to break away from the venomous forces of the party? The bigotry in the Republican Party did not begin with the forty-fifth president. Trump was the latest distillation of what Republicans have been brewing for decades.

General Colin Powell died at eighty-four years old in October 2021.[98] Obama showed his appreciation for Powell's support upon his death. He eulogized him and offered nuanced insight.

"General Powell was an exemplary soldier and an exemplary patriot," Obama said in a statement on his personal Twitter account. "Everyone who worked with General Powell appreciated his clarity of thought, insistence on seeing all sides, and ability to execute. And although he'd be the first to acknowledge that he didn't get every call right, his actions reflected what he believed was best for America and the people he served."[99]

Obama added that on a personal level, he was "deeply appreciative that someone like General Powell, who had been associated with Republican administrations in the past, was willing to endorse me in 2008. But what impressed me even more was how he did it. At a time when conspiracy theories were swirling, with some questioning my faith, General Powell took the opportunity to get to the heart of the matter in a way only he could."

Obama continued, "That's who Colin Powell was. He understood what was best in this country and tried to bring his own life, career, and public statements in line with that ideal."

Powell demonstrated that Black Republicans are not a monolith, but he revealed the limits of what Black Republicans could accomplish without compromising themselves.

Working in tandem with General Colin Powell during President George W. Bush's administration was Condoleezza Rice. She was the twentieth national security adviser from 2001 to 2005, the first Black woman in the role. Replacing Powell, Rice served as the sixty-sixth U.S. secretary of state from 2005 to 2009.

Rice was born in 1954 in Birmingham, Alabama. She grew up as the civil rights struggle was gathering strength and would reference her childhood in the Jim Crow South in political speeches.

In 2004, at the commencement for Michigan State University, Rice told the graduating class, "I grew up in Birmingham, Alabama, before the civil rights movement—a place that was once described, with no exaggeration, as the most thoroughly segregated city in the country. I know what it means to hold dreams and aspirations when half of your neighbors think of you as incapable of, or uninterested in, anything higher."[100]

The lesson Rice seemed to take from her childhood was self-reliance, which is admirable, but she would also push the harmful victim narrative. In her 2012 book, *A Memoir of My Extraordinary, Ordinary Family and Me*, Rice wrote, "I'd grown up in a family that believed there was no room for being a victim or depending on 'the white man' to take care of you… Despite the gross inequities my ancestors faced, there has been progress, and today race no longer determines how far one can go."[101]

These are redundant Black Republican talking points. Collectively, Black people have not depended on the "white man" to take care of them. Quite the opposite, from slavery to sharecroppers to domestic servants, Black people have been taking care of rich whites for decades. As Wiley A. Hall III wrote in 1991 when Supreme Court Justice Clarence Thomas was ranting about Black people being victims, "This myth that Black people have become obsessed with their role as history's victims is one of the more obnoxious developments."[102] Not only is the "victim" word obnoxious, it's deeply anti-Black, but Rice's game is a familiar one. Like Thomas and unlike Powell, Rice selectively calls on her roots to sell the "pull yourself up by your bootstraps" mantra. If she, raised in the Jim Crow South, could make history, why can't every Black person be as successful as her? If you aren't as magical as Rice, there must be something wrong with you. And she never seems to consider that being a rarity, a Black female Republican, contributed to being elevated in Republican ranks.

Rice, personally successful and with a story to tell about her upbringing in the segregated South, painted an image partly around the idea that any racial obstacle could be overcome if her example was followed or you simply work harder. The numbers tell a different story.

A 2015 report showed that white high school dropouts are wealthier than Black people with college degrees.[103] A 2017 study from Brookings stated that even though Black women are earning college degrees in higher numbers, that has not impacted the racial wealth gap.[104] Black women are three times more likely to die from a pregnancy-related cause compared to white women, according to the Centers for Disease Control and Prevention.[105] In 2021, *the New York Times* reported, "The median earnings for Black men in 2019 amounted to only 56 cents for every dollar earned by white men. The gap was wider than it was in 1970."[106] It would be more accurate for her to claim that race no longer determined how far *she* could go. Rice achieved her proximity to power.

Although Rice came of age in the Jim Crow South, she enjoyed a middle-class lifestyle. According to the *Birmingham News*, her maternal grandparents managed to push their way into the middle class, bought land, and sent their children to college.[107] Rice's paternal grandfather was a sharecropper turned minister who founded several churches and private schools. Her parents were educators at Fairfield Preparatory School. A 2001 feature in the *Washington Post* remarked that she was dressed "always like a vision in the finest clothes her middle-class parents could buy."

Rice herself said, "I was going to do all of these things that were revered in white society so well that I would be armored somehow from racism. I would be able to confront white society on its own terms."[108]

Obviously, there is nothing wrong with being a thriving, middle-class family in 1960s Jim Crow Birmingham. I salute anyone who finds success, but her comments come across as if there were no socioeconomic constraints that make it difficult for others to achieve her level of material success, regardless of the aspirations "to do all of these things that were revered in white society." Her outlook, which is celebrated by white conservatives, pushes the imaginary victim narrative. It's not only classist but clueless about others who aren't as successful.

Rice also knew one of the four little girls who died in the bombing of the Sixteenth Street Baptist Church in 1963. Rice's friend Denise McNair was murdered along with fourteen-year-olds Carole Robertson, Addie Mae Collins, and Cynthia Wesley. Yet the way that Rice drew on this history was callous. According to Rice, "Out of great tragedy, people began to recognize our humanity, and it brought people together."[109]

Children shouldn't be sacrificial lambs for bringing people together, and it is questionable whether the killing of the four little girls in Birmingham led to significant change. Although the Civil Rights Act was signed the following year, white terror continued throughout the South. Nine months later, in June 1964, Mount Zion Methodist Church in Longdale, Mississippi, was burned to the ground.[110] By 1967, Dr. Martin Luther King Jr. said his dream had "turned into a nightmare."[111] Moreover, no one was charged for the Sixteenth Street Baptist Church bombing until 1977.

Rice's perspective feeds today's GOP narrative that says let's skip from the Jim Crow era to a nonexistent color-blind era without taking stock of or responsibility for injustices that still occur and can't be explained by anything else but racism. Her willingness to make those kinds of statements helps other Republicans when they try to claim that MLK was a Republican,[112] even though he was a progressive.

Yes, Rice grew up in the Jim Crow South, but her middle-class life may have been a shield, which could have resulted in classism that created detachment, especially in the case of affirmative action.

In 1993, the same year Chevron named an oil tanker after Rice,[113] she became provost at Stanford University.[114] At thirty-eight years old, she was the first and only Black person in the role. Although highly qualified, she admitted that she was hired because of affirmative action. Rice was quoted as saying in 1998, "I am myself a beneficiary of a Stanford strategy that took affirmative action seriously, that took a risk in taking a young PhD from the University of Denver."[115]

Contrary to popular misconceptions and political myths, you do have to be qualified for an affirmative action hiring.[116] No one is handed a job because of a policy to create equal access for qualified individuals. And though Rice benefited from this policy, launched by Black Republicans like Arthur Fletcher, her actions at Stanford revealed much more ambiguity about affirmative action in practice, especially around teachers applying for tenure.

A 2005 story from the *Los Angeles Times*, which interviewed colleagues at Stanford, stated, "Some who believed that Rice would emerge as a champion of Blacks and women were disappointed."[117] Students protested Stanford University president Gerhard Casper for weeks when "the university's highest-ranking Latina administrator" was terminated. Students were also angered by "open hostility toward minorities" and Rice's unsuccessful attempt to consolidate the ethnic community centers into one building. Students camped out in tents[118] outside Rice's and Casper's offices, and five students went on a hunger strike. Rice's reaction: "I'm not hungry. I'm not the one who's not eating."[119]

Casper and Rice would eventually agree to a list of some student demands,[120] but this would not be her only conflict as provost at Stanford. Although Casper and Rice supported affirmative action for junior faculty, there were several high-profile denials for tenure. During a May 1998 meeting with the Faculty Senate, Rice was questioned as to why she wasn't advocating for affirmative action for tenure; she reportedly responded with, "I'm the chief academic officer now, and I am telling you that, in principle, I do not believe in, and in fact will not apply, affirmative-action criteria at time of tenure."[121]

Rice was granted tenure at Stanford University in 1987.[122] More on that later.

Some professors insisted the school was moving backward on diversity, but Rice argued that wasn't the case, presenting a report that contradicted a report from the Faculty Senate Women's Caucus. According to Marcus Mabry's *Twice as Good: Condoleezza Rice and Her Path to Power*, "Rice contended there was no structural problem at Stanford."[123] She even stated, "It's just that this is a very competitive and tough place." Kind of like when a company is questioned about why they have so little diversity and the response is, "We just couldn't find a [fill in the blank] who was qualified."

Yet it was clear that there was a race issue at Stanford. According to an April 1998 article from *Stanford Report*, protesters claimed women made up only 13 percent of tenured faculty and "Latinas and Latinos compose 2.4 percent of faculty; African Americans, 2.7 percent of faculty; and Asian Americans, 8.4 percent of the faculty at Stanford."[124]

Rice insisted affirmative action for tenure was not the university's policy. However, Ewart Thomas, former dean of the School of Humanities and Sciences, who is Black, said regardless of the policy, affirmative action was utilized in borderline tenure cases from at least 1983 to 1989. Thomas even sent a letter to Rice's office to notify her of this fact.[125] To make matters worse, former Stanford University president Donald Kennedy, who passed away in 2020,[126] agreed with Ewart and said so to the media, which prompted Stanford University president Gerhard Casper to have a hissy fit. "President Casper called me and read me the riot act," Kennedy told the *San Jose Mercury News*. "I said, 'Wait a minute, I'm reporting history here'... Essentially, his position was, 'You shouldn't have told a reporter; it made a problem for my provost and my administration.'"[127]

There is no doubt that Rice was a qualified scholar when she received tenure at Stanford University in 1987. She earned a PhD in political science at the University of Denver. She won a Ford Foundation dual expertise fellowship in Soviet studies and international security and took a year-long fellowship at Stanford University, which began her relationship with the school.[128] According to biographer Marcus Mabry, two professors on her tenure review said affirmative action was not considered. However, Coit Blacker, a Stanford University professor[129] and Rice's friend, told biographer Mabry that in social sciences, a candidate typically needs two published books and articles in the most prestigious journals to get tenure. Rice only wrote one book and "one very important journal article...in *World Politics.*" Blacker believed she was granted tenure due to that article.

Regardless of what motivated approval of her tenure and launched her high-profile career, the fact is that affirmative action was designed for someone like Condoleezza Rice. After all, countless Black and brown teachers have been denied tenure with credentials as impressive as Rice.[130] Being "twice as good" should not be the standard. If she earned the authority to level the playing field, especially for the Black or female professors coming after her, why wouldn't she? To instead deny there was a structural problem was harmful.

This is a conversation that still happens today. In 2021, Pulitzer Prize–winning journalist Nikole Hannah-Jones, who is Black, was denied tenure at the University of North Carolina, her alma mater.[131] The last two people in the role Hannah-Jones would have held, the Knight Chair in Race and Investigative Journalism at UNC's Hussman School of Journalism and Media, were granted tenure. Only after backlash was Hannah-Jones offered tenure, which she then declined, instead taking a position at Howard University.[132]

Rice could have been a vessel of change during her six years at Stanford. In 1998, a year before she left the university, the faculty at Stanford was 2.7 percent Black.[133] In 2020, the faculty was 2 percent Black.[134] There are many reasons for this worsening statistic, but Rice did not appear to have an enduring net positive effect on the women, Black, or brown people working within the institution.

As for Rice's embrace of Republicans, she was a Democrat

until 1982, allegedly changing her affiliation because she disagreed with the Carter administration on foreign policy.[135] Rice has also claimed she is a Republican because when growing up in Birmingham, Alabama, it was Democrats who were fighting against the right of her father to vote.[136] It's mind-boggling that as brilliant as Rice is, she doesn't know the basic history of the Republican Party, especially the ways that it absorbed the racists who left the Democratic Party during and after the 1964 Goldwater campaign. Stanford University professor Coit Blacker told Mabry, "You basically have to be ahistorical in order to be a Republican if you're a member of any minority group. She has chosen to be that way because she is forward-looking. And she likes the notion of being a positive agent for change."[137]

Rice is too smart to be ahistorical. Forward-looking? That is accurate, but not a positive agent for change, only for herself.

Rice began her work at the State Department under the Carter administration.[138] She would also serve on the National Security Council as the Soviet and Eastern Europe affairs adviser to President George H. W. Bush during the dissolution of the Soviet Union and German reunification from 1989 to 1991. In January 2001, a year after leaving Stanford University, she joined the Bush administration as President George W. Bush's national security adviser.[139]

Then there was 9/11. Thousands of Americans died due to the largest foreign terrorist attack in the United States, and fingers were pointed at the Bush administration's incompetence. Rice was right in the middle of that conversation. An August 6, 2001, presidential memo written by Rice was titled "Bin Laden Determined to Attack Inside the United States." While testifying at the 9/11 commission in April 2004, Rice claimed the memo was "information based on old reporting" and was not "a particular threat report."[140] Rice continually deflected whenever she was asked about the warnings and memos she had written.

A year before, in a 2003 interview with CNN, she made an infamous statement in support of going to war with Iraq. "The problem here is that there will always be some uncertainty about how quickly he can acquire nuclear weapons. But we don't want the smoking gun to be a mushroom cloud."[141]

Rice was a strong proponent of the unnecessary war in Iraq.[142] After the invasion and the discovery that there were indeed no weapons of mass destruction, Rice came under heavy scrutiny.[143] Like Powell, Rice was accused of aiding George Bush to pull America into an unjust war[144]—it was another GOP "big lie."

Nonetheless, Bush nominated Rice to be secretary of state on January 26, 2005.[145] She won confirmation in an 85–13 vote, although it was the highest number of nay votes cast against a candidate since 1825.[146] Critics felt her nomination was based on her allowing Bush to continue abusing his war powers beyond the executive branch.[147] Thomas E. Mann, a specialist at Washington's Brookings Institution on relations between the presidency and Congress, told the *Los Angeles Times*, "She is widely seen among Democrats and a few Republicans as being too loyal to the president and insufficiently forthcoming about problems encountered and mistakes made."[148] Senator Evan Bayh, a Democrat from Indiana, said, "The list of errors is lengthy and profound, and unfortunately many could have been avoided if Dr. Rice and others had only listened to the counsel [of lawmakers from both parties.]"[149] Senators Barbara Boxer of California, Mark Dayton of Minnesota, Robert Byrd of West Virginia, and Edward Kennedy of Massachusetts also spoke out against Rice.[150]

It wasn't just politicians who disapproved of Rice. Cartoonist Aaron McGruder depicted Rice as a "Female Darth Vader" in *The Boondocks* and called her a "mass murderer" to her face. Julian Bond, chairman of the NAACP, agreed with McGruder's assessment.[151]

The frustration over Rice wasn't just in foreign policy; she was meddling in domestic policy when it related to race. Rice's history at Stanford resurfaced as affirmative action came into play during the Bush administration.

Before Bush took office in 2000, Reverend Jesse Jackson had a message for Bush and his stance on affirmative action: "He must support affirmative action. Colin Powell would not have been considered for secretary of state if affirmative action had not allowed us to experience his leadership skills. We shouldn't burn the bridge that brought him over."[152]

Bush didn't listen.

In 2003, Bush spoke out against affirmative action at the University of Michigan, arguing it was a "quota system." He also used the reverse discrimination argument, saying, "The motivation for this administration policy may be very good, but the result is discrimination. And that discrimination is very wrong."[153]

Rice made a series of statements that appeared to support Bush's stance against the University of Michigan. "I could not be more supportive of what the president did." She would also say, "I've been a supporter of affirmative action that is not quota based and that does not seek to make race the only factor, but that considers race as one of many factors." There is no form of affirmative action that makes race the one and only factor, applicants still need to be qualified on various levels.[154]

It was a bizarre statement considering her role as the head of foreign policy in Bush's administration. Yet there were reports that she had taken a personal interest in the issue. The *Washington Post* stated, "The officials said Rice, in a series of lengthy one-on-one meetings with Bush, drew on her experience as provost at Stanford University to help convince him that favoring minorities was not an effective way of improving diversity on college campuses" and "officials described Rice as one of the prime movers behind Bush's announcement on Wednesday that he would urge the Supreme Court to strike down Michigan's affirmative action program."[155]

For her part, Rice denied that was the advice she gave to President Bush.[156]

The high court agreed with Bush and upheld a ban on affirmative action in Michigan in 2006.[157] Predictably, Black enrollment at the University of Michigan quickly nose-dived.[158] As of 2019, a study stated, "Michigan ranked the third-worst out of 41 states the report examined for Black student enrollment at four-year institutions in 2016."[159]

The dismantling of affirmative action is one of the many detrimental policy moves under an administration with an awful record in the Black community. By 2003, a study found that during the war in Iraq, 19.4 percent of the soldiers killed were Black, even though Black Americans represented only 13 percent of the country's overall population.[160]

Black unemployment hit 12.7 percent when Bush was in office[161]—a mess that Obama had to clean up. It was a record that challenges the claims of today's Black Republicans, particularly those who care about upward mobility. Moreover, it followed on the heels of the highest Black unemployment rate since the metric was recorded, a staggering 21.2 percent under President Ronald Reagan in 1983.[162]

Additionally, Bush refused to issue an apology for slavery

and allegedly said behind the scenes that Africans were also to blame because they sold their own and "participated" in slavery, a racist statement that shifts the bloody burden of chattel slavery to Africans who had no idea of Europeans' version of slavery.[163] In September 2001, just days before 9/11, on NBC's *Meet the Press*, Rice signaled that she agreed with this propaganda. While discussing the prospect of reparations for descendants of enslaved people, Rice said, "Given the fact that there's plenty of blame to go around for slavery, plenty of blame to go around among African and Arab states, plenty of blame to go around among Western states—I think we're better to look forward, not point fingers backward."[164]

As masterfully educated as Rice is, she could have benefited from multiple Black history courses at one of the many elite institutions she attended. She might then have learned there is a distinct difference in the practice of chattel slavery and how slavery existed in most parts of the world, including Africa. While slavery was practiced worldwide, Europeans used race-based slavery.[165] Europeans purchased enslaved people from African kingdoms after warfare. They often supplied guns to increase violence (war has always been profitable), creating refugees who would be put into slavery for Europeans to purchase.[166] As Africans were selling other Africans, they had no concept of a crucial distinction—chattel slavery.[167]

In chattel slavery, people were enslaved for life and considered property. In Africa, slavery was not based on race or color, and enslaved people were often reintegrated back into society.

Additionally, people were not born enslaved in Africa. In chattel slavery on plantations in the New World, a person was enslaved if their parent was enslaved, and every descendant after that was also enslaved unless they were somehow freed. Slavery of a person's offspring was specific to chattel slavery.[168]

Furthermore, by the 1860s, most enslaved people in the United States were third-, fourth-, or fifth-generation Americans.[169] During that time, the United States held the title of the most powerful and profitable system of slavery in the modern world.[170]

While Rice may have been an expert on the Soviet Union, she is miseducated on the history of slavery and its legacies.

Rice faced something of a scandal in August 2005 when, as the torrential rains of Katrina ripped through Louisiana and Mississippi, she was seen living the glamorous life in New York City. While she was shopping at Ferragamo, the luxury shoe store, a fellow shopper allegedly noticed Rice and said, "How dare you shop for shoes while thousands are dying and homeless!"

According to the *New York Daily News*, the woman, who happened to be white, was allegedly removed from the store: "A Ferragamo store manager confirmed to us that Rice did shop there yesterday, but refused to answer questions about whether the protester was removed, and whether by his own security or the Secret Service."[171]

Rice denied there was an encounter with an angry woman at the Ferragamo store,[172] but Ferragamo wasn't the end of her day on the town. She was later seen at the Broadway show *Spamalot* while people who looked like her were suffering from the aftermath of Katrina's storm surge.

The response from the Bush administration was deplorable. Bush dragged his feet and remained on vacation in Texas while people died.[173] He eventually traveled back to Washington, but Air Force One flew over New Orleans so he could gaze at the destruction as the press snapped photos.[174]

In his memoir, Bush wrote, "When the pictures were released, I realized I had made a serious mistake. The photo of me hovering over the damage suggested I was detached from the suffering on the ground."[175]

Many argued Bush would not have been so "detached from the suffering" if it were predominately white people begging for their lives in news footage. Before he was swallowed whole by the sunken place, rapper Kanye West said during a live relief telethon on NBC, "George Bush doesn't care about Black people."[176]

Rice infamously told the president during the Hurricane Katrina backlash, "We clearly have a race problem."[177] Yet at least while speaking to the public, she was flabbergasted that anyone would question President Bush's intentions toward Black people.

According to American Urban Radio Networks in 2011, Rice said, "It still makes me angry that people would even think that he [President Bush] would let people suffer because they were Black."[178] Did that make her angrier than people suffering in real time? Or more furious that she was part of an administration that didn't bother to assure Americans that the people of New Orleans were their priority? The delayed response to Hurricane Katrina and desperate people screaming for rescue off rooftops was rooted in a Republican administration's indifference to poverty and Black Americans. Instead of pushing Republicans to address these issues, Rice had been speaking out against reparations, cosigning the destruction of affirmative action, and drumming up support for the war.

Nevertheless, Rice blamed herself for the media nightmare of the Katrina aftermath. "I should have known better than to leave for New York with that hurricane approaching for the south of New Orleans," Rice said. "Yes, I was secretary of state. That was very much on my mind. I was one of the president's closest advisors and the highest-ranking African American. I really do feel I let him down in the first days of Katrina."

Interestingly, Rice still defended Bush and called her reaction "tone deaf." She claimed she "should've known better."[179]

How could she not? She is brilliant, a Soviet Union specialist who was rubbing elbows with the most influential people in the world. Was Rice, like Bush, too detached?

Rice was removed from how most Black Americans felt. According to a Gallup poll, more than 75 percent of Black Americans did not believe George W. Bush cared about Black people.[180] In Mabry's biography, Rice said about her reaction to Hurricane Katrina, "I responded like the secretary of state, which is [to] worry about the foreign contributions, worry about the [New Orleans] passport center... I'd be the first to say I learned something from that. I thought of myself as secretary of state, my responsibility is foreign policy. I didn't think about my role as a visible African American national figure. I just didn't think about it."[181]

This is a perfect example of how Rice behaved as a shapeshifter around race for the Republican Party. When it came to affirmative action and Bush cosigning to slam the door of education on countless Black and brown students in Michigan, Rice released a statement about the policy, even though her role in government was confined to foreign policy. But in the aftermath of Hurricane Katrina, Rice didn't "think about" being a Black national figure. She miraculously forgot her Blackness during one of the biggest news stories about Black citizens in the twenty-first century.

After the storm, Rice hit the road for the damage control tour, which included *The Tavis Smiley Show*, Fox News, and MTV News.

Bill O'Reilly asked her, "Does it hurt your feelings when some anti-Bush people say that you're a shill for him and [have] sold out your race?"

"Oh, come on," Rice reacted. "Why would I worry about something like that? Bill, the fact of the matter is I've been Black all my life. Nobody needs to tell me how to be Black."[182]

O'Reilly's question was a tactic to make Rice the victim with all the so-called radical Black people attacking her to his predominately white audience—and Rice's answer is pitch-perfect contemporary Republicanism.

Rice's race is not up for debate. She is and will always be a Black woman. Considering the record of Republicans stretching from the early 1960s to her boss's anti-Black and anti-poor policies, the real question is why is she defending the president without even the slightest nuance? Rice's individualism and cherry-picking around race will never make her "less Black." They make her a grifter and another model for the wave of grifters still to come.

When the Bush administration ended, Rice returned to academia but remained vocal about politics and America's culture wars. In 2017, just five months into the Trump administration, during the debate over Confederate monuments, Rice—who grew up with the racist monuments in the Jim Crow South—said the statues should not be removed because "I, myself, am not much for whitewashing history. I don't like the renamings. I don't like the taking down of the various monuments."[183]

It's bewildering that Rice believes removing white supremacist monuments would be a whitewashing of history—considering that erection of the monuments was a literal whitewashing of the Confederacy's history. The statues of treasonist white men were built all over the South, mainly in the early 1900s, to sell the lie that Confederates were good, patriotic Americans who fought for the country, a "lost cause" narrative that began right after the Civil War. As Jane Dailey, an associate professor of history at the University of Chicago, told NPR in 2017, "Most of the people who were involved in erecting the monuments were not necessarily erecting a monument to the past, but were rather, erecting them toward a white supremacist future."[184] Rice doesn't know or care that she was spitting out a white supremacist talking point, but it gives us a glimpse into how much Rice's loyalty to the modern-day Republican Party had captured her thinking.

Even after the Trump administration had ended in disgrace, she continued to offer cover for the GOP. In a June 2021 interview with NBC News, Rice fired back at anyone who said racism was worse under the Trump administration. "It sure doesn't feel worse than when I grew up in Jim Crow Alabama. So let's drop this notion that we're [in] worse race relations today than we were in the past. I think the hyperbole about how much worse it is isn't doing us any good."[185]

Either out of cynicism or naivete, her words miss the point. Life for Black Americans during the Trump years was not worse than in Jim Crow Alabama. But Trump's divisiveness froze in place progress that had been made since the Jim Crow era; his rhetoric dog-whistled to a time, if not the laws, of the Jim Crow era—when "the Blacks" knew their place. Just because life isn't as terrible as the segregated South doesn't mean racism should be ignored and doesn't mean it's not worth criticizing.

Rice told *Face the Nation* in 2019, "I think it's time to stop labeling each other and using explosive terms like 'She's a racist, he's a racist.' That stops the conversation. When you say that, that's meant to stop the conversation, and we need to have the conversation."[186]

Even if you don't want to call someone racist, how loudly did she call out Trump's housing discrimination lawsuits in the 1970s,[187] the racist birther movement against Obama,[188] the Muslim travel ban (a federal judge determined it was racist),[189] Trump's persecution of the Exonerated Five (he called for the execution of five Black teenagers with a full-page ad in the *New York Times* in 1989),[190] his statement that a judge of Mexican heritage could not do his job because he is Mexican,[191] his ban on racial sensitivity training for federal grantees,[192] the "patriotic education" commission,[193] and the lack of appointments of Black circuit judges by June 2020?[194]

This posture from Rice persisted. In October 2021, Rice appeared on *The View* and expressed her tone-deaf views on race and history. In response to a question about critical race theory, she said, "The way we're talking about race is that it either seems so big that somehow white people now have to feel guilty for everything that happened in the past—I don't think that's very productive—or Black people have to feel disempowered by race. I would like Black kids to be completely empowered, to know they are beautiful in their Blackness, but in order to do that, I don't have to make white kids feel bad for being white."

She continued, "In order for Black kids—who, quite frankly, for a long time the way they were portrayed, the way their history was portrayed, [it was] second-class citizenship. But I don't have to make white children feel bad about being white in order to overcome the fact that Black children were treated badly... Human beings aren't angels now and they weren't angels in the past."[195]

Never mind that none of this has anything to do with actual critical race theory—the legal school of thought that holds that the end of de jure discrimination did not end systemic racism—but it shows her impulse to downplay rather than confront the persistence of societal racism.

Cohost Sunny Hostin pushed back at Rice with, "I think that's been an issue that there's been this sort of rollback of history. People want to hide history."

"Oh, come now," Rice retorted.

Hostin held her ground, adding, "What we are seeing is this, this rollback of history; parents don't want children to hear about the real history. And when we teach children about the real history, I think that is when we will really have true racial reconciliation."

Hostin was correct. States like Texas were actively rewriting history,[196] yet Rice, in her dedication to GOP comfort, argued it was "part of the plan" to "make seven- and ten-year-olds feel that they are somehow bad people because of the color of their skin."[197] These comments indicate that Rice is far removed from the Alabama roots she trots out. Here, she appears more concerned with white children than with educating *all* children about American history.

General Colin Powell and Secretary Condoleezza Rice were both secretaries of state equally responsible for egregious decisions at home and abroad. The profound difference is Rice unapologetically continued to toe the Republican line while Powell found a moral high ground.

He endorsed Obama, criticized the direction of the Republican Party, and denounced Trump.

In later years, Powell channeled the Black Republicans before him who had no issue calling out GOP leadership. Additionally, he not only addressed Trump's racism, inefficiency, and inability to lead but narrowed in on the Republicans who continued to support Trump.[198] Powell knew it was necessary to vote Trump out to protect our democracy.

Rice, on the other hand, gave Trump the grace he didn't deserve. She said in June 2020, "The president has used some language that I really very much admire, like the resilience of the American people. Just be careful about those messages. I'm not advising the president, but if I were, I would say let's put tweeting aside for a little bit and—and talk to us, have a conversation with us. And I think we need that. And I think he can do it."[199]

Powell and Rice both have fallen victim to the same Republican flimflam, but at a point, there was a fork in the road where, despite past mistakes, Powell realized the Republican Party's racism could not be reformed. Powell said on *Meet the Press* in 2015 that there are still "unappealing shreds of old-fashioned racism" among segments of the GOP.[200] At this point, even if we are hesitant to paint the Republican Party with a broad brush, the post-Trump Republican Party is more than "unappealing shreds." It's the party of neo-Confederates. How so? Like the Confederacy, the GOP supports the erasure of history, dismisses violence—like the January 6 insurrection—and calls for a national divorce. As for Rice, she may have grown up in the Jim Crow South, but she flashes her race card when convenient. She appears to shame others who do not align with her version of Black Republicanism, becoming complicit in Trump's cult.

Powell was never a good fit for the Republican Party. Rice fits perfectly.

CHAPTER 8

STEELE

"Because I know it pisses them [Republicans] off."

—Michael Steele on why he stays in the Republican Party[1]

THE HISTORIC ELECTION OF PRESIDENT BARACK OBAMA IN 2008 ushered in a new wave of Black Republicans. Unlike any other Democratic president in recent history, Obama successfully managed to reshape the Republican Party. The ascension of a Black man to the nation's highest office ripped away the GOP's thin veneer of discretion, bringing deep-seated white fragility to the surface.

A slew of high-powered political figures threw temper tantrums, promising to obstruct Obama's presidency to the detriment of the American people.

When Obama spoke before a nationally televised joint session of Congress in defense of health care reform, South Carolina representative Joe Wilson screamed, "You lie!"[2] John Boehner, Speaker of the House, vowed, "We're going to do everything—and I mean everything we can do—to kill it, stop it, slow it down, whatever we can."[3] Kentucky senator Mitch McConnell assured reporters, "The single most important thing we want to achieve is for President Obama to be a one-term president."[4] Obama was elected to clean up the toxic, warmongering, economic recession Republicans created, yet the GOP pledged to stop him.

Black Republicans were divided. "I always knew it would have to be a Black president who was approved by the elites [and] the media," Justice Clarence Thomas said, "because anybody that they didn't agree with, they would take apart."[5] As if Justice Thomas wasn't himself hand-picked by the wealthy elite. Meanwhile, General Colin Powell endorsed Obama over his opponent Senator John McCain, and Oklahoma congressman J. C. Watts made glowing comments about the president and attended his 2008 inauguration.[6]

Other, less prominent Black Republicans declared war on Obama in an attempt to advance themselves. Alan Keyes was an early example. Having previously lost to Obama by more than forty points in the 2004 Illinois Senate race—when he was a resident of Maryland—Keyes subsequently became a birther, upholding the lie that Obama wasn't born in the United States.[7] In November 2008, Keyes filed a lawsuit challenging Obama's citizenship, which went as far as Keyes's political career—nowhere.[8] Keyes refused to call Obama his president. Instead, he used terms like "radical communist" and "an abomination." There was also this in 2009: "The person you call President Obama, and I frankly refuse to call him that, at the moment he is somebody who is kind of an alleged usurper, who is alleged to be someone who is occupying that office without Constitutional warrant to do so… This is insanity."[9] Keyes lost every single election he ran for—three presidential elections[10] and three Senate elections—but his rhetoric continued. Donald Trump would carry the birther conspiracy theory forward.[11]

White Republicans were eager to throw their support to Black Republicans willing to question Obama's identity, nationality, or race. Herman Cain, the former CEO of Godfather's Pizza, was briefly seen as the great Black Republican hope. In June 2011, when Cain attempted to run for president, the businessman claimed Obama "was raised in Kenya," and that was why "he's out of the mainstream."[12]

Obama was not raised in Kenya, and it's unclear what "mainstream" Cain was referring to, considering the forty-fourth president earned 69.5 million votes in 2008, the most for any presidential candidate until 2020.[13]

After sexual misconduct allegations surfaced,[14] Cain dropped out of the presidential race by December 2011.[15]

But the GOP was ready to elevate a Black Republican as never before. Michael Steele would make history in January 2009 as the first Black chairperson of the RNC.

However, the GOP power players once again faced their recurring conundrum. They were willing to uplift a Black face so long as the person involved would hold off from demanding policies that would help Black communities—and that wasn't Steele. The GOP wasn't prepared for a Black Republican critic, and after Steele, they were on the hunt for a new kind of media grifter, which would arrive in the form of a D-list actress.

As for Steele, he was well qualified for the position and called for a "hip-hop makeover" of the party.[16] A Republican since he was seventeen years old, Steele was a founding member of the Republican Leadership Council[17] and the first Black man elected to statewide office in Maryland, serving as lieutenant governor from 2003 to 2007.[18] In Maryland, although a conservative, he developed relationships with Black communities and, most importantly, wasn't pushing anti-Black policies. In January 2003, days before being sworn in as lieutenant governor, he spoke at a fundraiser for Delegate Howard P. Rawlings, a Baltimore Democrat and chairman of the Maryland House Appropriations Committee. Steele received a standing ovation from the mostly Black and Democratic crowd.[19]

In 2006, a Washington-based National Black Republican Association ran sixty-second radio ads claiming Democrats founded the Ku Klux Klan, an ahistorical claim that Republicans, especially Black Republicans, love to push even though it has been debunked.[20] The ad also declared Black voters were "bamboo-zled" by Democrats. Steele, who was running for the U.S. Senate, denounced the ad, saying it was "insulting to Marylanders and should come down immediately."[21] Steele lost the Senate race but refused to pathologize Black voters. Clearly and apprecia-tively, Steele was not a Gary Franks, Alan Keyes, Justice Clarence Thomas, or even J. C. Watts early in his congressional career.

Despite Steele's record, from the onset, his serving as RNC chair was critiqued as tokenism—that he was only named the chairman because of Obama's win. There could be some truth to that sentiment, but Steele was qualified. He wasn't a former NFL player or a random celebrity. In 2006, Curt Anderson, a political consultant and friend of Steele, warned him about being an "out-reach pawn." Anderson told the *New York Times*, "I have a dim view of the typical Republican outreach. It's like: Yeah, look, we have a Black guy. We have a Hispanic guy. Look over there, we have a Jewish guy. It's surface. It never bears fruit."[22]

Like others before him, Michael Steele believed he could

bear the fruit. Similar to Colin Powell, he was trying to reach Black voters without shaming them. There was no talk of the "Democratic plantation" or insults about social safety nets. He listened and understood why Black communities had a mistrust of the GOP. Steele acknowledged the Republican Party needed to do serious work to reach Black voters, attempting to release his party from the death grip of the Southern strategy. While he was sometimes mocked for the "hip-hop makeover" narrative, Steele was sincerely making an effort to expand the GOP's base. While his policies resembled some of the limitations of Black capitalism from Nixon, he was the last of the Black GOP leaders who believed in the roots of Douglass Republicans.

There were high hopes for Steele within the GOP. Senator Mitch McConnell was quoted as saying, "Chairman Steele will be judged on the basis of how much money did he raise and how many candidates did he elect."[23]

Judged by that standard, Steele was a success. Under his leadership, the Republican Party racked up historic wins during the 2010 midterms, broke fundraising records, and had the biggest GOP House victory in a midterm since 1938.[24] However, Steele had detractors, especially in the Tea Party, who believed those wins should not be credited to him.[25] Allegations of poor leadership[26] and excessive spending spread, including expenditures at a nightclub in Los Angeles. Karl Rove accused Steele of "bloated entourages, sweetheart deals."[27]

The problems came early on as Steele followed Colin Powell's example and tried to address issues within the party ahead of the midterms. In 2009, Steele said in a CNN interview with D. L. Hughley that radio host Rush Limbaugh, who Hughley said was the "de facto leader of the Republican Party," was "incendiary," an "entertainer," and not the leader of the GOP. All conservative hell broke loose.

Limbaugh fired back. He accused Steele of attempting to be a "talking-head media star." He also implied Steele was unfit to lead the party.

"I would be embarrassed to say that I'm in charge of the Republican Party in the sad-sack state that it's in," Limbaugh ranted. "If I were chairman of the Republican Party, given the state that it's in, I would quit. I might get out the hari-kari knife because I would have presided over a failure that is embarrassing to the Republicans and conservatives who have supported it and invested in it all these years."[28]

While it was reported Steele apologized to Rush Limbaugh, he did not, but he did say in a statement, "My intent was not to go after Rush—I have enormous respect for Rush Limbaugh. I was maybe a little bit inarticulate... There was no attempt on my part to diminish his voice or his leadership."[29]

In an October 2022 interview with me, Steele said about the conflict with Limbaugh, "For the first time in the recent history of the party, people were asking, 'Who is leading the Republican Party?'" He questioned why, when a Black man was the chair of the RNC, people asked who the leader was. Therefore, when he was told Limbaugh was the "de facto leader" during the Hughley interview, he explained the radio host was an entertainer, not a leader in the party. Due to the GOP heat, Steele called Limbaugh, who he said was a friend at the time. According to Steele, the shock jock laughed and replied, "No big deal. I knew exactly what you meant. It's not a big deal." But the next day, Limbaugh blasted Steele on the radio. Steele said Limbaugh was only pretending to be offended and described the moment as a "lesson learned."[30]

Steele told me he felt pressure to clarify his comments about Limbaugh because "for the next three weeks, we lost close to a third to half of our funders because Rush went on air and basically exercised the base." Limbaugh is the same man who frequently aired a racist parody song called "Barack, the Magic Negro"[31] and reportedly said, "Have you ever noticed how all composite pictures of wanted criminals resemble Jesse Jackson?"[32]

By March 2010, Republicans were distancing themselves from Steele. According to *The Hill*, "a GOP lawmaker who requested anonymity said the Republican National Committee chairman's relationship with House Minority Leader John Boehner (R-Ohio) and Senate Minority Leader Mitch McConnell (R-Ky) is 'not good at all.'"[33]

The final nail in Steele's Republican coffin was when he admitted race was a factor in how he and President Barack Obama were treated. In an April 2010 *Good Morning America* interview, Steele was asked if he had "a slimmer margin of error" because of race.

"The honest answer is, 'yes,'" Steele answered. "Barack Obama has a slimmer margin. A lot of folks do. It's a different role for me to play and others to play and that's just the reality of it. But you take that as part of the nature of it."[34]

Steele committed the cardinal sin that no Black Republican had explicitly done since Jackie Robinson. He admitted to the intersection of racism and politics. Plus, he acknowledged that our first Black president was experiencing racism when Republican leaders assured themselves that the existence of a Black president and a Black man heading the RNC proved that the country was magically post-racial. Steele revealed to me that was the moment the GOP truly turned on him. "It seemed like to them, I was defending Barack Obama and that was just untenable—[to the GOP] Barack Obama was an object. He wasn't a human being, and he certainly wasn't a Black man, in a sense that I could connect to him. The way they saw him as a Black man was very different than the way I saw him a Black man... They saw him as a threat, as a stereotype. Barack Obama was not some left-wing, ideologue progressive. That's how they wanted to project him because that's how they saw Black Democrats."

The GOP clearly had a racial obsession with Obama. Michael Steele explained that the RNC wanted him to push birtherism, the conspiracy theory that President Barack Obama was not an American citizen, in his speeches. Steele refused to be the GOP's puppet. In my interview, he slammed the birther narrative as profoundly racist and coded: "I don't even need to call you a nigger; you weren't even born right."[35]

Steele continued to go rogue. While speaking at DePaul University in Chicago, he admitted that the Republican Party had failed Black voters. "This party was cofounded by Blacks, among them Frederick Douglass. The Republican Party had a hand in forming the NAACP, and yet we have mistreated that relationship. People don't walk away from parties; their parties walk away from them."[36]

It wasn't the first time Steele spoke out about race in his party while chair of the RNC. In a November 2009 interview with Roland Martin, Steele admitted white Republicans are scared of Black voters—and him.

"I've been in the room, and they've been scared of me," Steele said. "I'm like, 'I'm on your side.'"[37]

Steele was attempting to thwart the rise of the Tea Party.[38] Previously he had embraced and even defended Tea Party activists when they were accused of racism.[39] Nonetheless, Tea Party Nation founder Judson Phillips had attacked Steele when he took credit for the 2010 midterms and fundraising while he was chair. He demanded that Steele not be reelected: "Michael Steele's incredible mismanagement of the party and his blatant ignoring of the Tea Party movement dictate that he cannot be reelected as RNC chair."[40]

Republicans, whether they were vocal about it or not, were disturbed by the doses of racial truth from their RNC chair. Michael Steele refused to be a grifter, he was ousted by January 2011, and Reince Priebus became the new chair of the RNC.[41] In 2012, Steele wasn't even invited to the Republican National Convention.[42]

Black voters rarely see an option for themselves in a Republican Party unwilling to deviate from their white base's refusal to acknowledge racism. When Colin Powell is booed for supporting affirmative action or Michael Steele, in a high-ranking position, can't get the party to see the value of the Black vote, Black folks cannot be blamed for voting Democratic in high numbers.

The Republican Party will never regain Black voters by ignoring or rejecting history. Shaving off just a few percentage points of the Black vote would significantly shift the electoral college. More than Colin Powell or J. C. Watts, Michael Steele had a chance at achieving this goal and making inroads with Black voters. But the party could not accept even mild criticism and self-reflection.

As Michael Steele was on the way out of the party, a new brand of Black Republicanism was taking shape. An early iteration of the celebrity-minded grifter we recognize today from television and social media became prominent as Obama ran for a second term: actress Stacey Dash.

Years before Trump, the erstwhile actress, who had no polit-ical experience, suddenly became a pundit on Fox News. After voting for President Barack Obama in 2008, Stacey Dash came out in support of Mitt Romney in 2012,[43] and—just like that—Fox News quickly put her in rotation.

By 2014, she was hired at the right-wing outlet for "cultural analysis and commentary."[44] Fox gave her a platform because they loved that a Black woman was giving her stamp of approval to what some white Republicans were thinking, and Dash was will-ing to play the role.

While appearing on Sean Hannity's show in 2014, she attacked Black voters in Louisiana for voting Democratic, employing lan-guage that has become all too familiar. "[Black voters] have a plan-tation mentality. As long as they give you this much money, you'll stay right there. You don't need to know too much because if you do, you might start thinking for yourself."[45] Dash doesn't know how a plantation worked. Enslaved people weren't given money. Enslaved people didn't "stay right there." Millions of enslaved people thought for themselves, which would explain uprisings from the United States to Haiti to Brazil.

Furthermore, Louisiana is a red state,[46] not to mention one of the poorest states in the Union.[47] In 2014, Louisiana had a Republican governor, and the state legislature was majority Republican. Claiming Black Louisianans were voting Democratic in response to some kind of payoff is to ignore that in 2014 it was reported that 33.7 percent of Black Louisianans lived in pov-erty.[48] But this was Stacey Dash. Her career was struggling, and she needed a new gig.

When challenged, her "expertise" would evaporate. In 2015, Dash appeared on *The Meredith Vieira Show* and embarrassed herself when she said the gender pay gap was a myth. When Vieira listed statistics, Dash froze like a deer caught in headlights and stated, "I don't know if that's true."

"It's true," Vieira shot back. "It's documented."[49]

What was interesting about this exchange, in the time before alternative facts, was the fact that Dash faced any challenge at all. Today, a pundit or even a politician can say data is a lie, and people will believe the lie over the truth.

That same year, Dash blamed the high divorce rate by saying "women don't know how to take care of their men anymore."[50] Dash has been married four times.[51]

In January 2016, Dash went viral for saying there shouldn't be Black History Month or BET (Black Entertainment Television). Dash told *Fox and Friends*, "We have to make up our minds. Either we want to have segregation or integration. And if we don't want segregation, then we need to get rid of channels like BET and the BET Awards and the Image Awards, where you're only awarded if you're Black. If it were the other way around, we would be up in arms. It's a double standard." She added, "Just like there shouldn't be a Black History Month. You know? We're Americans. Period. That's it."[52]

BET swatted back, tweeting an image of Dash in their hit show *The Game*, and captioned it with, "Can we get our check back... or nah?"[53] Dash wouldn't have had a career if not for the support from the Black community and Black media. But now that her career was on the ebb, she was willing to undercut the institutions that had built her up.

She continued lashing out. Later that year, when actor and activist Jesse Williams received the Humanitarian Award at the 2016 BET Awards, Dash wrote on her blog that Williams's response to receiving the award "for his Black activism was nothing short of an attack on white people." Dash continued, "You've just seen the perfect example of a HOLLYWOOD plantation slave! Sorry, Mr. Williams. But the fact that you were standing on that stage at THOSE awards tells people you really don't know what your [sic] talking about. Just spewing hate and anger."

Dash added, "That chip on the shoulders of people like you will weigh you down and keep you from flying free. But true freedom is never free. You have to know how to fly. If anyone is making you feel this way its [sic] you. Living in a psychological prison of your own making. If anyone is GHETTO-IZING anyone, it's people like you letting the BETs and other media outlets portray us in stereotypes."[54]

By January 2017, she had supported the Trump campaign, but Dash's novelty washed away amid a flood of new grifters. Fox News fired the actress.[55] Without her propaganda platform, Dash unsuccessfully attempted a run for Congress but quickly fell into obscurity.[56]

Four years later, in March 2021, Dash was apologizing for her sunken-place shenanigans. In an interview with the *Daily Mail*, she implied that she was typecast on Fox News. "I've lived my life being angry, which is what I was on Fox News. I was the angry, conservative, Black woman. And at that time in my life, it was who I was. I realized in 2016 that anger is unsustainable and it will destroy you. I made a lot of mistakes because of that anger."[57]

It was an anticlimactic end to someone who wasn't a skillful grifter. It must have been mind-boggling for Dash to witness many others perfecting her weak playbook to get hired at conservative organizations, work in the White House, gain millions of followers on social media, and land multimillion-dollar book deals.

What's most interesting of all, however, is the way that Dash's rise outraged sincere, hard-core Black Republicans. In 2014, conservative commentator Crystal Wright reprimanded Dash for her statements about Black voters in Louisiana. "Many Black people may want Obama to provide more productive policies, but to suggest, as Dash does, that Blacks are largely 'uneducated' and 'getting money for free' is a racist narrative that conservatives need to stop perpetuating. That kind of talk is an offensive nonstarter in getting Blacks to consider voting Republican."[58]

Longtime conservative Sonnie Johnson, who Candace Owens would later call "angry and washed up,"[59] wrote about Dash calling Williams a "plantation slave": "This is why we continue to lose, and there is a generation of us that are tired of this."

She continued, "If we can stop calling them slaves, stop talking about the plantation, and start talking about the American Dream—what it has to offer, what we as the right-wing have to offer! Freedom, liberty, financial independence, those are things that we can sell. But it's sad that we would rather pick and prod and call names, to try to fight Democrats, instead of actually accomplishing something."[60]

And that's the point. The grifters make it impossible for Black Republicans of integrity to operate. During an October 2021 episode of *The Michael Steele Podcast*, former Clinton White House aide Keith Boykin, a lifelong Democrat, suggested that Black people join the Republican Party "to help Republicans understand why it's in their interests to reach out to Black people."

Steele, a Republican for over four decades, disagreed with Boykin's strategy, saying, "I've had this battle for the forty-five years I've been in it."

When Boykin asked if he thought the Republican Party was

"irredeemable," Steele answered, "In this iteration? With this infection of Trumpism? Absolutely."

When questioned earlier in the podcast why he remained a Republican, Steele replied, "Because I know it pisses them [Republicans] off."[61]

Steele is correct. The party is irredeemable, and Trumpism is not dissipating; it's flourishing with or without him. However, Trump did not happen in a vacuum. As I stated before, Trump is the hate that Republicans created. The GOP has been irredeemable for decades. From Operation Dixie to the war on drugs, from the welfare queen narrative to the Willie Horton ad, from vetoing the civil rights acts to gutting the Voting Rights Act, the rap sheet is endless. The Democratic Party is imperfect and certainly has racist elements, but there are redeemable elements, especially with new, progressive Democrats on the rise. The Republican Party has shown us exactly who they are with impunity; let's believe them. As Steele expressed to me, "They [the GOP] love the idea of Blacks in the party, as long as they sound and act white. I don't mean that in the sense of white people; I just mean in terms of how the white power structure wants to talk about these issues."[62]

For all these reasons, Steele's original vision to bring in Black voters failed, and Dash signaled what was on the grifting horizon. More space had been cleared within the GOP for Black people to access power as Republicans if they were willing to excuse racism, withhold criticisms of party leadership, and stand against policies that most Black communities supported. With these terms understood, the first Black senator representing the Deep South since Reconstruction would emerge as another face of the Black Republican grift.

CHAPTER 9

COTTON TO CONGRESS

"Our family went from cotton to Congress in one lifetime."

—South Carolina senator Tim Scott[1]

WHEN SOUTH CAROLINA SENT TIM SCOTT TO THE HOUSE OF Representatives in 2011, he made history as the first Black Republican in Congress from the Palmetto State since the late 1800s. He was on track to be appointed as a U.S. senator just a year later. Scott's rise was made possible by the original Black Republicans during Reconstruction. Still, he was a far cry from former members of the House of Representatives Robert Smalls and Joseph Rainey. Scott is more like the Democrats of the late 1800s, who downplayed racism with a voting record that was fiercely against civil rights.

In the recent past, there were Supreme Court Justice Clarence Thomas, who the people did not elect, and a handful of Black Republicans in the House. Scott's level of power in Congress, coupled with his allegiance to the party of Trump, is stunning. If Clarence Thomas is the anti-Thurgood Marshall, then Scott is the anti-Edward Brooke, the first Black Republican officially elected to the U.S. Senate by voters.

Scott might be known now for giving a dramatic speech about being stopped by police[2] or for occasionally chastising, in the lightest possible way, former President Trump, but his chief role has been to lend cover to the antics of his fellow Republicans. A closer look at his background reveals troubling roots.

In 1995, Scott became the only Black man elected to the Charleston County Council in South Carolina. The *Post and Courier* applauded his win by calling him "intelligent, articulate"[3]—a framing that amounts to a racial pat on the head, whether it's being applied by Joe Biden to Barack Obama[4] or by Joe Rogan to Michelle Obama[5]—and pointing out that his victory came "with an overwhelming white vote." The reasons why a majority of white South Carolinians would cast a vote for a Black man would become clear soon enough.

Charleston County's structural racism would become the subject of legal action in just a few years. In 2001, the U.S. Department of Justice sued the county, more than 30 percent Black at the time, due to its at-large voting system.[6] The controversial at-large voting system makes several districts into one district, usually combining Black districts with multiple white districts, resulting in whites significantly outnumbering Blacks, making it nearly impossible to elect Black candidates.[7] These at-large voting systems were so effective at shrinking Black voting power that Supreme Court Justice Ruth Bader Ginsburg referred to them as "second-generation barriers" to ballot access.[8]

The DOJ believed smaller districts would allow for equal representation, but Barrett S. Lawrimore, the county council chairman at the time, insisted Scott's presence on the council was enough representation. As Lawrimore told the *New York Times*, "We've already got a minority on the council."

Scott backed his chairman up, claiming that smaller districts equaled segregation: "I don't like the idea of segregating everyone into smaller districts. Besides, the Justice Department assumes that the only way for African Americans to have representation is to elect an African American, and the same for whites. Obviously, my constituents don't think that's true." The irony of Scott's 2001 quote is that most Black voters in his area *did not* vote for him. As the *New York Times* stated, he was "rejected by voters in the county's Black precincts."[9]

Scott, who claimed his family had gone from "cotton to Congress," learned early on that the key to staying in Congress was suppressing voters who looked like him. His voting record, including not supporting the John Lewis Voting Rights Advancement Act, even calling it a "scheme,"[10] is reflective of just that.

By 2011, Scott was elected to the House of Representatives, representing South Carolina's First District. The last Black Republican to represent the South, George W. Murray, had been elected in that very same district in 1896. Murray had initially represented the Seventh District but was voted out due to redistricting and set his sights on the First District. He lost but contested the election, citing voter fraud, and was eventually declared the winner, but Murray was out of office within nine months. In 1895, South Carolina amended their state constitution, which equaled disenfranchising Black voters,[11] taking over one hundred years for another Black Republican to be elected.

Tim Scott is no George Murray. Endorsements from the likes of Sarah Palin[12] and former Arkansas governor Mike Huckabee[13] clearly showed who Scott would be working for in the House. Like

J. C. Watts before him, Scott refused to join the CBC as early as 2010, saying, "My campaign was never about race."[14] Quite the contrary, like many Black conservatives, Scott appears fanatically obsessed with race—just on the wrong side of the line.

He was part of the same class of congressional freshmen as Allen West, who was elected to Florida's Twenty-Second Congressional District.[15] West was notorious for incendiary comments like saying President Barack Obama was "probably the dumbest person walking around in America right now."[16] He claimed the mantle of a "modern-day Harriet Tubman" trying to rescue Black people from the Democratic Party. After only serving one term with few receipts in Congress, West lost reelection.[17] By 2021, West resigned as the chairman of the Texas Republican Party and was reduced to posting anti-vaccine rants even though he was hospitalized with the coronavirus.[18]

Scott was less of a loose cannon than West, which made all the difference. In 2012, South Carolina governor Nikki Haley appointed Tim Scott as U.S. senator of the Palmetto State. Replacing retired senator Jim DeMint,[19] Scott was the first Black American to be a U.S. senator from the South since Reconstruction.

Despite their friction with him in the House, the CBC attempted to be optimistic about Scott. Missouri representative Emanuel Cleaver II wrote a month before Scott's historic appointment that he was an "honorable man" whose "voting history seems to be in complete harmony with those of the majority of South Carolinians."[20]

It's unclear which South Carolinians' voting history Cleaver was referring to, but Scott's voting record was deeply conservative and Republican. Yet merely being conservative did not make Scott a grifter. To truly embrace the grift, someone needs to play a wicked game at the expense of their community to get ahead. Scott would qualify soon enough.

Fast-forward to April 28, 2021. President Joe Biden delivered his first address before a joint session of Congress—a speech full of policy priorities and an expansive vision for the future. It was no surprise that the Republican Party chose to put South Carolina senator Tim Scott forward for their "rebuttal"—in this case, fifteen minutes of pleading to voters that Democrats are the racists.

One of the main requirements for today's Black Republicans is navigating the tricky logic of downplaying racism while simultaneously playing the race card. This has been Senator Scott's battle cry for years, and he was ready to perform that number in his rebuttal. Scott quickly went viral for saying, "I get called 'Uncle Tom' and the n-word—by progressives, by liberals." Minutes later, he added, "Hear me clearly: America is not a racist country."[21] In one breath, Scott will cry, *See, I'm Black, just like you*, then in the next, he wants to make sure everyone knows he's not like the rest of those whining victims.

First, it's hard to imagine a country where people are calling you the n-word—no matter what side of the political aisle they sit on—as not being racist. Second, as much as Scott's pronouncement of an unracist America may have appealed to some voters—and endeared him to Republicans desperate for an alternative explanation for why their party can't get more than a paltry share of the Black vote—it wasn't a rebuttal to anything in Biden's speech. Biden never said America was a racist country. Scott created a straw-man talking point so he could tell his party's base what it wanted to hear.

His performance—and I do mean performance—wasn't quite as brazen as that of his Reconstruction-era predecessor Isaiah

Montgomery, who suggested that Black voters were uncivilized, but Scott's motivation is similar.

It's worth pausing here to set the record straight about Biden—or other elected leaders—calling America racist. National politicians rarely do. In January 2020, the *New York Times* asked presidential candidates at the time if the United States was a racist country, and not one of them said yes. Former New York City mayor Michael Bloomberg answered, "I don't think it's fair to categorize it as a racist country."[22]

Even Senator Elizabeth Warren said, "I think that racism is a serious problem in this country." Mayor Pete Buttigieg avoided saying the country was racist: "I am convinced that white supremacy is the force most likely to destroy the American dream." Vermont senator Bernie Sanders, the standard-bearer for the left wing of the Democratic Party, focuses more on class disparities rather than race and did not say America was racist.[23]

In July 2020, Biden came under fire for saying Trump was America's first racist president,[24] by which he meant that Trump was the first president to make a nakedly divisive appeal based on race as a central selling point. It was the presidential candidate's watered-down version of Ta-Nehisi Coates's argument that while Trump's predecessors may have "made their way to high office through the passive power of whiteness," Trump reached the White House by consistently embracing, over time, "white supremacy, in all its truculent and sanctimonious power," as his ideology.[25]

In that first address to Congress, Biden only mentioned racism when he called "to root out systemic racism in our criminal justice system"[26]—something Scott was supposedly trying to do when he negotiated (then smothered) the George Floyd Justice in Policing

Act[27]—and also said, "We have a real chance to root out systemic racism that plagues American life in many other ways."[28]

If Scott wanted to argue that there's no systemic racism, he could have done that, but he didn't. Scott wasn't there to rebut Biden's speech. He had one job: to soothe racial guilt at any cost, and he pursued it with precision.

Back to Scott's rebuttal… The Charleston, South Carolina, native repeatedly called on his Christianity, catnip to white evangelicals (those who supported an adulterer, a historic liar, and a person who never asked God for forgiveness at 80 percent),[29] after telling his audience that "the real story" for our souls and our nation isn't "original sin" but "redemption."[30] It was as if he was dismissing systemic racism by washing it away with holy water.

Republicans' racist policies, from a voter suppression bill that civil rights organizations sued over[31] to bills that grant immunity to drivers who hit protesters,[32] speak louder than their words. For all Scott's anxieties about delusions like "woke supremacy," the targets of Republican policies are apparent.[33]

In Scott's remarks, he defended Georgia's voter suppression bill by saying, "It will be easier to vote early in Georgia than in Democrat-run New York. But the left doesn't want you to know that." What Scott conveniently left out was that Senate Bill 202 limited ballot drop boxes in predominantly Black areas, criminalized handing out water to voters and, worst of all, gave more power over elections to the Republican state legislature.[34]

That said, defending racist policies isn't a shocker from Scott. He often brags about so-called opportunity zones. The Investing in Opportunity Act,[35] introduced by Scott and New Jersey Democratic senator Cory Booker in April 2016,[36] was a remixed version of trickle-down economics—make the rich richer and hope the wealth would trickle down to middle-class and low-income folks. The program was supposed to revitalize urban neighborhoods by giving tax breaks to corporations to invest in specific areas. In 2019, RealDeal.com reported that the program designated more than eight thousand census tracts across the United States as "distressed" communities. However, the so-called opportunity zones increased gentrification,[37] displacing Black people from their neighborhoods and giving a tax bonanza to corporations.[38]

In April 2019, the Institute on Taxation and Economic Policy reported, "Opportunity zones incent gentrification. Low-income communities can be defined by a comparison of income to the surrounding area, and opportunity zones can also qualify if they are adjacent to a low-income community. Thus, Opportunities Zones are in communities already vulnerable to gentrification. The program lacks adequate protections to ensure capital investors do not push out current residents or businesses." Areas for opportunity zones are "63 percent Black and only 28 percent white."[39]

In October 2019, the *New York Times* reported that friends of the Trump administration were profiting from the opportunity-zones tax break, specifically Michael Milken,[40] the man who partly inspired the character Gordon Gekko in the 1987 film *Wall Street*.[41] New Jersey senator Cory Booker, Missouri representative Emanuel Cleaver, and Wisconsin representative Ron Kind, all Democrats, called for an investigation,[42] but not Scott.

In November 2019, House majority whip Jim Clyburn released a statement about opportunity zones: "From the start, I've raised concerns that the opportunity zone incentive would turn out to be a tax credit for rich investors with limited benefits for low-income communities. This program needs to be tweaked if it is to accomplish its stated purpose, and this legislation makes the necessary reforms to ensure it is making an impact in the communities that need investments the most."

Clyburn wanted to prohibit investments in developments "such as casinos, stadiums, parking lots or luxury apartments and ensure the incentives only go to new investments within the zones, not projects that were already underway," according to the *Post and Courier*.[43] Clyburn was trying to prevent opportunity zones from creating more gentrification.

Scott complained that any changes are a "misguided attempt by congressional Democrats" that would "wreck the opportunity zone initiative under the guise of 'improvement.'" He also claimed Democrats "needlessly punish low-income communities who are hoping to use opportunity zones to transform areas left behind."[44]

By September 2020, John Harmon, CEO of the African American Chamber of Commerce of New Jersey and former chairman of the National Black Chamber of Commerce, told *Bloomberg*, "We see development occurring in the urban centers today, but the people who are doing the building and getting the benefits do not look like us."[45]

The facts backed up Harmon's claim. A feature that same month in *Bloomberg* reported how federal tax breaks via opportunity zones in Norfolk, Virginia, were being used to "plow under its historically Black neighborhoods."[46]

And in June 2020, *Bloomberg* reported, "Only a small percentage of the more than $10 billion invested as part of the program has benefited existing businesses."[47] A study by the Urban Institute stated, "It appears that [opportunity zones] are neither on a trajectory to democratize access to capital nor will they, at scale, incentivize mission-oriented projects that align with community goals and priorities."[48]

The facts made no difference. Scott refused to concede opportunity zones were not helping.[49]

Police reform is another area where Scott uses his Blackness when it's convenient but stops short of supporting a policy that would help Black people. He will say police have stopped him for "driving while Black" but then craft a weak Justice Act that doesn't end qualified immunity.[50] He had a chance to support the George Floyd Justice in Policing Act but instead went on national television to either lie or show he was wildly incompetent. In September 2021, Scott appeared on CBS News and claimed the bill defunded the police when even the International Association of Chiefs of Police and Fraternal Order of Police released a statement confirming that it gave more money to police departments.[51]

Scott voted with Trump over 90 percent of the time, including to weaken the Dodd-Frank Act, which aims to stop discrimination from mortgage lenders—with Black businesses and owners being disproportionately affected, a far cry from the days of Black Republicans in the Nixon era promoting Black capitalism and support for Black businesses.

What do grifters reap from the grift? For some, it's money. For those like Tim Scott, it's also power, which allows him to participate in blocking legislation that has material manifestations on the lives of all Americans, Black people in particular.

In June 2021, Scott did not support the For the People Act.[52] In November 2021, Scott joined Senate Republicans to block Democrats from advancing the John Lewis Voting Rights Advancement Act.[53] This is the same person who, in 2015, traveled to Selma, Alabama, for the fiftieth anniversary of Bloody Sunday, a 1965 demonstration for the right of Black people to vote.[54] The late John Lewis had his skull fractured. For Scott not to support a voting rights bill with Lewis's name on it, knowing the significance, is egregious.

Arguably, Scott's most shameful act is blocking the inquiry into the January 6 insurrection by voting against creating a bipartisan commission to investigate.[55] Domestic terrorists took over the U.S. Capitol and threatened to kill Scott's colleagues, and a man carried a Confederate flag in the Capitol. Scott didn't think a commission on the attempted coup was necessary.

Scott often mentions his family has gone from "cotton to Congress," a talking point to prove that he has pulled himself up by his bootstraps. The translation is if he could make it from cotton to Congress, so could any other Black person in America. Scott has stated his grandfather, Artis Ware, "dropped out of elementary school to work in the fields and pick cotton"[56]—hence, the cotton-to-Congress one-liner. It's a point that's popular with the GOP.

Here is where Scott's "cotton to Congress" one-liner gets complicated.

In April 2021, Glenn Kessler, a journalist from the *Washington Post*, claimed census records showed Scott's great-great-grandfather, Lawrence Ware, owned a farm and "a home without a mortgage." According to Kessler, Scott's great-grandfather, Willie Ware, would go on to be one of the biggest landowners, white or Black, in Aiken County, South Carolina. Also, census records in 1940 showed that Willie owned his home.[57]

Willie Ware died when Scott was ten or eleven. Was his grandfather, Artis Ware, picking cotton if the family owned more land than anyone in Aiken County, South Carolina? Kessler's reporting confirmed that Scott's grandfather dropped out of school to pick cotton, but presumably, he was picking cotton on his father's land.

Therefore, the "cotton to Congress" narrative feels disingenuous because it does not appear Scott's grandfather was living in the depths of southern poverty, which seems to be the story line Scott is attempting to push. He came from a family of landowners.

Picking cotton on your father's land is very different from suffering the exploitation of sharecropping and debt peonage. It's admirable that Scott's family appeared to be entrepreneurs, but it's disappointing that he might be manipulating the story to, once again, grift around the realities of class and race

While it's possible Scott did not know his complete family history—incorrect oral history can be passed down—Kessler said he gave Scott and his team four weeks to respond to the piece, but they declined.[58]

Scott was just as shameless in using his family background to disenfranchise Black people. In January 2022, Scott argued on the Senate floor—while referencing his grandfather, once again—that voting rights legislation isn't needed and that "it's hard to deny progress when two of the three [Black U.S. senators] come from the southern states which people say are the places where African American votes are being suppressed."[59] According to U.S. Virgin Islands delegate Stacey Plaskett on MSNBC, Scott's claim that because "he is in the Senate, the voting rights act is not necessary is the most ludicrous thing I could hear out of his mouth. Who told him that Black people voted for him in the first place?"[60]

She's right. In 2016, Scott received just 8 percent of the Black vote in South Carolina. It's clear he doesn't speak for most Black voters, even in his home state, but that isn't his role.[61] Scott is the mouthpiece to make white conservatives feel good about their anti-Black policies.

Scott's anti-voting-rights rant is equally outrageous if he

believes voter suppression has been washed away after only eleven Black U.S. senators in history as of 2022. The U.S. Senate first convened in 1789. Only four Black U.S. senators have represented southern states.

Former RNC chair Michael Steele had some pointed words for Scott: "The fact that he is embracing Donald Trump and Trumpism… When you value your party more than your own conscience, your own community… They'll have to live with that."[62]

In April 2022, Scott spoiled his legacy even further when he opposed Judge Ketanji Brown Jackson's nomination to the U.S. Supreme Court. Judge Jackson was the first Black woman nominated to the high court with a superb record and a "well-qualified" rating from the American Bar Association.[63]

It wasn't enough for Scott. He stated, "I cannot support her record of judicial activism."[64] The statement was creepily similar to what proud racist North Carolina senator Sam Ervin said when he refused to support Judge Thurgood Marshall for the U.S. Supreme Court in 1967: "It is clearly a disservice to the Constitution and the country to appoint a judicial activist to the Supreme Court."[65]

Later that month, Democratic South Carolina representative Wendell Gilliard called in to *The Karen Hunter Show* on SiriusXM and opened up about an experience with Scott. In a 2009 protest over a voter suppression bill in South Carolina,[66] former Representative David Mack, chairman of the South Carolina Black Caucus at the time, asked everyone to exit the chambers. According to Gilliard, Scott was the only Black person who remained.

Gilliard said he later saw Scott in the hallway and "reminded him of him being Black and the fact that he was standing on the shoulders of our ancestors." Gilliard said he told Scott he was supposed to represent the people, many of whom are Black in his state. Gilliard claimed Scott responded with, "That's the difference between you and me, Representative Gilliard... You come up here to represent the people; I came to make money."[67] In August 2022, Gilliard confirmed this alleged conversation with me.[68]

Lastly, in April 2023, Senator Tim Scott launched his exploratory campaign for president at Fort Sumter, where Confederates launched the war against the Union. It was a racist bullhorn from a Black man who stands by a political party that proudly celebrates the Confederacy.[69]

I would never call Scott an Uncle Tom. It's an insult to the character Uncle Tom, who was the opposite of Scott's buffoonery in Harriet Beecher Stowe's 1852 novel. While a problematic character in other ways, Tom is a man who sacrifices himself for the good of others. But in his unswerving devotion to party politics, Senator Scott is an embarrassment on his own—not just for his lies or cavalier dismissal of systemic racism but for his pursuit of political gain at the expense of our democracy.

CHAPTER 10

LOVE AND HURD

"This election experience and these comments [from Trump] shine a spotlight on the problems Washington politicians have with minorities and Black Americans—it's transactional, it's not personal."

—former Utah representative Mia Love[1]

EXCEPT FOR MADAM SECRETARY CONDOLEEZZA RICE, WHO was never an elected official, the story of Black Republican politicians, thus far, has mainly been a story of men. Those drawn to Black conservatism tend to be more preoccupied with "traditional gender roles" and might be less comfortable with Black women holding power in the halls of government.

In 2015, the GOP made history by electing Mia Love, the first Black woman to join the House of Representatives as a Republican, representing Utah's Fourth District. How was a Black woman finally elected? She used the Black Republican formula.

Around the same time Stacey Dash found her footing on Fox News, Love distinguished herself by spouting hyperconservative rhetoric. In 2012, Love vowed to destroy the CBC and made this bewildering comment: "Yes, yes. I would join the Congressional Black Caucus and try to take that thing apart from the inside out.

It's demagoguery. They sit there and ignite emotions and ignite racism when there isn't."[2]

That same year, Love utilized another tactic that would become a must-use tool for Black Republicans auditioning for the GOP—claim our first Black president was dividing America. While speaking at the 2012 Republican National Convention, Love roared, "President Obama's version of America is a divided one—pitting us against each other based on our income level, gender, and social status. His policies have failed!"[3] The crowd erupted, ecstatic that a Black woman was attacking a Black president. Love had the audacity to say this after Obama pulled us out of a recession, saved the auto industry,[4] killed Osama Bin Laden, and signed the Lilly Ledbetter Fair Pay Act[5]—all in his first term.

Love's speech was a success and the perfect performance for the GOP. She fundraised $250,000 within days after the anti-Obama rant and was the number one searched person on Google the next day.[6] In 2014, she continued to hit all the typical Black Republican notes, telling the *Salt Lake Tribune* that she had never experienced racism in Utah.[7] Ironically, in 2018, on the way to losing her reelection bid to her Democratic opponent, she claimed that her critics "do not like the fact that I am a Black female Republican."[8] She was a shape-shifter claiming that racism didn't exist when speaking about her allies and crying that racism was inescapable when speaking about her enemies. Love would succeed if she moved in a way that supported her white Republican voters' racist assumptions— but once the racism turned on her and she spoke out, Love would lose her base. Future Black Republicans would take note of the red lines as they crafted grifter personas of their own.

For a while, Love was able to thread the needle. In 2014, she was elected in a predominately white district of Utah.[9] Then, in what the *Washington Post* called "a move that seems at odds with much of her rhetoric," she joined the CBC.[10]

In January 2018, midway through her second congressional term, Love got a rude awakening about racism coming from her party. President Trump reportedly referred to Haiti, El Salvador, and African nations as "shithole" countries during a meeting about immigration and allegedly said, "Why do we need more Haitians?"[11]

Love, who is Haitian American, rebuked him. She issued a statement: "The President's comments are unkind, divisive, elitist, and fly in the face of our nation's values. This behavior is unacceptable from the leader of our nation. My parents came from one of those countries but proudly took an oath of allegiance to the United States and took on the responsibilities of everything that being a citizen comes with."[12] She called on Trump to apologize.[13]

Trump denied the comments—and months later, Representative Mia Love lost reelection. Trump famously said, "Mia Love gave me no love and she lost. Too bad. Sorry about that, Mia."[14]

For once, Trump may have had a point. What mattered to him as the leader of the GOP wasn't censoring his race-baiting but getting uncritical loyalty from the only Black female Republican in Congress. Additionally, Love is a member of the Church of Jesus Christ of Latter-day Saints, which has substantial support within the Republican Party in Utah.[15] The church did not allow Black men in their priesthood until 1978[16] and remains just 3 percent Black as of 2022. Over 75 percent of Mormons identify or lean Republican. Love skillfully positioned herself for leadership but could not sustain her residency in Trump's Republican Party.

In her concession speech, Love reversed course after years of emphasizing color-blind politics. She suggested racism ended her time in Congress. "The President's behavior towards me made me wonder: What did he have to gain by saying such a thing about a fellow Republican? It was not really about asking him to do more, was it? Or was it something else? Well, Mr. President," Love said, "we'll have to chat about that."

Sure enough, it was "something else"—the president didn't appear to value Mia Love as a person. Trump was accused of calling Haiti, the first Black nation, a shithole country. That's the "chat" she should have had—not with the former president but with herself—once Trump turned on her. She was a Black woman in a party drifting further toward white nationalism.

Love's concession speech continued, "This election experience and these comments [from Trump] shine a spotlight on the problems Washington politicians have with minorities and Black Americans—it's transactional, it's not personal."[17] She went on. "This election was horrible, and it has cost us greatly. I saw the media write uneducated, unfair, irresponsible stories. My ethics, my record, lied about, tarnished and repeated over and over again."[18]

Though Love may have belatedly recognized the truth about the transactional nature of her relationship with the Republican Party, she had no grounds to claim that her record was unclear. She voted to table articles against the impeachment of President Trump. She voted to give the government more power to deport immigrants "suspected" of being in gangs. She supported rolling back bank regulations by the Dodd-Frank Act. She voted to repeal the Department of Education rule on teacher preparation programs, an Obama-era rule to assist teachers.[19] Mia Love proudly tarnished her record, voted with the disgraced president 95.7 percent of the time,[20] all on her own.

Mia Love had the option to represent Black women or Haitian Americans. Instead, she supported a political party that trafficked in racism. Once she lost, she attempted to issue warnings and threats about the president to whom she had given racial cover. "I believe that we've elected a wolf in sheep's clothing, but the question remains at what cost to the people of Utah? The good news is, I'm not going away. But now I am unleashed. I am untethered. I am unshackled."[21]

She was never on a leash.

She was never tethered.

She was never shackled.

Most Black Republicans who rose to prominence during Obama's presidency are classic grifters. However, there was a Black Republican from Texas who briefly attempted to break the GOP mold.

In 2015, Will Hurd, a former undercover CIA officer,[22] was elected to represent the Twenty-Third Congressional District in Texas.[23] The Texas A&M grad[24] was a throwback Republican. There is no record of Hurd telling Black Democrats to get off the "plantation"; he did not racialize welfare and won an election in a predominately Hispanic district.[25] It is rare for a Black Republican to win a district that isn't white, and in some ways, Hurd was unique.

Hurd was known for his bipartisan efforts. In 2018, he was awarded the Prize for Civility in Public Life by Allegheny College, along with Beto O'Rourke.[26] But precisely because he refused to toe the party line, he would not be in office long.

The following year, Hurd, the only Black Republican in the House, attempted to warn the party about their lack of inclusivity and refusal to expand the base. He was quoted as saying, "This is a party that is shrinking. The party is not growing in some of the largest growing parts of our country. Why is that?... It's real simple... Don't be an asshole. Don't be a racist. Don't be a misogynist, right? Don't be a homophobe. These are real basic things that we all should learn when we were in kindergarten."[27] A few months after this comment, Hurd resigned in August 2019.[28]

This is an old-school move for Black Republicans in the tradition of Jackie Robinson, former Senator Edward Brooke, and Colin Powell—and Hurd would face the same woeful trajectory as all of them for daring to defy a party that had devoted itself to the Southern strategy.

Although Hurd did not vote to impeach Trump in 2019,[29] he publicly took him to task[30] and was one of four Republicans who voted for a resolution to condemn Trump's racist tweets after he attacked Representative Alexandria Ocasio-Cortez of New York, Representative Ilhan Omar of Minnesota, Representative Ayanna Pressley of Massachusetts, and Representative Rashida Tlaib of Michigan.[31] Hurd told CNN's Christiane Amanpour, "I'm the only Black Republican in the House of Representatives. I go into communities that most Republicans don't show up in [in] order to take a conservative message. This makes it harder in order to take our ideas, and our platform, to communities that don't necessarily identify with the Republican Party."[32]

Hurd's congressional career was running out of steam. In his last term, he only voted with Trump 64.8 percent of the time. However, Hurd's record is far from admirable. He did not support the Voting Rights Advancement Act of 2019, which will haunt his political career.[33]

In 2019, when he announced he would not run for reelection, Hurd wrote on Twitter, "I'm going to stay involved in politics to help make sure the Republican Party looks like America."[34] Hurd would not succeed. The Black Republicans who would come after him and Mia Love wouldn't look much like America. They were carbon copies of the worst of the MAGA movement.

I contacted Will Hurd's team for an interview, but they declined.

In 2020, two Black Republicans were voted into the House of Representatives. Byron Donalds, endorsed by the Tea Party,[35] represented Florida's Nineteenth District and was elected with a criminal past. In 1997, a misdemeanor arrest for distribution of marijuana. In 2000, a felony charge for receiving a bribe, which was later expunged.[36] Burgess Owens was elected to Utah's Fourth District, the same district Mia Love represented. Donalds and Owens stuck to the same Black Republican script, but they went a horrendous step further. They both fed into the big lie that Trump was the winner of the 2020 election and fought to overturn votes.[37]

On January 6, 2021, just hours before the hellacious insurrection, Donalds vowed to challenge the presidential election certification and was quoted as saying, "Actually, my plan is to object to the votes in several states."[38]

That morning, Congressman Donalds attended the Stop the Steal Rally,[39] which was hours before January 6 insurrection. He was on the House floor during the attack on the U.S. Capitol, ready to disenfranchise Americans. Thankfully, he failed.

Donalds's voting record in his first two years in office was reprehensible. He voted against the Build Back Better Act, the John R. Lewis Voting Rights Advancement Act of 2021, the American Rescue Plan Act of 2021, the For the People Act of 2021, the George Floyd Justice in Policing Act of 2021, the Right for Contraception Act, and the COVID-19 Hate Crimes Act, which even Senator Scott supported. Perhaps most disturbing, both Donalds and Owens did not support the Domestic Terrorism Prevention Act of 2022, which was legislation in reaction to the horrific mass shooting by a white supremacist in Buffalo, New York. The bill would have specifically combated extremism by white supremacists. That same year, Donalds voted against the Marijuana Opportunity Reinvestment and Expungement Act, which would decriminalize cannabis. His vote didn't match his criminal record, considering his 1997 marijuana arrest.[40]

After this alarming record and advocating to delegitimize the 2020 election, Donalds complained that he was denied entry to the CBC. The CBC said in a statement, "The Congressional Black Caucus remains committed to fighting for issues that support Black communities, including the police accountability bill, protecting voting rights, and a jobs bill that helps our communities. We will work with those who share our values and priorities for the constituents we serve."[41]

The CBC and Donalds shared different values, which was good enough for the kingmakers of the Republican Party. By December 2021, Trump endorsed Donalds for reelection.[42]

Owens was nearly a carbon copy of Donalds. In January 2021, the Trump-endorsed congressman said, "No question in my mind" that Trump won the election.[43] Maybe endorsing the "big lie" was the cost for remaining in the good graces of the supreme leader of the Republican Party.[44]

In January 2023, during the fiasco of California representative Kevin McCarthy begging Republicans to elect him as House Speaker, Donalds was nominated by Texas representative Chip Roy. Clearly unqualified to be Speaker, considering he had only been in the House one term, Donalds was deliberately used as a diversity prop. Yes, there were other representatives nominated, but only with Donalds was race mentioned. For Republicans who claim to detest identity politics, Roy offered up race, bragging that now two Black members had been nominated, then claimed it wasn't about race and quoted Dr. Martin Luther King Jr. Donalds was only nominated in response to well-qualified New York representative Hakeem Jeffries, who made history as the first Black person to be House minority leader. It was an eye-rolling performance, and Donalds insisted the nomination had nothing to do with race or diversity.[45]

Grifters all pay the price of admission. Hurd refused to pay, and Love's payment was insufficient. Black Republicans have been on a duplicitous downward spiral for decades, and those with integrity are pushed out of the party. The majority of Black Republicans in power, especially on a national level, oppose policies designed to advance Black communities. Being an outlier can get you far in politics, especially when your supporters are nurtured by decades of big lies and propaganda.

CHAPTER 11

TRUMPISM

"Girlfriend, I'm going to have to miss that train."

—Actress Sheryl Lee Ralph to Omarosa Manigault Newman[1]

DONALD TRUMP BEGAN HIS DEBASEMENT OF THE OVAL OFFICE on January 20, 2017. His administration introduced a newfangled era of politicians and conservative leaders bartering in lies to gain political clout. The racist rhetoric of his presidency was not shocking, but Trump ushered in high-octane foolishness and court jesters disguised as politicians and pundits. Yes, Supreme Court Justice Clarence Thomas was a trailblazer in profiting from the grift but possessed an understanding of government and policy. Today's motley crew of hucksters are grifters for attention who are more than willing to demean themselves to be the next buffoon.

The Trump era also flushed—willing or unwillingly—several Black Republicans out of the GOP. Social media stars or struggling actors were not in this bunch. These were political operatives with professional experience in the Republican Party. In 2015, the

RNC chaired by Reince Priebus employed a handful of Black staffers, including Tara Wall,[2] Kristal Quarker-Hartsfield,[3] Raffi Williams,[4] and Orlando Watson.[5] There were others as well, like Chelsi Henry, who, in 2014, was deemed a "rising star" in the Republican Party,[6] and conservative columnist Crystal Wright, who was making the rounds on cable news.

Yes, some brought the same exhausting rhetoric; Tara Wall told *Essence* in 2012, "There's no institutional racism in the Republican party. Show me a fact that shows it exists."[7] This language will consistently turn off Black voters, especially with endless facts, going back to the party of Lincoln. Nonetheless, their outreach, which comprised working with HBCUs, the National Urban League, and the National Association of Black Journalists and a joint venture with Black-owned Radio One, had shown some success. During the 2014 midterms, Republicans received a surprising 10 percent of the Black vote, still a small share but the highest the GOP had seen since 1996.[8]

But after years of some Black Republicans trying to convince Black voters that racism was not an issue in the Republican Party, along came Donald Trump. By April 2016, it was clear that Trump would be the Republican nominee for president. None of the staffers mentioned above remained with the RNC. NBC News described their departures as "a mass exodus of Black staff from the RNC" that was "undeniable."[9] Raffi Williams, son of Fox News analyst Juan Williams, claimed he didn't leave because of Trump.[10]

That same month, the RNC hired GOP communications strategist Telly Lovelace as the national director of Black initiatives.[11] Lovelace resigned in August 2017. Even Ruth Guerra, the RNC's director of Hispanic outreach, exited in June 2016 after saying she was "uncomfortable working for Mr. Trump."[12] Others, like lifelong Republican Tara Setmayer, blasted the party during the rise of Trump and left in November 2020 due to the "malignancy of Trumpism."[13]

Republican Shermichael Singleton, twenty-six years old at the time, briefly worked at HUD under Secretary Ben Carson in Trump's administration. Although a conservative, Singleton had a history of engaging Black communities, never chastised Black Democrats, and would freely call out racism in the party. He maintained his goal was never to convert all Black voters to the Republican Party, but like others before him, he hoped for Black people to have a voice in the GOP with their vote. In an interview with Singleton, he told me, "I always tried—when I was a strategist, when I was advising candidates—to [remind them], 'You need to do the things to reach Black people.' Unfortunately, I was not as effective as I would have hoped."[14]

Singleton's time at HUD didn't last long. He was fired after articles surfaced of him being critical of Trump. The *New York Times* reported Singleton was "led out of the department's headquarters by security."[15] Singleton considered Secretary Carson a hero of his, but his hero made no public comments when he was terminated.

In an interview with Singleton, I asked if he felt Carson sold him out by not making a statement. He hesitantly answered, "Knowing politics as well as I do, I don't know if I would have necessarily wanted him to say anything."

For the first time publicly, Singleton did reveal that Carson made sure he was financially stable and had jobs lined up for him. But after he was fired, Singleton said, "All of my political friends turned against me—from the Romney campaign,

from my time with Gingrich, all these campaigns I worked on."
Although Singleton was in a lesser role than Michael Steele,
Colin Powell, and J. C. Watts, just as with them, the GOP had
no loyalty to him.

Singleton has since left the Republican Party and identifies as
an independent. He conceded the rise of Black Republican grifters
ruined the work of sincere Black Republicans like Steele, Powell,
and former congressman Will Hurd. "I've never needed the
grift and insulting my people to elevate me for financial means,"
Singleton said.[16]

With actual Black Republicans who didn't have a grifter record
nearly extinct from the Republican Party in leadership roles, a flurry
of flash-in-the-pan celebrities and unknowns followed Stacey Dash's
playbook. Black Republicans who joined the party out of principle were replaced with dangerous, power-hungry escapists. Former
NFL player Herschel Walker, Pastor Darrell Scott,[17] Diamond and
Silk,[18] Candace Owens,[19] and Pastor Mark Burns[20] were just a few
of the ascendant grifters. They discovered there is a robust market
for the delusional Black Republican in the cult of Trump.

Kentucky attorney general Daniel Cameron is one of the
most horrific examples in the Trump era. In November 2019,
thirty-three-year-old Cameron made history as the first Black
man elected to statewide office in the Bluegrass State. Former
Democratic Kentucky attorney general Greg Stumbo warned a
month before the election, "My opponent has never even prose-
cuted a traffic ticket citation." He also claimed Cameron "admitted under oath how little law he has practiced."[21]

Rather than law experience, Cameron had something and
someone more important on his side—the support of Senator
Mitch McConnell.[22] Cameron was awarded a McConnell

scholarship and spent several years as a clerk and legal counsel for the Kentucky senator. McConnell would endorse his protégé for attorney general, despite his lack of experience.

McConnell and Cameron were a perfect match. Mitch McConnell groomed a Black man to execute his policy agenda throughout the state of Kentucky. As Cameron said in 2015 about one of the greatest political obstructionists in American history, "When I first met [McConnell] I knew he was somebody I wanted to emulate."[23]

And emulate he did.

Shortly after midnight on March 13, 2020, Louisville police officer Brett Hankison, Detective Myles Cosgrove, and Sergeant John Mattingly executed a botched "no-knock" warrant at Breonna Taylor's apartment. Her boyfriend, Kenneth Walker, a licensed gun owner, believed the officers were intruders and fired a single shot. The officers fired back, striking Taylor multiple times. The twenty-six-year-old emergency room technician died in a senseless act of police violence.

Kenneth Walker was charged with the attempted murder of a police officer. After the story of Taylor's death went viral, the charges were eventually dropped.[24]

Taylor was not the target of their investigation. Police were looking for her ex-boyfriend Jamarcus Glover. He was arrested the morning of March 13, after police killed Taylor.

The people were waiting for Kentucky attorney general Daniel Cameron to bring criminal charges against the officers.[25] But McConnell's protégé would perform just as his mentor would have wanted.

In August 2020, Cameron, who was taking his time investigating the Taylor case, was one of the few Black men who spoke at the Republican National Convention. He had the nerve to speak

Breonna Taylor's name over the course of a fiery speech condemning the Black Lives Matter activists and supporters who had been
fighting for justice for Taylor. "Even as anarchists mindlessly tear
up American cities while attacking police and innocent bystand-
ers, we Republicans do recognize those who work in good faith
towards peace, justice, and equality," Cameron said. "Whether you
are the family of Breonna Taylor or David Dorn, these are the
ideals that will heal our nation's wounds."[26]

David Dorn was a retired police captain who was fatally shot
in June 2020 after attempting to stop the burglary of a pawnshop
in St. Louis, Missouri.[27] The legal system moved swiftly for Dorn;
within five days of the senseless killing, a twenty-four-year-old
named Stephan Cannon was charged with his murder.[28]

Cameron's convention speech would reference Joe Biden disre-
spectfully saying "you ain't Black" if you weren't voting for him.[29]
Unlike Trump, who never apologized for saying Jewish people
who did not vote for him show "great disloyalty,"[30] Biden apologized for his statement within hours.[31]

"I think often about my ancestors who struggled for freedom,"
Cameron said. "And as I think of those giants and their broad
shoulders, I also think about Joe Biden, who says if you aren't
voting for me, 'you ain't Black.' Who argued that Republicans
would put us 'back in chains.' Who says there is no 'diversity' of
thought in the Black community."

He continued, "Mr. Vice President, look at me, I am Black.
We are not all the same, sir. I am not in chains. My mind is my
own. And you can't tell me how to vote because of the color of my
skin."

Breonna Taylor's mother, Tamika Palmer, reacted to
Cameron's speech by saying she hoped "the next time we see

him he's telling the country he's charging all officers responsible for my daughter's death."[32]

It was not to be. In September 2020, Cameron announced the grand jury's decision to issue counts of "wanton endangerment" in the first degree against Hankison for shooting into *another* apartment. A $15,000 cash bond was attached to the charges.[33] The other two officers were not charged.

At the time, no one was charged with homicide for the death of Breonna Taylor.

In a disturbing press conference on September 23, 2020, Cameron called on his roots to explain his failure to deliver justice for Taylor: "I understand that as a Black man, how painful this is…which is why it was so incredibly important to make sure that we did everything we possibly could to uncover every fact."[34]

"My heart breaks for the loss of Miss Taylor," Cameron continued. "And I've said that repeatedly. My mother, if something was to happen to me"—he took a dramatic pause, performatively holding back tears—"would find it very hard… I've seen that pain on Miss (Tamika) Palmer's face," he said, referring to Taylor's mother. "I've seen that pain in the community."[35]

Republicans had gotten exactly what they wanted. After the press conference, Trump praised Daniel Cameron as a "star" and "brilliant."[36]

Cameron may have seen "that pain in the community," but many in the Black community did not feel him. Weeks later, Megan Thee Stallion called out Cameron on an October 2020 appearance on *Saturday Night Live*. During a performance of her hit song "Savage," the Houston rapper made a strong statement about protecting Black women.

Megan stood with her fist in the air as the audio of activist

Tamika Mallory played: "Daniel Cameron is no different than the sellout negroes that sold our people into slavery."[37] Mallory famously made this statement after the grand jury's decision not to indict the officers involved in Taylor's death.[38]

Days after the performance, Cameron made appearances on Fox News. He complained about Megan Thee Stallion: "Let me just say that I agree that we need to love and protect our Black women. There's no question about that. But the fact that someone would get on national television and make disparaging comments about me because I'm simply trying to do my job is disgusting."[39]

Cameron's victim-playing after critique is a recurring pattern among Black Republican grifters. He whined that the performance showed "something that I've had to experience because I'm a Black Republican. Because I stand up for truth and justice as opposed to giving in to a mob mentality, and those are the sorts of things that will be hurled at me in this job." Cameron babbled on, "Obviously people preach about being tolerant (you've seen a lot of that from 'the left' about being tolerant), but what you saw there is inconsistent with tolerance. In fact, it's her espousing intolerance."

Cameron did not enlighten us on how demanding justice for Taylor was "intolerant" but instead shifted gears to complain about attorney Benjamin Crump, who was representing the Taylor family. "This is the Ben Crump model. He goes into a city, creates a narrative, cherry-picks to prove that narrative, creates chaos in the community, misrepresents the facts, and then he leaves with his money and then asks the community to pick up the pieces," he alleged. "It is terribly irresponsible on his part to push such narratives, such falsehoods."[40]

Whether trashing a Houston rapper or an attorney, Cameron's

playbook demands that he work to counter any Black political uprising while justifying himself as an "independent thinker." If Black people, or anyone who believes in a fair system, don't respond by singing "Kumbaya, My Lord," then we are not acknowledging progress.

But it's a twofold game; Cameron gives the Fox News audience the comfort of having a Black ally. He keeps his job and money. In Cameron, McConnell has a stone to throw in the political waters to get the right amount of ripple.

According to grand jurors, Cameron influenced the process to achieve his preferred end. Two grand jurors claimed that Cameron was pushing falsehoods. They demanded to be released from the gag order blocking them from speaking out about the Breonna Taylor case. An anonymous juror sued for the order to be lifted.[41]

Cameron aggressively opposed the juror's motion.[42] In early October 2020, he responded, "Allowing this disclosure would irreversibly alter Kentucky's legal system by making it difficult for prosecutors and the public to have confidence in the secrecy of the grand jury process going forward." Cameron claimed he didn't object to an opinion about how he oversaw the Taylor investigation but stated, "While the duty of a grand jury to meet in secret is firmly established, the right of the alleged grand juror to proceed anonymously is anything but."

Cameron insisted that the secrecy of the grand jury proceeding was "based on centuries of history, practice, and custom in the country and the commonwealth."[43] Like McConnell's approach to the filibuster, Cameron fell back on custom and tradition when it suited his agenda.

Breonna Taylor's family asked Cameron to recuse himself from the case, but he declined.[44]

By late October 2020, Kentucky governor Andy Beshear demanded in a public statement that Cameron release everything from the grand jury. "The current situation raises serious concerns, as multiple grand jurors are now claiming Attorney General Cameron has not been truthful to the public about what occurred in the grand jury process," Beshear stated. "I trust Kentuckians with the truth, and the next step should be to release all information, evidence, grand jury conversations, recorded or not—everything."[45]

A juror identified only as "Anonymous Grand Juror #1" claimed in a statement released by their attorney that Cameron had not allowed them to consider homicide charges. "The grand jury was not presented with any charges other than the three wanton endangerment charges against Detective Hankison," the juror said. "The grand jury did not have homicide charges explained to them. The grand jury never heard anything about those laws. Self-defense or justification was never explained either. Questions were asked about additional charges and the grand jury was told there would be none because the prosecutors didn't feel they could make them stick."[46] Two other grand jurors confirmed this account.

By January 2021, three grand jurors called for Cameron to be impeached. Attorney Kevin Glogower said in a statement, "He [Cameron] lied about what was presented to the grand jurors, he lied about what options were given to the grand jurors, and he lied about the decisions the grand jury made."[47] Cameron was never impeached, and Brett Hankison was acquitted on the three felony counts of wanton endangerment.[48]

Attorney General Daniel Cameron was able to dodge any reckoning for his actions. Cameron would have people believe his handling of the Breonna Taylor case was a sober application of the law, and the angry Black mob was unfairly attacking him.

The fight for justice did not stop with Cameron. In August 2022, the Department of Justice charged the four officers involved in Taylor's death. Charges included unlawful conspiracies, unconstitutional use of force, and civil rights offenses.[49] Cameron defended his work in several tweets. "I'm proud of the work of our investigators & prosecutors. There are those, however, who want to use this moment to divide Kentuckians, misrepresent the facts of the state investigation, and broadly impugn the character of our law enforcement community."

Cameron also stated he would not "participate in that sort of rancor."[50]

But in November 2020, Cameron participated in another kind of rancor by supporting the big lie that Trump won the election. He fought to disenfranchise voters, many of whom are Black and helped to secure Biden's win. The Louisville *Courier-Journal* reported Cameron's efforts to challenge the legitimacy of Pennsylvania's mail-in ballots. The Keystone State is nearly five hundred miles outside Cameron's jurisdiction. Republicans argue for small government, but calling for elections to be overturned in states they do not represent—that sounds like big government. On November 9, Cameron, McConnell, and others planned to take "major legal action."[51]

Republican state legislatures in Pennsylvania tried to block mail-in votes from being counted when they arrived.[52] Votes were still being counted days after the election because Pennsylvania allowed universal mail-in voting for the first time due to the COVID pandemic.[53] Republicans refused to allow ballots to be processed when they arrived, only on Election Day, which caused the delay.

Cameron joined McConnell and other attorneys general from

Louisiana,[54] Texas,[55] and Missouri to challenge the validity of Biden's win in Pennsylvania.[56] "The Republican AGs are already stepping up to the frontlines as 'America's insurance policy' against the possibility of a Biden-Harris administration and their liberal extremist agenda," a Cameron spokesperson said in a statement provided to the *Courier-Journal*.[57]

There was no evidence of widespread voter fraud in Pennsylvania or any other state.[58]

Cameron's efforts in support of the big lie failed, but he should not be ignored. With the backing of Mitch McConnell, he could easily rise in political ranks.

Don't dismiss Cameron as a sellout; that oversimplifies his impact as a grifter. Justice for Breonna Taylor should not have been elusive for an attorney general who claims to be so familiar with the needs of the Black community. He is materially dangerous because his actions manifest in Black communities. Sadly, Cameron's shape-shifting logic is what we have seen from too many Black Republicans over the decades. It's a strategy Reagan, Bush (both), and Trump used masterfully, harming Black people with a Black person willing to do their work. This brings us to the most loyal Trump administration member and the only Black person who served in his presidential cabinet, Dr. Ben Carson.

Carson was appointed secretary of HUD, an illogical role for a doctor with zero housing experience. In November 2016, according to business manager and close friend Armstrong Williams, Carson felt he had "no government experience, he's never run a federal agency."[59] Experience obviously meant nothing to Trump; it was all about loyalty, and Carson was loyal.

Carson was raised by a single mom in working-class Detroit, briefly living in public housing, but he was by no means a subject matter expert. Section 8 housing, for example, is not an exclusively Black issue. Nearly 50 percent of Section 8 recipients are white.[60] Carson seemed to view his role in conjunction with the Black Republican who demands people who look like him pull themselves up by their overworked bootstraps. Although Carson insisted he provided self-sufficiency to Black communities, slashing resources does not facilitate independence for the working poor of any color.

Under Carson, there was a proposal to cut the HUD budget by 14 percent.[61] He also fought to reverse Obama-era policies that required cities to prevent housing segregation and create equitable housing.[62] In 2017, he grumbled that low-income people are "too comfortable."[63] A year later, Carson sought to remove the word *discrimination* from HUD's mission statement.[64] President Lyndon B. Johnson launched HUD in 1965 to mitigate discriminatory housing practices.

Like most people in the Trump administration, Dr. Ben Carson appeared in over his head. In early 2018, he said brain surgery was easier than his role at HUD.[65] Yes, Carson was blessed with gifted hands as a brain surgeon, but he operated with no bedside manner as the secretary of HUD. Wearing Christianity on his sleeve, his approach to service wasn't Christlike.

Carson's tenure was not without scandal. HUD was investigated for his family's involvement and "using his position for private gain."[66] A lawsuit accused his team of demoting a HUD official, Helen Foster,[67] for refusing to approve pricey office renovations. Marcus Smallwood, another HUD official, confirmed these accusations in an email saying that HUD employees "have operated in fear."[68] In February 2018, the *New York Times* reported on the expensive renovations after HUD announced plans to slash

$8 million in funding for the homeless, elderly, and poor. Carson would blame the upgrades on his wife, Candy Carson.[69] Carson said at a House hearing in March 2018, "The next thing that I, quite frankly, heard about it was that this $31,000 table had been bought."[70] Under pressure, grifters reliably fold, casting blame on the nearest target to protect themselves.

Katrina Hubbard, an executive assistant to HUD's chief information officer, Johnson Joy, claimed she was fired in January 2018 for reporting "misuse of public funds." Hubbard told the *Guardian*, "I reported information about fraud, waste and abuse, and as a result I was retaliated against." Joy would "resign" by March 2018.[71]

There were also accusations of taxpayer dollars being used for private planes and White House bible study sessions.[72]

Corruption and inexperience were the new normal in the Trump era. Carson was such a disservice that he was even kicked off the grounds of a Black church in Baltimore. He was attempting to hold a press conference to celebrate Trump after the president attacked the late Representative Elijah Cummings, who represented Baltimore. Trump called his district a "disgusting rat and rodent-infested mess" and a "very dangerous and filthy place."[73] Ironically, Trump labeled Cummings a "brutal bully" for speaking out against detention centers on the U.S. southern border.[74]

Carson's predecessor, Julián Castro, appeared on my SiriusXM show in July 2019 and said, "It just doesn't seem like he really believes in the mission of the organization. This administration thinks that if you're poor, there's something wrong with you."

He added, "Secretary Carson, in his own upbringing… He grew up in tough circumstances… I wish that they would extend that ladder down and help folks be able to rise and climb. Instead of pulling that ladder out."[75]

Extending the ladder, whether it's through affirmative action, voting rights, or housing, is not the way of Black Republican grifters.

Carson stayed with Trump until the bitter end. After the January 6 insurrection, there were several resignations—from Secretary of Transportation Elaine Chao to Secretary of Education Betsy DeVos. Not Carson. He condemned the violence but insisted Trump was not to blame.[76] Like Samuel Riley Pierce Jr., President Ronald Reagan's HUD secretary, Carson's loyalty to his boss spoiled his legacy. His allegiance to Trumpism overshadows his record as a groundbreaking pediatric neurosurgeon.

Even after Trump left office, Carson used his platform to say there is too much talk about race while screaming racism. In a May 2022 interview with *Politico*, Carson complained everything is "circling back to race these days." Yet in the same interview, he compared "cancel culture" to race. Disturbingly, Carson defended an analogy that cancel culture and "Jim Crow racism have much in common."[77] This comment is reminiscent of when Carson compared the Affordable Care Act to slavery.[78] I asked former HUD staffer Shermichael Singleton about Carson's history of vile and anti-Black rhetoric. He said when he worked with Carson and assisted with press releases or statements, he "was always very conscientious of how he would articulate certain things as it pertains to issues of race." Singleton added while he has a "tremendous amount of respect" for Carson, he doesn't always agree with him. In a telling statement, he added, "I know my experience with Dr. Carson, and then I know the political version of Dr. Carson."[79]

Although not a politician in any sense, Minister Omarosa Manigault Newman worked for the Trump administration and rode the gravy train as far as she could.

The Youngstown, Ohio, native is undoubtedly a trailblazer who paved the way for the likes of Candace Owens. It's unclear if Newman is a Republican, Democrat, or independent,[80] but she is a grifter who campaigned for a proud racist.

In the 1990s, she worked for the Clinton administration in the office of Vice President Al Gore. Mary Margaret Overbey, Gore's former office administrator, told the *New York Times* in 2017, "She was the worst hire we ever made." Newman was eventually transferred to the Commerce Department. Cheryl Shavers, the Commerce Department's undersecretary for technology administration and the first Black woman in the position, described Newman as "unqualified and disruptive" and needing to be "removed."[81]

Newman's claim to fame was in 2004 with the first season of Donald Trump's *The Apprentice*. The breakout star from the reality series, Newman was cast as the villain, a role she would continue to play. She famously feuded with Wendy Williams, La Toya Jackson, model Claudia Jordan, and others.

In 2014, Newman had a weak presence in media but tweeted out her support of Hillary Clinton. By 2016, she was no longer supporting Clinton. Newman was on board with her boss at *The Apprentice*, despite her alleged knowledge of him using the n-word. That didn't stop the opportunist from jumping on the Trump train.[82] The reality star, who was once fired from Clinton's administration,[83] proudly wore the "Make America Great Again" hat.[84] She also declared that all Trump's detractors would "bow down" to him, establishing her role in Trump's cult.[85]

After Trump's win, Newman joined the White House as assistant to the president and director of communications in the White House Office of Public Liaison. She immediately made it clear that she was out for herself alone. Reports emerged that she was blocking other Black Republicans from joining the administration. In 2018, Black Republican Eugene Craig, chair of the Maryland Republican Party at the time, stated to the *Cincinnati Herald*, "I was blocked personally. Essentially, my file was pulled, and I wasn't deemed pro-Trump enough." In true Newman fashion, there could only be one winner in her White House reality show.

Newman proceeded to bend the rules as she saw fit. "The floodgates were opened, but Omarosa held all of us to a different standard," Craig said. "She had a say over a lot of the Black résumés. I know for a fact from promises that she made us directly." According to Craig, there was a January 2017 conference call "specifically for African American activists and party loyalists." Newman "bogarted on" and "made us these promises that this would be the most diverse administration in history. And she'll help us with whatever we needed and wherever we wanted to go into government and to shoot our résumés over to her and she gave us her official transition email. She said this administration has a goal of having 25 percent minority hiring... She positioned herself as the end-all, be-all for Black things, for Black people in the administration."

But the reality of Newman's White House was much stingier when it came to hiring Black people. Ayshia Connors, the former deputy director of African American engagement at the RNC, claimed résumés of Black Republicans were ignored: "Omarosa, she didn't want other Black Republicans there. She wanted to be the big shot. She wanted to be the only one." Newman was also accused of blocking Kay Coles James, the first Black woman to serve as president of the conservative Heritage Foundation.[86]

Kwame Jackson, also on the first season of *The Apprentice* with Newman, said about her role in the Trump administration, "The master plan of Omarosa's vision for African American outreach. Deny reality, laugh it off with a fake and venomous smile, implore and praise Mr. Trump like the smiley butler Sam Jackson played in the film *Django Unchained*."[87]

Then there was Newman's alleged attack on Black women like veteran White House reporter April Ryan. According to the *Washington Post*, Newman and Ryan got into a heated confrontation outside Press Secretary Sean Spicer's office in February 2017. The *Washington Post* reported that several staffers and Abby Phillip, a *Washington Post* reporter at the time, witnessed the argument. Phillip didn't hear the entire exchange, but she said Ryan explained that Newman's behavior was "Secret Serviceable." Ryan told the *Washington Post* about the incident. "She stood right in my face like she was going to hit me. I said, 'You better back up.' She thought I would be bullied. I won't be." Newman also supposedly warned that President Trump was keeping a running list of Black journalists who were the subject of negative "dossiers," according to Ryan.

The grudge had been long in the making. In fall 2016, Newman reportedly sent two emails to Ryan. One email allegedly implied that Ryan accepted money from the Clintons for favorable coverage, which Ryan denied. Another email from Newman allegedly read, "Protect your legacy!! You have worked too hard to have people question your ethics as a journalist. People talking trash about the reporters on that list having NO integrity. It's hurtful to hear people say those things about you." Ryan spoke out against the smears: "She's trying to harm my integrity and my career. I've been [covering the White House] for 20 years. I plan to be here for the next 20 years. You don't mess with someone's livelihood." Newman responded in an email to the *Post*, calling Ryan's claims "fake news."[88]

Newman's disturbing behavior continued at the National Association of Black Journalists convention in August 2017. Newman was working for the Trump White House and sat on a panel about police brutality along with the mother of Philando Castile, who was fatally shot by police in July 2016. Newman was reportedly added at the "eleventh hour."[89] It's unclear why the National Association of Black Journalists thought Newman would be a good fit for the panel.

Symone Sanders, who was a CNN commentator at the time, tweeted on August 10, 2017, "Who at #NABJ17 said Omarosa and Philando Castile's mother belong on the same panel? Does the President even believe black lives matter?"[90]

According to TheGrio, veteran journalist Ed Gordon agreed to moderate the panel after other moderators—like Nikole Hannah-Jones, the creator of the 1619 Project—pulled out due to learning of Newman's participation.[91] During the panel, while Newman was talking, some attendees turned their backs, and others walked out.[92]

Gordon, who had interviewed everyone from Tupac Shakur to President Barack Obama, asked Newman about Trump's comments around policing in Black communities. Trump was calling for more police and rapidly rolling back Obama-era police reform policies, including restricting consent decrees.[93] Newman became unhinged.

At one point, she stood from her chair and accused Gordon of being "aggressive" because he stepped away from his podium. Newman paced around the stage and demanded, "Ask about my story; I'm not going to stand here and defend every single word or decision." She professed, "I fight on the front lines every day," which made the audience laugh. Gordon responded with, "I've seen you do this, and you're not going to railroad this," which received claps and cheers from the audience. Newman also referred to Freddie Gray, who died in police custody in April 2015, as a "boy." He was twenty-five years old at the time of his death.[94]

After that performance and accusing Gordon of being "aggressive," according to American Urban Radio Networks, "Omarosa cornered CNN commentator Symone Sanders and verbally accosted her for talking trash on social media, suggesting Omarosa shouldn't have been there at all."[95]

Gordon told TheGrio in 2018 about the exchange with Newman. "I knew what her MO was and felt like, 'Not today.'"[96]

Newman was too explosive and self-aggrandizing even for Donald Trump. By December 2017, the reality star was terminated from the White House.[97]

After she was fired from the Trump administration, Newman dropped a mixtape of damning recordings of Trump aides, promising an n-word recording would drop before the 2018 midterms. It never did.[98] It appeared she was willing to tell any story to sell a product, just as Trump taught her. That shamelessness is what propelled her 2018 book, *Unhinged*, to the *New York Times* bestsellers list.

In September 2018, I interviewed Newman live on SiriusXM for *Unhinged* and got to experience firsthand what it was like when a grifter was held accountable.[99]

I came prepared. During her press tour for the book, Newman repeatedly defended standing by Trump because she was "blindsided" by him—even though she had known Trump for fifteen years. Therefore, my first question was, "In *Unhinged*, you talk about your journey, you talk about growing up in the projects and experiencing gun violence. You went to three HBCUs, so you're clearly a smart woman. So I guess I'm confused. How does someone as smart as you get blindsided by someone like Trump?"

Newman shot me the death stare. She was stumped. I used her own talking point to ask the question. "I wasn't the only one in America. Donald Trump was a successful businessman who was running an amazing company and who was a very interesting person, as we saw on *The Apprentice*," she said. "I was duped but I wasn't alone."

That wasn't a real answer to my question, and I wasn't convinced someone as sharp as Newman could be duped. Nevertheless, I moved on.

I asked her about sisters Diamond and Silk, whose real names are Herneitha and Ineitha Hardaway. The YouTubers became famous for their worship of Trump and bizarre monologues at his rallies. They were also fixtures on Fox News for years and, in grifter fashion, cried racism when they were no longer with the network.[100]

I began, "You campaigned with Diamond and Silk."

Newman quickly interjected, "No, they campaigned with *me*."

I corrected myself and continued, "I think they are really dangerous propaganda. What was your impression working with them? Are they sincere or are they just trying to get attention and make money?"

Newman answered, "I thought they were nice girls. I'm never gonna knock anybody's hustle so if that's their hustle, and they want to make money, why knock them?"

"But do you think it was sincere?" I asked. "Because people feel like it's a joke, it's a gimmick."

"It was sincere to them," she replied. "But I'm never gonna knock another sister's hustle. That's not my position."

Moments later, she was knocking the hustle of April Ryan who, unlike Diamond and Silk, had a real job as a White House press reporter.

The week before, April Ryan was a guest on *The Karen Hunter Show*, also on SiriusXM Urban View, and went into detail about how Newman tried to have her fired.[101]

When I asked about attempting to fire Ryan, Newman denied any truth to her comments and added with sarcasm, "I don't have a beef with her. I wish her well... I heard she has a project out. I haven't seen much about it. God bless her. Hopefully, people will read it." She added it was "ignorant" for anyone to believe she could get Ryan terminated, even though the question was whether she *tried* to get her fired.

Newman continued, "It's surprising she gives me that much power in her life. But I didn't have that power nor was she even on my radar at all. I like her. So I hope that people will find some benefit in the stuff that she's saying. But I think if you look at our two projects, our books came out around the same time. I'm number one on the bestsellers list."

"That's a very Trump line," I said with a laugh.

"I'm not being shady," she shot back. "I'm number one on the *New York Times* bestsellers list. I don't know where she is."

Newman became more frustrated when I questioned her infamous "bow down" comment, suggesting that it reeked of a dictatorship. She argued it was "hyperbolic" and "hyperdramatic" but added, "Everything that I say, I support with facts. I don't just pull it out of the air. Politics is a rough game. If you can't deal with it, don't step in the arena." Newman couldn't explain how "bow down" was supported with facts and clearly didn't like the arena she was stepping into with me.

I asked about her claims that Trump made advances to her, but she could not specify what he said.

I questioned her insistence that she knew of a tape of Trump using the n-word. In August 2018, Newman told NPR she had heard the tape, despite saying in *Unhinged* that she had only *heard of* the tape.[102] Newman said that the slur had been directed toward Black *Apprentice* cast members but could give no specifics, at least not in my interview.

Newman's bizarre claims of an n-word tape expose a shape-shifter in motion. In August 2018, she released an audio clip from October 2016 of a discussion she had with Trump campaign aides Katrina Pierson and Lynne Patton, two other Black women. They appeared to discuss the possibility of Trump using the racial slur on tape.[103] That means Newman was having this conversation about the n-word tape less than a month before the 2016 presidential election. It's alarming that she recorded this conversation, appearing to know or at least have an idea that the tape existed, and still supported him as president on the campaign trail.

If she truly cared about the republic, why didn't Newman release this audio of Pierson, Patton, and herself before the November election? This could have been another "October surprise." The recording could have changed the election's outcome, considering Trump won by such a small margin in swing states. Newman strategically sat on the audio for her own opportunistic purposes.

The interview continued to go left when I questioned her advocating for the Trump administration. She began talking over me and asked a question, trying to turn the tables on me: "What's your point?"

I calmly answered, "Here's my point, Omarosa. I don't believe you. I don't believe that you went in the White House thinking you were going to help Black people. I believe that you knew he was a con artist, and I believe you're a con artist as well. I believe that you were being an opportunist. I'm speaking for a lot of African Americans and the majority of Black women who voted 96 percent for the other candidate."

Newman went full Trumpian. She stood up with her phone recording and got extremely close to me, right in my personal space. I was immediately reminded of when April Ryan said she thought Newman might hit her. Her physical behavior would have been considered threatening if I were a woman and she was a man. She attempted to bully me like she bullied Symone Sanders, Ed Gordon, and many other Black people in the media.

Just like her 2017 performance at the National Association of Black Journalists and Gordon saying, "not today," that is how I felt: not today and not on my radio show.

I told Newman she was in the same category as Sean Spicer and Sarah Huckabee Sanders, which was accurate, considering she worked in the same administration.

She accused me of being part of "petty Black people," "lowbrow," and then claimed I had a Jheri curl, which I thought was hilarious.

At one point in the interview, I played a 2017 clip of legendary actress and Broadway icon Sheryl Lee Ralph saying Newman offered for her to join the "Trump train."

"Omarosa and I met at this church event," Ralph recalled on *Hollywood Today*. "And I say, 'Girlfriend, please don't tell me you're taking...you're doing...what, why?' And she said, 'Sheryl, I am going to the White House. I will have an office in the White

House. I am riding this train and I've got a ticket for you, if you would like to come along.' And I was like, 'Girlfriend, I'm going to have to miss that train.'"[104]

I asked for a response to the clip, which obviously called her out for being a grifter. Newman was mortified that I played the clip, calling me "gutter" and saying, "An actress! An actress!"

I replied, "Sheryl Lee Ralph is a national treasure."

She refused to leave the SiriusXM studio and insisted I end the show, which I couldn't because it was live radio. My final words to her were, "Have a great day. Good luck with *Unhinged*, good luck with your bestseller. I look forward to the next book, the next reality show. Sell out as many Black folks as you can."

The minister responded by calling me a "bitch" and used a favorite line from Black conservatives—telling me to get off the "plantation."

Newman continued to fume outside the SiriusXM studio as she recorded me through the glass walls. I was later told SiriusXM talent reps asked if she wanted to cancel her next interview. She reportedly said no and conducted the following interview like nothing had happened.

Just a year before the interview, Newman had been defending Trump's comments about Charlottesville.[105] She left the White House in December 2017, nine months before my interview with her. She was fresh off the Trump train. In today's culture, things move quickly, and con artists rely on short memories and revisionist history, but I was prepared—as we all need to be when facing off against con artists.

Newman and Trump have many things in common. They are both hungry for fame and money. They each respond to being held accountable by hurling insults. They are both anti-Black. Yes,

Newman is a Black woman, but she's not for Black people. She's solely for herself.

I tell this story because I don't think every Black Republican is a traitor. As I've detailed in this book, there are Black people with sincere Republican views who believed they could change the GOP from within, but those who joined the cult of Trump cannot claim to be sincere or truthful about anything. For the children at the border who were locked in cages, for the people living in public housing who were threatened with massive rent increases under Ben Carson's HUD,[106] for the Black people who are disproportionately affected by gun violence as Republicans bowed down to the NRA, for the threat to our democracy via Vladimir Putin and Russian interference, for the Black and brown people who felt less safe under the Trump administration, it was my job to hold anyone accountable, if I were interviewing them, who advocated for that atrocious man.

Moreover, any person who vouched for this president has blood on their hands.[107] Minister Newman stood by Trump, knowing who he was, all while smiling like a game show host. It will take decades to recover from Trump's tragic legacy. Anyone who helped that contagion infect the White House while conveniently recording people for an upcoming book should never be sanitized.

Newman is a textbook grifter, and many others have followed in her footsteps, especially in the Trump era.

There is Candace Owens, Omarosa 2.0. Before she became famous, she was the CEO of a website called Degree180, which frequently published anti-Trump posts.[108] Even after the site stopped publishing in 2016, no one knew her name until she "came out" as a conservative on YouTube a few months later.

Her videos quickly went viral, and soon she was on Fox News.

Owens called the NAACP "one of the worst groups for Black people," even though the organization helped her win a $37,500 settlement over racial discrimination in 2007. Owens accused white children at her high school of leaving her racist and threatening voicemails. Connecticut NAACP president Scot X. Esdaile, who helped with the case, told *Mic* in April 2018, "We're very saddened and disappointed in her. It seems to me that she's now trying to play to a different type of demographic." Esdaile compared her to Supreme Court Justice Clarence Thomas. "It's the same type of thing Clarence Thomas did. [Thomas] reaped all the benefits of affirmative action and then tried to roll over on it. It's that kind of mentality and disrespect."[109]

Owens once falsely claimed on Fox News that the NRA was founded as a civil rights organization that protected Black people from the KKK.[110] She was rewarded with airtime that wouldn't have been given to her as a liberal commentator or via her failed doxing site.[111] In 2018, she launched Blexit, her self-indulgent movement for Black people to leave the Democratic Party, which failed. A 2023 feature from the Center for Media and Democracy stated Blexit was "bankrolled by wealthy conservatives" with Owens getting a six-figure salary, probably more than she ever earned before she came out as a conservative.[112] She now speaks all over the country and has millions of followers on Twitter.

Outside attacking Black men who were murdered, like Ahmaud Arbery[113] and George Floyd,[114] another vile moment was when she blathered that she would be okay if Adolf Hitler just wanted to "make Germany great."[115] After comments like these, though she later tried to clarify them,[116] Owens was still invited by Republicans to speak before the House Judiciary Committee hearing on "Hate Crimes and the Rise of White Nationalism."[117] In late 2022, Owens, along with rapper Kanye West, proudly wore "White Lives Matter" shirts, a popular slogan for white supremacists.

Candace Owens may have given up her soul for fame with white Republicans, but arguably the saddest casualty of the Trump administration is Herman Cain, former CEO of Godfather's Pizza.

Along with leading the National Restaurant Association for several years, the successful businessman ran for the Republican nomination for president in 2000 and for U.S. Senate in Georgia in 2004. Sexual misconduct claims derailed his second run for president in 2011, but he remained outspoken in GOP politics and was a Tea Party activist.

The rise of Trump gave Cain newfound political legs. He quickly boarded the Trump train and was named the cochair of Black Voices for Trump. In June 2016, despite Trump's extensive record of bigotry, Cain called on his Georgia roots to insist that Trump was not racist: "I grew up in Atlanta, Georgia. I know what a racist looks like when I see one. Donald Trump is not a racist."[118]

As COVID-19 ravaged the country in 2020, many people refused to wear masks, even at crowded Trump rallies. Cain, a cancer survivor, was one of them. On June 20, 2020, Cain was reportedly flown in by the Trump campaign to a rally in Tulsa, Oklahoma. He was pictured maskless and smiling. After nine days, Cain tested positive for COVID. Two days later, the seventy-four-year-old was hospitalized. On July 2, Cain's staff released a statement, saying there was "no way of knowing for sure how or where" he contracted COVID.[118]

On July 30, 2020, Herman Cain died due to complications

from COVID-19. Trump's reaction? "Unfortunately, he passed away from a thing called the China virus." He also called Cain a "very special person."[119]

Do Republicans know what they are doing in the name of Trump is wrong? According to journalist Jonathan Karl, the Tulsa rally was a toxic super-spreader event. Trump staffers reportedly blamed themselves for Cain's death. One senior staffer reportedly stated, "We killed Herman Cain."[120] Like members of a cult, people were willing to risk their lives for loyalty.

Shilling for Trump and courting his worshippers has consequences, but for some frauds, the rewards are worth it—if they can avoid being exposed. Sunlight is the best disinfectant, as an unknown twenty-six-year-old wannabe politician learned the hard way. In May 2021, Alex Stovall announced he was running for Congress in Arizona. His announcement tweet said he was "running for Congress to take on AOC."[121] Even though Representative Alexandria Ocasio-Cortez represents a district in New York City, Stovall coveted her name recognition.

A press release read, "We are proud to launch this historic campaign for Congress. Alex was spurred into running by seeing the actions of AOC and her squad. He knew that our nation needed a young conservative voice in Congress to counter her socialist agenda. Alex loves this country and will fight to make sure that it continues to be the greatest country in the world."[122]

By mid-July, Stovall had "collected $33,000 and had $18,000 in cash"[123] and was on the rowdy Black Republican train. Stovall said in an interview about the Arizona audit, which was a wasteful deep dive into ballots cast in Maricopa County during the 2020 presidential election, "I try and tell people the audit is paramount. Once the audit is done, and the truth will come to light, we can

make those corrections and make sure it never happens again."
However, a right-wing site exposed Stovall. An insider from his
campaign leaked audio of him saying the exact opposite. "The
whole audit bull-crap thing that they're doing, it's just another way
to funnel money from the American people. Do you know how
much money they raised from this audit? Over $10 million."[124]
Stovall knew his possible constituents were being scammed.

He was also caught saying there was no significant election
fraud to have overturned the 2020 election, but "I'm not going to
broadcast that everywhere." Stovall gave another interview stating,
"We need guys or girls to implement policies and bills that are
going to make America stronger, continue what Trump's started."
But when he didn't know he was being recorded, he called out
the people continuing Trump's lies and dropped the truth of why
anyone would vote for him. "The stuff that they're doing should
be criminal, and they should all be thrown in prison. They want
to vote for me just so they can say that they elected the youngest
Black Republican in American history." Stovall knew his conservative Blackness was an asset. He eagerly raised his hand to be a
token for profit.

Stovall also said when he didn't know he was on camera that
Trump would more than likely endorse him "but I'm not going to
publicly advertise it." He dragged Candace Owens. "No, I don't
have respect for Candace Owens anymore. Will I take her dona-
tion and take her donors? Absolutely, but it goes no further than
that. I would never invite her to a Christmas party." The video
showed a photo of him smiling with Candace Owens.

Stovall made it clear his only goal was to win and even referred
to himself as a monkey. "You don't win Arizona by being super
right, Republican. You never show all your cards, right? Yes, I'm a

conservative. But I'm not gonna beat on my big old monkey chest running around telling a whole bunch of people I am. It's gonna turn people off and no one's going to want to give me money."[125]

As for racism, which his party consistently downplays, Stovall admitted, "Racism is real. What the news is telling you, what Tucker Carlson is telling you, what Candace Owens is telling you, it's a bunch of baloney."

The last piece caught on camera was "You want to be less white? Vote for the young Black candidate." Stovall didn't know that if you are a hustler and in charge, everyone around you is going to be a hustler as well. That's why he was exposed.

He is an obvious grifter, but it didn't take a secret recording to prove that fact. Conservative media knew who he was from start to finish, just as they knew Candace Owens, Pastor Darrell Scott, and Diamond and Silk were also grifting.

The stunt Stovall pulled is a shortcut to Black Republican relevance. It's not to be a Colin Powell. It's to be a buffoon and defend white supremacy at any cost. He was copying the clownery that has proven successful.

Most importantly, if Stovall hadn't been outed and had made it to Congress, he would have voted against Black and brown people. Why would he do that? Because there is a price to be paid to climb further in the ranks. Stovall was an opportunist, and there are more coming.

Consider State Representative Walter Blackman, the first Black Republican elected to the Arizona legislature.[126] During his 2020 campaign, he said, "This is my thought on Black Lives Matter—first of all, it's a terrorist organization because it's been deemed, or it's been identified by the FBI already."[127]

He also thought it would be winning politics to insult a man killed by a police officer with a knee in his neck in May 2020, George Floyd. While Blackman wished the family justice, he posted a Facebook video with a title that read in part, "I do not support George Floyd and I refuse to see him as a martyr."[128] The American Civil Liberties Union of Arizona and the American Friends Services Committee-Arizona, a justice reform organization that once worked with Blackman, denounced him.

In January 2021, the former combat veteran supported the "Stop the Steal" movement, which was behind the lie that Trump won the presidential election nationwide and in Arizona.[129] Eight months later, Blackman also praised the far-right group the Proud Boys, saying it was "one of the proudest moments of my life" when the group attended one of his events. He added, "Not because of what the media portrayed them to be, but the patriots they showed young people: the example on how to be an American." After backlash, Blackman, sixty-two at the time, claimed he "wasn't familiar with the totality and breadth of the Proud Boys' conduct" and condemned the group.[130]

Fast-forward to January 2022, Blackman was crying racism.[131] The combat vet said it wasn't possible to decertify the 2020 presidential election—not that he didn't want to, just that he didn't believe it was possible. A right-wing site complained, "Blackman sounded like a Democrat."[132] Blackman's family began receiving racist messages, according to him, due to a story on the right-wing site. A text message to his daughter allegedly read, "Your nigger dad is RINO." RINO stands for "Republican in Name Only."

The site accused Blackman of sending the message to himself, which he denied. Blackman said, "This is what happens when your opponents can't run a campaign on the issues. They resort to disgusting smear attacks with a word that has no place in our Republican Party or society in general."[133]

This is what happens when you support the Proud Boys and rally to overturn an election for a congressional seat. By 2022, Blackman was running for the Second Congressional District in Arizona. He lost to Trump-endorsed Eli Crane by over nine points.[134]

In 2020 and 2021, we saw many losers in the land of Black Republicans, including Kimberly Klacik (lost Maryland's Seventh Congressional District by more than forty points),[135] Angela Stanton (lost Georgia's Fifth Congressional District by seventy points),[136] and Larry Elder (California rejected a recall of Governor Gavin Newsom by over thirty points).[137] In the 2022 midterms, former Newsmax host Joe Pinion lost the New York U.S. Senate race against Charles Schumer by over ten points.[138] I interviewed Pinion in October 2022 on my SiriusXM radio show, and he ahistorically called Schumer a "modern day George Wallace," to the disgust of the listening audience and obviously the people of New York. Trump-endorsed candidate Kristina Karamo, a former trivia host who received press in 2020 on conservative media for claiming she witnessed fraud in Michigan, lost Michigan's secretary of state race to Jocelyn Benson by double digits. Over twenty-four hours after Karamo's clear loss, she was refusing to concede.[139] Another loser was Kathy Barnette, whose abhorrent history included hateful comments about Muslims, peddling conspiracy theories about President Barack Obama, and marching near Proud Boys on January 6. In 2022, she was rejected twice over, losing to Dr. Mehmet Oz in the Republican primary for Pennsylvania's Senate seat and then again in her bid to represent Pennsylvania's Fourth Congressional District.[140] Being in the gutter of the sunken place didn't even get them a seat at the white supremacist table.

At the same time, in 2022, there were some significant wins. After John James, endorsed by Trump, was a two-time loser for the Michigan U.S. Senate race, in 2022, he narrowly won the Tenth Congressional District in Michigan.[141] Wesley Hunt, also endorsed by Trump, lost Texas's Seventh Congressional District in 2020, but in 2022, he won a seat in the House in Texas's predominately white Thirty-Eighth Congressional District, which was newly created due to redistricting.[142] Hunt has hit all the current Black Republican talking points. In 2021 and 2022, he frequently appeared on conservative media and ranted about "woke" culture and critical race theory and accused the "left" of trying to defund the military, even though President Joe Biden has done the exact opposite.[143]

There was also the unruly absurdity of Herschel Walker's Senate campaign in Georgia, which was a warning. The former NFL player was the shameful face of Black Republicanism in 2022—incoherent, a proven liar according to his son, and deeply hypocritical on issues ranging from abortion to fatherhood. Walker's political success among southern white Republicans is yet another reminder of how original Black Republicanism has been pulverized. In the 2022 midterms, despite his far from Christlike behavior, including abortions with alleged receipts, he received a whopping 88 percent of support from white evangelicals.[144] Walker earned a higher percentage of the evangelical vote than Senator Ted Budd, who voted against certifying the 2020 election, in North Carolina,[145] showing the ability of a Black Republican, even one tarnished by scandal, to command even greater support than a conservative white candidate. This so-called Christian demographic supported Walker over Democratic senator Raphael Warnock, a longtime faith leader who is the senior pastor of Ebenezer Baptist,

Dr. Martin Luther King Jr.'s church. Politics is more important than their Jesus, and the elevation of the Black Republican grift is blaring in Walker. Shamefully, Walker and Warnock headed to a run-off due to neither reaching the 50 percent threshold of votes. In the end, Walker lost by ninety-nine thousand votes, but considering his nauseating record, the race should have never been so close.

Although not Black—even though he claimed to be part Black in a July 2020 tweet[146]—George Santos was elected to represent New York's Third Congressional District, defeating Democrat Robert Zimmerman, helping to give Republicans a slim majority in the House. The first openly gay Latin person elected to Congress as a Republican gave Herschel Walker a run for his grifting money with an endless train wreck of lies: education, employment, property ownership, and even questions about his sexual orientation. There were reports that senior House Republicans knew he was a chronic liar, but they didn't care. On the campaign trail, Santos loved to remind people he was Latin, gay, and an immigrant, when in reality, he was a hustler. Just like today's Black Republicans, Santos provided cover for bigotry. The party of alleged "morals" wouldn't demand that Santos step down—until after he was sworn in—because they knew he would do their bidding in the House. It's the GOP's version of identity politics:, find a "token" in a "minority" group to downplay their hate, and hopefully, their base will be incentivized. If Santos attempted to pull this stunt as a Democrat, he would have been thrown out of the party faster than former Minnesota senator Al Franken.[147]

The Republican Party is actively recruiting grifters. In October 2022, Pam Keith, a Florida native and CEO of the Center for Employment Justice, revealed on SiriusXM's *The Karen*

Hunter Show that she was "solicited by the Florida GOP to run as a Republican, and their view was that they could fund me to the moon and beyond because I was an articulate, conservative-looking Black woman that they could have made a star." Keith, who is a Democrat, refused to take the GOP blood dollars and underscored that the money came with a price: "You are Stepin Fetchit when you take that money. Look at Herschel Walker." She also said while South Carolina senator Tim Scott isn't a "Stepin Fetchit," he was "neutered."[148]

Reginald Grant, who began identifying as a Republican in the early 2000s as a teenager, was once a rising political star in the Texas GOP. He formed a Black Republican group in college and was making connections in the Republican Party. The former Marine supported Obama in 2008, but dissatisfied with his decisions on foreign policy, he supported Mitt Romney in 2012. The power players in the Texas GOP took notice and so did Grant. He began to play the Black Republican game. Grant told me that he shaped himself into the mold of what white Republicans required, using "misleading" and "intellectually dishonest" talking points like "Lincoln freed the slaves," quoting Booker T. Washington saying "pull yourself by your bootstraps," and downplaying racism. Grant acknowledged he "played the role" for white Republicans: "tout my military service, try to be over the top with the talking points, let them know, 'I'm the safe guy.'"

Grant was rewarded for his performance. He was elected as a delegate at the 2016 Republican National Convention, beating out a founder of the Tea Party in the Harris County, Texas, area. Grant said he was strategically selected to be on stage with Texas lieutenant governor Dan Patrick. He claimed the RNC representative for Texas told him, "We want to showcase how diverse and youthful our party is here, so we want you to stand next to the lieutenant governor as he reads out the Texas delegate count for our presidential nomination." Grant was fully aware he was being used as a "prop" but believed "this is going to propel me to political stardom. This is the type of exposure I need. Yeah, they are using me but I'm also going to use them too."

Grant's hustle would soon fold. In 2018, he primaried Texas state representative Dan Huberty to represent House District 127. He claimed the GOP quickly turned on him. According to Grant, he was told by white Republicans, "Don't forget you're Black. You need to stay in your place." His Black Republican colleagues demanded that he not challenge Huberty. "They told me, 'If you don't drop out of this race, they are going to paint you out to be as the typical Black man who walked out on his family.'" Grant was in the middle of a divorce.[149]

Huberty's campaign challenged his residency. A judge eventually ruled against Grant, which, according to him, impacted the election, and he lost to Huberty.[150] Like many Black Republicans before him, Grant believed he was ultimately pushed out because he didn't "know his place." He said if he had obeyed the Black Republican rules, he could have possibly had a huge political career.

Reginald Grant officially left the Republican Party in 2019. He insisted that he was not intentionally grifting. He felt there needed to be a Black presence in the Texas GOP and said he would have supported policies that helped Black communities. I asked for his reaction to critics who might say he only left the party once he saw and experienced the GOP's bigotry. "In a sense, that is absolutely true," Grant conceded. But he stressed he was naive to the racist power structure of the Republican Party. He said Black people cannot exist in the GOP unless they are "saying the right things and championing policies of white supremacy."[151]

The GOP appreciates the optics of a Black Republican, but only if they know their place. During Black History Month, the Republican Party bragged in a 2022 tweet about "a record number of Black Republicans running for office and winning at all levels." According to their count, "Over 40 Black Republicans are running in GOP primaries for both local and federal office."[152] This is their "record." There were thousands of federal and state races in 2022, and the GOP celebrated forty.[153] No matter how small the percentage, the GOP seeks Black Republican coconspirators in their plan to subvert democracy. On the likes of Candace Owens, Herschel Walker, and the other Black Republicans in the cult of Trump, former Republican Shermichael Singleton remarked, "I've never needed the grift and insulting my people to elevate me for financial means. It becomes a question of character. It becomes a question of values for the Owens and the Walkers of the world."[154] Michael Steele, the one and only Black man to be chair of the RNC, said, "They are very dangerous because they are not moored to anything that is identifiable in the traditions of the Republican Party… It's about the grift; there is money to be made here. Identify the Black person, prop them up, put them out there, and they'll spew out what you want them to spew out."[155]

Days before the 2020 election, California representative Maxine Waters said on SiriusXM's *The Joe Madison Show*, "It just hurts me so bad to see Blacks talking about supporting Trump." Waters added, "Any of them showing their face, I will never ever forgive them for undermining the possibility to help their own people and their own communities. It is absolutely unconscionable."[156]

Waters is right. These charlatans should never be forgotten.

Thankfully, Joe Biden won the 2020 presidential election. Polls indicate Biden and Vice President Kamala Harris were victorious partly due to Black voters.[157] Black women and men supported the former vice president in historic numbers.[158] Despite how Black male Trump supporters were presented in early exit polls,[159] Black men voted for Biden more than any other male demographic.[160]

During the distressing four years of the Trump administration, we saw a flock of disingenuous opportunists gain notoriety by supporting a president with a long history of racism. There were Black Trump supporters who proudly went viral after insulting Black men who were killed by police,[161] claiming people like Representative Maxine Waters had a "low IQ,"[162] and telling Congress white nationalism was not an issue,[163] despite reports from the FBI.[164]

Let's not forget the hip-hop-pop stars who allegedly had secret meetings with Trump's son-in-law outside the White House.[165] Or Kanye West, who ran for president with a history of insulting freedom fighters like Harriet Tubman, and his publicist, who reportedly harassed a sixty-two-year-old Georgia election worker, which resulted in death threats.[166]

Trump's cult brought the grifters out of the closet, and most disappointingly, the work of Black Republicans who were not snakes was undermined. I spoke to Black Republicans who worked for the Republican Party before Trump with the promise our conversations remain off the record. They made biting statements about the racism in the GOP and the existing crop of Black Republicans. When I questioned why they only spoke off the record, I was told more than once they had moved on from politics.

I walked away not believing they had truly moved on. I was convinced they hoped to one day reenter GOP politics in a post-Trump Republican Party. They witnessed the racism from the inside but refused to speak out publicly. While they appeared to believe they were perched on moral high ground, how much better are they than a Candace Owens or a Herschel Walker? Their deafening silence is complicity.

WHAT'S NEXT?

"They are taking your rights away as you sleep."

—*Legendary actress Jenifer Lewis*[1]

THE REPUBLICAN PARTY IS HOPELESS IN ITS CURRENT STATE. IF there was doubt, the January 6 insurrection at the U.S. Capitol was bloody proof. The cult of Trump is not a small cluster within the GOP's base, and it's feeble-minded to doubt Trump's influence. As Republican Kevin McCarthy said after finally being elected Speaker of the House in January 2023, "I don't think anybody should doubt his [Trump's] influence."[2] QAnon conspiracy theories are the fundamental principles. Regardless of their failures in the 2022 midterms, Republicans are not moving away from the ideology of Trumpism. Repulsive behavior is normalized. Make America Great Again rage is a strong voting bloc, and the next insurrection won't be as loud as January 6. Expect the sequel to play out within local governments under the veil of states' rights, and elected officials, like a secretary of state or a governor, will follow their demands. With a propaganda infrastructure, the GOP seeks to rule, not govern. Like the Confederacy, the Republican Party is establishing torment by policy. There is a thin line between MAGA Republicans and mainstream Republicans. We must stop them.

It might surprise you that I think there is an answer in Black Republicanism, but not the kind pushed by the grifters of today. Can a Black leader function in the current Republican Party and not be an accomplice to the GOP's gruesome agenda? No. There is no saving the GOP—full stop. Privacy rights, voting, marriage, education, health care, democracy—the Republican ranks are plotting to reverse settled law. GOP leaders would sooner establish easier access to military-style rifles than to voting. Colin Powell, J. C. Watts, Will Hurd, Michael Steele, and others have proven that Black Republicans are not welcome if they are invested in helping diverse communities. As Watts stated nearly twenty years ago, the GOP expects Black Republicans to "denounce the experiences" they have as Black Americans. In October 2022, Steele told me he sees no space for Black people in the GOP. "The reality of it is, the party needs to account for its sins against the Black community."[3]

In 1864, the country would not have survived a Democratic administration. Incumbent president Abraham Lincoln was running against Democratic nominee George B. McClellan. At the time, the Democratic Party was a haven for white supremacy. Was Frederick Douglass begging for bipartisanship with Democrats in the 1860s? Was he trying to "understand where they are coming from," like many passive, liberal pundits argue today? Absolutely not. We must stop coddling Republicans with narratives like, "They're not all bad," and we must hear the "other side."

Were all Democrats terrible in the 1860s? Who cares? Our political crisis cannot be measured in degrees of anecdotal goodness. Douglass knew the danger of apathy for bigotry. He was visionary enough to mobilize citizens who believed in liberation, freedom, and a collective America. The pluralistic America of today, where Black Americans' aspirations and rights are respected, will not survive a Republican administration in 2024. The current GOP is as threatening as the Democratic Party was 160 years ago.

America is at the edge, but all is not lost just yet. My call to action is not to Black Republican grifters; this book has exposed them for who they are. My ask is to the people who can save humanity, not just democracy. We can reshape the current Democratic Party, where we have the most power, to push for an inclusive agenda that accepts no residue of worker exploitation, inhumane housing, poisonous health care, and white supremacy. Not just for Black people but for poor whites, the middle class, women, Native American communities, and every marginalized group beaten down by corporate goons disguised as leaders. Whether we are Douglass Republicans or post-Obama Democrats, we can win the long game if we learn from our past and play to win.

Many of us do not know our power or refuse to capitalize on it. Combined, nearly 180 million eligible voters did not participate in the 2016 and 2020 elections.[4] Grabbing just 10 percent of nonvoters, we can reimagine America to the Reconstruction vision intended to repair the country after the Civil War. How do we activate a nonvoter? I understand the nonvoter; I used to be one.

In 1995, I turned eighteen years old. I lived in West Philadelphia, watching drug wars ravage the city, infrastructure in shambles, and violent crime normalized. I would complain about my city, but when I was eligible to vote, I didn't register. I was convinced the system would never work for me or anyone in my community. This wasn't about partisan politics. In 1995, Philadelphia had Democratic mayor Ed Rendell, and Pennsylvania elected Republican governor Tom Ridge.

I knew of Mayor Rendell but had no clue who my two U.S. senators were, both Republicans and one being the horror that was Rick Santorum. I couldn't name Pennsylvania's attorney general and was unaware of who represented my district in the House of Representatives. How could I criticize my city but not know who represented me nationally or locally? I soon learned that politics will impact your life, regardless of your engagement.

My disengagement began with miseducation. While I was a solid student in school, I knew nothing about my history. Every February, I could predict our redundant Black History Month lessons. I heard the line, "People died for your right to vote," but there was no context. The Philadelphia school system did not teach me civics. I didn't know how the electoral college functioned. I didn't see the haunting 1964 congressional speech on voting rights from Fannie Lou Hamer. I would wear Malcolm X gear without knowing one line of his 1964 "The Ballot or the Bullet" speech. I saw Dr. Martin Luther King Jr.'s "I Have a Dream" speech, but no one told me that by 1967, he said the dream "turned into a nightmare."[5]

I was taught Black history began with enslaved people, and there was no mention of ancient Africa.

I was taught drug abuse was a Black issue, even though more whites were reported using drugs than Black people.[6]

I was taught welfare was a Black issue when more white people received federal assistance than any other demographic.[7]

I was purposely taught lies with the hopes I would remain uninformed. Being informed is too dangerous.

Regardless of race or nationality, millions of young people across America are exposed to propaganda steeped in education, which is the beginning of political detachment. When the principles of civic engagement are properly taught, a proactive electorate is a reasonable expectation. As a young person, I disengaged from the "system" because we believed it was a farce. In my neighborhood, voting was nearly inaccessible. Registering to vote, especially before widespread access to the internet, was not readily available. Lack of access to voting is another way to suppress the vote.

My circle of friends and I foolishly believed we were revolutionaries, bucking the system by not voting. My first memory of government intervention in Philadelphia was the 1984 bombing of MOVE, a Black liberation group. The City of Brotherly Love dropped a bomb on a block in Philadelphia to kill MOVE members living in a row house. Men, women, and children were killed, and more than sixty homes were destroyed.[8] We were rightfully angry but with no strategy.

We attended marches for Mumia Abu-Jamal, a Philadelphia man convicted of the 1982 killing of a police officer.[9] We worshipped Nina Simone, quoting every line to "Mississippi Goddam." We gathered our pennies and trekked to New York City to see Angela Davis or Cornell West speak. We joined community organizations. I was a member of a Black youth group titled 40 Acres, inspired by the term "forty acres and a mule." Yet we weren't using one of many tools in our toolbox—voting.

By September 2001, at twenty-four years old, I was living in the New York City area and saw the horrific terrorist attack on Manhattan's World Trade Center. I was terrified but still not able to tie politics with terrorism. I remember being profoundly disturbed when I saw President George Bush sitting in a Florida classroom for seven long minutes as the country was in turmoil. It further proved that most politicians are criminals, and we choose between the lesser of the two evils.

It took three more years for it all to click. In June 2004, during the Bush-Kerry presidential election, a friend took me to see Michael Moore's documentary *Fahrenheit 9/11*, which covered the 2000 election, 9/11, and the profit of war.[10]

I was revolted by President Bush in a tuxedo, saying, "Some people call you the elite; I call you my base."[11]

Michigan representative John Conyers floored me when he admitted, "We don't read most of the bills."[12]

I was moved when Corporal Abdul Henderson, refusing to go back to Iraq, said, "I will not let anyone send me back over there to kill other poor people, especially when they pose no threat to me and my country."[13]

The film was a demand for civic engagement without shaming you into voting. I walked out of the theater and immediately registered. I promised myself I would never dismiss my right to vote again. I was suppressing my own vote.

Right before my sophomore year at Rutgers University, Hurricane Katrina hit. Bush showed us in plain sight that he did not care about Black or poor people. I changed my major to Black studies; not only would I vote, but I would be informed, even if it cost me thousands in student loan debt. By 2008, I was a political junkie and volunteered for the Obama campaign in Philadelphia.

For too long, I accepted lies that my vote was useless. A vote is a voice, which is why the fight for representation is so vicious. Voting is not always about being the winner or attaining everything you want. Voting is a long game.

If you thought the last two presidential election cycles were brutal, 2024 will be a political bloodbath. Just as Democrats schemed to regain control over the South during Reconstruction, Republicans are plotting to reclaim power over the entire country, no matter the cost. Over 50 percent of Americans expect civil war, and I would argue many are craving war.[14]

We do not need violence. Violence is a cheap shot; political leverage is the endgame.

VOTER TURNOUT

In 1868, Black voter registration reached 80 percent.[15] The turnout elected Black and white leaders throughout the South who believed in biracial coalitions and upward mobility via federal policies and self-reliance. No one begged for handouts; they demanded economic justice after an economy based on slavery ended. The power of the Black vote changed the political landscape. The response was a strategic assault on the pursuit of life and liberty. Thankfully, we are not in the 1800s. The voting electorate is more diverse, and our power in the Democratic Party is stronger than ever. We are not maximizing this advantage.

Since 1964, Black voter turnout has surpassed 65 percent twice: in 2008 (65 percent) and 2012 (66.6 percent).[16] The numbers are even more dismal during midterm elections, never reaching above 50 percent since 1970.[17] In the 2020 election, when voting was made easier due to COVID, Black voter turnout hit 62.6 percent,[18] with 12 percent voting Republican.[19] Georgia went blue,[20] prompting the former president of the United States to ask Georgia's Republican secretary of state to "find" votes.[21]

Republicans were so petrified of Black voter turnout during the presidential election that the response was voter suppression laws, even with 12 percent voting for the GOP. By 2021, more than four hundred bills with provisions that restricted voting were introduced in forty-nine states.[22] How did the GOP accomplish this? Local elections, where policy that personally impacts you is crafted. When Republicans lose nationally, they strategize their politics beyond the White House: school boards, state legislatures, county commissioners, district attorneys, comptroller, dogcatcher; the list is endless.

If we want to effect change, we need consistent high voter turnout, especially in midterms and primaries. Yes, there is voter suppression, which should be accounted for, but Black men in the 1860s and 1870s endured life-threatening suppression and still managed to vote. You cannot declare, "Nothing ever changes!" when we have not collectively used the power of our vote to its fullest potential. High voter turnout will create local change with a national impact.

Suppose you don't know where to start. In that case, countless organizations are fighting for voter rights: Black Voters Matter, Color of Change, Stacey Abrams's Fair Fight Action, and Reverend Al Sharpton's National Action Network, just to name a few. Longtime organizations like the National Urban League and the NAACP are on the ground in nearly every major city. It's a myth that no one is doing the work. On my SiriusXM radio show, I have interviewed the leaders of these organizations. Their efforts may not be headline news, but they are fighting and need engagement to combat the GOP.

Many are calling for an end to the two-party system. While it's possible on a local level, it appears implausible on a national level, and the effect a third-party candidate has on election outcomes is splitting the vote.

In 1992, Ross Perot's candidacy pulled votes away from Bush, partially helping President Bill Clinton to win.[23]

In 2000, the Green Party contributed to Gore's loss, with Ralph Nader earning nearly three million votes. Nader won over ninety-seven thousand in Florida, where the election recount nightmare occurred.[24]

Even in 1864, Frederick Douglass and several hundred Republicans formed the Radical Democracy Party hoping not to reelect Lincoln. When it was clear Lincoln's proslavery challenger could win, the Radical Democracy Party pulled out of the election.

I understand the sentiment for a multiparty system, but expanding the two-party system will not solve our political ills. Austria has a multiparty system; in 2019, 90 percent of Austrians said their political system was corrupt.[25] Brazil has a multiparty system and is rife with corruption; the same goes for Pakistan. A two-party or multiparty system is useless if the people in power are crooked. Instead of the lesser of the two evils—a concept I reject; only one party is the party of evil—voters will complain about the lesser of the three, four, or five evils.

There is a solution in history. Founded in 1854, the Radical Republican Party was a party within the Republican Party. With leaders like John Frémont, Charles Sumner, Thaddeus Stevens, and Ulysses S. Grant, the Fourteenth Amendment and the Fifteenth Amendment passed. These amendments ushered in Black elected officials throughout the South. They believed in working within the party to create change.

In *The Devil You Know: A Black Power Manifesto*, author Charles Blow suggested that Black people should migrate back to the South in large numbers and vote Republican to overtake the party.[26] He called it a second Great Migration that would be "the most audacious power play by Black America in the history of the country." There is already a large population of Black people

in states like Texas, Alabama, and Mississippi, but that has not
shifted or diminished Republican dominance. As a base, Black
voters already hold substantial power as Democrats in states like
Georgia. Consider the Radical Republican Party of the 1860s or
the Tea Party of the 2000s. The Tea Party didn't create a third
party; they infiltrated the GOP to advance their policy platform.

At this point, a third-party option or a Republican Party take-
over is not a strategic use of our vote on a national level. There
are elected officials on the rise who are much different from the
Democrats of the 1990s or the early 2000s. Take a page from the
Tea Party or the MAGA Party: mobilize within, and support the
plethora of candidates who will make neo-Dixiecrats nonfactors.

BLACK CAPITALISM AND FREEDOM

From Nixon Black Republicans to celebrities, it's a classist lie
that opening more Black businesses and buying Black will trickle
down to the average Black worker. Even with the title "buying
Black" attached, trickle-down economics has never translated into
long-standing community success. I am not saying there shouldn't
be Black-owned businesses, but helping the working poor is more
than entrepreneurship.

A disproportionate 20 percent of Black people are employed
in the public sector.[27] Being a business owner might not be for
everybody. Some people want a pension and health care attached
to their employment. It's misleading to tell people that they can
simply save their pennies and crawl out of poverty as a business
owner. What about people who cannot launch a small business?
Sadly, many people living in poverty, Black or white, will not reach
middle-class status. For Black men, it's worse. Black men are less

likely, out of any demographic, to rise out of poverty or more likely to fall into poverty.[28] The people who work the hardest get paid the least. Capitalism does not reward hard work. Why? Because the federal government does not protect quality of opportunity, and Black communities are severely impacted.

Am I against capitalism? No. I'm against the kind of exploitative capitalism that has found Black Americans disproportionately at the bottom. But demanding an end to capitalism in these United States is like saying there should be no two-party system. It's not practical. There can be a form of equality in capitalism with proper support from the federal government, which has been done before under the administrations of Lincoln and Grant, both Republicans. The country is very different than it was in the 1860s. Even so, the answers are in the not-too-distant past; let's go back to 1967.

According to Bayard Rustin, the limitation of the civil rights movement of that era was a focus only on three issues: voting, the right to public accommodations, and allowing parents to send their children to the school they chose. In 1979, Rustin explained, "It [the civil rights movement] did not invest itself, in any way, in the economic and social problems of Black people."[29] Twelve years before, in 1967, A. Philip Randolph and Rustin attempted to shift the focus with "A Freedom Budget for All Americans," endorsed by Dr. Martin Luther King Jr. and the basis for his Poor People's Campaign.[30]

In the introduction, King wrote, "The tragedy is that the workings of our economy so often pit the white poor and the Black poor against each other at the bottom of society. The tragedy is that groups only one generation removed from poverty themselves, haunted by the memory of scarcity and fearful of slipping back, step on the fingers of those struggling up the ladder."

He continued. "This is what the 'Freedom Budget' is. It is not visionary or utopian. It is feasible. It is concrete. It is specific. It is quantitative. It talks dollars and cents. It sets goals and priorities. It tells how these can be achieved. And it places the responsibility for leadership with the Federal Government, which alone has the resources equal to the task. The 'Freedom Budget' is not a call for a handout. It is a challenge to the best traditions and possibilities of America."

The Freedom Budget included many solutions, but one of the most critical proposals was the minimum wage. Randolph and Rustin demanded a $2 minimum wage; the federal minimum wage was a shameful $1.40 in 1967.[31] The pushback against the minimum wage was the same argument we hear today: "Small businesses can't afford a higher minimum wage!"

The Freedom Budget had an answer: subsidies from the government. Before elite Republicans say, "The government can't afford that!" note that the rich have been receiving subsidies for decades—corporate welfare. Pharmaceutical companies, airlines, and the country's biggest retail stores receive billions that rarely reach the average worker.[32]

Dr. King's Poor People's Campaign also presented an "economic bill of rights" with five planks: "a meaningful job at a living wage," a secure and adequate income "for those who can't find work," "access to land," "access to capital," and the "ability for ordinary people to play a truly significant role in the government." He demanded a federal government investment of $30 billion for the anti-poverty package.[33] Reverend William Barber has continued the work of the Poor People's Campaign, which can be reached at PoorPeoplesCampaign.org.

When revisiting the economic vision of the party of Lincoln

and the Radical Republican Party, under the umbrella of including Black and brown people, we cannot forget the importance of the federal government. As historian Heather Cox Richardson stated, Lincoln created an activist government "for America that is designed to guarantee that every man has an equal opportunity to rise… It's a fundamental reworking of what America is supposed to do and a fundamental reworking of the relationship between individuals and the government."[34]

An activist government does not start with the elite. It is not about rugged individualism; it's not a grift. It doesn't focus on the upper or middle class, abandoning low-income communities. Most poor people, Black or white, work jobs for starvation wages.

The Freedom Budget is not a panacea; it's an economic infrastructure for fighting poverty. The answers aren't innovative or elusive. There are several blueprints, from the Radical Republican Party to the Poor People's Campaign, for a working community with the federal government's assistance to cultivate property ownership, equal access to education, and fair wages. As Philadelphia teacher and activist Paul Prescod stated, "Build the labor movement and a strong welfare state. The majority of Black people have only made significant progress when there has been strong federal policies to redistribute wealth and power."[35] We need elected officials in office who can execute the blueprint, if not nationally, then locally.

BET ON BLACK

Black candidates need the support of the Democratic Party. I've interviewed many candidates for public office who say the Democratic establishment is not supporting them, partly because they are not seen as "winning" candidates. Too many Democrats still think the traditional, moderate white candidate is the winning formula.

In July 2019, failed presidential candidate New York senator Kirsten Gillibrand said she could talk to other white women because she is a white woman.[36] By August, she dropped out of the race.

Another failed presidential candidate, Minnesota senator Amy Klobuchar, often said that she was from the Midwest so she could gain the "real America" vote.

Vermont senator Bernie Sanders and former presidential candidate insisted Democrats should commit to spending more resources in traditionally red states. So much so he was in Mississippi in January 2020 and complained that President Barack Obama only received 10 percent of the white vote in the state. He claimed this showed the "very bad work" by Democrats and the belief that "90 percent of white people in Mississippi are not racist."[37] I am surprised Obama got 1 percent of the white vote in Mississippi. For a state that didn't officially abolish slavery until 2013,[38] a Black candidate winning 10 percent of the vote is a miracle.

When do you hear Republicans claim they will win New York or California? The GOP rarely campaigns, unless there is redistricting, in blue states and never talks about their "very bad work" of barely grabbing the Black vote. Democrats can learn from Republicans: Passionately speak to the base.

Republicans sell the lies of critical race theory, the scary transgender community, and the dangers of "wokeness" as bait. How are Democrats going to bait their base to make their most loyal voting bloc feel heard and seen? Bet and invest in qualified Black candidates. Black voter turnout increases with Black candidates who, most importantly, will address the nuanced issues of our communities.

Whites have voted majority Republican in every presidential election since the signing of the Civil Rights Act of 1964.[39] Hillary Clinton, John Kerry, and Al Gore failed with the white vote. President Bill Clinton didn't nab the majority of the white vote and won twice. Therefore, why would Democrats think they have the power to convert whites who consistently vote along party lines? There is a base of whites who vote Democrat, but Black and brown voters swing elections. The talk of appealing to the majority of white voters is delusional, especially with coded language like "the real America," "rural America," "the soccer mom," or "working class"—as if Black people can't be real, rural, soccer moms, or working class.

Today, Republicans recognize the power of promoting Black candidates. Experience is not a prerequisite if they stick to the GOP game plan. Republican leaders do not need or want Black voters. They use Black Republicans as racial cover and a veil of inclusion to entice their base. On the other hand, Democrats still doubt the power of a Black, experienced candidate.

In 2016, when then Minnesota representative Keith Ellison, who is Black and Muslim, was campaigning to be the Democratic National Committee chairman, a supporter of Tom Perez, who would become the DNC chair in 2017, said, "We like Keith. But is he really the guy we need right now when we are trying to get all of those disaffected white working-class people to rally around our message of economic equality?" [40]

The perspective that Black candidates are unappealing to white voters is outdated. As racial demographics shift in the country, the

Democratic Party needs as much diversity in their elected officials as they have in their base. In 2024, to maintain our democracy, the power brokers in the Democratic Party must support and energetically invest in Black candidates.

Lastly, once our elected officials are in office, we must force them to keep their promises. Attend city council and school board meetings, call your local representative, and, if possible, run for office. Voting is one of the numerous steps to power. That said, "hold them accountable" can be a loaded, trite one-liner. In today's politics, the GOP is rarely ever held accountable, and party loyalty is unwavering. When the GOP loses, they strategize. It took fifty years to overturn *Roe v. Wade*, and GOP voters weren't declaring, "Overturn abortion now or we won't vote!" Loss is only temporary for Republicans. Their voters stand by their side, even if policy isn't passed in their lifetime. Democrats are quickly held accountable for the slightest infraction and cannibalize their own. With a more diversified base, it is a challenge to give solutions to everybody. I hear demands for "Tangibles!"—but tangibles are also a long game that many refuse to play. So yes, hold Democrats accountable, and push for legislation that moves the needle, but do not forget to embrace the victories. Nearly every piece of progressive policy since the 1930s has come from the Democratic Party: the New Deal, the Civil Rights Act of 1964, voting rights, hate crimes legislation, and the Affordable Care Act. The Democratic Party is far from perfect, but we must celebrate and sell our wins. If we don't, then even a win can be spun as a loss—a game wishy-washy pundits play—which suppresses our voice, only giving more power to the party that consistently dodges accountability, even when crimes are committed in plain sight.

IN CLOSING

Months before the 2022 midterm elections, legendary actress Jenifer Lewis warned, "They are taking your rights away as you sleep."[41]

The "they" is the Republican Party. Whether people will admit it or not, one party is actively plotting, through obstruction, to chip away at our freedoms. This isn't partisan; this is truth. We must accept that reality and identify the enemy and its enablers. If not, we are doomed. The GOP is digging into the archives of white supremacy, not just to harm Black communities but anyone and anything that improves the lives of people of all backgrounds.

Adversaries who look like us are gaining access to power with an unprecedented level of poison. From social media to the ballot box, beware of grifters; they cannot be trusted. Study your history. Vote, locally and nationally, like it's 1868, when 80 percent of Black voters were registered.

I understand everybody doesn't agree with me on every issue, but there are some areas where we must be on the same page. Our votes cannot be overturned. Our rights cannot be reversed. Our guns cannot be more valuable than our lives. To un-grift the grift, we must become a monolith against white supremacy. Without that agreement and with Black Republicans not applying pressure to their party, there is no solution to their grift. There is also no way to hide the truth that one party fundamentally does not care about or respect the interests of marginalized people.

The United States of America was originally created for a narrow group of wealthy white men, but America was built to change. The Constitution was made to evolve, and so were the American people. On my SiriusXM radio show in August 2022, Doug Jones, former Democratic senator of Alabama, said something I will never forget. While he expressed serious concerns about the country's direction, especially the U.S. Supreme Court, Jones told me on live radio, "The United States was destined to be a multicultural, multiracial society."[42] Jones's comment restored my faith in America. Regardless of the framers' hateful vision, our country's greatest survival skill is our multiethnic and multifaceted citizens. The cardinal sin of this century would be the undoing of progress that has been built into policies.

I love my country because it was built on the broken backs of enslaved people, Africans, poor whites, Native Americans, immigrants, and more. Therefore, my message is two-pronged. I am both calling out and calling in. Every election, a fresh group of unapologetic and brilliant citizens are elected to Congress, but they need our support. There are firebrand candidates who do the work, ready to replace grifters. In them, I see hope. Finally, to Black Republicans who are willing Judases, may history be ruthless to the legacy of betrayal you left behind.

Acknowledgments

MY HOPE WITH THIS BOOK WAS TO RECLAIM REVISIONIST HIStory, expose opportunists, and honor heroes. It was no easy journey. There are many people, experiences, conversations, interviews, and heated debates that allowed me to make this book a reality.

I would like to specifically express gratitude to my representation at Collective 5 Entertainment (Yona Deshommes, Jeff Rivera, Rockelle Henderson, Lavaille Lavette), my phenomenal editor Brandon Proia, fact-checker Alexander Johnson, and Karen Hunter for blessing me with a platform when very people few believed in me. Also, thanks to former and current Republicans who I interviewed, Shermichael Singleton, Reginald Grant, Michael Steele, and several others who would only talk off the record.

This book would not be possible without my teachers from many years ago at Rutgers University. Barbara Foley, Dr. Wendell Hoolbrook, and Dr. Zain Abdullah, it has been over a decade, but your passion for history and analysis changed my life.

Thank you to my friends, family, and brilliant minds who gave me invaluable feedback, Keith Boykin, Lurie Daniel Favors, Qasim Rashid, Dr. Ted Johnson, Patrick Lynn Washington, GeColby Youngblood, Reecie Colbert, Allen Orr, Richard Fowler, Antar

Bush, Alexa Munoz, Charles Stein, Nicole Ray, Jeremiah Jones, Smriti Mundhra, Shani Saxon, Andrew McCaskill, Ameshia Cross, Ted Winn, and Monroe France. Endless love to my mother and father who were always clear about race. They armed me with affirmations and passed on their life lessons, which I have never forgotten.

Big thanks to the phenomenal work of great historians, educators, and leaders like W. E. B. DuBois, Bayard Rustin, Eric Foner, Leah Wright Rigueur, Joshua Farrington, Tim Wise, Lawrence Otis Graham, Julius E. Thompson, Philip Dray, Reverend Jesse Jackson, Reverend Al Sharpton, Jane Elliott, Roland Martin, Dr. Michael Eric Dyson, and Lerone Bennett Jr. Their work, whether in the classroom or on the streets, have helped to free people from dangerous misinformation.

Lastly, to the original Black Republicans, the first progressives, who saw a country where people of all backgrounds flourished, I hope I added to the work of countless others who have attempted to rescue history from liars and snakes. The United Daughters of the Confederacy, William A. Dunning, D. W. Griffith, and too many others set this country back with their racist propaganda. Sadly, their Lost Cause narratives are resurfacing from Virginia to Florida to Texas, but we shall not be moved.

Notes

INTRODUCTION

1   Martin Luther King Jr. "The Summer of Our Discontent," speech, New School for Social Research, Amherst College, February 6, 1964, Amherst, MA, transcript, https://www.amherst.edu/library/archives/holdings/mlk/transcript.

2   Robert E. Hemenway, *Zora Neale Hurston: A Literary Biography* (Champaign: University of Illinois Press, 1980), 285.

3   Gillian Brockel, "Gabriel's Revolt: In 1800, He Was Savvy, Armed and Determined to End Slavery in Virginia's Capital," *Washington Post*, August 23, 2019, https://www.washingtonpost.com/history/2019/08/23/gabriels-revolt-he-was-savvy-armed-determined-end-slavery-virginias-capital.

4   "Death or Liberty: Gabriel's Conspiracy," Library of Virginia, accessed June 1, 2022, https://www.lva.virginia.gov/exhibits/deathliberty/gabriel/index.htm.

5   Thomas Wentworth Higginson, "The Story of Denmark Vesey," *Atlantic*, June 1861, https://www.theatlantic.com/magazine/archive/1861/06/denmark-vesey/396239.

6   James O'Neil Spady, "Power and Confession: On the Credibility of the Earliest Reports of the Denmark Vesey Slave Conspiracy," *William and Mary Quarterly* 68, no. 2 (April 2011): 287–304, http://doi.org/10.5309/willmaryquar.68.2.0287.

7   "Love, Ludmya Bourdeau (Mia)," History, Art & Archives, United States House of Representatives, accessed August 1, 2022, https://history.house.gov/People/Detail/15032411201.

8   "J.C. Watts on Why the 'Race Issue' Is Costing Republicans Black Voters," Yahoo Life, August 13, 2020, https://www.yahoo.com/lifestyle/j-c-watts-why-race-233429005.html.

9   Frederick Douglass, "The Race Problem," speech, Bethel Literary and Historical Association, October 21, 1890, Washington, DC, National Humanities Center, transcript, http://nationalhumanitiescenter.org/pds/maai2/politics/text2/douglass.pdf.

10   Tim Scott, "Sen. Tim Scott: S.1 Is Not a Voting Rights Bill, It's a Partisan Power Grab That Will Harm Faith in Elections," Fox News, May 20, 2021, https://www.foxnews.com/opinion/s-1-voting-rights-elections-sen-tim-scott.

11   "Sen. Tim Scott Defends Vote to Repeal Affordable Care Act," WIS-TV, Columbia, SC, January 12, 2017, https://www.wistv.com/story/34242811/sen-tim-scott-defends-vote-to-repeal-affordable-care-act.

12   "Tim Scott Criticizes Democrats for 'George Floyd' Bill after Filibustering His Police Reforms," Senator Tim Scott (website), March 2, 2021, https://www.scott.senate.gov/media-center/in-the-news/tim-scott-criticizes-democrats-for-george-floyd-bill-after-filibustering-his-police-reforms.

13   Julie Carey, "Va. GOP Nomination for Lt. Gov. Draws Controversy with Campaign Photo of Rifle," WRC-TV, Washington, DC, May 15, 2021, https://www.nbcwashington.com/news/va-gop-nomination-for-lt-gov-draws-controversy-with-campaign-photo-of-rifle/2672742/.

14   Joshua Q. Nelson, "Virginia GOP Lieutenant Governor Nominee Slams Critical Race Theory Curriculum as 'Nonsense,'" Fox News, May 13, 2021, https://www.foxnews.com/media/virginia-republican-winsome-sears-critical-race-theory-nonsense.

15   "Fox News's Gutfeld Says Winsome Sears 'Dared to Leave the Plantation of Ideology,'" Media Matters, November 3, 2021, https://www.mediamatters.org/greg-gutfeld/fox-news-gutfeld-says-winsome-sears-dared-leave-plantation-ideology.

16   Annie Karni and Jonathan Weisman, "'I Will Not Sit Quietly': 3 Black Senators in Spotlight on Voting Rights," New York Times, January 20, 2022, https://www.nytimes.com/2022/01/20/us/politics/voting-rights-cory-booker-tim-scott.html.

17   "Herschel Walker Testifies to Congress against Reparations Bill," Forbes Breaking News, February 17, 2021, YouTube video, 5:56, https://youtu.be/o9di_2l21As.

18   King, "Summer of Our Discontent."

19   "Edward Brooke: A Featured Biography," United States Senate, accessed June 1, 2022, https://www.senate.gov/senators/FeaturedBios/Featured_Bio_Brooke.htm.

20   "Watts, Julius Caesar Jr. (J. C.)," History, Art & Archives, United States House of Representatives, accessed May 30, 2023, https://history.house.gov/People/Detail/23468.

21   Chris Canipe and Jason Lange, "The Republicans Who Voted to Overturn the Election," Reuters Graphics, February 4, 2021, https://www.reuters.com/graphics/USA-TRUMP/LAWMAKERS/xegpbedzdvq/.

22   The Clay Cane Show, aired April 15, 2021, on SiriusXM Urban View.

23   "Trump: I've Done More for Black People Than Anyone, Maybe Lincoln," NBC News, July 22, 2020, video, 1:18, https://www.nbcnews.com/now/video/trump-says-he-has-done-more-for-black-people-than-anyone-with-possible-exception-of-lincoln-88141381811.

24   Tom Dreisbach, "RNC Speaker Facing Federal Charges of Insider Trading," NPR, August 25, 2020, https://www.npr.org/2020/08/25/905953942/rnc-speaker-facing-federal-charges-of-insider-trading.

25   Ed Kilgore, "Why White Racists Can Vote for Black Republicans," New York Magazine, November 12, 2021, https://nymag.com/intelligencer/2021/11/why-white-racists-can-vote-for-black-republicans.html.

26   Pat Moran, "'I'm Not Ashamed': Republican Candidate for Lieutenant Governor Blast-

ed for Racist, Homophobic Posts," *Cardinal & Pine*, October 1, 2020, https://cardinalpine.com/story/im-not-ashamed-meet-the-gop-lieutenant-governor-candidate-under-fire-for-homophobic-racist-posts.

27 "Results of SurveyUSA News Poll #26290," SurveyUSA, April 11, 2022, https://www.surveyusa.com/client/PollReport.aspx?g=1908f972-2f76-48ec-9a89-7f421e135e05.

28 Kesley Koberg, "Fight against Critical Race Theory Will Be 'Long and Bitter Struggle,' Says NC Lieutenant Governor," Fox News, October 8, 2021, https://www.foxnews.com/media/mark-robinson-critical-race-theory-struggle-north-carolina.

29 Lauren Windsor (@lawindsor), "NEW: Trump strategist Steve Bannon told PA Republicans in Gettysburg: 'African-American males are also another central part of our coalition,'" Twitter, November 8, 2021, 5:30 p.m., https://twitter.com/lawindsor/status/1457837943201189895.

30 Advertisement for an Ida B. Wells public speech, *Washington Bee*, October 22, 1892, https://chroniclingamerica.loc.gov/lccn/sn84025891/1892-10-29/ed-1/seq-3/.

CHAPTER 1: DOUGLASS

1 Frederick Douglass, "An Oration in Memory of Abraham Lincoln," April 14, 1876, Washington, DC, University of Rochester Frederick Douglass Project, transcript, https://rbscp.lib.rochester.edu/4402.

2 Edward Steers Jr., "Reconsidering Abraham Lincoln's Legacy Is All Well and Good—But You Can't Argue With Results," *Time*, April 15, 2021, https://time.com/5954962/abraham-lincoln-historical-revision.

3 Kate Masur, "What 6 Historians Want You to Know about Abraham Lincoln," CNN, February 14, 2021, https://www.cnn.com/2021/02/14/opinions/abraham-lincoln-divided-we-stand-roundup/index.html.

4 Andrew Lang, "Trump Betrays the Party of Lincoln," *Atlantic*, January 5, 2021, https://www.theatlantic.com/ideas/archive/2021/01/trump-betrays-party-lincoln/617547.

5 Francis Clines, "Powell Rules Out '96 Race; Cites Concerns for Family and His Lack of 'a Calling,'" *New York Times*, November 9, 1995, https://www.nytimes.com/1995/11/09/us/powell-decision-announcement-powell-rules-96-race-cites-concerns-for-family-his.html.

7 Jon Meacham, "Henry Louis Gates Jr. on African-American Religion," review of *The Black Church: This Is Our Story, This Is Our Song*, by Henry Louis Gates Jr., *New York Times*, February 16, 2021, https://www.nytimes.com/2021/02/16/books/review/henry-louis-gates-jr-the-black-church.html.

8 Henry Louis Gates Jr. and John Stauffer, "Five Myths about Frederick Douglass," *Washington Post*, February 10, 2017, https://www.washingtonpost.com/opinions/five-myths-about-frederick-douglass/2017/02/10/0aaeb592-ea3b-11e6-bf6f-301b6b443624_story.html.

9   "Oration in Memory of Abraham Lincoln."

10   Jon Greenberg, "Napolitano: Lincoln Enforced the Fugitive Slave Act," PolitiFact, March 18, 2014, https://www.politifact.com/factchecks/2014/mar/18/andrew -napolitano/napolitano-lincoln-enforced-fugitive-slave-act.

11   "Fugitive Slave Law of 1850," Ohio History Central, accessed March 1, 2022, https://ohiohistorycentral.org/w/Fugitive_Slave_Law_of_1850.

12   "Mr. Lincoln and Negro Equality," *New York Times*, December 28, 1860, https:// www.nytimes.com/1860/12/28/archives/mr-lincoln-and-negro-equality.html.

13   John Stauffer, "Lincoln and Douglass Shared Uncommon Bond," interview by Michael Martin, *Tell Me More*, NPR, February 16, 2009, https://www.npr.org /templates/story/story.php?storyId=100694897.

14   William C. Davis, "Life in Civil War America," in *A Concise History of the Civil War* (Fort Washington, PA: Eastern National, 2007), http://npshistory.com /publications/civil_war_series/4/sec1.htm.

15   Curtis Harris, "#NeverLincoln: Abolitionists and the 1860 Election," President Lincoln's Cottage, August 9, 2016, https://www.lincolncottage.org/neverlincoln -abolitionists-and-the-1860-election/.

16   Abraham Lincoln, "First Inaugural Address," March 4, 1861, Lillian Goldman Law Library of Yale University, transcript, https://avalon.law.yale.edu/19th_century /lincoln1.asp.

17   Greenberg, "Napolitano."

18   "Civil War Begins," United States Senate, accessed June 1, 2022, https://www .senate.gov/artandhistory/history/minute/Civil_War_Begins.htm.

19   "April 15, 1861: President Lincoln Calls Congress into Emergency Session," United States Senate, accessed June 1, 2022, https://www.senate.gov/artandhistory/history /common/civil_war/LincolnEmergencySession_FeaturedDoc.htm.

20   "Black Soldiers in the U.S. Military during the Civil War," National Archives, last reviewed September 1, 2017, https://www.archives.gov/education/lessons/blacks -civil-war.

21   "Black Soldiers in the U.S. Military."

22   James McPherson, "Lincoln as Commander in Chief," *Smithsonian Magazine*, January 2009, https://www.smithsonianmag.com/history/lincoln-as-commander -in-chief-131322819/.

23   Vincent Harding, *There is a River: The Black Struggle for Freedom in America* (Boston: Houghton Mifflin Harcourt, 1981), 221.

24   "African Americans and the Defenses of Washington," Civil Defenses of Washington, DC, National Park Service, last updated August 27, 2020, https:// www.nps.gov/cwdw/learn/historyculture/african-americans-and-the-defenses-of -washington.htm.

25   "Living Contraband—Former Slaves in the Nation's Capital during the Civil War," National Park Service, last updated August 15, 2017, https://www.nps.gov/articles/living -contraband-former-slaves-in-the-nation-s-capital-during-the-civil-war.htm.

26   Dave Davies, "From Slavery to 'American Wonder': Revisiting Frederick Doug-
      lass' Remarkable Life," *Fresh Air*, NPR, December 17, 2018, https://www.npr
      .org/2018/12/17/677350952/from-slavery-to-american-wonder-revisiting
      -frederick-douglass-remarkable-life.

27   "Proclamation Revoking General David Hunter's General Order No. 11 on
      Military Emancipation of Slaves, May 19, 1862," Iowa Department of Cul-
      tural Affairs, accessed June 2, 2022, https://iowaculture.gov/sites/default/files
      /history-education-pss-afamcivil-hunter-transcription.pdf.

28   James M. McPherson, *Battle Cry of Freedom: The Civil War Era* (New York: Oxford
      University Press, 2003), 354.

29   "District of Columbia Emancipation Act of 1862," C-SPAN, April 16, 2019, video,
      1:27:54, https://www.c-span.org/video/?459859-1/district-columbia-emancipation
      -act-1862#.

30   Damani Davis, "Slavery and Emancipation in the Nation's Capital," *Prologue* 42,
      no. 1 (Spring 2010), https://www.archives.gov/publications/prologue/2010/spring
      /dcslavery.html.

31   Paul Finkelman, "The Revolutionary Summer of 1862," *Prologue* 49, no. 4 (Winter
      2017–18), https://www.archives.gov/publications/prologue/2017/winter/summer
      -of-1862.

32   Jon Greenberg, "Jon Stewart: Lincoln Tried to Buy Slaves to Free Them," PolitiFact,
      March 18, 2014, https://www.politifact.com/factchecks/2014/mar/18/jon-stewart
      /jon-stewart-lincoln-tried-buy-slaves-free-them/.

33   Gideon Welles, *Diary of Gideon Welles*, vol. 1, *1861–March 30, 1864* (New York:
      Houghton Mifflin, 1911), 70.

34   *Encyclopaedia Britannica*, s.v. "Confiscation Acts," last updated July 30, 2020, https://
      www.britannica.com/event/Confiscation-Acts.

35   Lerone Bennett Jr., *Forced Into Glory: Abraham Lincoln's White Dream* (Chicago:
      Johnson, 2007), 448.

36   James F. Rhodes, *History of the United States from the Compromise of 1850*, vol. 4,
      1862–1864 (London: Macmillan, 1920), 63–64.

37   James McPherson, "What Did He Really Think about Race?," *New York Re-
      view of Books*, March 29, 2007, https://www.nybooks.com/articles/2007/03/29
      /what-did-he-really-think-about-race/.

38   Horace Greeley, "A Prayer for Twenty Millions," *New York Tribune*, August 20,
      1862, https://www.americanantiquarian.org/Manuscripts/greeley.html.

39   Abraham Lincoln, "A Letter from the President," clipping from the *Daily Na-
      tional Intelligencer*, Washington, DC, August 23, 1862, Abraham Lincoln Pa-
      pers, Library of Congress, https://www.loc.gov/resource/mal.4233400/?st=text&r
      =0.036,-0.144,1.126,1.049,0.

40   "Preliminary Emancipation Proclamation, 1862," American Originals, Nation-
      al Archives and Records Administration, https://www.archives.gov/exhibits
      /american_originals_iv/sections/preliminary_emancipation_proclamation.html.

41 "An Appeal from the Colored Men of Philadelphia to the President of the United States, 1862," in Herbert Aptheker, ed., *A Documentary History of the Negro People in the United States*, vol. 1, *From the Colonial Times through the Civil War* (New York: Citadel, 1960), 474.

42 Louis Jacobson, "Did Abraham Lincoln Plan to Send Ex-Slaves to Central America after the Civil War?," PolitiFact, June 26, 2015, https://www.politifact.com /factchecks/2015/jun/26/blog-posting/did-abraham-lincoln-plan-send-ex-slaves -central-am/.

43 Tera Hunter, "When Slaveowners Got Reparations," *New York Times,* April 16, 2019, https://www.nytimes.com/2019/04/16/opinion/when-slaveowners-got-reparations .html.

44 Graham D. Welch, "Île à Vache and Colonization: The Tragic End of Lincoln's 'Suicidal Folly,'" *Gettysburg College Journal of the Civil War Era* 4, (April 2014): 45–81, https://cupola.gettysburg.edu/gcjcwe/vol4/iss1/5/.

45 Charles H. Wesley, "Lincoln's Plan for Colonizing the Emancipated Negroes," *Journal of Negro History* 4, no. 1 (January 1919): 7–21, https://doi.org/10.2307/2713705.

46 Benjamin F. Butler, *Butler's Book* (Boston: A. M. Thayer, 1892), 903.

47 Abraham Lincoln, "The Emancipation Proclamation," National Archives, last reviewed January 28, 2022, https://www.archives.gov/exhibits/featured-documents /emancipation-proclamation.

48 Bennett, *Forced Into Glory*, 448.

49 Janell Ross, "America's Understanding of Emancipation Proclamation on Its 150th Anniversary Too Simple for Country's Own Good," HuffPost, January 1, 2013, https:// www.huffpost.com/entry/emancipation-proclamation-150th-anniversary_n_2392876.

50 "The Emancipation Proclamation: Eric Foner and Julie Golia in Conversation," Center for Brooklyn History, January 26, 2016, YouTube video, 1:21:07, https:// youtu.be/We9rnHa4iiI.

51 Nina Strochlic, "How Slavery Flourished in the United States," *National Geographic*, August 23, 2019, https://www.nationalgeographic.com/culture/article/how -slavery-flourished-united-states-chart-maps.

52 Sarah Pruitt, "5 Things You May Not Know About Abraham Lincoln, Slavery and Emancipation," History, September 21, 2012, https://www.history.com/news /5-things-you-may-not-know-about-lincoln-slavery-and-emancipation.

53 Nicholas Wu et al., "'Insensitive and Isolated': Rev. Sharpton Slams Trump at Tulsa Juneteenth Celebration," *USA Today*, June 19, 2020, https://www .usatoday.com/story/news/politics/elections/2020/06/19/trump-tulsa-rally -curfew-imposed-mayor/3221319001.

54 "NIST Builds a Secure Home for the 'Second Declaration of Independence,'" NIST, April 11, 2018, https://www.nist.gov/nist-time-capsule/making-nist-case -preservation/nist-builds-secure-home-second-declaration.

55 "Black Soldiers in the Civil War," National Archives, last reviewed March 19, 2019, https://www.archives.gov/education/lessons/blacks-civil-war/douglass-sons.html.

56 DeNeen L. Brown, "Frederick Douglass Needed to See Lincoln: Would the President Meet with a Former Slave?," *Washington Post*, February 14, 2018, https://www.washingtonpost.com/news/retropolis/wp/2018/02/14/frederick -douglass-needed-to-see-lincoln-would-the-president-meet-with-a-former -slave/.

57 "With Malice Toward None: The Abraham Lincoln Bicentennial Exhibition," Library of Congress, accessed September 1, 2022, https://www.loc.gov/exhibits/lincoln /lincoln-and-frederick-douglass.html.

58 Kate Masur, "The African American Delegation to Abraham Lincoln: A Reappraisal," *Civil War History* 56, no. 2 (June 2010): 117–44, http://doi.org/10.1353 /cwh.0.0149.

59 Brown, "Frederick Douglass Needed."

60 "The Fort Pillow Massacre," *New York Times*, May 3, 1864, https://www.nytimes .com/1864/05/03/archives/the-fort-pillow-massacre.html.

61 "1864: The Civil War Election," Campaigning for the U.S. Presidency (exhibit), Cornell University Library, 2004, https://rmc.library.cornell.edu/vote/1864 /index.html.

62 "Hannibal Hamlin Takes Vice Presidential Oath," United States Senate, accessed June 2, 2022, https://www.senate.gov/artandhistory/history/minute/Hannibal _the_corporal.htm.

63 David Priess, "How a Difficult, Racist, Stubborn President Was Removed From Power—If Not From Office," Politico, November 13, 2018, https://www.politico .com/magazine/story/2018/11/13/andrew-johnson-undermined-congress-cabinet -david-priess-book-222413/.

64 Jules Witcover, "Lincoln's Vice-Presidential Switch Changed History," *Chicago Tribune*, November 16, 2014, https://www.chicagotribune.com/columns /sns-201411141300--tms--poltodayctnyq-a20141116-20141116-column.html; Jules Witcover, "Lincoln's Successor Problem," Politico, April 13, 2015, https://www .politico.com/magazine/story/2015/04/lincoln-vice-president-hamlin-116930/.

65 "Wade-Davis Bill (1864)," National Archives, last reviewed May 10, 2022, https:// www.archives.gov/milestone-documents/wade-davis-bill.

66 Philip Sheldon Foner, *The Life and Writings of Frederick Douglass* (New York: International Publishers, 1950), 404.

67 Michael E. Ruane, "Civil War Gen. George McClellan: Deemed a Savior, Then a Failure," *Washington Post*, October 7, 2011, https://www.washingtonpost .com/lifestyle/style/civil-war-gen-george-mcclellan-deemed-a-savior-then-a -failure/2011/09/21/gIQAfpF6SL_story.html.

68 "Gen. Fremont Withdraws from the Canvass. Gen. Cochrane Follows His Example. Their Letters and Explanations," *New York Times*, September 23, 1864, https:// www.nytimes.com/1864/09/23/archives/the-presidential-campaign-gen-fremont -withdraws-from-the-canvass.html.

69 "Gen. Fremont Withdraws."

70 "Lincoln and Douglass Shared Uncommon Bond," *Tell Me More*, NPR, February 16, 2009, https://www.npr.org/templates/story/story.php?storyId=100694897.

71 David Blight, *Frederick Douglass: Prophet of Freedom* (New York: Simon and Schuster, 2018), 407.

72 Clint Smith, "In 1864, Like in 2020, America Just Got Lucky," *Atlantic*, November 22, 2020, https://www.theatlantic.com/ideas/archive/2020/11/election-when -america-narrowly-avoided-disaster/617176/.

73 "Political Caricature No. 4, The Miscegenation Ball," lithograph published in 1864, Prints & Photographs Online Catalog, Library of Congress, accessed July 1, 2022, https://www.loc.gov/pictures/item/2008661682/.

74 "The Lincoln Catechism Wherein the Eccentricities and Beauties of Despotism Are Fully Set Forth: A Guide to the Presidential Election of 1864," pamphlet published in 1864, Gilder Lehrman Institute of American History, accessed August 1, 2022, https://www.gilderlehrman.org/collection/glc08632.

75 Philip Kadish, "The Race-Mixing Hoax That Dogged Lincoln," CNN, February 18, 2014, https://www.cnn.com/2014/02/15/opinion/kadish-lincoln-hoax/index.html.

76 "Fact Check—Abraham Lincoln Quote about Slavery Is Missing Context," Reuters, July 14, 2021, https://www.reuters.com/article/factcheck-lincoln-lee/fact-check -abraham-lincoln-quote-about-slavery-is-missing-context-idUSL1N2OQ1LE.

77 "Ulysses S. Grant," White House, accessed October 1, 2022, https://www.whitehouse .gov/about-the-white-house/presidents/ulysses-s-grant/.

78 "African-American Soldiers during the Civil War," Library of Congress, accessed May 31, 2023, https://www.loc.gov/classroom-materials/united-states-history-primary-source -timeline/civil-war-and-reconstruction-1861-1877/african-american-soldiers-during -the-civil-war/.

79 "Black Soldiers in the U.S. Military."

80 Joe Servis, "The Surrender Meeting," Appomattox Court House, National Park Service, last updated June 14, 2022, https://www.nps.gov/apco/learn/history culture/the-surrender-meeting.htm.

81 Nathan Cooper, "A Call for Reconciliation: Lincoln's Final Speech," Abraham Lincoln Presidential Library and Museum, July 29, 2020, https://presidentlincoln .illinois.gov/Blog/Posts/20/Abraham-Lincoln/2020/7/A-Call-for-Reconciliation -Lincolns-Final-Speech/blog-post/.

82 "Examining Lincoln's Views on African Americans and Slavery," Abraham Lincoln Presidential Library and Museum, accessed April 1, 2022, https:// presidentlincoln.illinois.gov/learn/educators/educator-resources/teaching-guides /lincolns-evolving-views-on-race/.

83 Sarah Pruitt, "What Lincoln Said in His Final Speech," History, April 10, 2015, https://www.history.com/news/what-lincoln-said-in-his-final-speech.

84 Steve Moyer, "Remarkable Radical: Thaddeus Stevens," *Humanities* 33, no. 6 (November-December 2012), https://www.neh.gov/humanities/2012/novemberdecember /feature/remarkable-radical-thaddeus-stevens.

85   "Charles Sumner: After the Caning," United States Senate, May 4, 2020, https://
www.senate.gov/artandhistory/senate-stories/charles-sumner-after-the-caning.htm.

86   Herman Belz, "Salmon P. Chase and the Politics of Racial Reform," *Journal of the Abraham Lincoln Association* 17, no. 2 (Summer 1996): 22–40, https://
quod.lib.umich.edu/j/jala/2629860.0017.204?view=text;rgn=main.

87   *Encyclopaedia Britannica*, s.v. "John Wilkes Booth," last updated November 9, 2022,
https://www.britannica.com/biography/John-Wilkes-Booth.

88   "With Malice toward None: The Abraham Lincoln Bicentennial Exhibition,"
Library of Congress, accessed May 1, 2022, https://www.loc.gov/exhibits/lincoln
/lincoln-and-frederick-douglass.html.

89   "Oration in Memory of Abraham Lincoln."

90   "Frederick Douglass's Tribute to Abraham Lincoln, 1880," Gilder Lehrman Institute of American History, accessed June 1, 2022, https://www.gilderlehrman
.org/history-resources/spotlight-primary-source/frederick-douglass%E2
%80%99s-tribute-abraham-lincoln-1880.

91   Tricia Noel, "Looking Back: The Slaveholders' Rebellion: Frederick Douglass' Fourth of July in Himrod," *Finger Lakes Times*, June 20, 2021, https://www
.fltimes.com/lifestyle/local_history/looking-back-the-slaveholders-rebellion
-frederick-douglass-fourth-of-july-in-himrod/article_3da57f09-29d5-5ba2
-b602-3bd5474910a1.html.

CHAPTER 2: RECONSTRUCTION

1   Hiram R. Revels, "The State of Georgia," Senate speech, March 16, 1870, United States Senate, transcript, https://www.senate.gov/artandhistory/history/resources
/pdf/RevelsGeorgia.pdf.

2   "Jim Crow and Reconstruction," African American Heritage, National Park Service,
last updated August 17, 2018, https://www.nps.gov/subjects/africanamericanheritage
/reconstruction.htm.

3   John William Gorman, "The Crucible of Freedom: Reconstruction Violence in Texas, 1865–1868" (PhD diss., Texas A&M University, August 2019), Appendix A, 146, https://oaktrust.library.tamu.edu/bitstream/handle/1969.1/186314
/GORMAN-DISSERTATION-2019.pdf?sequence=1.

4   Rick Condon, "An Absolute Massacre—The New Orleans Slaughter of July 30, 1866," Reconstruction Era National Historical Park, National Park Service, last updated July 30, 2020, https://www.nps.gov/articles/000/neworleansmassacre.htm.

5   "Explore Pine Bluff: City's Lynchings Teach about Mobs of Today," *Arkansas Democrat Gazette*, February 15, 2021, https://www.arkansasonline.com/news/2021/feb/15
/citys-lynchings-teachabout-mobs-of-today/; "Documenting Reconstruction Violence," in *Reconstruction in America: Racial Violence after the Civil War, 1865–1876* (Equal Justice Initiative, 2020), https://eji.org/report/reconstruction-in-america
/documenting-reconstruction-violence.

6   Joshua Zeitz, "When Congress Almost Ousted a Failing President," Politico, May 20, 2017, https://www.politico.com/magazine/story/2017/05/20/andrew-johnson-impeachment-donald-trump-215166/.

7   "Andrew Johnson, One of the Worst U.S. Presidents," *Talk of the Nation*, NPR, January 17, 2011, https://www.npr.org/2011/01/17/133000855/andrew-johnson-one-of-the-worst-u-s-presidents.

8   Zeitz, "When Congress Almost Ousted."

9   Andrew Glass, "Lincoln Imposes First Federal Income Tax: Aug. 5, 1861," Politico, August 5, 2009, https://www.politico.com/story/2009/08/lincoln-imposes-first-federal-income-tax-aug-5-1861-025787.

10   ""Featured Document: The Revenue Act of 1861," United States Senate, accessed February 1, 2023, https://www.senate.gov/artandhistory/history/common/civil_war/RevenueAct_FeaturedDoc.htm.

11   "Homestead Act (1862)," National Archives, last reviewed June 7, 2022, https://www.archives.gov/milestone-documents/homestead-act.

12   Roger L. Geiger and Nathan M. Sorber, eds., *The Land-Grant Colleges and the Reshaping of Higher Education* (New Brunswick, NJ: Transaction Publishers, 2013), 29.

13   "Landmark Legislation: The Pacific Railway Act of 1862," United States Senate, accessed September 1, 2022, https://www.senate.gov/artandhistory/history/common/generic/PacificRailwayActof1862.htm.

14   Andrew Johnson, "Proclamation of Amnesty," May 29, 1865, UNC School of Education, transcript, https://cwnc.omeka.chass.ncsu.edu/items/show/13.

15   Patricia C. Click, "How Andrew Johnson Doomed the Roanoke Island Freedmen's Colony," *Slate*, November 8, 2017, https://slate.com/human-interest/2017/11/how-president-johnson-doomed-efforts-to-secure-land-for-former-slaves.html.

16   *Encyclopaedia Britannica*, s.v. "Black Code," last updated April 18, 2023, https://www.britannica.com/topic/black-code.

17   Nadra Kareem Nittle, "How the Black Codes Limited African American Progress after the Civil War," History, October 1, 2020, https://www.history.com/news/black-codes-reconstruction-slavery.

18   Ann McColl, "In Observance of Juneteenth: 'Their First Political Act,'" Education-NC, June 19, 2020, https://www.ednc.org/in-observance-of-juneteenth-their-first-political-act.

19   *Official Proceedings of the Mississippi State Colored Convention held at Vicksburg, Miss, Wednesday, Thursday, Friday and Saturday, Nov. 22, 23, 24 & 25, 1865* (Mississippi: Freedmen's Bureau Press Print, 1865), https://curiosity.lib.harvard.edu/slavery-abolition-emancipation-and-freedom/catalog/74-990061072160203941.

20   McColl, "In Observance of Juneteenth."

21   Darlene Clark Hine, William C. Hine, and Stanley Harrold, *The African-American Odyssey* (Upper Saddle River, NJ: Pearson Prentice Hall, 2008), 304.

22   McColl, "In Observance of Juneteenth."

23   "James Walker Hood Died," NC Department of Natural and Cultural Resources,

October 30, 2016, https://www.ncdcr.gov/blog/2015/10/30/bishop-j-w-hood-of
-the-ame-zion-church.

24 George P. Sanger, ed., *The Statutes at Large, Treaties and Proclamations of the
United States of America from December, 1865, to March, 1867* (Boston: Lit-
tle, Brown, 1868), 28, http://memory.loc.gov/cgi-bin/ampage?collId=llsl&file
Name=014/llsl014.db&recNum=59.

25 "Andrew Johnson's Veto of the Civil Rights Act, 1866," Bill of Rights Institute, accessed January 1, 2023, https://billofrightsinstitute.org/activities/andrew-johnsons
-veto-of-the-civil-rights-act-1866.

26 "Landmark Legislation: The Reconstruction Act of 1867," United States Senate,
accessed February 1, 2023, https://www.senate.gov/artandhistory/history/common
/generic/Civil_War_AdmissionReadmission.htm.

27 "The First Reconstruction Act Is Passed," History Engine, accessed March 1, 2023,
https://historyengine.richmond.edu/episodes/view/1431.

28 "Before the Voting Rights Act," United States Department of Justice, updated August 16, 2018, https://www.justice.gov/crt/introduction-federal-voting-rights-laws.

29 "Landmark Legislation: The Fourteenth Amendment," United States Senate,
accessed July 1, 2022, https://www.senate.gov/about/origins-foundations/senate
-and-constitution/14th-amendment.htm.

30 Manisha Sinha, "Donald Trump, Meet Your Precursor," *New York Times*, November 29, 2019, https://www.nytimes.com/2019/11/29/opinion/sunday/andrew
-johnson-donald-trump.html.

31 Edmund Drago, "Black Legislators during Reconstruction," New Georgia Encyclopedia, last modified September 24, 2020, https://www.georgiaencyclopedia.org
/articles/history-archaeology/black-legislators-during-reconstruction/; *Reconstruction: America after the Civil War*, directed by Julia Marchesi, featuring Henry Louis Gates Jr., aired April 9 and April 16, 2019, on PBS, https://www.pbs.org/weta
/reconstruction/.

32 John F. Kowal and Wilfred U. Codrington III, "How a Nation Recovering from
Total War Completed the Nation's 'Second Founding,'" Brennan Center for
Justice, September 21, 2021, https://www.brennancenter.org/our-work/analysis
-opinion/how-nation-recovering-total-war-completed-nations-second-founding.

33 "15th Amendment to the U.S. Constitution: Voting Rights (1870)," National Archives, last modified February 8, 2022, https://www.archives.gov/milestone-docu-
ments/15th-amendment.

34 Amber Phillips, "Republicans Want to Change the 14th Amendment. But That
Often Requires War, Crisis or Death," *Washington Post*, August 19, 2015, https://
www.washingtonpost.com/news/the-fix/wp/2015/08/19/republicans-want-to
-change-the-14th-amendment-but-that-often-requires-war-crisis-or-death/.

35 "Why the Women's Rights Movement Split over the 15th Amendment," National
Park Service, accessed March 1, 2022, https://www.nps.gov/articles/000/why-the
-women-s-rights-movement-split-over-the-15th-amendment.htm.

36 Louis Menand, "How Women Got in on the Civil Rights Act," *New Yorker*, July 14, 2014, https://www.newyorker.com/magazine/2014/07/21/sex-amendment; "Black Women & The Suffrage Movement: 1848–1923," Wesleyan University, accessed June 2, 2022, https://www.wesleyan.edu/mlk/posters/suffrage.html.

37 "African American Suffrage," Voting Rights, student website, Baylor University, accessed July 1, 2022, https://blogs.baylor.edu/votingrights/documents-page-1/.

38 "Why the Women's Rights Movement."

39 "Frederick Douglass' Take on Independence Day," *News and Notes*, NPR, July 4, 2007, https://www.npr.org/templates/story/story.php?storyId=11734985.

40 "Frederick Douglass," History, October 27, 2009, https://www.history.com/topics/black-history/frederick-douglass.

41 "Black Women & The Suffrage Movement."

42 "Ku Klux Klan," Southern Poverty Law Center, accessed June 1, 2022, https://www.splcenter.org/fighting-hate/extremist-files/ideology/ku-klux-klan.

43 "Hiram Revels: First African American Senator," United States Senate, February 25, 2020, https://www.senate.gov/artandhistory/senate-stories/First-African-American-Senator.htm.

44 "Revels, Hiram Rhodes," Biographical Directory of the United States Congress, accessed January 1, 2022, https://bioguide.congress.gov/search/bio/R000166.

45 "Revels, Hiram Rhodes."

46 "The First African-American Congressman: Hiram Rhodes Revels," Arthur Ashe Legacy at UCLA, February 1, 2016, https://arthurashe.ucla.edu/2016/02/01/the-first-african-american-congressman-hiram-rhodes-revels/.

47 "U.S. Census Bureau History: Hiram Rhodes Revels," United States Census Bureau, February 2020, https://www.census.gov/history/www/homepage_archive/2020/february_2020.html.

48 Eric Foner, "There Have Been 10 Black Senators Since Emancipation," *New York Times*, February 14, 2020, https://www.nytimes.com/2020/02/14/opinion/sunday/hiram-revels-reconstruction-150.html.

49 "Senators Elected by State Legislatures," United States Senate, accessed August 1, 2022, https://www.senate.gov/artandhistory/history/common/generic/Feature_Homepage_ElectedStateLegislatures.htm.

50 "Voting Rights and Political Representation in the Mississippi Delta," in *Racial and Ethnic Tensions in American Communities: Poverty, Inequality, and Discrimination*, vol. 7, *The Mississippi Delta Report*, U.S. Commission on Civil Rights, February 2001, https://www.usccr.gov/files/pubs/msdelta/ch3.htm.

51 Bennett, *Forced Into Glory*, 212.

52 Philip Dray, *Capitol Men: The Epic Story of Reconstruction Through the Lives of the First Black Congressmen* (Boston: Houghton Mifflin, 2008), 108.

53 W. E. B. Du Bois, *Black Reconstruction: An Essay Toward a History of the Part Which Black Folk Played in the Attempt to Reconstruct Democracy in America, 1860–1880* (New York: Harcourt, Brace 1935), 469.

54 "Hiram Revels."

55 "Dred Scott v. Sandford," Primary Documents in U.S. History, Library of Congress, accessed June 2, 2022, https://www.loc.gov/rr/program//bib/ourdocs/dredscott .html.

56 "Davis, Jefferson," History, Art & Archives, United States House of Representatives, accessed June 2, 2022, https://history.house.gov/People/Detail/11970.

57 Henry Louis Gates Jr., "Cory Booker and the First Black Senators," *The African Americans*, PBS, accessed June 2, 2022, https://www.pbs.org/wnet/african -americans-many-rivers-to-cross/history/cory-booker-and-the-first-black-senators/.

58 "Revels, Hiram Rhodes."

59 "Charles Douglass Calls Swearing-In of Senator Hiram Revels 'One of the Greatest Days in the History of This Country,'" Ghosts of DC, May 22, 2012, https:// ghostsofdc.org/2012/05/22/hiram-rhodes-revels/.

60 John R. Lynch, *The Facts of Reconstruction* (Washington, DC: Neale 1913; Project Gutenberg, 2005), chap. 3, https://www.gutenberg.org/ebooks/16158.

61 Lerone Bennett Jr., *Black Power U.S.A.: The Human Side of Reconstruction* (Chicago: Johnson, 1967), 212.

62 Nicholas Gilmore, "The First Black U.S. Senator Argued for Integration after the Civil War," *Saturday Evening Post*, February 25, 2020, https://www.saturdayeveningpost .com/2020/02/the-first-black-u-s-senator-argued-for-integration-after-the-civil-war/.

63 Revels, "State of Georgia."

64 Lynch, *Facts of Reconstruction*, chap. 1.

65 "Hiram Revels: The Nation's First African American Senator, featuring Eric Foner," Mississippi Department of Archives and History, February 11, 2020, YouTube video, 1:08:55, https://youtu.be/A45VcbZXKLk?t=3266.

66 GeColby Youngblood, in discussion with the author, March 2023.

67 "Hiram Revels: First African American Senator."

68 Julius E. Thompson, "Hiram Rhodes Revels, 1827–1901: A Reappraisal," *Journal of Negro History* 79, no. 3 (Summer 1994): 297–303, https://doi.org/10.2307/2717508.

69 Bennett, *Black Power U.S.A.*, 194.

70 "MFDP Brief to House Cites Past Unseatings," 1965, Robert W. Park Papers, Wisconsin Historical Society, https://content.wisconsinhistory.org/digital/collection /p15932coll2/id/21140.

71 "The Vicksburg Troubles," *New York Times*, December 14, 1874, https:// timesmachine.nytimes.com/timesmachine/1874/12/14/82745923.pdf.

72 Dray, *Capitol Men*, 191.

73 Dray, *Capitol Men*, 192.

74 "Mississippi: The Origin of the Vicksburg Conflict," *New York Times*, December 18, 1874, https://www.nytimes.com/1874/12/18/archives/mississippi-the-origin -of-the-vicksburg-conflict-statement-of-the.html.

75 Dray, *Capitol Men*, 205.

76 Dray, *Capitol Men*, 216.

77 "Hiram Revels' Letter to Pres. Grant," Ncpedia, accessed February 1, 2023, https://www.ncpedia.org/Biography/RevelsLetter.

78 *Mississippi in 1875: Report of the Select Committee to Inquire Into the Mississippi Election of 1875, With the Testimony And Documentary Evidence*, vol. 1 (Washington: Government Printing Office, 1876), 1016, 1120.

79 Bennett, *Black Power U.S.A.*, 366.

80 George A. Sewell, "Hiram Rhodes Revels: Another Evaluation," *Negro History Bulletin* 38, no. 1 (1974): 336, http://www.jstor.org/stable/44175632.

81 Lawrence Otis Graham, *The Senator and the Socialite: The True Story of America's First Black Dynasty* (New York: HarperCollins, 2009), 57.

82 Thompson, "Hiram Rhodes Revels."

83 Bennett, *Black Power U.S.A.*, 366.

84 E. Merton Coulter, "Aaron Alpeoria Bradley, Georgia Negro Politician During Reconstruction Times, Part I," *Georgia Historical Quarterly* 51, no. 1 (March 1967): 15–41, http://www.jstor.org/stable/40578873.

85 "Elliott, Robert Brown," History, Art & Archives, United States House of Representatives, accessed June 2, 2022, https://history.house.gov/People/Detail/12753.

86 Robert B. Elliot, "Addressing the Ku Klux Klan Bill of 1871", speech, House of Representatives, April 1, 1971, NYU School of Law, transcript, http://www.law.nyu.edu/sites/default/files/ElliotR.pdf

87 "Elliott, Robert Brown."

88 "South Carolina Representative Robert Elliott's Rousing Oratory," History, Art & Archives, United States House of Representatives, accessed June 2, 2022, https://history.house.gov/HistoricalHighlight/Detail/35183.

89 "Neglected Voices: Speeches of African-American Representatives Addressing the Civil Rights Bill of 1875," NYU Law, accessed June 2, 2022, http://www.law.nyu.edu/sites/default/files/civilrightsactspeeches.pdf.

90 "Bruce, Blanche Kelso," History, Art & Archives United States House of Representatives, accessed June 2, 2022, https://history.house.gov/People/Detail/10029.

91 Bennett, *Black Power U.S.A.*, 366.

92 Graham, *Senator and the Socialite*, 114.

93 Graham, *Senator and the Socialite*, 52.

94 "Blanche Kelso Bruce House," National Park Service, last updated August 11, 2017, https://www.nps.gov/places/blanche-kelso-bruce-house.htm.

95 "Bruce, Blanche Kelso."

96 "Southern Violence during Reconstruction," *American Experience*, PBS, accessed June 2, 2022, https://www.pbs.org/wgbh/americanexperience/features/reconstruction-southern-violence-during-reconstruction/.

97 "Bruce, Blanche Kelso."

98 Bennett, *Black Power U.S.A.*, 302.

99 Graham, *Senator and the Socialite*, 85.

100 Graham, *Senator and the Socialite*, 7.

101 "The True Story of America's First Black Dynasty: Real Estate, U.S. Senate," Way Back (video), April 16, 2018, https://www.youtube.com/watch?v=vKGV 9JyqhCk.

102 Graham, *Senator and the Socialite*, 86.

103 Dray, *Capitol Men*, 320.

104 "Bruce, Blanche Kelso."

105 Daniel Byman, "White Supremacy, Terrorism, and the Failure of Reconstruction in the United States," *International Security* 46, no. 1 (Summer 2021): 53–103, https://direct.mit.edu/isec/article/46/1/53/102853/White-Supremacy-Terrorism-and -the-Failure-of.

106 Heather Cox Richardson, "Killing Reconstruction." *Jacobin*, August 19, 2015, https://jacobin.com/2015/08/racism-reconstruction-homestead-act-black -suffrage.

107 "Financial Panic of 1873," U.S. Department of the Treasury, accessed June 2, 2022, https://home.treasury.gov/about/history/freedmans-bank-building/financial -panic-of-1873.

108 Greg Daugherty, "President Ulysses S. Grant: Known for Scandals, Overlooked for Achievements," History, April 24, 2020, https://www.history.com/news/ulysses -s-grant-president-accomplishments-scandals-15th-amendment.

109 Robert Mitchell, "The First Midterm 'Wave' Election That Ended Total Republican Control of Government," *Washington Post*, November 4, 2018, https://www.washington post.com/history/2018/11/04/midterm-wave-election-that-set-standard-them -all/.

110 "The Electoral Vote Count of the 1876 Presidential Election,"History, Art & Archives, United States House of Representatives, accessed June 2022, https://history.house .gov/Historical-Highlights/1851-1900/The-electoral-vote-count-of-the-1876 -presidential-election/.

111 Jerry Schwartz, "Explainer: 1876 Election Holds Record for Highest Turnout," AP News, November 3, 2020, https://apnews.com/article/ap-explains-1876-election -voter-record-fa49a19958231294f820517e3c0478f4.

112 "Electoral Vote Count."

113 Ronald G. Shafer, "The Ugliest Presidential Election in History: Fraud, Voter Intimidation and a Backroom Deal," *Washington Post*, November 24, 2020, https://www.washingtonpost.com/history/2020/11/24/rutherford-hayes-fraud-election -trump/.

114 "The Compromise of 1877," Khan Academy, accessed June 2, 2022, https://www.khanacademy.org/humanities/us-history/civil-war-era/reconstruction/a /compromise-of-1877.

115 Hillel Italie, "Frederick Douglass' July 4 Speeches Trace American History," AP News, July 1, 2018, https://apnews.com/article/north-america-ap-top-news -slavery-rochester-entertainment-393ae428732c4cc8905f3e3af01128d7.

116 Frederick Douglass, "The Color Question," speech, Hillsdale College, July 5,

1875, Washington, DC, Library of Congress, transcript, https://www.loc.gov/item /mss1187900415/.

117 Douglass, "Color Question."

CHAPTER 3: MONTGOMERY AND WASHINGTON

1 "Mississippi Disenfranchisement a Disgrace to the Race," *Cleveland Gazette*, October 25, 1890, 2.

2 Ben Paviour, "Virginia's First Black Woman Lieutenant Governor Says We Need to Move on from Slavery," *Morning Edition*, NPR, January 13, 2022, https://www.npr .org/2022/01/13/1072153233/virginias-first-black-woman-lieutenant-governor -says-we-need-to-move-on-from-sla.

3 Heather Long and Andrew Van Dam, "The Black-White Economic Divide Is as Wide as It Was in 1968," *Washington Post*, June 4, 2020, https://www.washingtonpost.com /business/2020/06/04/economic-divide-black-households/.

4 "Freedom to Fear," in *Reconstruction in America: Racial Violence after the Civil War, 1865–1876* (Equal Justice Initiative, 2020), https://eji.org/report/reconstruction -in-america/freedom-to-fear/.

5 Aaron Morrison, "100 Years after Tulsa Race Massacre, the Damage Remains," AP News, May 25, 2021, https://apnews.com/article/tulsa-race-massacre-1921-100 -years-later-3bc13e842c31054a90b6d1c81db9d70c.

6 Stephen A. Jones, *Presidents and Black America: A Documentary History* (Los Angeles: CQ Press, 2012), 218, https://archive.org/details/presidentsblacka0000jone /page/218/mode/2up.

7 "Elliott, Robert Brown."

8 "Rainey, Joseph Hayne," History, Art & Archives, United States House of Representatives, accessed June 2, 2022, https://history.house.gov/People/Listing /R/RAINEY,-Joseph-Hayne-(R000016)/.

9 "Haralson, Jeremiah," History, Art & Archives, United States House of Representatives, accessed June 2, 2022, https://history.house.gov/People/Detail/14507.

10 "The Civil Rights Cases," Oyez, accessed August 9, 2022, https://www.oyez.org /cases/1850–1900/109us3.

11 Jonathan K. Stubbs, "Modern Sappers and Miners: The Rehnquist and Roberts Courts and the Civil Rights Act of 1964," *Richmond Journal of Law and the Public Interest* 18, (2014): 461, https://scholarship.richmond.edu/cgi/viewcontent .cgi?article=2160&context=law-faculty-publications.

12 Henry McNeal Turner, *The Barbarous Decision of the United States Supreme Court Declaring the Civil Rights Act Unconstitutional and Disrobing the Colored Race of All Civil Protection* (Atlanta: HM Turner, 1893).

13 Turner, *Barbarous Decision*.

14 Ronald G. Shafer, "The 'Mississippi Plan' to Keep Blacks from Voting in 1890: 'We Came Here to Exclude the Negro,'" *Washington Post*, May 1, 2021, https://

www.washingtonpost.com/history/2021/05/01/mississippi-constitution-voting
-rights-jim-crow/.

15 Neil R. McMillen, "Isaiah T. Montgomery, 1847–1924 (Part II)," *Mississippi History Now*, February 2007, https://www.mshistorynow.mdah.ms.gov/issue/isaiah-t
-montgomery-1847-1924-part-ii.

16 Neil R. McMillen, "Isaiah T. Montgomery, 1847–1924 (Part I)," *Mississippi History Now*, February 2007, https://www.mshistorynow.mdah.ms.gov/issue/isaiah-t
-montgomery-1847-1924-part-I.

17 McMillen, "Isaiah T. Montgomery (Part I)."

18 Catherine Clinton, *Civil War Stories* (Athens: University of Georgia Press, 1998), 67.

19 Neil Kinghan, "A Brief Moment in the Sun: Francis Cardozo and Reconstruction in South Carolina" (PhD diss., University College London, 2019), 86, https://discovery
.ucl.ac.uk/id/eprint/10084666/1/A%20Brief%20Moment%20in%20the%20
Sun%20-%2030%20October.pdf.

20 DeeDee Baldwin, "Albert Johnson," *Against All Odds: The First Black Legislators in Mississippi* (virtual exhibit), Mississippi State University Libraries, accessed June 2, 2022, http://msstate-exhibits.libraryhost.com/exhibits/show/legislators
/albert-johnson--warren-county-.

21 James Tyson Currie, "Benjamin Thornton Montgomery," *Mississippi Encyclopedia*, July 11, 2017, https://mississippiencyclopedia.org/entries/benjamin-thornton
-montgomery/; Graham, *Senator and the Socialite*, 42.

22 "Mound Bayou Mourns Slave Who Founded Negro City: Isaiah T. Montgomery," *New York Times*, April 27, 1924, https://www.nytimes.com/1924/04/27/archives
/mound-bayou-mourns-slave-who-founded-negro-city-isaiah-t-montgomery.html.

23 Shafer, "Mississippi Plan."

24 Vernon Lane Wharton, *The Negro in Mississippi, 1865–1890* (Chapel Hill: University of North Carolina Press, 1947), 211.

25 "Address by Isaiah T. Montgomery Delegate from Bolivar County Mississippi Constitutional Convention on September 15, 1890," *Mississippi History Now*, accessed March 1, 2022, https://www.mshistorynow.mdah.ms.gov/sites/default/files
/imported-images/115.gif.

26 McMillen, "Isaiah T. Montgomery (Part II)."

27 "Mississippi Disenfranchisement a Disgrace."

28 Herb Boyd, "Thomas McCants Stewart, Jurist, Educator, Author, and Civil Rights Leader," *Amsterdam News*, April 18, 2019, https://amsterdamnews.com
/news/2019/04/18/thomas-mccants-stewart-jurist-educator-author-and/.

29 Ida B. Wells-Barnett, *Crusade for Justice: The Autobiography of Ida B. Wells* (Chicago: University of Chicago Press, 1972), 34–35.

30 Douglass, "Race Problem."

31 Lynne Feldman and John Ingham, *African-American Business Leaders: A Biographical Dictionary* (Westport, CT: Greenwood Press, 1994), 46; "Delegate Montgom-

ery: The Colored Delegate in the Mississippi Constitutional Convention," *Washington Post*, October 20, 1890, 4; "A Negro Municipality," *Friends' Intelligencer, October* 26, 1907, 676, https://www.proquest.com/magazines/negro-municipality /docview/90903156/se-2.

32 Tyler D. Parry, "How the 'Democratic Plantation' Became One of Conservatives' Favorite Slurs," *Washington Post*, January 8, 2019, https://www.washingtonpost.com/out look/2019/01/08/how-democratic-plantation-became-one-conservatives-favorite-slurs/.

33 Joshua Q. Nelson, "Virginia GOP Lieutenant Governor Nominee Slams Critical Race Theory Curriculum as 'Nonsense,'" Fox News, May 13, 2021, https://www.foxnews .com/media/virginia-republican-winsome-sears-critical-race-theory-nonsense.

34 "Tim Scott Criticizes Obama on Race Relations: America 'Has Not Made as Much Progress,'" *Face the Nation*, March 8, 2015, YouTube video, 6:08, https://www.youtube.com /watch?v=HUztrH3IfFs.

35 Rebecca Nelson, "Candace Owens Is the New Face of Black Conservatism," *Washington Post Magazine*, March 6, 2019, https://www.washingtonpost.com/news /magazine/wp/2019/03/06/feature/candace-owens-is-the-new-face-of-black -conservatism-but-what-does-that-really-mean/.

36 Jessie Carney Smith, "Montgomery, Isaiah T.," in *Notable Black American Men, Book II* (Farmington Hills, MI: Gale, 2007), https://www.encyclopedia.com/african -american-focus/news-wires-white-papers-and-books/montgomery-isaiah-t.

37 Norman L. Crockett, "Frustration and Failure," in *The Black Towns* (Lawrence: University Press of Kansas, 2021), 155–88, https://doi.org/10.2307/j.ctv1p2gkjr.9.

38 Leon F. Litwack and August Meier, eds., *Black Leaders of the Nineteenth Century* (Champaign: University of Illinois Press, 1991), 303.

39 Gene Dattel, *Cotton and Race in the Making of America: The Human Costs of Economic Power* (Lanham, MD: Rowman and Littlefield, 2009), 341.

40 McMillen, "Isaiah T. Montgomery (Part II)."

41 "Cheatham, Henry Plummer," History, Art & Archives, United States House of Representatives, accessed June 2, 2022, https://history.house.gov/People/Detail/10878.

42 "Langston, John Mercer," History, Art & Archives, United States House of Representatives, accessed June 2, 2022, https://history.house.gov/People/Detail/16682.

43 "Miller, Thomas Ezekiel," History, Art & Archives, United States House of Representatives, accessed June 2, 2022, https://history.house.gov/People/Detail/18276.

44 "Murray, George Washington," History, Art & Archives, United States House of Representatives, accessed June 2, 2022, https://history.house.gov/People/Detail/18709.

45 "White, George Henry," History, Art & Archives, United States House of Representatives, accessed June 2, 2022., https://history.house.gov/People/Detail/23657.

46 Smith, "Montgomery, Isaiah T."

47 Booker T. Washington, speech to the Atlanta Cotton States and International Exposition, October 18, 1895, Atlanta, GA, America Radio Networks, transcript,

http://americanradioworks.publicradio.org/features/blackspeech/btwashington
.html.

48 Norman Coombs, "The New Negro," in *The Black Experience in America: The Immigrant Heritage of America* (ebook, 1993), https://www.gutenberg.org/files/67/67-h/67-h.htm.

49 Thomas Joseph Frusciano, "Theodore Roosevelt and the Negro in the Age of Booker T. Washington, 1901–1912" (master's thesis, University of Montana, 1975), 19, https://scholarworks.umt.edu/etd/3866/.

50 Frusciano, "Roosevelt and the Negro," 19.

51 Henry McNeal Turner, "Critique of 'The Atlanta Compromise (1895),'" in *Respect Black: The Writings and Speeches of Henry McNeal Turner,* ed. Edwin S. Redkey (New York: Arno Press, 1971), 166.

52 *Cleveland Gazette*, quoting *Atlanta Advocate*, November 2, 1895.

53 "John Hope: A Critique of the Atlanta Compromise (1896)," in *The Story of John Hope* (New York: Macmillan, 1948), 114–15, https://rivercity.wusd.k12.ca.us /documents/Academics/Social-Science/GRADE-11-US-HISTORY/PRIMARY -SOURCE-DOCUMENTS/3787774444067282158.pdf.

54 Paula Cochran, "Boston Riot," Oxford African American Studies Center, December 1, 2009, https://oxfordaasc.com/view/10.1093/acref/9780195301731.001.0001 /acref-9780195301731-e-45307.

55 Booker T. Washington, *Address of Booker T. Washington: Delivered at the Alumni Dinner of Harvard University Cambridge, Mass., after Receiving the Honorary Degree of "Master of Arts,"* in Daniel Murray Pamphlet Collection, Library of Congress, https:// www.loc.gov/item/91898144/.

56 Booker T. Washington, *Up from Slavery: An Autobiography* (New York: Doubleday, Page, 1907), 3.

57 Peggy Hardman, "Pittman, Portia Marshall Washington," Handbook of Texas Online, accessed August 9, 2022, https://www.tshaonline.org/handbook/entries /pittman-portia-marshall-washington; Graham, *Senator and the Socialite*, 233.

58 Wells-Barnett, *Crusade for Justice*, 283.

59 "Trotter's Guardian Newspaper Advocated African American Advancement," *Bay State Banner*, February 26, 2015, https://www.baystatebanner.com/2015/02/26 /trotters-guardian-newspaper-advocated-african-american-advancement/.

60 Alexander Street, "Cheerful Journey through Mississippi" (essay on the National Negro Business League), *World's Work* 17, (February 1909), http://blackfreedom. proquest.com/wp-content/uploads/2020/09/nnbl13.pdf.

61 Booker T. Washington, "A Protest against the Burning and Lynching of Negroes," *Birmingham Age-Herald*, February 29, 1904, in Daniel Murray Pamphlet Collection, Library of Congress, https://www.loc.gov/item/91898237/.

62 W. E. B. Du Bois, *The Souls of Black Folks* (Chicago: A. C. McClurg, 1908), 58.

63 Booker T. Washington, "A Town Owned by Negroes," John Hopkins University Press, https://pwb01mw.press.jhu.edu/books/supplemental/booker_t/ch07_02_booker _t_washington_rediscovered.pdf.

64 George H. White, "Defense of the Negro Race—Charges Answered," House of Representatives speech, January 29, 1901, Documenting the American South, transcript, https://docsouth.unc.edu/nc/whitegh/whitegh.html.

CHAPTER 4: ROBINSON, BROOKE, AND NIXON CAPITALISM

1 Thomas J. Foley, "Brooke Appears Winner," *Atlanta Journal and Atlanta Constitution*, November 6, 1966.

2 Terry Gross, "A 'Forgotten History' of How the U.S. Government Segregated America," *FreshAir*, NPR, May 3, 2017, https://www.npr.org/2017/05/03/526655831/a-forgotten-history-of-how-the-u-s-government-segregated-america.

3 Larry DeWitt, "The Decision to Exclude Agricultural and Domestic Workers from the 1935 Social Security Act," *Social Security Bulletin* 70, no. 4 (2010), https://www.ssa.gov/policy/docs/ssb/v70n4/v70n4p49.html.

4 "Party Realignment and the New Deal," History, Art, & Archives, United States House of Representatives, accessed June 2, 2022, https://history.house.gov/Exhibitions-and-Publications/BAIC/Historical-Essays/Keeping-the-Faith/Party-Realignment--New-Deal/.

5 Don Amerman, "Brotherhood of Sleeping Car Porters," in *St. James Encyclopedia of Labor History Worldwide: Major Events in Labor History and Their Impact*, ed. Neil Schlager (Detroit, MI: St. James Press, 2004), https://www.encyclopedia.com/history/encyclopedias-almanacs-transcripts-and-maps/brotherhood-sleeping-car-porters-1.

6 Avik Roy, "No, Trump Didn't Win 'The Largest Share Of Non-White Voters Of Any Republican In 60 Years,'" Forbes, November 9, 2020, https://www.forbes.com/sites/theapothecary/2020/11/09/no-trump-didnt-win-the-largest-share-of-non-white-voters-of-any-republican-in-60-years/?sh=5b53a3294a09.

7 Earl Brown, "Big Negro Vote Backs FDR as New Deal Sweeps Nation: Negroes Elected Placed at 25," *New York Amsterdam News*, November 7, 1936, https://www.proquest.com/historical-newspapers/big-negro-vote-backs-f-d-r-as-new-deal-sweeps/docview/226153069/se-2.

8 Kenneth Eugene Mann, "Oscar Stanton De Priest: Persuasive Agent for the Black Masses," *Negro History Bulletin* 35, no. 6 (October 1972): 134, https://www.proquest.com/scholarly-journals/oscar-stanton-de-priest-persuasive-agent-black/docview/1296738042/se-2.

9 Mann, "Oscar Stanton De Priest."

10 "De Priest, Oscar Stanton," History, Art & Archives, United States House of Representatives, accessed June 2, 2022, https://history.house.gov/People/Detail/12155.

11 "Crafting an Institutional Identity," History, Art, & Archives, United States House of Representatives, accessed June 2, 2022, https://history.house.gov/Exhibitions-and-Publications/BAIC/Historical-Essays/Keeping-the-Faith/Crafting-Institutional-Identity/.

12 "Oscar Stanton De Priest's Lonely Fight," Arthur Ashe Legacy at UCLA, February 12, 2016, https://arthurashe.ucla.edu/2016/02/12/february-12th-2016/.

13 Herbert Hoover, *The Memoirs of Herbert Hoover*, vol. 2, The Cabinet and the Presidency, 1920–1933 (New York: Macmillan, 1952), 324.

14 "Illinois: Oscar Stanton De Priest House," National Park Service, January 5, 2021, https://www.nps.gov/places/illinois-oscar-stanton-de-priest-house.htm; "De Priest, Oscar Stanton."

15 Mann, "Oscar Stanton De Priest."

16 *Black Americans in Congress, 1870–2007* (Washington, DC: U.S. Government Printing Office, 2008), 260, https://www.govinfo.gov/content/pkg/GPO-CDOC-108hdoc224/pdf/GPO-CDOC-108hdoc224.pdf.

17 Brooks Jackson, "Blacks and the Democratic Party," Fact Check, April 18, 2008, https://www.factcheck.org/2008/04/blacks-and-the-democratic-party.

18 Michael G. Long, "Jackie Robinson Fought for a Racially Inclusive GOP," *Chicago Tribune*, January 30, 2019, https://www.chicagotribune.com/opinion/commentary/ct-perspec-jackie-robinson-100-politics-mlk-nixon-0131-20190130-story.html.

19 "Breaking the Color Line: 1940 to 1946," Library of Congress, accessed June 2, 2022, https://www.loc.gov/collections/jackie-robinson-baseball/articles-and-essays/baseball-the-color-line-and-jackie-robinson/1940-to-1946/.

20 "A Letter from Jackie Robinson: Civil Rights Advocate," National Archives, last reviewed April 16, 2021, https://www.archives.gov/exhibits/featured-documents/jackie-robinson.

21 "Letter, Jackie Robinson to President John F. Kennedy, February 9, 1961," National Archives, last reviewed October 9, 2016, last reviewed October 9, 2016, https://www.archives.gov/education/lessons/jackie-robinson/letter-1961.html.

22 Steven Levingston, "Before Trump vs. the NFL, There Was Jackie Robinson vs. JFK," *Washington Post*, September 24, 2017, https://www.washingtonpost.com/news/retropolis/wp/2017/09/24/before-trump-vs-the-nfl-there-was-jackie-robinson-vs-jfk/.

23 Steven Levingston, "John F. Kennedy, Martin Luther King Jr., and the Phone Call That Changed History," *Time*, June 20, 2017, https://time.com/4817240/martin-luther-king-john-kennedy-phone-call/.

24 John F. Kennedy to Jackie Robinson, May 15, 1959, Gilder Lehrman Institute of American History, https://www.gilderlehrman.org/sites/default/files/09754.04.pdf.

25 Jackie Robinson, *First Class Citizenship: The Civil Rights Letters of Jackie Robinson* (New York: Henry Holt, 2007), 83–85.

26 Robinson, *First Class Citizenship*, 107.

27 Levingston, "Before Trump vs. the NFL."

28 "52 Individuals, Including Dr. Martin Luther King Jr., Arrested in Atlanta Sit-In Protest," Equal Justice Initiative, accessed June 1, 2022, https://calendar.eji.org/racial-injustice/oct/19.

29 "King Receives Four-Month Sentence for Sit-In," King Encyclopedia, Martin Luther King Jr. Research and Education Institute, Stanford University, accessed June 2, 2022, https://kinginstitute.stanford.edu/encyclopedia/king-receives-four -month-sentence-sit.

30 Steven Levingston, *Kennedy and King: The President, the Pastor, and the Battle Over Civil Rights*, (New York: Hachette Books, 2017), 21.

31 Levingston, *Kennedy and King*, 23.

32 Levingston, *Kennedy and King*, 24.

33 Martin Luther King Jr., "Statement on Presidential Endorsement," press release, November 1, 1960, Martin Luther King Jr. Research and Education Institute, Stanford University, https://kinginstitute.stanford.edu /king-papers/documents/statement-presidential-endorsement.

34 Levingston, *Kennedy and King*, 23.

35 Michael O'Brien, *John F. Kennedy : A Biography* (New York: Thomas Dunne Books/ St. Martin's Press, 2005), 487.

36 Levingston, *Kennedy and King*, 26.

37 Bennett, *Forced Into Glory*, title page.

38 Adam Serwer, "Lyndon Johnson Was a Civil Rights Hero. But Also a Racist," MSNBC, April 11, 2014, https://www.msnbc.com/msnbc/lyndon-johnson-civil -rights-racism-msna305591.

39 Juan Williams, "Jackie Robinson Fought for Justice in Baseball and in America," *Los Angeles Times*, May 3, 1987, https://www.latimes.com/archives/la-xpm-1987 -05-03-sp-8534-story.html.

40 Matthew Delmont, "When Jackie Robinson Confronted a Trump-Like Candidate," *Atlantic*, March 19, 2016, https://www.theatlantic.com/politics/archive/2016/03 /goldwater-jackie-robinson/474498/.

41 Angie Maxwell, "What We Get Wrong about the Southern Strategy," *Washington Post*, July 26, 2019, https://www.washingtonpost.com/outlook/2019/07/26 /what-we-get-wrong-about-southern-strategy/.

42 Delmont, "When Jackie Robinson Confronted."

43 Joshua Farrington, "Farrington on Wright Rigueur, 'The Loneliness of the Black Republican: Pragmatic Politics and the Pursuit of Power,'" review of *The Loneliness of the Black Republican: Pragmatic Politics and the Pursuit of Power*, by Leah Wright Rigueur, H-Net, December 2016, https://networks.h-net.org/node/2606 /reviews/156544/farrington-wright-rigueur-loneliness-black-republican -pragmatic.

44 "Judge Harry A. Cole," *Baltimore Sun*, February 24, 2007, https://www .baltimoresun.com/features/bal-blackhistory-cole-story.html.

45 "Hobson R. Reynolds," Archives, Pennsylvania House of Representatives, accessed June 2, 2022, https://www.legis.state.pa.us/cfdocs/legis/BiosHistory /MemBio.cfm?ID=2207&body=H.

46 Martin Luther King Jr. to Hobson R. Reynolds, May 23, 1956, Martin Luther King

Jr. Research and Education Institute, Stanford University, https://kinginstitute .stanford.edu/king-papers/documents/hobson-r-reynolds.

47 David T. Beito and Linda Royster Beito, "An Unlikely, Unsung Civil Rights Champion," *Los Angeles Times*, August 28, 2009, https://www.latimes.com/archives /la-xpm-2009-aug-28-oe-beito28-story.html.

48 "Miller, William Edward," History, Art & Archives, United States House of Representatives, accessed June 2, 2022, https://history.house.gov/People/Listing /M/MILLER,-William-Edward-(M000762)/.

49 Scott Farris, *Almost President: The Men Who Lost the Race But Changed the Nation* (Essex, CT: Lyons Press, 2013), 193.

50 Brent D. Glass and Wiley J. Williams, "Civil Rights Unionism, 'Operation Dixie,' and the Birth of the ACTWU," in *Encyclopedia of North Carolina*, ed. William S. Powell (Chapel Hill: University of North Carolina Press, 2006), https://www .ncpedia.org/labor-unions-part-4-civil-rights.

51 "Negro Fails in Bid to Upset Seating; G.O.P. Unit Backs All White Delegation of Tennessee," *New York Times*, July 14, 1964, https://www.nytimes.com/1964/07/14 /archives/negro-fails-in-bid-to-upset-seating-gop-unit-backs-allwhite.html.

52 Joshua D. Farrington, *Black Republicans and the Transformation of the GOP* (Philadelphia: University of Pennsylvania Press, 2016), 133.

53 "George W. Lee Says Fixed Vote Beat Him," *Michigan Chronicle*, August 15, 1964.

54 John H. Britton, "The Great Purge of the Negroes," *Jet*, July 9, 1964, 10.

55 "The Increasing Racial and Ethnic Diversity in the House and Senate," Face the Nation, January 15, 2023, YouTube video, 1:24 https://www.youtube.com /watch?v=3EhpwtOgUu0.

56 Tom Wicker, "Convention Ends; Extremism in Defense of Liberty 'No Vice,' Arizonan Asserts," *New York Times*, July 17, 1964, https://www.nytimes .com/1964/07/17/archives/convention-ends-extremism-in-defense-of-liberty-no -vice-arizonan.html.

57 "Goldwater Show Is Jolting," *New Pittsburgh Courier*, July 25, 1964, https://www .proquest.com/newspapers/goldwater-show-is-jolting/docview/371594124/se-2.

58 Jerry Roberts, "California Pioneer," *Santa Barbara Independent*, April 21, 2011, https://www.independent.com/2011/04/21/california-pioneer.

59 Delmont, "When Jackie Robinson Confronted."

60 "Goldwater, Barry M.," King Encyclopedia, Martin Luther King Jr. Research and Education Institute, Stanford University, accessed June 2, 2022, https:// kinginstitute.stanford.edu/encyclopedia/goldwater-barry-m.

61 Jeremy D. Mayer, "LBJ Fights the White Backlash," *Prologue* 33, no. 1 (Spring 2001), https://www.archives.gov/publications/prologue/2001/spring/lbj-and-white -backlash-2.html.

62 "Goldwater Show Is Jolting."

63 Leah Wright Rigueur, "Conscience of a Black Conservative: The 1964 Election and the Rise of the National Negro Republican Assembly," *Federal History Journal* 1,

(2009): 32–45, https://dash.harvard.edu/bitstream/handle/1/24890953/4-Wright -final-design-pp32-45(1).pdf.

64 Alice Patterson, *Bridging the Racial & Political Divide: How Godly Politics Can Transform a Nation* (San Jose, CA: Transformational Publications, 2010), 133.

65 Tommy Christopher, "WATCH: Full Context of Viral 2015 Mitch McConnell Clip Proclaiming He's 'Proud' GOP Does 'Really Good With White People,'" *Mediaite*, January 22, 2022, https://www.mediaite.com/news/watch-full-context-of-viral-2015-mitch -mcconnell-clip-proclaiming-hes-proud-gop-does-really-good-with-white-people/.

66 Paul Kendrick and Stephen Kendrick, "If Only Richard Nixon Had Listened to Jackie Robinson—The GOP Might Be Doing Better Than Trump Today," *Chicago Sun-Times*, October 26, 2020, https://chicago.suntimes.com/2020/10/26/21534624 /jackie-robinson-dr-martin-luther-king-trump-gop-history-black-voters-civil -rights-movement.

67 "Jackie Robinson's Daughter Slams Trump for Using Father's Image in Campaign Ad," BET, October 9, 2020, https://www.bet.com/article/2tjt11/jackie-robinson-s -daughter-slams-trump-ad.

68 Allan Morrison, "Negro Political Progress in New England," *Ebony*, October 1963, 27, https://books.google.com/books?id=X_WsIHH8ugEC&pg=PA27.

69 Leah Wright Rigueur, *The Loneliness of the Black Republican: Pragmatic Politics and the Pursuit of Power* (Princeton, NJ: Princeton University Press, 2014), 102.

70 Chuck Stone, *Black Political Power in America* (New York: Dell, 1968), 171.

71 Justin Driver, "The Report on Race That Shook America," *Atlantic*, May 2018, https://www.theatlantic.com/magazine/archive/2018/05/the-report-on-race-that -shook-america/556850/.

72 Robert Healy, "Brooke Deals with Backlash," *Boston Globe*, October 2, 1966.

73 Rigueur, *Loneliness of the Black Republican*, 112.

74 "Brooke Says Black Power's Failed, Makes Plea for Negro Moderation," *Harvard Crimson*, October 8, 1966, https://www.thecrimson.com/article/1966/10/8 /brooke-says-black-powers-failed-makes/.

75 "Watts Rebellion (Los Angeles)," King Encyclopedia, Martin Luther King Jr. Research and Education Institute, Stanford University, accessed June 2, 2022, https:// kinginstitute.stanford.edu/encyclopedia/watts-rebellion-los-angeles.

76 "The Bold Strokes of Edward Brooke," Arthur Ashe Legacy at UCLA, February 17, 2016, https://arthurashe.ucla.edu/2016/02/17/the-bold-strokes-of-edward-brooke/.

77 "Brooke Says Black Power's Failed."

78 "Brooke, Edward William, III," History, Art, & Archives, United States House of Representatives, accessed June 1, 2022, https://history.house.gov/People/Detail /9905.

79 "Nation: The Senate: An Individual Who Happens To Be a Negro," *Time*, February 17, 1967, http://content.time.com/time/subscriber/printout/0,8816,839437,00.html.

80 Edward W. Brooke, *The Challenge of Change: Crisis in Our Two-Party System* (Boston: Little, Brown, 1966), quoted in Leah M. Wright, "'The Challenge of Change':

Edward Brooke, the Republican Party, and the Struggle for Redemption," *Souls* 13, no. 1 (2011): 91–118, https://www.tandfonline.com/doi/abs/10.1080/10999949 .2011.551479.

81   "Remembering Former Massachusetts Sen. Ed Brooke," WBUR Radio, Boston, January 5, 2015, https://www.wbur.org/radioboston/2015/01/05/ed-brooke.

82   "Rental Burdens: Rethinking Affordability Measures," *PD&R Edge*, accessed June 2, 2022, https://www.huduser.gov/portal/pdredge/pdr_edge_featd_article_092214. html.

83   Stone, *Black Political Power in America*, 268.

84   Simone Esters, "Blunt's Wrong: Trump Did Not Get the Highest Minority Vote Percentage in 100 Years," PolitiFact, December 8, 2020, https://www.politifact .com/factchecks/2020/dec/08/roy-blunt/blunts-wrong-trump-did-not-get -highest-minority-vo/.

85   Richard Nixon, "Bridges to Human Dignity, The Concept," remarks on CBS Radio, April 25, 1968, American Presidency Project, transcript, https://www.presidency .ucsb.edu/documents/remarks-the-cbs-radio-network-bridges-human-dignity -the-concept.

86   Tracy Jan, "The Biggest Beneficiaries of the Government Safety Net: Working-Class Whites," *Washington Post*, February 16, 2017, https://www.washingtonpost.com /news/wonk/wp/2017/02/16/the-biggest-beneficiaries-of-the-government-safety -net-working-class-whites/.

87   Kelefa Sanneh, "The Plan to Build a Capital for Black Capitalism," *New Yorker*, February 1, 2021, https://www.newyorker.com/magazine/2021/02/08/the-plan-to -build-a-capital-for-black-capitalism.

88   "Floyd B. McKissick," in *Encyclopedia of World Biography*, ed. James Craddock (Farmington Hills, MI: Gale, 2014), https://www.encyclopedia.com/history /encyclopedias-almanacs-transcripts-and-maps/floyd-b-mckissick.

89   Milton Viorst, "The Blacks Who Work for Nixon," *New York Times*, November 29, 1970, https://www.nytimes.com/1970/11/29/archives/the-blacks-who-work-for -nixon-the-blacks-who-work-for-nixon.html.

90   Rigueur, *Loneliness of the Black Republican*, 141.

91   Rigueur, *Loneliness of the Black Republican*, 140.

92   Jane Holzka, "Philadelphia Plan," in Schlager, *St. James Encyclopedia*, https://www.ency-clopedia.com/history/encyclopedias-almanacs-transcripts-and-maps/philadelphia-plan.

93   Mike Flynn, "Remembering Arthur Fletcher, Father of Affirmative Action," *Seattle Times*, November 9, 2018, https://www.seattletimes.com/opinion/remembering -arthur-fletcher-father-of-affirmative-action/.

94   "A New Administration Takes Shape," *Time*, December 20, 1968, http://content.time .com/time/subscriber/article/0,33009,844682,00.html.

95   "Senator Thurmond Backs Nixon in University of Montana Speech," December 5, 1969, *University of Montana News Releases, 1928, 1956–Present*, https://scholarworks .umt.edu/cgi/viewcontent.cgi?article=6379&context=newsreleases.

96 Maxwell, "What We Get Wrong."

97 Dean Kotlowski, "Black Power—Nixon Style: The Nixon Administration and Minority Business Enterprise," *Business History Review* 72, no. 3 (1998): 409–45, https://doi.org/10.2307/3116216.

98 "Executive Order 11478—Equal Employment Opportunity in the Federal Government," National Archives, last reviewed August 15, 2016, https://www.archives .gov/federal-register/codification/executive-order/11478.html.

99 "The History of the MBDA," Minority Business Development Agency, accessed June 2, 2022, https://www.mbda.gov/about/history.

100 "Event Recap: Robert J. Brown," Richard Nixon Foundation, March 20, 2019, https://www.nixonfoundation.org/2019/03/event-recap-robert-j-brown/.

101 "Races: America's Rising Black Middle Class," *Time*, June 17, 1974, http:// content.time.com/time/subscriber/article/0,33009,879319–2,00.html.

102 Michael Sheetz, "Black Unemployment Falls to the Lowest Level since 1972," CNBC, June 1, 2018, https://www.cnbc.com/2018/06/01/black-unemployment -falls-to-the-lowest-level-since-1972.html.

103 Jon Nordheimer, "'The Dream,' 1973: Blacks Move Painfully toward Full Equality," *New York Times*, August 26, 1973, https://www.nytimes.com/1973/08/26/archives /-the-dream-1973-blacks-move-painfully-toward-full-eq-quality-death-.html.

104 Rigueur, *Loneliness of the Black Republican*, 150.

105 "James Henry Hammond," National Park Service, June 17, 2015, https://www.nps .gov/people/james-henry-hammond.htm.

106 Zack O'Malley Greenburg, "Artist, Icon, Billionaire: How Jay-Z Created His $1 Billion Fortune," *Forbes*, June 3, 2019, https://www.forbes.com/sites /zackomalleygreenburg/2019/06/03/jay-z-billionaire-worth/?sh=29579c293a5f.

107 Thomas Healy, "The 1970s Black Utopian City That Became a Modern Ghost Town," *Atlantic*, February 2021, https://www.theatlantic.com/ideas /archive/2021/02/lost-dream-soul-city/618012/.

108 Robert J. Brown, "Soul City," speech, July 21, 1972, Stanley S. Scott Papers, Gerald R. Ford Presidential Library, https://www.fordlibrarymuseum.gov/library /document/0315/1181435.pdf.

109 Pat Stith, "I Reported on Soul City in the 1970s. What the N&O Said Then Is Still True Now," *News & Observer* (Raleigh, NC), March 7, 2021, https://www.news observer.com/opinion/article249728563.html.

110 Farrington, *Black Republicans*, 207.

111 James Conaway, "Sammy Davis Jr. Has Bought the Bus," *New York Times*, October 15, 1972, https://www.nytimes.com/1972/10/15/archives/sammy-davis-jr -has-bought-the-bus-sammy-davis-the-new-sammy-drinks.html.

112 Farrington, *Black Republicans*, 205.

113 Robert A. Jordan, "Sammy Davis Hugs Dick Nixon," *Bay State Banner*, September 7, 1972, https://www.proquest.com/docview/371285617/3C27915883434ECFPQ /1?accountid=35635.

114 "The Hardest Working Man: How James Brown Saved the Soul of America," *Billboard*, October 16, 2008, https://www.billboard.com/music/music-news/the -hardest-working-man-how-james-brown-saved-the-soul-of-america-1043762/.

115 "Have Pro Nixon Blacks Really Sold Their Souls?," *Washington Afro-American*, October 24, 1972, https://news.google.com/newspapers?nid=2238&dat=197Q1024&id =7nslAAAAIBAJ&sjid=HfUFAAAAIBAJ&pg=712,2072292.

116 Paul Delaney, "Blacks for Nixon Sharply Rebuked," *New York Times*, August 3, 1972, https://www.nytimes.com/1972/08/03/archives/blacks-for-nixon-sharply -rebuked-julian-bond-labels-them-political.html.

117 Viorst, "Blacks Who Work for Nixon."

118 Viorst, "Blacks Who Work for Nixon."

119 "Nixon Adviser Admits War on Drugs Was Designed to Criminalize Black People," Equal Justice Initiative, March 25, 2016, https://eji.org/news/nixon-war-on -drugs-designed-to-criminalize-black-people/.

120 Dan Baum, "Legalize It All," *Harper's Magazine*, April 2016, https://harpers.org /archive/2016/04/legalize-it-all/.

121 John Nichols, "Edward Brooke and the Republican Party That Might Have Been," *Nation*, January 7, 2015, https://www.thenation.com/article/archive /edward-brooke-and-republican-party-might-have-been/.

122 "The Last Time Republicans Duked It Out to the Last, Heated Minute," *Weekend Edition Sunday*, NPR, March 13, 2016, https://www.npr .org/2016/03/13/470271684/1976-the-last-time-republicans-duked-it-out-to -the-last-heated-minute.

123 Farrington, *Black Republicans*, 233.

124 Alan Flippen, "Black Turnout in 1964, and Beyond," *New York Times*, October 16, 2014, https://www.nytimes.com/2014/10/17/upshot/black-turnout-in-1964 -and-beyond.html.

125 "Edward Brooke, First Black Elected US Senator, Dies," CBS Boston, January 3, 2015, https://boston.cbslocal.com/2015/01/03/edward-brooke-first-black-elected -us-senator-dies/.

CHAPTER 5: REAGAN, PIERCE, AND THOMAS

1 Julia Jacobs, "Anita Hill's Testimony and Other Key Moments from the Clarence Thomas Hearings," *New York Times*, September 20, 2018, https://www.nytimes .com/2018/09/20/us/politics/anita-hill-testimony-clarence-thomas.html.

2 Renée Graham, "Why Is Anyone Surprised by Reagan's Racism?," *Boston Globe*, August 2, 2019, https://www.bostonglobe.com/opinion/2019/08/02/why -anyone-surprised-reagan-racism/wVSXLxvnSXV2WlUJ3rbcQL/story.html.

3 Leon Wynter, "The 'Black Elephant:' Growth for the GOP," *Washington Post*, June 25, 1981, https://www.washingtonpost.com/archive/local/1981/06/25/the-black -elephant-growth-for-the-gop/cd4a8efb-1f8f-4f8a-8420-8f1a1686b93b/.

4   "Reagan's Exit Stirs Negro G.O.P. Parley," *New York Times*, March 7, 1966, https://www.nytimes.com/1966/03/07/archives/reagans-exit-stirs-negro-gop-parley.html.

5   Farrington, *Black Republicans*, 233.

6   "Ronald Reagan's Neshoba County Speech," C-SPAN, April 10, 2010, video, 1:35:35, https://www.c-span.org/video/?293124-1/ronald-reagans-neshoba-county-speech.

7   "Murder in Mississippi," American Experience: Freedom Summer, PBS, accessed June 2, 2022, https://www.pbs.org/wgbh/americanexperience/features/freedomsummer-murder/.

8   Rick Perlstein, "Exclusive: Lee Atwater's Infamous 1981 Interview on the Southern Strategy," *Nation*, November 13, 2012, https://www.thenation.com/article/archive/exclusive-lee-atwaters-infamous-1981-interview-southern-strategy/.

9   "'Welfare Queen' Becomes Issue in Reagan Campaign," *New York Times*, February 15, 1976, https://www.nytimes.com/1976/02/15/archives/welfare-queen-becomes-issue-in-reagan-campaign-hitting-a-nerve-now.html.

10 Bryce Covert, "The Myth of the Welfare Queen," *New Republic*, July 2, 2019, https://newrepublic.com/article/154404/myth-welfare-queen.

11 Josh Levin, *The Queen: The Forgotten Life Behind an American Myth* (Boston: Little, Brown, 2019), 130.

12 "Welfare Queen Becomes Issue."

13 Covert, "Myth of the Welfare Queen."

14 Covert, "Myth of the Welfare Queen."

15 Francine D. Blau and Andrea H. Beller, "Black-White Earnings over the 1970s and 1980s: Gender Differences in Trends," *Review of Economics and Statistics* 74, no. 2 (May 1992): 276–86, https://www.jstor.org/stable/2109659.

16 Aaron C. Catlin and Cathy A. Cowan, *History of Health Spending in the United States, 1960–2013* (Baltimore, MD: Centers for Medicare and Medicaid Services, 2015), 5.

17 "U.S. Spent $141 Billion in Vietnam in 14 Years," *New York Times*, May 1, 1975, https://www.nytimes.com/1975/05/01/archives/us-spent-141billion-in-vietnam-in-14-years.html.

18 Harry F. Rosenthal, "Reagan Administration Plagued with Ethical Problems," AP News, December 19, 1987, https://apnews.com/article/9255cf25155fca5abdd58d94388d3e60.

19 "Allied with Apartheid: Reagan Supported Racist South African Gvt," Democracy Now!, June 11, 2004, https://www.democracynow.org/2004/6/11/allied_with_apartheid_reagan_supported_racist.

20 Justin Elliott, "Reagan's Embrace of Apartheid South Africa," Salon, February 5, 2011, https://www.salon.com/2011/02/05/ronald_reagan_apartheid_south_africa/.

21 Rudy Abramson, "S. Africa Clerics Ask for Reforms : U.S. Scolds Tutu for Criticizing Reagan Policy," *Los Angeles Times*, August 20, 1985, https://www.latimes.com/archives/la-xpm-1985-08-20-mn-1916-story.html.

22 Sarah Mervosh and Niraj Chokshi, "Reagan Called Africans 'Monkeys' in Call With Nixon, Tape Reveals," *New York Times*, July 31, 2019, https://www.nytimes.com/2019/07/31/us/politics/ronald-reagan-richard-nixon-racist.html.

23 Gerhard Peters and John T. Woolley, "Ronald Reagan, Nomination of Samuel R. Pierce, Jr., to Be Secretary of Housing and Urban Development," American Presidency Project, University of California at Santa Barbara, accessed June 2, 2022, https://www.presidency.ucsb.edu/documents/nomination-samuel-r-pierce-jr-be-secretary-housing-and-urban-development.

24 Philip Shenon, "Samuel R. Pierce Jr., Ex-Housing Secretary, Dies at 78," *New York Times*, November 3, 2000, https://www.nytimes.com/2000/11/03/nyregion/samuel-r-pierce-jr-ex-housing-secretary-dies-at-78.html.

25 Shenon, "Samuel R. Pierce Jr."

26 "Cabinet Aide Greeted by Reagan as 'Mayor,'" *New York Times*, June 19, 1981, https://www.nytimes.com/1981/06/19/us/cabinet-aide-greeted-by-reagan-as-mayor.html; Shenon, "Samuel R. Pierce Jr."

27 "Samuel Pierce (1981–1989)," Miller Center, University of Virginia accessed June 2, 2022, https://millercenter.org/president/reagan/essays/pierce-1981-secretary-of-housing-and-urban-development.

28 J. Y. Smith, "HUD Secretary Samuel Pierce Jr., 78, Dies," *Washington Post*, November 4, 2000, https://www.washingtonpost.com/archive/local/2000/11/04/hud-secretary-samuel-pierce-jr-78-dies/c145b4ef-26da-4165-aefe-fb797d1c1f56/.

29 "As Black-Owned Harlem Bank Dies, So Does a Symbol," *Baltimore Sun*, November 14, 1990, https://www.baltimoresun.com/news/bs-xpm-1990-11-14-1990318052-story.html.

30 Leslie Maitland, "Files Show Pierce Was Busy With Social Details," *New York Times*, August 4, 1989, https://www.nytimes.com/1989/08/04/us/files-show-pierce-was-busy-with-social-details.html.

31 Howard Kurtz, "In Pierce's Past, Seeds of His Failure at HUD," *Washington Post*, July 26, 1989, https://www.washingtonpost.com/archive/politics/1989/07/26/in-pierces-past-seeds-of-his-failure-at-hud/03eb90f6-7572-4c4e-b4a8-ed2040a6a540/.

32 David Johnston, "Pierce Helped His Old Law Firm on H.U.D. Requests, Files Show," *New York Times*, August 6, 1989, https://www.nytimes.com/1989/08/06/us/pierce-helped-his-old-law-firm-on-hud-requests-files-show.html.?pagewanted=all.

33 Margie Bonnett Sellinger, "Housing's Down—and Blacks Are Down on Reagan—but Sam Pierce of H.U.D. Is Plunging Ahead," *People*, November 2, 1981, https://people.com/archive/housings-down-and-blacks-are-down-on-reagan-but-sam-pierce-of-h-u-d-is-plunging-ahead-vol-16-no-18/.

34 William Tucker, "The Source of America's Housing Problem: Look in Your Own Back Yard," *Policy Analysis* 127, Cato Institute, February 6, 1990, https://www.cato.org/sites/cato.org/files/pubs/pdf/pa127.pdf.

35 Peter Dreier, "Reagan's Legacy: Homelessness in America," Shelterforce, May 1, 2004, https://shelterforce.org/2004/05/01/reagans-legacy-homelessness-in-america/.

36 Smith, "HUD Secretary Samuel Pierce Jr."

37 Farrington, *Black Republicans*, 227.

38 Louis Jacobson, "Was Ronald Reagan's Record on Black Unemployment Better Than Barack Obama's?," PolitiFact, May 22, 2015 https://www.politifact.com /factchecks/2015/may/22/facebook-posts/was-ronald-reagans-record-black -unemployment-bette/.

39 "The Great Eliminator: How Ronald Reagan Made Homelessness Permanent," *SFWeekly*, June 29, 2016, https://www.sfweekly.com/news/the-great-eliminator -how-ronald-reagan-made-homelessness-permanent/.

40 "Great Eliminator."

41 Juan Williams, "Homeless Choose to Be, Reagan Says," *Washington Post*, February 1, 1984, https://www.washingtonpost.com/archive/politics/1984/02/01/homeless -choose-to-be-reagan-says/781996b6-ab3b-499b-96ea-38155d1c5127/.

42 Kurtz, "In Pierce's Past."

43 Robert L. Jackson, "Samuel R. Pierce Jr.; Reagan HUD Chief Was Investigated but Never Charged," *Los Angeles Times*, November 4, 2000, https://www.latimes.com /archives/la-xpm-2000-nov-04-me-47066-story.html.

44 Shenon, "Samuel R. Pierce Jr."

45 Smith, "HUD Secretary Samuel Pierce Jr."

46 Marjorie Williams, "The Real Louis Sullivan Stands Out," *Washington Post*, May 14, 1989, https://www.washingtonpost.com/archive/lifestyle/magazine/1989/05/14 /the-real-louis-sullivan-stands-out/4eb6b474-1793-4ebb-8198-18e9090a2d12/.

47 Ellen Warren and Owen Ullmann, "Abortion Foes Clear Sullivan for Cabinet," *Philadelphia Inquirer*, December 22, 1988, https://www.proquest.com/newspapers /abortion-foes-clear-sullivan-cabinet/docview/1833049860/se-2.

48 William J. Eaton, "Stark Admits Using Race to Attack Sullivan Was Wrong," *Los Angeles Times*, August 4, 1990, https://www.latimes.com/archives/la-xpm-1990 -08-04-mn-1067-story.html.

49 Felicia Sonmez and John Wagner, "Trump Says Any Jewish People Who Vote for Democrats Are Showing 'Great Disloyalty' or 'Lack of Knowledge,'" *Washington Post*, August 21, 2019, https://www.washingtonpost.com/politics/trump-says-that-jewish -people-who-vote-for-democrats-are-very-disloyal-to-israel-denies-his-remarks -are-anti-semitic/2019/08/21/055e53bc-c42d-11e9-b5e4-54aa56d5b7ce_story.html.

50 "Joe Biden on Black Woman Running Mate, Democrats Taking Black Voters for Granted + Wiping Weed Crime," Breakfast Club Power 105.1 FM, May 22, 2020, YouTube video, 18:19, https://www.youtube.com/watch?v=KOIFs_SryHI&ab _channel=BreakfastClubPower105.1FM.

51 Long, "Jackie Robinson Fought."

52 McMillen, "Isaiah T. Montgomery (Part II)."

53 "National Response to the Atlanta Address," Booker T. Washington National Monument, Virginia, National Park Service, February 26, 2015, https://www.nps .gov/bowa/learn/historyculture/in-black-and-white.htm.

54 Clarence Thomas, *My Grandfather's Son: A Memoir* (New York: Harper, 2007), 12.

55 William Grimes, "The Justice Looks Back and Settles Old Scores," *New York Times*, October 10, 2007, https://www.nytimes.com/2007/10/10/books/10grim.html.

56 Thomas, *My Grandfather's Son*, 30–31.

57 Elaine Woo, "Dr. Henry Lucas Dies at 77; Republican Activist Was One of First African Americans on the RNC," *Los Angeles Times*, June 8, 2009, https://www.latimes.com/local/obituaries/la-me-henry-lucas8-2009jun08-story.html.

58 Herbert Denton, "Meese Pledges Cabinet, Top Jobs for Blacks," *Washington Post*, December 15, 1980, https://www.washingtonpost.com/archive/politics/1980/12/15/meese-pledges-cabinet-top-jobs-for-blacks/5ea2268f-358f-411f-ba79-80ce602a07fa/.

59 Juan Williams, "Black Conservatives, Center Stage," *Washington Post*, December 16, 1980, https://www.washingtonpost.com/archive/politics/1980/12/16/black-conservatives-center-stage/c5b44552-ad84-4a40-9b3c-3e88fdfa3589/.

60 Clarence Page, "Thomas' Sister's Life Gives Lie to His Welfare Fable," *Chicago Tribune*, July 24, 1991, https://www.chicagotribune.com/news/ct-xpm-1991-07-24-9103220246-story.html.

61 Karen Tumulty, "Sister of High Court Nominee Traveled Different Road," *Los Angeles Times*, July 24, 1991, https://www.latimes.com/archives/la-xpm-1991-07-05-mn-1766-story.html.

62 Page, "Thomas' Sister's Life."

63 Kevin Merida and Michael A. Fletcher, "Justice Thomas's Life a Mix of Poverty, Privilege," NBC News, April 22, 2007, https://www.nbcnews.com/id/wbna18255941.

64 Emma Mae Martin, in discussion with the author, July 2022.

65 Neil A. Lewis, "On Thomas's Climb, Ambivalence about Issue of Affirmative Action," *New York Times*, July 14, 1991, https://www.nytimes.com/1991/07/14/us/on-thomas-s-climb-ambivalence-about-issue-of-affirmative-action.html.

66 *Encyclopaedia Britannica*, s.v. "Clarence Thomas," by Brian P. Smentkowski, last updated May 30, 2023, https://www.britannica.com/biography/Clarence-Thomas.

67 "Anita Hill," Iowa State University Archives of Women's Political Communication, accessed June 2, 2022, https://awpc.cattcenter.iastate.edu/directory/anita-hill/.

68 Herbert H. Denton and Bill Peterson, "Reagan Picks Black Lawyer for EEOC," *Washington Post*, February 13, 1982, https://www.washingtonpost.com/archive/politics/1982/02/13/reagan-picks-black-lawyer-for-eeoc/428e2659-4359-496f-ada6-74fd91771a35/.

69 William M. Welch, "Thomas Presided over Shift in Policy at EEOC, Records Show," AP News, July 25, 1991, https://apnews.com/article/b419883e871b5117649d1f3fdacf6f95.

70 Lewis, "On Thomas's Climb."

71 Scott Pendleton, "NAACP Takes Long Look at Thomas as High Court Nominee," *Christian Science Monitor*, July 10, 1991, https://www.csmonitor.com/1991/0710/10092.html.

72 "Remarks of Thurgood Marshall at the Annual Seminar of the San Francisco Patent and Trademark Law Association," May 6, 1987, https://books.google.com/books/about/Remarks_of_Thurgood_Marshall_at_the_Annu.html?id=LJP-tgAACAAJ.

73 Clarence Thomas, "Black Americans Based Claim for Freedom on Constitution," *San Diego Union*, October 6, 1987.

74 Nathaniel R. Jones, *Answering the Call: An Autobiography of the Modern Struggle to End Racial Discrimination in America* (New York: New Press, 2010), 329.

75 Maureen Dowd, "The Supreme Court; Conservative Black Judge, Clarence Thomas, Is Named to Marshall's Court Seat," *New York Times*, July 2, 1991, https://www.nytimes.com/1991/07/02/us/supreme-court-conservative-black-judge-clarence-thomas-named-marshall-s-court.html.

76 "Excerpt from News Conference Announcing Court Nominee," The Supreme Court, New York Times, July 2, 1991, https://www.nytimes.com/1991/07/02/us/the-supreme-court-excerpts-from-news-conference-announcing-court-nominee.html.

77 Courtland Milloy, "The Complexities of Clarence Thomas," *Washington Post*, July 14, 1991, https://www.washingtonpost.com/archive/local/1991/07/14/the-complexities-of-clarence-thomas/6d96b990-be72-4901-935b-9df78b242851/.

78 Robert Chrisman and Robert L. Allen, eds., *Court of Appeal: The Black Community Speaks Out on the Racial and Sexual Politics of Clarence Thomas vs. Anita Hill* (New York: Ballantine Books, 1992), 177.

79 Ann Devroy, "Bush Vetoes Civil Rights Bill," *Washington Post*, October 23, 1990, https://www.washingtonpost.com/archive/politics/1990/10/23/bush-vetoes-civil-rights-bill/cd68a6c4-8529-471a-b4f7-08c26cf65ac0/.

80 Linda Greenhouse, "Justice Clarence Thomas's Solitary Voice," *New York Times*, June 8, 2016, https://www.nytimes.com/2016/06/09/opinion/justice-clarence-thomass-solitary-voice.html.

81 "Justice Clarence Thomas '74 Visits the Law School; Meets with Student Groups, Teaches Class," *Yale Law School Today*, December 14, 2011, https://law.yale.edu/yls-today/news/justice-clarence-thomas-74-visits-law-school-meets-with-student-groups-teaches-class.

82 "About the Court," Supreme Court of the United States, accessed June 2, 2022, https://www.supremecourt.gov/about/biographies.aspx.

83 "Biography of Associate Justice Ruth Bader Ginsburg," Supreme Court of the United States, accessed June 2, 2022, https://www.supremecourt.gov/about/biographyginsburg.aspx.

84 Neil A. Lewis, "Bar Association Splits on Fitness of Thomas for the Supreme Court," *New York Times*, August 28, 1991, https://www.nytimes.com/1991/08/28/us/bar-association-splits-on-fitness-of-thomas-for-the-supreme-court.html.

85 Anthony Lewis, "Abroad at Home; Which Judge Thomas?," *New York Times*, Sep-

tember 16, 1991, https://www.nytimes.com/1991/09/16/opinion/abroad-at-home
-which-judge-thomas.html.

86 Welch, "Thomas Presided over Shift."

87 Welch, "Thomas Presided over Shift."

88 John Hope Franklin, "Booker T. Washington, Revisited," *New York Times*, August
1, 1991, https://www.nytimes.com/1991/08/01/opinion/booker-t-washington
-revisited.html.

89 Rosa Parks, "Statement on the Nomination of Clarence Thomas to the United States
Supreme Court," September 13, 1991, Rosa Parks Papers, Library of Congress,
https://www.loc.gov/item/mss859430237/.

90 Madeline Carlisle and Julia Zorthian, "Clarence Thomas Signals Same-Sex Marriage and Contraception Rights at Risk after Overturning *Roe v. Wade*," *Time*,
June 24, 2022, https://time.com/6191044/clarence-thomas-same-sex-marriage
-contraception-abortion/.

91 Sean Illing, "The Racial Pessimism of Clarence Thomas," Vox, October 15,
2019, https://www.vox.com/policy-and-politics/2019/10/15/20893737/clarence
-thomas-supreme-court-corey-robin.

92 Marc Fisher, "The Private World of Justice Thomas," *Washington Post*, September 11, 1995, https://www.washingtonpost.com/archive/lifestyle/1995/09/11/the
-private-world-of-justice-thomas/fd434eb3-9226-4885-a4ef-afc6a9ddde1a/.

93 Dennis Hevesi, "William T. Coleman Jr., Who Broke Racial Barriers in Court
and Cabinet, Dies at 96," *New York Times*, March 31, 2017, https://www.nytimes
.com/2017/03/31/us/politics/william-coleman-jr-dies.html.

94 "William T. Coleman Jr. '46: 1920–2017," *Harvard Law Today*, May 1, 2017,
https://today.law.harvard.edu/william-t-coleman-jr-46-1920-2017/.

95 "LDF Commemorates William T. Coleman Jr., 1920–2017," *NAACP Legal Defense
Fund*, April 1, 2017, https://www.naacpldf.org/press-release/ldf-commemorates
-william-t-coleman-jr-1920-2017/.

96 "Senators Reintroduce Bill to Name Transportation Department Headquarters after First African American Secretary," Senate Committee on Commerce, Science,
and Transportation, February 24, 2021, https://www.commerce.senate.gov/2021/2
/senators-reintroduce-bill-to-name-transportation-department-headquarters
-after-first-african-american-secretary.

97 Al Kamen and Edward Walsh, "3 Black Leaders, GOP Senator Voice Opposition
to Bork," *Washington Post*, September 22, 1987, https://www.washingtonpost.com
/archive/politics/1987/09/22/3-black-leaders-gop-senator-voice-opposition-to
-bork/a1e25324-20ae-44ab-970a-0df62be2ca44/.

98 Hevesi, "William T. Coleman Jr."

99 Hevesi, "William T. Coleman Jr."

100 Michael Fletcher and Kevin Merida, *Supreme Discomfort: The Divided Soul of
Clarence Thomas* (New York: Crown, 2008), 258.

101 Fletcher and Merida, *Supreme Discomfort*, 258.

102 Clarence Page, "Justice Thomas May Be 'Color Blind,' but His Mentor Wasn't," *Baltimore Sun*, March 13, 2007, https://www.baltimoresun.com/news/bs-xpm-2007-03-13-0703130090-story.html.

103 Corey Robin, "Clarence Thomas's Radical Vision of Race," *New Yorker*, September 10, 2019, https://www.newyorker.com/culture/essay/clarence-thomass-radical-vision-of-race.

104 "Clarence Thomas Interviewed by Julian Bond: Explorations in Black Leadership Series," University of Virginia, February 16, 2009, YouTube video, 1:32:43, https://www.youtube.com/watch?v=gfAZUYCZSLQ&t=2358s.

105 Robin, "Clarence Thomas's Radical Vision."

106 Dave Davies, "How Ginni Thomas, Wife of Justice Clarence Thomas, Influences the Supreme Court," *Fresh Air*, NPR, January 27, 2022, https://www.npr.org/2022/01/27/1076097533/how-ginni-thomas-wife-of-justice-clarence-thomas-influences-the-supreme-court.

107 Kenneth P. Vogel, John Bresnahan, and Marin Cogan, "Justice Thomas's Wife Now Lobbyist," Politico, February 4, 2011, https://www.politico.com/story/2011/02/justice-thomass-wife-now-lobbyist-048812.

108 Laura Blumenfeld, "The Nominee's Soul Mate," *Washington Post*, September 10, 1991, https://www.washingtonpost.com/archive/lifestyle/1991/09/10/the-nomineess-soul-mate/3e0a9aa9-fdee-41f3-b5be-a6af468d89cc/.

109 Fisher, "Private World of Justice Thomas."

110 Asawin Suebsaeng and Adam Rawnsley, "Inside Ginni Thomas' 'Insane' Hiring Memos for Trump," Daily Beast, April 1, 2022, https://www.thedailybeast.com/inside-ginni-thomas-insane-hiring-memos-for-former-president-donald-trump.

111 Jane Mayer, "Is Ginni Thomas a Threat to the Supreme Court?," *New Yorker*, January 21, 2022, https://www.newyorker.com/magazine/2022/01/31/is-ginni-thomas-a-threat-to-the-supreme-court.

112 Robert Barnes, "Ginni Thomas Apologizes to Husband's Supreme Court Clerks after Capitol Riot Fallout," *Washington Post*, February 2, 2021, https://www.washingtonpost.com/politics/courts_law/ginni-thomas-apology-clarence-thomas-clerks-trump-rally/2021/02/02/a9818cce-6496-11eb-8c64-9595888caa15_story.html.?tid=pm_pop.

113 Mayer, "Is Ginni Thomas a Threat."

114 Bob Woodward and Robert Costa, "Virginia Thomas Urged White House Chief to Pursue Unrelenting Efforts to Overturn the 2020 Election, Texts Show," *Washington Post*, March 24, 2022, https://www.washingtonpost.com/politics/2022/03/24/virginia-thomas-mark-meadows-texts/.

115 Meaghan Ellis, "Clarence Thomas Complains Roe Leak Hurt 'Trust' in Supreme Court: 'It's Like Infidelity,'" Salon, May 16, 2022, https://www.salon.com/2022/05/16/clarence-thomas-complains-roe-leak-hurt-trust-in-its-like-infidelity_partner/.

116 "About the Court."

117 Jan Crawford Greenburg, "Clarence Thomas: A Silent Justice Speaks Out,"

ABC News, September 30, 2007, https://abcnews.go.com/TheLaw/story?id=3664572&page=1.

118 Martin, discussion.

119 Clarence Thomas, "Speech to the National Bar Association," July 28, 1998, Memphis, TN, Teaching American History, transcript, https://teachingamericanhistory.org/document/speech-to-the-national-bar-association/.

120 Thomas, "Speech to the National Bar Association."

121 Robert E. Terrill, ed., *The Cambridge Companion to Malcolm X* (Cambridge, UK: Cambridge University Press, 2010), 94.

122 Michael McGouch, "Clarence Thomas and the Gospel of Colorblindness," *Los Angeles Times*, June 26, 2013, https://www.latimes.com/opinion/la-xpm-2013-jun-26-la-ol-clarence-thomas-supreme-court-race-20130626-story.html.

123 Malcolm X, "Message to the Grass Roots," speech, Northern Negro Grass Roots Leadership Conference, November 10, 1963, Detroit, MI, Columbia Center for New Media Teaching and Learning, transcript, https://ccnmtl.columbia.edu/projects/mmt/mxp/speeches/mxa29.html.

124 Malcolm X, "The Race Problem," speech, African Students Association and NAACP Campus Chapter, January 23, 1963, East Lansing, MI, Columbia Center for New Media Teaching and Learning, transcript, https://ccnmtl.columbia.edu/projects/mmt/mxp/speeches/mxt14.html.

125 Paul Butler, in discussion with the author, December 2021.

126 Adam Clymer, "About That Flag on the Judge's Desk," *New York Times*, July 19, 1991, https://www.nytimes.com/1991/07/19/us/about-that-flag-on-the-judge-s-desk.html.

127 Clymer, "About That Flag."

128 Thomas, *My Grandfather's Son*, 103.

129 "Rebel Flag Pits Issue of Racism vs. History," *Houston Chronicle*, April 23, 1987.

128 Clymer, "About That Flag."

131 Fisher, "Private World of Justice Thomas."

132 "Curtis Flowers Sues the DA Who Put Him on Trial 6 Times," NPR, September 3, 2021, https://www.npr.org/2021/09/03/1034198690/curtis-flowers-mississippi-lawsuit-prosecutor-da-freed-prisoner.

133 Will Craft, "Mississippi D.A. Doug Evans Has Long History of Striking Black People from Juries," *APM Reports*, Minnesota Public Radio, June 12, 2018, https://features.apmreports.org/in-the-dark/mississippi-da-doug-evans-striking-black-people-from-juries/.

134 Nina Totenberg, "Supreme Court Strikes Down Conviction of Mississippi Man on Death Row for 22 Years," *Morning Edition*, NPR, June 21, 2019, https://www.npr.org/2019/06/21/732159330/supreme-court-strikes-down-conviction-of-mississippi-man-on-death-row-for-22-yea.

135 *Flowers v. Mississippi*, No. 17-9572, 588 U.S. ___ (2019), https://www.supremecourt.gov/opinions/18pdf/17-9572_k536.pdf.

136 Paul Butler, "Mississippi Goddamn: Flowers v Mississippi's Cheap Racial Justice," *Supreme Court Review* 2019, (2019), https://www.journals.uchicago.edu/doi/full/10.1086/708458#fn154.

137 John Schwartz, "Between the Lines of the Voting Rights Act Opinion," *New York Times*, June 25, 2013, https://archive.nytimes.com/www.nytimes.com/interactive/2013/06/25/us/annotated-supreme-court-decision-on-voting-rights-act.html.

138 Jason Slotkin, "After 6 Trials, Prosecutors Drop Charges Against Curtis Flowers," NPR, September 5, 2020, https://www.npr.org/2020/09/05/910061573/after-6-trials-prosecutors-drop-charges-against-curtis-flowers.

139 "Curtis Flowers," National Registry of Exonerations, University of Michigan, accessed June 2, 2022, https://www.law.umich.edu/special/exoneration/Pages/casedetail.aspx?caseid=5808.

140 "Curtis Flowers Sues the DA."

141 Jesus Jiménez, "Curtis Flowers Sues Prosecutor Who Tried Him Six Times," *New York Times*, September 4, 2021, https://www.nytimes.com/2021/09/04/us/curtis-flowers-doug-evans.html.

142 Lisa Lerer, "Joe Biden Says He Regrets Role in Anita Hill Hearing," *New York Times*, March 26, 2019, https://www.nytimes.com/2019/03/26/us/politics/biden-anita-hill.html.

143 Krissah Thompson, "For Anita Hill, the Clarence Thomas Hearings Haven't Really Ended," *Washington Post*, October 6, 2011, https://www.washingtonpost.com/politics/for-anita-hill-the-clarence-thomas-hearings-havent-really-ended/2011/10/05/gIQAy2b5QL_story.html.

144 Danielle Genet et al., "Anita Hill Reflects on Clarence Thomas Testimony, Her 30-Year Fight against Gender Violence," ABC News, September 27, 2021, https://abcnews.go.com/GMA/News/anita-hill-reflects-clarence-thomas-testimony-30-year/story?id=80256745.

145 *Hearings before the Committee on the Judiciary on the Nomination of Clarence Thomas to Be Associate Justice of the Supreme Court of the United States*, 102nd Cong. (1991), https://www.govinfo.gov/content/pkg/GPO-CHRG-THOMAS/pdf/GPO-CHRG-THOMAS-4.pdf.

146 Jacobs, "Anita Hill's Testimony."

147 Angela Wright, interview by Jim Gilmore, *Frontline*, PBS, July 8, 2020, https://www.pbs.org/wgbh/frontline/interview/angela-wright/.

148 Jacobs, "Anita Hill's Testimony"; "Clip of Thomas Second Hearing Day 1, Part 4," C-SPAN, October 12, 1991, video, 3:18, https://www.c-span.org/video/?c3945290/user-clip-clarence-thomas-lynching.

149 Bob Secter, "Veteran Illinois Senator Dixon Defeated," *Los Angeles Times*, March 18, 1992, https://www.latimes.com/archives/la-xpm-1992-03-18-mn-3844-story.html.

150 Paul Delaney, "The Nation; 'Black and Conservative' Takes Many Different Tones," *New York Times*, December 22, 1991, https://www.nytimes.com/1991/12/22/weekinreview/the-nation-black-and-conservative-takes-many-different-tones.html.

CHAPTER 6: FRANKS AND WATTS

1 "J.C. Watts on Why the 'Race Issue' Is Costing Republican Black Voters," Yahoo Finance, August 13, 2020, video, 7:13, https://www.yahoo.com/lifestyle/j-c-watts-why-race-233429005.html.

2 "Black-American Members by Congress," History, Art & Archives, United States House of Representatives, accessed June 2, 2022, https://history.house.gov/Exhibitions-and-Publications/BAIC/Historical-Data/Black-American-Representatives-and-Senators-by-Congress/.

3 "Franks, Gary A.," History, Art, & Archives, United States House of Representatives, accessed June 2, 2022, https://history.house.gov/People/Detail/13411.

4 Theodore Rueter, *The Politics of Race: African Americans and the Political System* (Armonk, NY: M. E. Sharpe, 1995), 92.

5 Gregg Zoroya, "The Sunday Profile: Against the Grain: Gary Franks' Stand on Affirmative Action Pits Him against Other Blacks in Congress—and the Leaders of His Own Party," *Los Angeles Times*, August 6, 1995, https://www.latimes.com/archives/la-xpm-1995-08-06-ls-31993-story.html.

6 "Black Congressman Slams March,"UPI Archives,October 12,1995,https://www.upi.com/Archives/1995/10/12/Black-congressman-slams-march/3520813470400/.

7 Nick Ravo, "New Star for G.O.P. Is Conservative and Black," *New York Times*, November 25, 1990, https://www.nytimes.com/1990/11/25/nyregion/new-star-for-gop-is-conservative-and-black.html.

8 Ann Devroy, "Bush Vetoes Civil Rights Bill," *Washington Post*, October 23, 1990, https://www.washingtonpost.com/archive/politics/1990/10/23/bush-vetoes-civil-rights-bill/cd68a6c4-8529-471a-b4f7-08c26cf65ac0/.

9 Jacqueline Trescott,"Rep. Gary Franks, Unexpected Republican," *Washington Post,* July 31, 1991, https://www.washingtonpost.com/archive/lifestyle/1991/07/31/rep-gary-franks-unexpected-republican/7ce692c5-ec04-439f-9a05-20aacf075d85/.

10 Gary Franks, "I Was Shunned by the Congressional Black Caucus. It Hasn't Changed," *Connecticut Post*, June 23, 2021, https://www.ctpost.com/opinion/article/Gary-Franks-opinion-I-was-shunned-by-the-16267734.php.

11 Franks, "I Was Shunned."

12 Zoroya, "Sunday Profile: Against the Grain."

13 Stuart Rothenberg, "Dem, GOP Tests in Connecticut, Arizona," CNN, April 9, 1997, https://edition.cnn.com/ALLPOLITICS/1997/04/09/spotlight/.

14 Mike McIntire and Michael Remez, "Franks Blames GOP, Liberals, Labor and Rat Ads for His Loss," *Hartford Courant*, November 7, 1996, https://www.courant.com/news/connecticut/hc-xpm-1996-11-07-9611070214-story.html.

15 McIntire and Remez, "Franks Blames GOP."

16 Franks, "I Was Shunned."

17 Juliet Eilperin, "Watts Walks a Tightrope on Affirmative Action," *Washington Post*, May 12, 1998, https://www.washingtonpost.com/wp-srv/politics/special/affirm/stories/aa051298.htm.

18   Dewey M. Clayton, *African Americans and the Politics of Congressional Redistricting* (New York: Routledge, 2004), 21.

19   Lally Weymouth, "J. C. Watts: No Excuses," *Washington Post*, February 15, 1995, https://www.washingtonpost.com/archive/opinions/1995/02/15/j-c-watts-no -excuses/26f80e0d-f66f-46fd-9a3b-5f4159ff3e35/.

20   Clarence Lusane, "Alan Keyes and Other False Prophets," *Baltimore Sun*, May 12, 1995, https://www.baltimoresun.com/news/bs-xpm-1995-05-12-1995132022-story .html.

21   Weymouth, "J. C. Watts: No Excuses."

22   "State of the Union Response," C-SPAN, February 4, 1997, video, 17:18, https:// www.c-span.org/video/?78505–1/state-union-response.

23   Ken Ringle, "Carrying the GOP Ball," *Washington Post*, February 4, 1997, https:// www.washingtonpost.com/archive/lifestyle/1997/02/04/carrying-the-gop-ball /dfa39ec0-bbbd-41b3-9d3d-db0e25f5e77a/.

24   Sandra Evans, "Mayor Promises Summer Jobs to D.C. Youth," *Washington Post*, April 17, 1985, https://www.washingtonpost.com/archive/local/1985/04/17/ mayor-promises-summer-jobs-to-dc-youth/6a52dbf9-274e-45c2-8d22- da6ad4a67b93/.

25   Chris Casteel, "Controversy over Comment Doesn't Have Watts Worried," *Oklahoman*, February 6, 1997, https://www.oklahoman.com/story/news/1997/02/06 /controversy-over-comment-doesnt-have-watts-worried/62324735007/.

26   Tom Pendergast and Sara Pendergast, "Jackson, Jesse Jr. 1965–," in *Contemporary Black Biography*, vol. 14 (Farmington Hills, MI: Gale, 1997), https://www.encyclopedia .com/education/news-wires-white-papers-and-books/jackson-jesse-jr-1965–0.

27   Casteel, "Controversy over Comment."

28   Casteel, "Controversy over Comment."

29   Eilperin, "Watts Walks a Tightrope on Affirmative Action."

30   Eilperin, "Watts Walks a Tightrope."

31   Jake Tapper, "Fade to White," *Washington Post*, January 5, 2003, https://www.washington post.com/archive/lifestyle/magazine/2003/01/05/fade-to-white/0caf4763-0665 -4603-acee-63a1bad17089/.

32   Tom DeLay, "The Message or the Machine?," Politico, February 12, 2007, https:// www.politico.com/story/2007/02/tom-delay-the-message-or-the-machine-002722.

33   Jake Tapper, "Fade to White," Washington Post, January 5, 2003, https://www. washingtonpost.com/archive/lifestyle/magazine/2003/01/05/fade-to-white /0caf4763-0665-4603-acee-63a1bad17089/.

34   Tapper, "Fade to White."

35   Tapper, "Fade to White."

36   "2002 U.S. House Ratings," Acuratings, accessed June 2, 2022, https://web .archive.org/web/20080209140708/http://www.acuratings.org/ratingsarchive /2002/2002House.htm.

37   David Espo, "Analysis: A Vote with Unforeseen Consequences?," Associated Press,

October 1, 2008, https://usatoday30.usatoday.com/news/washington/2008-10-01
-484084648_x.htm.

38   Bob Wheaton, "Gay Marriage, Removal of God from 'Public Square' Will Hurt America, J. C. Watts Says," MLive Media Group, February 21, 2012, https://www.mlive
.com/news/jackson/2012/02/gay_marriage_removal_of_god_fr.html.

39   Paighten Harkins, "Ex-Congressman J.C. Watts Calls Out Politicians for Silence on President Trump, Racism," *Tulsa World*, August 20, 2017, https://tulsaworld.com
/news/ex-congressman-j-c-watts-calls-out-politicians-for-silence-on-president
-trump-racism/article_4aa53bd9-d3b7-5e78-88d7-e93ec671f794.html.

40   "J.C. Watts on Why."

41   Julia Mueller, "Former GOP Rep. J.C. Watts Endorses Democrat in Oklahoma Governor's Race," *Hill*, October 31, 2022, https://thehill.com/homenews/campaign/3712933
-former-gop-rep-j-c-watts-endorses-democrat-in-oklahoma-governors-race/.

CHAPTER 7: RICE, POWELL, AND BUSH

1   Condoleezza Rice, interview by Bill O'Reilly, *O'Reilly Factor*, Fox News, September 14, 2005, https://2001-2009.state.gov/secretary/rm/2005/53155.htm.

2   "Can Bush Mend His Party's Rift with Black America?," *New York Times*, December 17, 2000, https://www.nytimes.com/2000/12/17/opinion/can-bush-mend-his
-party-s-rift-with-black-america.html.

3   Julian Borger, "US Inquiry into Claims Black Voters Were Stripped of Rights," *Guardian*, December 4, 2000, https://www.theguardian.com/world/2000/dec/04
/uselections2000.usa1.

4   Dan Keating and John Mintz, "Florida Black Ballots Affected Most in 2000," *Washington Post*, November 13, 2001, https://www.washingtonpost.com/archive
/politics/2001/11/13/florida-black-ballots-affected-most-in-2000/16784e7d
-439a-4b96-9653-1b7362312d2a/.

5   "U.S. Sues Black Activist on Voting Act Violation," NBC News, May 2, 2006, https://www.nbcnews.com/id/wbna12597671.

6   Ko Bragg, "Unapologetically Ike Brown," *Scalawag*, October 29, 2018, https://
scalawagmagazine.org/2018/10/mississippi-voter-rights/.

7   Adam Nossiter, "U.S. Says Blacks in Mississippi Suppress White Vote," *New York Times*, October 11, 2006, https://www.nytimes.com/2006/10/11/us/politics
/11voting.html.

8   "U.S. Sues Black Activist."

9   Bragg, "Unapologetically Ike Brown."

10   "Alphonso Jackson, Former Secretary of Housing & Urban Development," White House, accessed June 2, 2022, https://georgewbush-whitehouse.archives.gov
/government/ajackson-bio.html.

11   "Education Secretary Paige Reportedly to Resign," NBC News, November 12, 2004, https://www.nbcnews.com/id/wbna6471630; "Rod Paige, U.S. Secretary

of Education—Biography," U.S. Department of Education, February 13, 2004, https://www2.ed.gov/news/staff/bios/paige.html.

12 Sean F. Reardon et al., "Left Behind? The Effect of No Child Left Behind on Academic Achievement Gaps," Center for Education Policy Analysis, Stanford University, 2013, https://cepa.stanford.edu/content/left-behind-effect-no-child -left-behind-academic-achievement-gaps.

13 "Rod Paige | Conversations | MPB," Mississippi Public Broadcasting, May 7, 2017, YouTube video, 26:46, https://www.youtube.com/watch?v=w5h_kvsv9EY.

14 Julia E. Koppich, "A Tale of Two Approaches: The AFT, the NEA, and NCLB," *Peabody Journal of Education* 80, no. 2 (2005): 137–155, http://www.jstor.org /stable/3497064.

15 "President Bush Discusses No Child Left Behind," policy address given at General Philip Kearny School, January 8, 2009, Philadelphia, PA, White House, transcript, https://georgewbush-whitehouse.archives.gov/news/releases /2009/01/20090108-2.html.

16 Jennifer Imazeki and Andrew Reschovsky, "Is No Child Left Behind an Un (or Under) Funded Federal Mandate? Evidence from Texas," *National Tax Journal* 57, no. 3 (2004): 571–88, http://www.jstor.org/stable/41790231.

17 Lily Eskelsen García and Otha Thornton, "'No Child Left Behind' Has Failed," *Washington Post*, February 13, 2015, https://www.washingtonpost.com/opinions /no-child-has-failed/2015/02/13/8d619026-b2f8-11e4-827f-93f454140e2b _story.html.

18 "Faith in the Public Sphere," *New York Times*, April 11, 2003, https://www .nytimes.com/2003/04/11/opinion/faith-in-the-public-sphere.html.

19 "Release of Transcript Fails to Vindicate Education Secretary Paige, Says Amer- icans United," Americans United for Separation of Church and State, April 15, 2003, https://web.archive.org/web/20060720152942/https://www.commondreams .org/news2003/0415-11.htm.

20 Ori Nir, "Schools Chief Boosts Christian Values," *Forward*, April 18, 2003, https:// forward.com/news/8632/schools-chief-boosts-christian-values/.

21 Robert Pear, "Education Chief Calls Union 'Terrorist,' Then Recants," *New York Times*, February 24, 2004, https://www.nytimes.com/2004/02/24/us/education -chief-calls-union-terrorist-then-recants.html.

22 "Education Secretary Paige."

23 "Lawsuit Targets Bush Education Law," CBS News, April 20, 2005, https:// www.cbsnews.com/news/lawsuit-targets-bush-education-law/.

24 Valerie Strauss, "A Decade of No Child Left Behind: Lessons from a Policy Fail- ure," *Washington Post*, January 7, 2012, https://www.washingtonpost.com/blogs /answer-sheet/post/a-decade-of-no-child-left-behind-lessons-from-a-policy -failure/2012/01/05/gIQAeb19gP_blog.html.

25 Maureen Downey, "An architec of No Child Left Behind Looks Back on Failed Reforms and Says, 'We Forgot the Why'" *Atlanta Journal-Constitution*, October 20,

2014, https://www.ajc.com/blog/get-schooled/architect-child-left-behind-looks -back-failed-reforms-and-says-forgot-the-why/OLq1hGth5iSt7Ed5mL6g5H/.

26 Mary Bowerman, "George W. Bush: C Students, You Too Can Be President," *USA Today*, May 17, 2015, https://www.usatoday.com/story/news/nation-now/2015/05 /17/george-w-bush-c-students-president-graduation/27488795/.

27 Harold Gater, "Rod Paige on Betsy DeVos hearing," Jackson, MS *Clarion Ledger* Jackson, MS, January 19, 2017, https://www.clarionledger.com/videos/news /politics/2017/01/19/rod-paige-betsy-devos-hearing/96798278/.

28 Valerie Strauss, "Six Astonishing Things Betsy DeVos Said—and Refused to Say—at Her Confirmation Hearing," *Washington Post*, January 18, 2017, video, 2:42, https:// www.washingtonpost.com/news/answer-sheet/wp/2017/01/18/six-astonishing -things-betsy-devos-said-and-refused-to-say-at-her-confirmation-hearing/.

29 "Alphonso Jackson," Bureau of Educational and Cultural Affairs, accessed June 2, 2022, https://eca.state.gov/fulbright/about-fulbright/fulbright-foreign -scholarship-board-ffsb/ffsb-members/alphonso-jackson.

30 Rachel Swarns, "Official's Journey Ends in a Swirl of Accusations," *New York Times*, April 1, 2008, https://www.nytimes.com/2008/04/01/washington/01jack son.html.

31 "Profile: Secretary of Housing and Urban Development Alphonso Jackson," ABC News, 2004, https://abcnews.go.com/Politics/Inauguration/story?id=406759.

32 Libby Lewis, "HUD Secretary Jackson Steps Down amid Probe," *All Things Considered*, NPR, March 31, 2008, https://www.npr.org/2008/03/31/89248516/hud -secretary-jackson-steps-down-amid-probe.

33 "HUD Chief Says He Made Up Story of Rejecting Bush Foe," *Washington Post*, May 11, 2006, https://www.washingtonpost.com/archive/politics/2006/05/11 /hud-chief-says-he-made-up-story-of-rejecting-bush-foe/0d349cf3-8ff0-4b57 -a09d-a4d66542bafb/.

34 "HUD Chief Says He Made Up Story."

35 "A Made-Up Story?," *East Bay Times*, May 15, 2006, https://www.eastbaytimes .com/2006/05/15/a-made-up-story-2/.

36 Elizabeth Williamson, "Probe Finds Jackson Urged Favoritism in HUD Contracts; No Evidence That Staff Complied" *Washington Post*, September 22, 2006, https://www .proquest.com/newspapers/probe-finds-jackson-urged-favoritism-hud/docview /410066244/se-2.

37 "Report Says HUD Secretary Will Resign," *New York Times*, March 31, 2008, https://www.nytimes.com/2008/03/31/washington/31jack.html.

38 Sam Thielman, "Black Americans Unfairly Targeted by Banks before Housing Crisis, Says ACLU," *Guardian*, June 23, 2015, https://www.theguardian.com /business/2015/jun/23/black-americans-housing-crisis-sub-prime-loan.

39 "Officials: FBI Probing HUD Secretary Alphonso Jackson over Katrina Contracts," Fox News, January 13, 2015, https://www.foxnews.com/story/officials-fbi-probing -hud-secretary-alphonso-jackson-over-katrina-contracts.

40   "Philadelphia Housing Authority Files Lawsuit against Federal Housing Secre-
     tary," Multi-Housing News, February 5, 2008, https://www.multihousingnews.com
     /philadelphia-housing-authority-files-lawsuit-against-federal-housing-secretary/;
     Swarns, "Official's Journey Ends."

41   "HUD Chief Jackson Resigns under Pressure," NPR, March 31, 2008, https://
     www.npr.org/templates/story/story.php?storyId=89244878.

42   Victoria McGrane, "Dodd, Murray Call for HUD Chief to Resign," Politico, March
     21,   2008,   https://www.politico.com/blogs/politico-now/2008/03/dodd-murray
     -call-for-hud-chief-to-resign-007219.

43   "HUD Resignation a Chance to Fix Housing Crisis?," NPR, April 1, 2008, https://
     www.npr.org/transcripts/89266042.

44   Douglas Rice and Barbara Sard, "Decade of Neglect Has Weakened Federal
     Low-Income Housing Programs," Center on Budget and Policy Priorities, February
     24, 2009, https://www.cbpp.org/sites/default/files/atoms/files/2-24-09hous.pdf.

45   Todd Gillman, "Dallas' Alphonso Jackson Vouches for HUD Nominee Ben Car-
     son, While Housing Advocates Fret," Dallas Morning News, December 29, 2016,
     https://www.dallasnews.com/news/politics/2016/12/29/dallas-alphonso-jackson
     -vouches-for-hud-nominee-ben-carson-while-housing-advocates-fret/.

46   "Does Gen. Colin Powell Have Presidential Aspirations? 'Watch This Space,' He
     Tells DePauw Audience," DePauw University, November 2, 1994, https://web
     .archive.org/web/20210514203109/https://www.depauw.edu/news-media/latest
     -news/details/13936/.

47   Clines, "Powell Rules Out '96 Race."

48   Encyclopaedia Britannica, s.v. "Democratic Party," last updated June 1, 2023, https://
     www.britannica.com/topic/Democratic-Party.

49   Lee Drutman, "How Race and Identity Became the Central Dividing Line
     in American Politics," Vox, August 30, 2016, https://www.vox.com/polyarchy
     /2016/8/30/12697920/race-dividing-american-politics.

50   Harry J. Enten, "Were Republicans Really the Party of Civil Rights in the 1960s?,"
     Guardian, August 28, 2013, https://www.theguardian.com/commentisfree/2013
     /aug/28/republicans-party-of-civil-rights.

51   Maxwell, "What We Get Wrong."

52   Andrew Glass, "House Overrides Reagan Apartheid Veto, Sept. 29, 1986," Po-
     litico, September 29, 2017, https://www.politico.com/story/2017/09/29/house
     -overrides-reagan-apartheid-veto-sept-29-1986-243169.

53   Howell Raines, "Reagan and States' Rights; News Analysis," New York Times,
     March 4, 1981, https://www.nytimes.com/1981/03/04/us/reagan-and-states-rights
     -news-analysis.html.

54   "Congressional Override of a Veto by President Ronald Reagan, March 22, 1988,"
     History, Art & Archives, United States House of Representatives, accessed June 2,
     2022,   https://history.house.gov/Historical-Highlights/1951-2000/Congressional
     -override-of-a-veto-by-President-Ronald-Reagan/.

55 Nkechi Taifa, "Race, Mass Incarceration, and the Disastrous War on Drugs," Brennan Center for Justice, May 10, 2021, https://www.brennancenter.org/our-work /analysis-opinion/race-mass-incarceration-and-disastrous-war-drugs.

56 Ann Devroy, "Bush Vetoes Civil Rights Bill," *Washington Post*, October 23, 1990, https://www.washingtonpost.com/archive/politics/1990/10/23/bush-vetoes-civil -rights-bill/cd68a6c4-8529-471a-b4f7-08c26cf65ac0/.

57 Peter Baker, "Bush Made Willie Horton an Issue in 1988, and the Racial Scars Are Still Fresh," *New York Times*, December 3, 2018, https://www.nytimes .com/2018/12/03/us/politics/bush-willie-horton.html.

58 Colin L. Powell and Joseph E. Persico, *My American Journey* (New York: Random House, 1995), 400.

59 Bob Woodward, "The Powell Predicament," *Washington Post*, September 24, 1995, https://www.washingtonpost.com/archive/lifestyle/magazine/1995/09/24 /the-powell-predicament/aa7a50da-d997-4c02-bae2-25987e7a6c13/.

60 Wright, "'Challenge of Change.'"

61 Woodward, "Powell Predicament."

62 Woodward, "Powell Predicament."

63 Will Dunham, "Colin Powell, U.S. Military Leader and First Black Secretary of State, Dies," Reuters, October 18, 2021, https://www.reuters.com/world/us /obituary-colin-powell-us-military-leader-first-black-secretary-state-dies-2021 -10-18/.

64 Dave Roos, "How Colin Powell's Service in Vietnam Shaped His Leadership," History, October 20, 2021, https://www.history.com/news/colin-powell-vietnam-war.

65 "My Lai Massacre," History, November 9, 2009, https://www.history.com/topics /vietnam-war/my-lai-massacre-1.

66 Matthew Dallek, "How the Army's Cover-Up Made the My Lai Massacre Even Worse," History, August 30, 2018, https://www.history.com/news/my-lai-massacre -1968-army-cover-up.

67 Seymour Hersh, "Lieutenant Accused of Murdering 109 Civilians," *St. Louis Post-Dispatch*, November 13, 1969, reproduced in "'I Sent Them a Good Boy and They Made Him a Murderer,'" Pulitzer Prizes, https://www.pulitzer.org/article/i-sent -them-good-boy-and-they-made-him-murderer.

68 Peter Ross Range, "Only One Man Was Found Guilty for His Role in the My Lai Massacre. This Is What It Was Like to Cover His Trial," *Time*, March 16, 2018, https://time.com/5202268/calley-trial-my-lai-massacre/.

69 David Corn, "Colin Powell's Vietnam Fog," *Nation*, May 2, 2001, https:// www.thenation.com/article/politics/colin-powells-vietnam-fog/.

70 Bradley Graham, "Colin L. Powell, Former Secretary of State and Military Leader, Dies at 84," *Washington Post*, October 18, 2021, https://www.washingtonpost .com/local/obituaries/colin-powell-dead/2021/10/18/fdc71fde-c5db-11df-94e1 -c5afa35a9e59_story.html.

71 Powell and Persico, My American Journey, 144.

72   Jeffrey J. Matthews, "Powell: The Vietnam War Years," HistoryNet, October 18, 2021, https://www.historynet.com/colin-powell-the-vietnam-war-years.htm.

73   Clines, "Powell Rules Out '96 Race."

74   Clines, "Powell Rules Out '96 Race."

75   Reihan Salam, "Why Isn't Colin Powell a Democrat?," CNN, October 26, 2012, https://www.cnn.com/2012/10/26/opinion/salam-partisan-colin-powell/index.html.

76   Scott Lindaw, "Powell Says He Disagrees with Bush's Position on Affirmative Action Case," *Washington Post*, January 20, 2003, https://www.washingtonpost.com/archive/politics/2003/01/20/powell-says-he-disagrees-with-bushs-position-on-affirmative-action-case/0f6867d1-448c-4956-9db8-4158fa5e96b6/.

77   Andrea Mitchell, "Colin Powell Had No Party Loyalty. For That, He Was Booed by Some Republicans," NBC News on Yahoo, October 19, 2021, https://www.yahoo.com/now/colin-powell-had-no-party-225349952.html.

78   "Party Realignment and the New Deal," History, Art, & Archives, United States House of Representatives, accessed June 2, 2022, https://history.house.gov/Exhibitions-and-Publications/BAIC/Historical-Essays/Keeping-the-Faith/Party-Realignment--New-Deal/.

79   Elizabeth Myong, "What Being 'Anti-Racist' Looks Like for FDR's Descendants," KERA News, Dallas, TX, November 24, 2021, https://www.keranews.org/news/2021-11-24/what-being-anti-racist-looks-like-for-fdrs-descendants.

80   Encyclopaedia Britannica, s.v. "United States Presidential Election of 2000," *by Michael Levy, last updated March 10, 2023*, https://www.britannica.com/event/United-States-presidential-election-of-2000.

81   Roy, "No, Trump Didn't Win."

82   "Biographies of the Secretaries of State: Colin Luther Powell (1937–2021)," Office of the Historian, U.S. Department of State, accessed June 2, 2022, https://history.state.gov/departmenthistory/people/powell-colin-luther.

83   "CIA's Final Report: No WMD Found in Iraq," NBC News, April 25, 2005, https://www.nbcnews.com/id/wbna7634313.

84   "Chilcot Report: What Blair Said to Bush in Memos," BBC News, July 6, 2016, https://www.bbc.com/news/uk-36722312.

85   Julian Borger, "Colin Powell's UN Speech: A Decisive Moment in Undermining US Credibility," *The Guardian*, October 18, 2021, https://www.theguardian.com/us-news/2021/oct/18/colin-powell-un-security-council-iraq.

86   Jeffrey M. Jones, "Blacks Showing Decided Opposition to War," Gallup, March 28, 2003, https://news.gallup.com/poll/8080/blacks-showing-decided-opposition-war.aspx.

87   John King et al., "Powell Resigns with Three Other Cabinet Secretaries," CNN, November 16, 2004, https://edition.cnn.com/2004/ALLPOLITICS/11/15/powell/index.html.

88   "Colin Powell Endorses Senator Obama," C-SPAN, October 19, 2008, video, 1:54, https://www.c-span.org/video/?281880-1/colin-powell-endorses-senator-obama.

89 Dan Glaister, "Colin Powell Endorses Barack Obama for President," *Guardian*, October 19, 2008, https://www.theguardian.com/world/2008/oct/19/colin-powell -endorses-barack-obama.

90 Chris Rovzar, "So Who Thought Colin Powell Only Endorsed Obama Because He's Black?," *New York Magazine*, October 20, 2008, https://nymag.com/intelligencer /2008/10/so_who_thought_colin_powell_on.html.

91 Tal Kopan, "Colin Powell Slams N.C. Voting Law," Politico, September 22, 2013, https://www.politico.com/story/2013/08/colin-powell-north-carolina-voting -law-095813.

92 Donald Trump (@realDonaldTrump), "Obama is about to destroy the mililtary [sic] through the sequester. The Middle East is a mess. Yet Colin Powell still endorses him. Wonder why?," Twitter, October 26, 2012, 1:45 p.m., https://twitter.com /realdonaldtrump/status/261901502430461953.

93 Daniella Diaz and Elise Labott, "Colin Powell Says He's Voting for Clinton," CNN, October 25, 2016, https://www.cnn.com/2016/10/25/politics/colin-powell-hillary -clinton-endorsement/index.html.

94 "A High Honor: Women Secretaries of State," National Museum of American Diplomacy, accessed June 2, 2022, https://diplomacy.state.gov/exhibits/explore -online-exhibits/herdiplomacy/a-high-honor-secretaries-of-state/.

95 "Colin Powell Endorses Joe Biden for US President," *Guardian*, June 7, 2020, https://www.theguardian.com/us-news/2020/jun/07/colin-powell-endorses-joe -biden-for-us-president.

96 Allan Smith, "Colin Powell Calls Trump a Liar, Says He Skirts the Constitution, Will Vote Biden," NBC News, June 7, 2020, https://www.nbcnews.com/politics/donald -trump/colin-powell-calls-trump-liar-says-he-skirts-constitution-will-n1227016.

97 Chandelis Duster, "Colin Powell Says He No Longer Considers Himself a Republican," CNN, January 11, 2021, https://www.cnn.com/2021/01/11/politics/colin-powell -no-longer-republican-cnntv/index.html.

98 Eric Schmitt, "Colin Powell, Who Shaped U.S. National Security, Dies at 84," *New York Times*, October 18, 2021, https://www.nytimes.com/2021/10/18/us/politics /colin-powell-dead.html.

99 Barack Obama (@BarackObama), "General Colin Powell understood what was best in this country, and tried to bring his own life, career, and public statements in line with that ideal," Twitter, October 18, 2021, 1:15 p.m., https://twitter.com/BarackObama /status/1450148473295228929/photo/1.

100 "Dr. Rice Speaks at Michigan State University," White House, May 7, 2004, https:// georgewbush-whitehouse.archives.gov/news/releases/2004/05/20040507-17.html.

101 Condoleezza Rice, *Condoleezza Rice: A Memoir of My Extraordinary, Ordinary Family and Me* (New York: Delacorte Press, 2010), 158–59.

102 Wiley A. Hall III, "Thomas Thomas Debate Feeds Myth: Blacks Obsessed with Role as History's Victims," *Sun Sentinel (South Florida)*, September 14, 1991, https://www.sun-sentinel.com/news/fl-xpm-1991-09-14-9102050323-story.html.

103 Michael A. Fletcher, "White High School Dropouts Are Wealthier Than Black and Hispanic College Graduates. Can a New Policy Tool Fix That?," Washington Post, March 10, 2015, https://www.washingtonpost.com/news/wonk/wp/2015/03/10 /white-high-school-dropouts-are-wealthier-than-black-and-hispanic-college -graduates-can-a-new-policy-tool-fix-that/.

104 Richard V. Reeves and Katherine Guyot, "Black Women Are Earning More College Degrees, but That Alone Won't Close Race Gaps," Brookings Institution, December 4, 2017, https://www.brookings.edu/blog/social-mobility-memos/2017/12/04/black -women-are-earning-more-college-degrees-but-that-alone-wont-close-race-gaps/.

105 "Working Together to Reduce Black Maternal Mortality," Centers for Disease Control and Prevention, April 6, 2022, https://www.cdc.gov/healthequity/features /maternal-mortality/index.html.

106 Eduardo Porter, "Black Workers Stopped Making Progress on Pay. Is It Racism?," *New York Times*, June 28, 2021, https://www.nytimes.com/2021/06/28/business /economy/black-workers-racial-pay-gap.html.

107 Thomas Spencer, "Condoleezza Rice's Book Tells All about Her Parents' Lives in Titusville," Alabama Media Group, November 6, 2010, https://www.al.com/spotnews /2010/11/condoleezza_rices_book_tells_a.html.

108 Dale Russakoff, "Lessons of Might and Right," *Washington Post Magazine*, September 9, 2001, https://www.washingtonpost.com/wp-dyn/articles/A54664-2001Sep6 .html.

109 Verna Gates, "Condoleezza Rice Recalls Racial Blast That Killed Childhood Friend," Reuters, September 14, 2013, https://www.reuters.com/article/us-usa -alabama-memorial/condoleezza-rice-recalls-racial-blast-that-killed-childhood -friend-idUSBRE98C11720130914.

110 "A Byte Out of History: Mississippi Burning," FBI, February 26, 2007, https:// archives.fbi.gov/archives/news/stories/2007/february/miburn_022607.

111 Andrew K. Franklin, "King in 1967: My Dream Has 'Turned into a Nightmare,'" NBC News, August 27, 2013, https://www.nbcnews.com/nightly-news/king-1967 -my-dream-has-turned-nightmare-flna8c11013179.

112 *Encyclopaedia Britannica*, s.v.Encyclopaedia Britannica, s.v. "Was Martin Luther King, Jr., a Republican or a Democrat?," last updated January 11, 2019, https://www .britannica.com/story/was-martin-luther-king-jr-a-republican-or-a-democrat.

113 "Chevron Takes 'Condoleezza Rice' off the Seas," *Gulf News*, May 8, 2001, https://gulfnews.com/business/energy/chevron-takes-condoleezza-rice-off-the -seas-1.416198.

114 "Condoleezza Rice," Faculty Profiles, Stanford Graduate School of Business, accessed June 2, 2022, https://www.gsb.stanford.edu/faculty-research/faculty /condoleezza-rice.

115 Mark Z. Barabak, "Not Always Diplomatic in Her First Major Post," *Los Angeles Times*, January 16, 2005, https://web.archive.org/web/20160410111510/http: /articles.latimes.com/2005/jan/16/local/me-rice16/2.

116 Anthony Walesby, "Facts and Myths of Affirmative Action," Higher Ed Jobs, December 16, 2010, https://www.higheredjobs.com/articles/articledisplay.cfm?ID =246.

117 Barabak, "Not Always Diplomatic."

118 Andrew Vogeley, "Fighting for the Future: A History of the May 1994 Hunger Strike," *Stanford Daily*, May 23, 2014, https://stanforddaily.com/2014/05/23/fighting-for -the-future-a-history-of-the-1994-hunger-strike/.

119 Marcus Mabry, *Twice as Good: Condoleezza Rice and Her Path to Power* (New York: Modern Times, 2007), 131.

120 "The Creation of Stanford's Program in Comparative Studies in Race and Ethnicity," School of Education, Stanford University, December 13, 2006, https:// caselib.stanford.edu/sites/default/files/cases/clarke_case.pdf.

121 Mabry, *Twice as Good*, 137.

122 "Casper Selects Condoleezza Rice to Be Next Stanford Provost," Stanford University News Service, May 19, 1993, https://news.stanford.edu/pr/93/930519Arc3267.html.

123 Mabry, *Twice as Good*, 136.

124 Diane Manuel, "Students Rally for Faculty Diversity," *Stanford Report*, April 29, 1998, https://web.archive.org/web/20210609131035/https://news.stanford.edu /news/1998/april29/rally429.html.

125 Mabry, *Twice as Good*, 138.

126 Kathleen J. Sullivan, "Donald Kennedy, Stanford's Eighth President, Dead at 88," *Stanford News*, April 21, 2020, https://news.stanford.edu/2020/04/21/donald -kennedy-stanfords-eighth-president-dead-88/.

127 Mabry, *Twice as Good*, 138.

128 Matt Palumbo, "Dr. Condoleezza Rice, Former U.S. Secretary of State, Visits the Cornell Club-NY," LinkedIn, May 11, 2017, https://www.linkedin.com/pulse /dr-condoleezza-rice-former-us-secretary-state-visits-cornell-palumbo/.

129 "Coit D Blacker," Stanford Center for African Studies, accessed June 2, 2022, https://africanstudies.stanford.edu/people/coit-d-blacker.

130 Lourdes Torres, "The Struggle Continues: Women of Color Faculty and Institutional Barriers," in *Persistence Is Resistance*, ed. Julie Shayne (Seattle: University of Washington Libraries, 2020), https://uw.pressbooks.pub/happy50thws/chapter /the-struggle-continues-women-of-color-faculty-and-institutional-barriers/; Kate Taylor, "Denying a Professor Tenure, Harvard Sparks a Debate Over Ethnic Studies," *New York Times*, January 2, 2020, https://www.nytimes.com/2020/01/02/us /harvard-latinos-diversity-debate.html; Tory Lysik, "CU Boulder Students Protest Demotion of Latina Faculty Member," CUIndependent, University of Colorado Boulder, February 14, 2020, https://www.cuindependent.com/2020/02/14/cu -boulder-protest-latina-professor-demotion/.

131 Katie Robertson, "Nikole Hannah-Jones Denied Tenure at University of North Carolina," *New York Times*, May 19, 2021, https://www.nytimes.com/2021/05/19 /business/media/nikole-hannah-jones-unc.html.

132 Laurel Wamsley, "After Tenure Controversy, Nikole Hannah-Jones Will Join Howard Faculty Instead of UNC," NPR, July 6, 2021, https://www.npr.org/2021/07/06/1013315775/after-tenure-controversy-nikole-hannah-jones-will-join-howard-faculty-instead-of.

133 Manuel, "Students Rally for Faculty Diversity."

134 "Faculty Profile: Fall 2021," Stanford Facts, accessed June 2, 2022, https://facts.stanford.edu/academics/faculty-profile/.

135 Dan Balz, "The Republicans Showcase a Rising Star," *Washington Post*, August 1, 2000, https://www.washingtonpost.com/archive/politics/2000/08/01/the-republicans-showcase-a-rising-star/430295bb-7c08-4c39-b7ab-36a0a3de8c57/.

136 "Text: Condoleezza Rice at the Republican National Convention," *Washington Post*, August 1, 2000, http://www.washingtonpost.com/wp-srv/onpolitics/elections/ricetext080100.htm.

137 Mabry, *Twice as Good*, 161.

138 Sara Spieth, "Celebrating State Department Interns," *DipNote* (blog), U.S. Department of State, July 29, 2021, https://www.state.gov/dipnote-u-s-department-of-state-official-blog/celebrating-state-department-interns/; Condoleezza Rice, interview by Peter Feaver, Meghan O'Sullivan, and Timothy Sayle, July 20, 2015, Center for Presidential History, Southern Methodist University, https://www.smu.edu/Dedman/Research/Institutes-and-Centers/Center-for-Presidential-History/CMP/The-Surge-in-Iraq/Condoleezza-Rice.

139 Condoleezza Rice, interview by Peter Kenyon, *All Things Considered*, NPR, December 17, 2000, https://www.npr.org/2000/12/17/1115648/condoleezza-rice.

140 "Transcript of Rice's 9/11 Commission Statement," CNN, May 19, 2004, https://www.cnn.com/2004/ALLPOLITICS/04/08/rice.transcript/.

141 Wolf Blitzer, "Search for the 'Smoking Gun,'" CNN, January 10, 2003, https://www.cnn.com/2003/US/01/10/wbr.smoking.gun/.

142 Condoleezza Rice, "Why We Know Iraq Is Lying," *New York Times*, January 23, 2003, https://www.nytimes.com/2003/01/23/opinion/why-we-know-iraq-is-lying.html.

143 Peter Maass, "Colin Powell Was a Nice Man Who Helped Destroy Iraq," The Intercept, October 18, 2021, https://theintercept.com/2021/10/18/colin-powell-dead-iraq/.

144 Dylan Matthews "No, Really, George W. Bush lied about WMDs," Vox, July 9, 2016, https://www.vox.com/2016/7/9/12123022/george-w-bush-lies-iraq-war.

145 "Biographies of the Secretaries of State: Condoleezza Rice (1954–)," Office of the Historian, U.S. Department of State, accessed June 2, 2022, https://history.state.gov/departmenthistory/people/rice-condoleezza.

146 Sheryl Gay Stolberg, "Rice Is Sworn in as Secretary after Senate Vote of 85 to 13," *New York Times*, January 27, 2005, https://www.nytimes.com/2005/01/27/world/rice-is-sworn-in-as-secretary-after-senate-vote-of-85-to-13.html.

147 Stolberg, "Rice Is Sworn In."

148 Richard B. Schmitt and Tyler Marshall, "Rice Is Confirmed Despite Opposi-

tion," *Los Angeles Times*, January 27, 2005, https://www.latimes.com/archives
/la-xpm-2005-jan-27-na-confirm27_-story.html.

149 Charles Babington, "Democrats Criticize Rice Over Iraq War," *Washington Post*, January 26, 2005, https://www.washingtonpost.com/archive
/politics/2005/01/26/democrats-criticize-rice-over-iraq-war/0ccd1811-39df
-4f51-b2ba-98d77d88480d/.

150 Michele Keleman, "Heated Senate Debate Slows Rice Confirmation," *Morning Edition*, NPR, January 26, 2005, https://www.npr.org/templates/story/story
.php?storyId=4466375; Babington, "Democrats Criticize Rice."

151 John Leo, "Don't Care for Bush? He Must Be a Nazi," *Tampa Bay Times*, December 20, 2003, https://www.tampabay.com/archive/2003/12/20/don-t-care-for-bush
-he-must-be-a-nazi/.

152 Jesse Jackson et al., "Can Bush Mend His Party's Rift with Black America?," *New York Times*, December 17, 2000, https://www.nytimes.com/2000/12/17/opinion
/can-bush-mend-his-party-s-rift-with-black-america.html.

153 "Pres. Bush Calls Affirmative Action Policy Unconstitutional," *NewsHour*, PBS, January 15, 2003, https://www.pbs.org/newshour/politics/law-jan-june03-affirmative
_01–15.

154 Ron Fournier, "Security Adviser for Bush Offers Views on Racial Issue," Southeast Missourian, January 18, 2003, https://web.archive.org/web/20170927031115
/https://www.semissourian.com/story/99178.html.

155 Mike Allen and Charles Lane, "Rice Helped Shape Bush Decision on Admissions," *Washington Post*, January 17, 2003, https://www.washingtonpost.com/archive
/politics/2003/01/17/rice-helped-shape-bush-decision-on-admissions/3fbd9282
-11d1-47e0-ab0f-f75b7bd30f3c/.

156 Mabry, *Twice as Good*, 280.

157 Bill Mears, "Michigan's by Supreme Court," CNN, April 23, 2014, https://www
.cnn.com/2014/04/22/justice/scotus-michigan-affirmative-action/index.html.

158 Adam Harris, "What Happens When a College's Affirmative-Action Policy Is Found Illegal," *Atlantic*, October 26, 2018, https://www.theatlantic.com
/education/archive/2018/10/when-college-cant-use-race-admissions/574126/.

159 Kim Kozlowski, "Study: Michigan among Worst in Black University Enrollment," *Detroit News*, April 1, 2019, https://www.detroitnews.com/story/news/local
/michigan/2019/04/02/michigan-universities-black-enrollment/3290299002/.

160 Thomas Hargrove, "Conflict with Iraq: Study Shows 20 Percent of War Deaths Are Blacks," *Naples Daily News*, April 12, 2003, http://www.latinamericanstudies.org
/immigration/iraq.htm.

161 Eugene Kiely, "Fact Check: Rand Paul, Obama and Black Unemployment," *USA Today*, December 11, 2013, https://www.usatoday.com/story/news
/politics/2013/12/11/fact-check-rand-paul-obama-black-unemployment/3988561/.

162 Jacobson, "Ronald Reagan's Record on Black Unemployment."

163 April Ryan, "Grading the Presidents on Race," *Politico Magazine*, March 1, 2015,

https://www.politico.com/magazine/story/2015/03/grading-the-presidents-on
-race-115639/.

164 "Rice Dismisses Reparations for Slavery," CNN, September 9, 2001, https://
www.cnn.com/2001/ALLPOLITICS/09/09/rice.reparations/index.html.

165 Molefi Kete Asante, "Slavery Remembrance Day," speech, Liverpool Town
Hall, August 21, 2007, National Museums Liverpool, transcript, https://www
.liverpoolmuseums.org.uk/ideological-origins-of-chattel-slavery-british-world.

166 "Implications of the Slave Trade for African Societies," BBC, accessed June 2, 2022,
https://www.bbc.co.uk/bitesize/guides/zxt3gk7/revision/2.

167 "African Passages, Lowcountry Adaptations," Lowcountry Digital History Initiative, accessed June 2, 2022, https://ldhi.library.cofc.edu/exhibits/show
/africanpassageslowcountryadapt/introductionatlanticworld/slaverybeforetrade.

168 Jennifer L. Morgan, "*Partus sequitur ventrem*: Law, Race, and Reproduction in
Colonial Slavery," *Small Axe: A Caribbean Journal of Criticism* 22, no. 1 (March
2018): 1–17, http://blogs.law.columbia.edu/abolition1313/files/2020/08/Morgan
-Partus-1.pdf.

169 Steven Mintz, "Historical Context: Facts about the Slave Trade and Slavery," Gilder Lehrman Institute of American History, accessed June 2, 2022, https://www
.gilderlehrman.org/history-resources/teaching-resource/historical-context-facts
-about-slave-trade-and-slavery.

170 Ta-Nehisi Coates, "Slavery Made America," *Atlantic*, June 24, 2014, https://www
.theatlantic.com/business/archive/2014/06/slavery-made-america/373288/.

171 David Mikkelson, "Condoleezza Rice Shops for Shoes," Snopes, October 25, 2011,
https://www.snopes.com/fact-check/shoe-stopper/.

172 Mabry, *Twice as Good*, 271.

173 Kenneth T. Walsh, "The Undoing of George W. Bush," *U.S. News and World Report*,
August 28, 2015, https://www.usnews.com/news/the-report/articles/2015/08/28
/hurricane-katrina-was-the-beginning-of-the-end-for-george-w-bush.

174 Nick Wing, "Bush Admits Katrina Air Force One Photo Was 'Huge Mistake,'"
HuffPost, November 6, 2010, https://www.huffpost.com/entry/bush-katrina
-photo-mistake_n_779527.

175 George W. Bush, *Decision Points* (New York: Crown, 2010), 318.

176 "'George Bush Doesn't Care about Black People': Reflections on Kanye West's Criticism 10 Years After," Democracy Now!, August 28, 2015, YouTube video, 13:08, https://
www.youtube.com/watch?v=lTuRPuhneAs&ab_channel=DemocracyNow%21.

177 Kim Geiger, "Condoleezza Rice Regrets Vacationing, Shoe-Shopping during Katrina," *Los Angeles Times*, November 1, 2011, https://www.latimes.com/archives
/la-xpm-2011-nov-01-la-pn-rice-katrina-20111101-story.html.

178 "Condoleezza Rice on Katrina: 'I Should Have Known Better,'" TheGrio, November
4, 2011, https://thegrio.com/2011/11/04/condoleezza-rice-i-should-have-known
-better-on-katrina/.

179 "Condoleezza Rice on Katrina."

180 "Reaction to Katrina Split on Racial Lines," CNN, September 13, 2005, http://www.cnn.com/2005/US/09/12/katrina.race.poll/.

181 Mabry, *Twice as Good*, 271.

182 Rice, interview by O'Reilly.

183 "Condoleezza Rice Talks Religion, Confederate Monuments, and Energy Policy," AL.com, May 18, 2017, YouTube video, 20:01, https://www.youtube.com/watch?v=HoCY69iP4fk.

184 Miles Parks, "Confederate Statues Were Built to Further a 'White Supremacist Future,'" NPR, August 20, 2017, https://www.npr.org/2017/08/20/544266880/confederate-statues-were-built-to-further-a-white-supremacist-future.

185 Ryan Saavedra (@RealSaavedra), "Condoleezza Rice shuts down an NBC reporter for suggesting race relations are worse under Trump," Twitter, June 21, 2019, 12:54 a.m., https://twitter.com/RealSaavedra/status/1141932381152010240.

186 "Transcript: Condoleezza Rice on *Face the Nation*, September 15, 2019," CBS News, September 15, 2019, https://www.cbsnews.com/news/transcript-condoleezza-rice-on-face-the-nation-sept-15-2019/.

187 "Decades-Old Housing Discrimination Case Plagues Donald Trump," *All Things Considered*, NPR, September 29, 2016, https://www.npr.org/2016/09/29/495955920/donald-trump-plagued-by-decades-old-housing-discrimination-case.

188 Alana Abramson, "How Donald Trump Perpetuated the 'Birther' Movement for Years," ABC News, September 16, 2016, https://abcnews.go.com/Politics/donald-trump-perpetuated-birther-movement-years/story?id=42138176.

189 Jennifer Rubin, "Opinion: Fourth Circuit Finds Racist Motivation in Travel Ban," *Washington Post*, February 15, 2018, https://www.washingtonpost.com/blogs/right-turn/wp/2018/02/15/fourth-circuit-finds-racist-motivation-in-travel-ban/.

190 Sarah Burns, "Why Trump Doubled Down on the Central Park Five," *New York Times*, October 17, 2016, https://www.nytimes.com/2016/10/18/opinion/why-trump-doubled-down-on-the-central-park-five.html.

191 Z. Byron Wolf, "Trump's Attacks on Judge Curiel Are Still Jarring to Read," CNN, February 27, 2018, https://www.cnn.com/2018/02/27/politics/judge-curiel-trump-border-wall/index.html.

192 Katherine Mangan, "Trump Bars Federal Grants for 'Divisive and Harmful' Racial-Sensitivity Training," *Chronicle of Higher Education*, September 24, 2020, https://www.chronicle.com/article/trump-bars-federal-grants-for-divisive-and-harmful-racial-sensitivity-training.

193 Alana Wise, "Trump Announces 'Patriotic Education' Commission, A Largely Political Move," NPR, September 17, 2020, https://www.npr.org/2020/09/17/914127266/trump-announces-patriotic-education-commission-a-largely-political-move.

194 Madison Alder and Jasmine Ye Han, "Trump Nears Post-Nixon First: No Black Circuit Judges (Corrected)," Bloomberg Law, June 24, 2020, https://news.bloomberglaw.com/us-law-week/no-black-judges-among-trumps-appeals-court-confirmations.

195 "Condoleezza Rice on The View Transcript: Critical Race Theory," Rev, October 20, 2021, https://www.rev.com/blog/transcripts/condoleezza-rice-on-the-view-transcript-critical-race-theory.

196 Simon Romero, "Texas Pushes to Obscure the State's History of Slavery and Racism," *New York Times*, May 20, 2021, https://www.nytimes.com/2021/05/20/us/texas-history-1836-project.html.

197 "Condoleezza Rice on *The View* Transcript."

198 Azi Paybarah, "Colin Powell Says He 'Can No Longer Call Himself a Republican,'" *New York Times*, January 11, 2021, https://www.nytimes.com/2021/10/18/us/colin-powell-gop.html.

199 Melissa Quinn, "Condoleezza Rice Urges Trump to 'Put Tweeting Aside for a Little Bit,'" *Face the Nation*, CBS News, June 7, 2020, https://www.cbsnews.com/news/condoleezza-rice-george-floyd-black-lives-matter-face-the-nation-interview/.

200 Joseph Epstein, "Why Not Colin Powell?," *Chicago Tribune*, September 8, 2015, https://www.chicagotribune.com/opinion/commentary/ct-colin-powell-condoleezza-rice-dick-cheney-president-perspec-0909-20150908-story.html.

CHAPTER 8: STEELE

1 "I Keep the Flame Burning on What Republicanism Is: With Guest Keith Boykin," October 2021, in The Michael Steele Podcast, produced by Two Squared Media, podcast, 1:05:34, https://open.spotify.com/episode/6LRGhMLfMuo8Kv9RRPojDM.

2 "Crowd Shouts 'You Lie' at Joe Wilson, Who Shouted at Obama," AP News, April 11, 2017, https://apnews.com/article/4bcb12cd995d48719a81273f071e7f6f.

3 Michael O'Brien, "Boehner: 'Not a Time for Compromise,'" *Hill*, October 27, 2010, https://thehill.com/blogs/blog-briefing-room/news/126153-boehner-this-is-not-a-time-for-compromise.

4 Glenn Kessler, "When Did Mitch McConnell Say He Wanted to Make Obama a One-Term President?," *Washington Post*, January 11, 2017, https://www.washingtonpost.com/news/fact-checker/wp/2017/01/11/when-did-mitch-mcconnell-say-he-wanted-to-make-obama-a-one-term-president/.

5 David Jackson, "Thomas: 'Elites' Like Obama," *USA Today*, May 3, 2013, https://www.usatoday.com/story/theoval/2013/05/03/obama-clarence-thomas-duquesne-elites-cspan/2132043/.

6 Chris Castell, "Former U.S. Rep. J. C. Watts Talks of Historic 'Firsts,'" *Oklahoman*, January 25, 2009, https://www.oklahoman.com/article/3340557/former-us-rep-jc-watts-talks-of-historic-firsts.

7 Andrew Malcolm, "Opinion: Alan Keyes Stokes Obama Birth Certificate Controversy," *Los Angeles Times*, February 21, 2009, https://latimesblogs.latimes.com/washington/2009/02/obama-birth-cer.html.

8 James Janega, "Suit Contesting Barack Obama's Citizenship Heads to U.S. Supreme

Court," *Chicago Tribune*, December 5, 2008, https://www.chicagotribune.com/chi-obama-birth-certificatedec04-archive-story.html.

9   Eric Zorn, "Another Stale Breath of Crazy from Alan Keyes," *Chicago Tribune*, February 22, 2009, https://blogs.chicagotribune.com/news_columnists_ezorn/2009/02/another-stale-breath-of-crazy-from-alan-keyes-.html.

10 *Encyclopaedia Britannica*, s.v. "Alan Keyes," last updated August 3, 2022, https://www.britannica.com/biography/Alan-Keyes.

11 Adam Serwer, "Birtherism of a Nation," *Atlantic*, May 13, 2020, https://www.theatlantic.com/ideas/archive/2020/05/birtherism-and-trump/610978/.

12 Elspeth Reeve, "Herman Cain: Obama 'Was Raised in Kenya,'" *Atlantic*, June 13, 2011, https://www.theatlantic.com/politics/archive/2011/06/herman-cain-obama-was-raised-kenya/351678/.

13 Maria Cramer, "Biden Surpasses Obama's 2008 Popular-Vote Total (with Asterisks)," *New York Times*, November 4, 2020, https://www.nytimes.com/2020/11/04/us/politics/biden-surpasses-obamas-2008-popular-vote-total-with-asterisks.html.

14 Lucy Madison and Brian Montopoli, "Herman Cain Preemptively Denies New Sex Allegation," CBS News, November 29, 2011, https://www.cbsnews.com/news/herman-cain-preemptively-denies-new-sex-allegation/.

15 James Oliphant, "Herman Cain Drops Out of Presidential Race," *Los Angeles Times*, December 3, 2011, https://www.latimes.com/archives/la-xpm-2011-dec-03-la-pn-cain-announcement-20111203-story.html.

16 Ari Melber, "The GOP's Hip-Hop Makeover," *Nation*, March 3, 2009, https://www.thenation.com/article/archive/gops-hip-hop-makeover/.

17 Michael Steele, "Michael Steele: It's Time to Start Restoring the Party of Lincoln," *Hill*, August 31, 2020, https://thehill.com/opinion/white-house/514380-michael-steele-its-time-to-start-restoring-the-party-of-lincoln.

18 "Michael S. Steele," Maryland Manual On-Line, accessed June 1, 2023, https://msa.maryland.gov/msa/mdmanual/08conoff/ltgov/former/html/msa13921.html.

19 Laura Vozzella, "Democrats Give Steele a Place at Their Table," *Baltimore Sun*, January 3, 2003, https://www.baltimoresun.com/news/bs-xpm-2003-01-04-0301040187-story.html.

20 Chloe Kim, "Ku Klux Klan Not Founded by the Democratic Party," AP News, October 23, 2018, https://apnews.com/article/archive-fact-checking-2336745806.

21 Kristen Wyatt, "Democrats Started the KKK," *Chicago Tribune*, September 21, 2006, https://www.chicagotribune.com/chinews-mtblog-2006-09-democrats_started_the_kkk-story.html.

22 Michael Sokolove, "Why Is Michael Steele a Republican Candidate?," *New York Times*, March 26, 2006, https://www.nytimes.com/2006/03/26/magazine/326steele.html.

23 Molly K. Hooper and Bob Cusack, "GOP Leaders Seek to Distance Themselves from Michael Steele," *Hill*, March 31, 2010, https://thehill.com/homenews/campaign/65601-gop-leaders-seek-to-distance-themselves-from-michael-steele/.

24   Devin Dwyer, "Republicans Win Control of House with Historic Gains," ABC News, November 2, 2010, https://abcnews.go.com/Politics/republicans-win -control-house-abc-news-projects-vote-2010-election-results/story?id=12035796; Andy Barr, "RNC Tries to Calm Fundraising Fears," Politico, January 8, 2010, https:// www.politico.com/story/2010/01/rnc-tries-to-calm-fundraising-fears-031269.

25   Sean Miller, "Tea Party Activist Blasts Steele for Touting 2010 Success," *Hill*, January 14, 2011, https://thehill.com/blogs/ballot-box/other-races/137953-tea-party -activist-blasts-steele-for-touting-2010-success-/.

26   Claire Shipman, "Is RNC Chairman Michael Steele's Job in Jeopardy?," ABC News, March 31, 2010, https://abcnews.go.com/GMA/Politics/rnc-chairman-michael -steeles-job-jeopardy/story?id=10247675.

27   Karl Rove, "Cleaning Up after Steele," Daily Beast, January 17, 2011, https:// news.yahoo.com/cleaning-steele-20110117-194306-190.html.

28   Jonathan Martin, "Limbaugh Blasts Steele, the GOP," Politico, March 3, 2009, https://www.politico.com/story/2009/03/limbaugh-blasts-steele-the-gop-019498.

29   Mike Allen, "Steele to Rush: I'm Sorry," Politico, March 2, 2009, https:// www.politico.com/story/2009/03/steele-to-rush-im-sorry-019517.

30   Michael Steele, in discussion with the author, October 2022.

31   Christi Parsons, "Limbaugh Draws Fire on Obama Parody," *Seattle Times*, May 6, 2007, https://www.seattletimes.com/nation-world/limbaugh-draws-fire-on-obama-parody/.

32   David Mikkelson, "Did Rush LImbaugh Utter All These 'Racist' Statements?" Snopes, October 2, 2003, updated Febraury 4, 2020, https://www.snopes.com/fact -check/rush-limbaugh-racist-quotes/.

33   Hooper and Cusack, "GOP Leaders Seek to Distance."

34   Huma Khan, Jonathan Karl, and Polson Kanneth, "White House: Michael Steele's Comments on Race Are 'Silly,'" ABC News, April 4, 2010, https://abcnews .go.com/GMA/Politics/michael-steele-obama-slimmer-margins-error-african -american/story?id=10283514.

35   Steele, discussion.

36   Stephanie Condon, "Do Blacks Have a Reason to Vote GOP? Michael Steele Says No," CBS News, April 22, 2010, https://www.cbsnews.com/news/do-blacks -have-a-reason-to-vote-gop-michael-steele-says-no/.

37   Jordan Fabian, "Steele: White Republicans Are Scared of Me," *Hill*, November 9, 2009, https://thehill.com/blogs/blog-briefing-room/news/67009-steele-white -republicans-are-scared-of-me.

38   Brad Knickerbocker, "Michael Steele: On His Way Out as Republican Party Chair?," *Christian Science Monitor*, December 12, 2010, https://www.csmonitor.com/USA /Politics/2010/1212/Michael-Steele-On-his-way-out-as-Republican-Party-chair.

39   Michael O'Brien, "Steele Condemns Allegations of Racism against Tea Party," *Hill*, July 14, 2010, https://thehill.com/blogs/blog-briefing-room/news/108825 -steele-condemns-allegations-of-racism-against-tea-party.

40   Miller, "Tea Party Activist Blasts Steele."

41   Sean Sullivan, "The Story of Michael and Reince: A Friendship Turned Sour,"
     Washington Post, March 27, 2013, https://www.washingtonpost.com/news/the-fix
     /wp/2013/03/27/the-story-of-michael-and-reince-a-friendship-turned-sour/.

42   Hamil Harris, "Michael Steele at the RNC: 'We Have Work to Do' to Attract
     People of Color to the GOP," *Washington Post*, August 28, 2012, https://www
     .washingtonpost.com/blogs/therootdc/post/michael-steele-at-the-rnc-we
     -have-work-to-do-to-attract-blacks-to-the-gop/2012/08/28/d2f96308-f134
     -11e1-a612-3cfc842a6d89_blog.html.

43   "Stacey Dash Shares Reasons behind her Romney Endorsement," *Piers Morgan To-
     night*, CNN, October 10, 2012, https://cnnpressroom.blogs.cnn.com/2012/10/10
     /piers-morgan-tonight-stacey-dash-shares-reasons-behind-her-endorsement/.

44   "Fox News Hires Stacey Dash as Contributor," Deadline, May 28, 2014, https://
     deadline.com/2014/05/fox-news-hires-stacey-dash-as-contributor-736874/.

45   Crystal Wright, "Black Republican Actress' Racist Remarks Hurt GOP," CNN,
     October 21, 2014, https://www.cnn.com/2014/10/21/opinion/wright-stacey-dash
     -black-republicans-fox/.

46   Melinda Deslatte, "Analysis: Election Reminds Just How Red Louisiana Has Become,"
     Associated Press, November 8, 2020, https://apnews.com/article/election-2020-donald
     -trump-john-bel-edwards-elections-louisiana-fe71643c51b9e5cc57deba99188a6ca9.

47   "Census: Louisiana Remains 1 of Nation's Poorest States," Associated Press, Septem-
     ber 27, 2019, https://apnews.com/article/1068e41cc2374eb9a3457b807de011f0.

48   Steve Spires, "No Drop in Poverty in 2014," Louisiana Budget Project, September
     17, 2015, https://www.labudget.org/2015/09/no-drop-in-poverty-in-2014/.

49   "Stacey Dash on Gender Inequality In Pay," *The Meredith Vieira Show*, April 29,
     2015, YouTube video, 2:18, https://www.youtube.com/watch?v=68rpl0rFQTU;
     Rosalyn Oshmyansky, "Stacey Dash and Meredith Vieira Argue over Equal Pay
     in Very Uncomfortable Interview," ET, April 29, 2015, https://www.etonline.com
     /news/163654_stacey_dash_and_meredith_vieira_argue_over_equal_pay.

50   David Edwards, "Fox Host: The Role of Modern Women Is to 'Engage in a Little
     Horizontal Hula and Then Make Him a Sandwich,'" Raw Story, July 30, 2015,
     https://www.rawstory.com/2015/07/fox-host-the-role-of-modern-women-is-to
     -engage-in-a-little-horizontal-hula-and-then-make-him-a-sandwich/.

51   Alexia Fernández, "Stacey Dash Files for Divorce 9 Months After Alleged Do-
     mestic Violence Incident," *People*, June 16, 2020, https://people.com/movies/stacey
     -dash-files-for-divorce/.

52   Moriba Cummings, "Stacey Dash Doesn't Want a Black History Month or the
     BET Awards," BET, January 20, 2016, https://www.bet.com/article/2blhj2
     /stacey-dash-doesn-t-want-black-history-month-or-bet.

53   BET (@BET), "Soooooo @REALStaceyDash can we get our check back...
     or nah?," Twitter, January 20, 2016, 2:40 p.m., https://twitter.com/BET/status
     /689910485060288513.

54   Stacey Dash, "Racist Speech at BET Awards Attacked White People," Stacey Dash

(blog), June 29, 2016, https://www.patheos.com/blogs/staceydash/2016/06/racist -speech-at-bet-awards-attacked-white-people/.

55 Minyvonne Burke, "Stacey Dash Fired from Fox News, Won't Return as Contributor," *New York Daily News*, January 23, 2017, https://www.nydailynews.com/news /national/stacey-dash-fired-fox-news-article-1.2953529.

56 Saba Hamedy, "'Clueless' Star Stacey Dash Withdraws from Congressional Race," CNN, March 31, 2018, https://www.cnn.com/2018/03/30/politics/stacey -dash-withdraws-congressional-race/index.html.

57 Josh Boswell, "Exclusive: 'That's Not Who I Am Anymore!' Actress and Former Fox News Pundit Stacey Dash Apologizes for Her Offensive Comments as She Turns on Donald Trump, Quits Politics and Blames the Network for Type Casting Her as the 'Angry Black Woman,'" *Daily Mail*, March 10, 2021, https://www.dailymail .co.uk/news/article-9342409/Stacey-Dash-apologizes-offensive-comments-turns -Donald-Trump-quits-politics.html.

58 Wright, "Black Republican Actress' Racist Remarks."

59 Candace Owens (@RealCandaceO), "You have been obsessively tweeting about me & @TheOfficerTatum for almost a year. I'm blocking you for your own mental health," Twitter, May 11, 2020, 11:10 p.m., https://twitter.com/i/web/status /1260044700582641665.

60 John Hayward, "Sonnie Johnson on Blacks for Donald Trump," Breitbart, July 1, 2016, https://www.breitbart.com/radio/2016/07/01/sonnie-johnson-blacks-trump -want-greatness-not-want-free-sht/.

61 "I Keep the Flame Burning."

62 Steele, discussion.

CHAPTER 9: COTTON TO CONGRESS

1 "Tim Scott: 'Our Family Went from Cotton to Congress in One Lifetime,'" Politico, August 24, 2020, video, 11:40, https://www.politico.com/video/2020/08/24 /tim-scott-our-family-went-from-cotton-to-congress-in-one-lifetime-086109.

2 "GOP Senator Shares Struggle with Police Prejudice (2016)," CNN, June 11, 2020, video, 2:04, https://www.cnn.com/videos/politics/2020/06/11/tim-scott-police-black -men-orig-jk.cnn.

3 "Tim Scott's Significant Victory," *Post and Courier* (Charleston, SC), February 9, 1995, https://archive.ph/20130124135048/http:/news.google.com/newspapers?id =1ThSAAAAIBAJ&sjid=pDYNAAAAIBAJ&pg=4278,2512392&dq=tim+scott +charleston&hl=en.

4 Lynette Clemson, "The Racial Politics of Speaking Well," *New York Times*, February 4, 2007, https://www.nytimes.com/2007/02/04/weekinreview/04clemetson.html.

5 Darragh Roche, "Michelle Obama for President? What Polls Say About Her 2024 Chances," *Newsweek*, December 29, 2021, https://www.newsweek.com/michelle -obama-president-what-polls-say-about-her-2024-chances-1663937.

6   "Justice Department Sues Charleston County, South Carolina over Its Method of Electing County Council," U.S. Department of Justice, January 17, 2001, https://www.justice.gov/archive/opa/pr/2001/January/024cr.htm.

7   David Firestone, "U.S. Sues Charleston County, S.C., Alleging Violation of Black Voting Rights," *New York Times*, January 19, 2021, https://www.nytimes.com/2001/01/19/us/us-sues-charleston-county-sc-alleging-violation-of-black-voting-rights.html.

8   Adam Liptak, "Supreme Court Invalidates Key Part of Voting Rights Act," *New York Times*, June 25, 2013, https://www.nytimes.com/2013/06/26/us/supreme-court-ruling.html.

9   Firestone, "U.S. Sues Charleston County."

10 Tim Scott (@votetimscott), "Your 'voting rights' scheme is about two insidious things: undermining the security of our elections and changing the rules to fit your agenda," Twitter, January 18, 2022, 3:00 p.m., https://twitter.com/votetimscott/status/1483529634922729474; Carl Hulse, "After a Day of Debate, the Voting Rights Bill Is Blocked in the Senate," *New York Times*, January 19, 2022, https://www.nytimes.com/2022/01/19/us/politics/senate-voting-rights-filibuster.html.

11 "Freedoms Lost: The Constitutional Convention of 1895," Freedoms Gained and Lost, College of Charleston, accessed May 1, 2022, https://speccoll.cofc.edu/freedoms-gained-and-lost/the-constitutional-convention-of-1895/.

12 Alex Isenstadt, "Palin Backs Scott," Politico, June 19, 2010, https://www.politico.com/story/2010/06/palin-backs-scott-038757.

13 Alexander Burns, "Huckabee to Back Texas Slate, Tim Scott—McCollum Tears into Rick Scott—EMILY's List Launching EMPower—Biden to Calif. for Boxer—NYT Hits Kirk Teaching—Romanoff Takes on Milbank," Politico, June 17, 2010, https://www.politico.com/tipsheets/morning-score/2010/06/huckabee-to-back-texas-slate-tim-scott-mccollum-tears-into-rick-scott-emilys-list-launching-empower-biden-to-calif-for-boxer-nyt-hits-kirk-teaching-romanoff-takes-on-milbank-005656.

14 Marin Cogan, "Black Republican Rejects CBC Invite," Politico, December 1, 2010, https://www.politico.com/story/2010/12/black-republican-rejects-cbc-invite-045824.

15 Corey Dade, "Meet the Freshmen: Rising Stars of the GOP," NPR, January 4, 2011, https://www.npr.org/2011/01/09/132087663/meet-the-freshmen-rising-stars-of-the-gop.

16 Alex Isenstadt, "Allen West's Smashmouth Politics," Politico, October 15, 2012, https://www.politico.com/story/2012/10/allen-wests-smashmouth-politics-082433.

17 Isenstadt, "Allen West's Smashmouth Politics."

18 Lindsey Ellefson, "Texas GOP Governor Candidate Allen West Still Anti-Vax After Hospitalization for COVID," *The Wrap*, October 21, 2012, https://www.thewrap.com/allen-west-covid-19-vaccine/.

19 Aaron Blake and Chris Cillizza, "Nikki Haley Appoints Rep. Tim Scott to Senate," *Washington Post*, December 17, 2021, https://www.washingtonpost.com/news /the-fix/wp/2012/12/17/nikki-haley-to-appoint-rep-tim-scott-to-senate/.

20 Emanuel Cleaver II, "Scott Pick Is First Step for GOP," Politico, December 21, 2012, https://www.politico.com/story/2012/12/for-gop-scott-appointment-is-first -step-085369.

21 "Read Republican Sen. Tim Scott's Response to Biden's Address to Congress," CNN, April 28, 2021, https://www.cnn.com/2021/04/28/politics/tim-scott-response -transcript/index.html.

22 "Candidates Up Close: Do You Think the United States Is a Racist Country?," *New York Times*, 2020, https://www.nytimes.com/interactive/2020/us/politics /racism-in-america-20-questions.html.

23 Christopher S. Parker and Christopher Towler, "Why Bernie Sanders Isn't Winning Over Black Voters," Politico, March 7, 2020, https://www.politico.com/news /magazine/2020/03/07/why-bernie-sanders-economic-message-isnt-enough-to -win-over-black-voters-118197.

24 Colby Itkowitz and John Wagner, "Biden Says Trump Is America's First 'Racist' President," *Washington Post*, July 22, 2020, https://www.washingtonpost.com/politics /biden-says-trump-is-americas-first-racist-president/2020/07/22/867017e8-cc4b -11ea-bc6a-6841b28d9093_story.html.

25 Ta-Nehisi Coates, "The First White President," *Atlantic*, October 2017, https:// www.theatlantic.com/magazine/archive/2017/10/the-first-white-president-ta -nehisi-coates/537909/.

26 "President Biden: We Need to Root Out Systemic Racism in Our Criminal Justice System," CNBC, April 28, 2021, video, 3:47, https://www.cnbc.com/video /2021/04/28/president-biden-we-need-to-root-out-systemic-racism-in-our -criminal-justice-system.html.

27 Dareh Gregorian and Leigh Ann Caldwell, "Bipartisan Police Reform Legislation Talks End without a Deal, Sen. Booker Says," NBC News, September 22, 2021, https://www.nbcnews.com/politics/congress/bipartisan-police-reform-legislation -talks-end-without-deal-sen-booker-n1279880.

28 Cleve R. Wootson Jr., "Biden Boasts of Early Accomplishments. But Now Comes the Hard Part—On Equity, Voting, Guns and Immigration," *Washington Post*, April 29, 2021, https://www.washingtonpost.com/politics/immigration-guns-equity-after -biden-address/2021/04/28/edd6677a-a797-11eb-8c1a-56f0cb4ff3b5_story.html.

29 Tom Gjelten, "2020 Faith Vote Reflects 2016 Pattern," NPR, November 8, 2020, https://www.npr.org/2020/11/08/932263516/2020-faith-vote-reflects-2016 -patterns.

30 "President Biden: We Need."

31 Michelle Stoddart, "Civil Rights Groups Sue Georgia over New Voting Law," ABC News, March 30, 2021, https://abcnews.go.com/Politics/civil-rights-group-sue -georgia-voting-law/story?id=76775186.

32 Reid J. Epstein and Patricia Mazzei, "G.O.P. Bills Target Protesters (and Absolve

Motorists Who Hit Them)," *New York Times*, April 21, 2021, https://www.nytimes
.com/2021/04/21/us/politics/republican-anti-protest-laws.html.

33 Lexi Lonas, "Tim Scott Defends Saying 'Woke Supremacy' Is as Bad as White
Supremacy," *Hill*, March 23, 2021, https://thehill.com/homenews/senate/544550
-tim-scott-fires-back-after-criticism-for-saying-woke-supremacy-is-as-bad-as/.

34 Dan Merica, "Stacey Abrams Calls Georgia Elections Bill 'Nothing Less Than Jim
Crow 2.0,'" CNN, March 25, 2021, https://www.cnn.com/politics/live-news/georgia
-voting-restrictions-bill-03-25-21/h_299f27574b50c49515e01520521768d9.

35 "Senator Tim Scott Discusses Investing in Opportunity Act—Fox Business," Senator Tim Scott, February 6, 2018, YouTube video, 4:10, https://www.youtube.com
/watch?v=zBzSQ-fYJbE.

36 "Senators Booker and Scott and Congressmen Tiberi and Kind Introduce the Investing in Opportunity Act," Senator Cory Booker (website), April 27, 2016, https://
www.booker.senate.gov/news/press/senators-booker-and-scott-and-congressmen
-tiberi-and-kind-introduce-the-and-147investing-in-opportunity-act-and-148.

37 Caleb Melby, "A Virginia City's Playbook for Urban Renewal: Move Out the
Poor," Bloomberg, September 22, 2020, https://www.bloomberg.com/news
/features/2020-09-22/how-norfolk-virginia-is-using-tax-breaks-to-demolish
-black-neighborhoods.

38 Jesse Drucker and Eric Lipton, "How a Trump Tax Break to Help Poor Communities Became a Windfall for the Rich," *New York Times*, August 31, 2019, https://
www.nytimes.com/2019/08/31/business/tax-opportunity-zones.html.

39 Misha Hall and Lorena Roque, "So-Called Opportunity Zones Provide Opportunity For Whom?," Institute on Taxation and Economic Policy, April 23, 2019,
https://itep.org/so-called-opportunity-zones-provide-opportunity-for-whom/.

40 Jesse Drucker and Eric Lipton, "Symbol of '80s Greed Stands to Profit From Trump
Tax Break for Poor Areas," *New York Times*, October 26, 2019, https://www.nytimes
.com/2019/10/26/business/michael-milken-trump-opportunity-zones.html.

41 "Michael Milken's Career," *New York Times*, October 26, 2019, https://www
.nytimes.com/2019/10/26/business/michael-milken-career.html.

42 Jesse Drucker, "Trump Tax Break That Benefited the Rich Is Being Investigated,"
New York Times, January 15, 2020, https://www.nytimes.com/2020/01/15/business
/trump-opportunity-zone-investigation.html.

43 James Lovegrove, "2 Powerful SC Lawmakers, Jim Clyburn and Tim Scott, Feud over
'Opportunity Zone' Changes," *Post and Courier* (Charleston, SC), November 13, 2019,
https://www.postandcourier.com/politics/powerful-sc-lawmakers-jim-clyburn-and
-tim-scott-feud-over/article_42432520-062f-11ea-a582-4fc1f2bd894f.html.

44 "Scott Responds to Democrat Efforts to Destroy Opportunity," Senator Tim
Scott (website), November 13, 2019, https://www.scott.senate.gov/media-center
/press-releases/scott-responds-to-democrat-efforts-to-destroy-opportunity.

45 Lydia O'Neal, Patrick Ambrosio, and John Dunbar, "Opportunity Zones Get Big Push
as Critics Question Who They Help," Bloomberg Tax, September 8, 2020, https://

news.bloombergtax.com/daily-tax-report/opportunity-zones-get-big-push-as -critics-question-who-they-help.

46 Melby, "Virginia City's Playbook for Urban Renewal."

47 Alex Wittenberg, "The Biggest Problem with Opportunity Zones," Bloomberg, June 25, 2020, https://www.bloomberg.com/news/articles/2020-06-25/opportunity -zones-don-t-work-can-they-be-fixed.

48 Brett Theodos et al., "An Early Assessment of Opportunity Zones for Equitable Development Projects: Nine Observations on the Use of the Incentive to Date," Urban Institute, July 28, 2020, https://www.urban.org/sites/default/files/publication/102348 /early-assessment-of-opportunity-zones-for-equitable-development-projects .pdf.

49 "ICYMI: Tim Scott's 'Opportunity Zones' Drew $29B to Low-Income Areas: 'Changing the Game,'" Senator Tim Scott (website), November 21, 2021, https:// www.scott.senate.gov/media-center/press-releases/icymi-tim-scotts-opportunity -zones-drew-29b-to-low-income-areas-changing-the-game.

50 "ACLU Statement of Opposition to Sen. Tim Scott's So-Called 'Justice Act,'" ACLU, June 24, 2020, https://www.aclu.org/press-releases/aclu-statement -opposition-sen-tim-scotts-so-called-justice-act; Jason Lemon, "Tim Scott Wants Police Reform Because He's Been Stopped 18 Times for 'Driving While Black,'" *Newsweek*, May 2, 2021, https://www.newsweek.com/tim-scott- wants-police-reform-because-hes-been-stopped-18-times-driving-while- black-1588150.

51 Margaret Brennan and Jake Miller, "Senator Tim Scott Says Police Reform Talks Collapsed Because Democrats Supported 'Defunding the Police,'" CBS News, September 25, 2021, https://www.cbsnews.com/news/senator-tim-scott-police-reform-talks -collapsed-democrats-defund-the-police/.

52 "Tim Scott's Voting Records on Issue: Civil Liberties and Civil Rights," Vote Smart, accessed June 1, 202, https://justfacts.votesmart.org/candidate/key -votes/11940/tim-scott/13/civil-liberties-and-civil-rights.

53 Ari Berman, "Republicans Once Supported the Voting Rights Act. Today, They Voted Against Its Restoration," *Mother Jones*, November 3, 2021, https://www .motherjones.com/politics/2021/11/republicans-once-supported-the-voting-rights -act-today-they-voted-against-its-restoration/.

54 "Senator Tim Scott to Co-Chair Congressional Pilgrimage to Selma This Weekend," Senator Tim Scott (website), March 6, 2015, https://www.scott.senate.gov/media -center/press-releases/senator-tim-scott-to-co-chair-congressional-pilgrimage-to -selma-this-weekend.

55 Jamie Lovegrove, "Graham, Scott Vote Against Commission to Probe Jan. 6 Capitol Riot as Proposal Dies," *Post and Courier* (Charleston, SC), May 28, 2021, https://www.postandcourier.com/politics/graham-scott-vote-against-commission -to-probe-jan-6-capitol-riot-as-proposal-dies/article_c6329414-bfca-11eb-9caa -7bcd69fc8541.html.

56 Glenn Kessler, "Tim Scott Often Talks about His Grandfather and Cotton. There's More to that Tale," Washington Post, April 23, 2021, https://www.washingtonpost.com/politics/2021/04/23/tim-scott-often-talks-about-his-grandfather-cotton-theres-more-tale/.

57 Glenn Kessler, "Tim Scott Often Talks about His Grandfather and Cotton. There's More to That Tale," *Washington Post*, April 23, 2021, https://www.washingtonpost.com/politics/2021/04/23/tim-scott-often-talks-about-his-grandfather-cotton-theres-more-tale/.

58 "Journalist Digs Into Sen. Tim Scott's 'Tidy' Origin Story After Comments on Racism," All Things Considered, NPR, May 2, 2021, https://www.npr.org/2021/05/02/992922648/journalist-digs-into-sen-tim-scotts-tidy-origin-story-after-comments-on-racism.

59 Jonathan Weisman and Annie Karni, "'I Will Not Sit Quietly': 3 Black Senators in Spotlight on Voting Rights," *New York Times*, January 20, 2022, https://www.nytimes.com/2022/01/20/us/politics/voting-rights-cory-booker-tim-scott.html.

60 "Rep. Plaskett on Sen. Tim Scott: 'Who Told Him That Black People Voted for Him in the First Place?,'" MSNBC, January 23, 2022, https://www.msnbc.com/ali-velshi/watch/rep-plaskett-on-sen-tim-scott-who-told-him-that-black-people-voted-for-him-in-the-first-place-131501637560.

61 "Election 2016 Results, South Carolina," CNN, November 9, 2016, https://www.cnn.com/election/2016/results/exit-polls/south-carolina/senate.

62 Steele, discussion.

63 "ABA Standing Committee on the Federal Judiciary Rates Judge Ketanji Brown Jackson 'Well Qualified,'" American Bar Association, March 18, 2022, https://www.americanbar.org/news/abanews/aba-news-archives/2022/03/aba-committee-rates-judge-ketanji-brown-jackson-well-qualified/.

64 "Senator Scott to Vote 'No' on Biden Supreme Court Nominee," Senator Tim Scott (website), April 4, 2022, https://www.scott.senate.gov/media-center/press-releases/_senator-scott-to-vote-no-on-biden-supreme-court-nominee.

65 "Thurgood Marshall's Unique Supreme Court Legacy," National Constitution Center, August 30, 2022, https://constitutioncenter.org/blog/thurgood-marshalls-unique-supreme-court-legacy.

66 Tony Santaella, "Black Lawmakers Walk Out During Debate on Voter ID," WLTX, Columbia, SC, February 26, 2009, https://www.wltx.com/article/news/black-lawmakers-walk-out-during-debate-on-voter-id/101-380873348.

67 *The Karen Hunter Show*, aired April 7, 2022, on SiriusXM Urban View.

68 Wendell Gilliard, in discussion with the author, August 2022.

68 Ashton Pittman, "Gov. Reeves Declares Confederate Heritage Month, a 30-Year-Old Mississippi Tradition," *Mississippi Free Press*, April 4, 2023, https://www.mississippifreepress.org/32351/gov-reeves-declares-confederate-heritage-month-a-30-year-old-mississippi-tradition.

CHAPTER 10: LOVE AND HURD

1   Sydney Ember, "Mia Love Criticizes Trump in Scathing Concession Speech," *New York Times*, November 26, 2018, https://www.nytimes.com/2018/11/26/us/politics/mia-love-trump-utah.html.

2   Dennis Romboy, "Love Would 'Take Apart' Congressional Black Caucus If Elected in Utah's 4th District," Deseret *News*, January 5, 2012, https://www.deseret.com/2012/1/5/20391127/love-would-take-apart-congressional-black-caucus-if-elected-in-utah-s-4th-district.

3   "Mia Love RNC Speech," Politico, August 30, 2012, https://www.politico.com/story/2012/08/mia-love-rnc-speech-transcript-080490.

4   David Kiley, "As Obama Takes Victory Lap over Auto Industry Rescue, Here Are the Lessons of the Bailout," *Forbes*, January 20, 2016, https://www.forbes.com/sites/davidkiley5/2016/01/20/obamas-takes-victory-lap-over-auto-industry-rescue/?sh=82fb87f3e830.

5   Megan Slack, "From the Archives: President Obama Signs the Lilly Ledbetter Fair Pay Act," Obama White House Archives, January 30, 2012, https://obamawhitehouse.archives.gov/blog/2012/01/30/archives-president-obama-signs-lilly-ledbetter-fair-pay-act.

6   Dennis Romboy, "Mia Love Nominated for National Campaign Award for 'Love Bomb' Fundraiser," KSL-TV, Salt Lake City, UT, January 12, 2013, https://www.ksl.com/article/23676762/mia-love-nominated-for-national-campaign-award-for-love-bomb-fundraiser.

7   Annie Knox, "Mia Love: Utahns Care Little about Race," *Salt Lake Tribune*, November 10, 2014, https://www.sltrib.com/news/politics/2014/11/10/mia-love-utahns-care-little-about-race/.

8   Lee Davidson, "Mia Love Tells Fox News That Democrats Target Her Because 'I Am a Black Female Republican' and They Want to Control Everything," *Salt Lake Tribune*, September 24, 2018, https://www.sltrib.com/news/politics/2018/09/24/mia-love-says-dems-target/.

9   Astead W. Herndon, "The Districts Are Mostly White. The Candidates Are Not," *New York Times*, July 19, 2018, https://www.nytimes.com/2018/07/19/us/politics/minority-candidates.html.

10 Nia-Malika Henderson, "Mia Love Joins a Group She Promised to Dismantle," *Washington Post*, January 6, 2015, https://www.washingtonpost.com/news/the-fix/wp/2015/01/06/mia-love-joins-the-cbc-the-group-she-vowed-to-dismantle/.

11 Ali Vitali, Kasie Hunt, and Frank Thorp V, "Trump Referred to Haiti and African Nations as 'Shithole' Countries," NBC News, January 11, 2018, https://www.nbcnews.com/politics/white-house/trump-referred-haiti-african-countries-shithole-nations-n836946.

12 Abigail Abrams, "'The President Must Apologize': Haitian-American GOP Rep. Mia Love Slams Trump's 'Shithole Countries' Comment," *Time*, Jan-

uary 11, 2018, https://time.com/5100217/mia-love-donald-trump-shithole
-remark/.

13 Caroline Kenny, "Trump Denies Making 'Shithole Countries' Comment," CNN,
January 12, 2018, https://www.cnn.com/2018/01/12/politics/donald-trump-tweet
-daca-rejection/index.html.

14 Devan Cole, "Mia Love Slams Trump in Concession Speech: 'No Real Relationships, Just Convenient Transactions,'" CNN, November 26, 2018, https://www
.cnn.com/2018/11/26/politics/mia-love-donald-trump-concession/index.html.

15 Mary C. Curtis, "Mia Love Is Black, Mormon, Republican and Blowing People's
Minds," *Washington Post*, November 12, 2014, https://www.washingtonpost.com
/blogs/she-the-people/wp/2014/11/12/mia-love-is-black-mormon-republican
-and-blowing-peoples-minds/.

16 Jason Horowitz, "The Genesis of a Church's Stand on Race," *Washington Post*, February 28, 2012, https://www.washingtonpost.com/politics/the-genesis-of-a-churchs
-stand-on-race/2012/02/22/gIQAQZXyfR_story.html.

17 Ember, "Mia Love Criticizes Trump."

18 "Rep. Mia Love Calls Ben McAdams a 'Wolf in Sheep's Clothing,'" KSL-TV, Salt
Lake City, UT, November 26, 2018, https://ksltv.com/404031/rep-mia-love-calls
-successor-wolf-sheeps-clothing/.

19 Andrew Keighbaum, "New Accountability for Teacher Prep," Inside Higher Ed, October
13, 2016, https://www.insidehighered.com/news/2016/10/13/obama-administration
-releases-final-rules-teacher-preparation-programs; "Teacher Preparation Issues: A
Rule by the Education Department," *Federal Register*, October 13, 2016, https://www
.federalregister.gov/documents/2016/10/31/2016-24856/teacher-preparation
-issues.

20 "Tracking Congress in the Age of Trump: Mia B. Love," FiveThirtyEight, last updated January 13, 2021, https://projects.fivethirtyeight.com/congress-trump-score
/mia-b-love/.

21 John Wagner, "Mia Love Gives Trump No Love as She Concedes a Narrow Loss
in Utah," *Washington Post*, November 26, 2018, https://www.washingtonpost.com
/politics/mia-love-gives-trump-no-love-as-she-concedes-a-narrow-loss-in-utah
/2018/11/26/2062c158-f1a5-11e8-80d0-f7e1948d55f4_story.html.

22 "The Future of the GOP with Former Congressman Will Hurd," *Washington Post*, May 18, 2021, https://www.washingtonpost.com/washington-post
-live/2021/05/18/future-gop-with-former-congressman-will-hurd/.

23 "Watch Former U.S. Rep. Will Hurd Discuss the Republican Party, the Nation's
Challenges and More at the Texas Tribune Festival," *Texas Tribune*, September 20,
2021, https://www.texastribune.org/2021/09/20/will-hurd-congress-gop/.

24 Keith Randall, "Will Hurd: U.S. Must Streamline Immigration Procedures," *Texas
A&M Today*, October 3, 2019, https://today.tamu.edu/2019/10/03/will-hurd-u-s
-must-streamline-immigration-procedures/.

25 "Texas Congressional District 23, Representative Will Hurd," U.S. Census Bureau,

January 1, 2010, https://www2.census.gov/geo/maps/cong_dist/cd115/cd_based/ST48/CD115_TX23.pdf.

26 "2018 Allegheny College Prize for Civility in Public Life," Allegheny College, July 18, 2018, https://sites.allegheny.edu/civilityaward/2018-allegheny-college-prize-for-civility-in-public-life/.

27 Lou Chibbaro Jr., "GOP Congressman Urges: 'Don't Be an Asshole, Don't Be a Homophobe,'" *Washington Blade*, June 26, 2019, https://www.washingtonblade.com/2019/06/26/gop-congressman-urges-dont-be-an-asshole-dont-be-a-homophobe/.

28 Emily Cochrane, "Will Hurd, Only Black Republican in House, Is Retiring from Congress," *New York Times*, August 1, 2019, https://www.nytimes.com/2019/08/01/us/politics/will-hurd-retires.html.

29 J. Edward Moreno, "U.S. Rep. Will Hurd Sticks with Republicans during Last Public Impeachment Hearing of the Week," *Texas Tribune*, November 21, 2019, https://www.texastribune.org/2019/11/21/will-hurd-says-hell-vote-no-impeachment-disappointing-democrats/.

30 Kate Sullivan, "GOP Congressman Says Trump Tweets Are 'Racist and Xenophobic,'" CNN, July 15, 2019, https://www.cnn.com/2019/07/15/politics/will-hurd-gop-trump-racist-xenophobic-cnntv/index.html.

31 Sheryl Gay Stolberg, "The Republicans Who Voted to Condemn Trump's Remarks (and Other Things to Know)," *New York Times*, July 16, 2019, https://www.nytimes.com/2019/07/16/us/politics/republicans-who-voted-for-resolution.html.

32 Sullivan, "GOP Congressman."

33 "Tracking Congress in the Age of Trump: Will Hurd," FiveThirtyEight, last updated January 13, 2021, https://projects.fivethirtyeight.com/congress-trump-score/will-hurd/; "Will Hurd's Voting Records on Issue: Civil Liberties and Civil Rights," Vote Smart, accessed, June 27, 2023, https://justfacts.votesmart.org/candidate/key-votes/116911/will-hurd/13/civil-liberties-and-civil-rights?p=1.

34 Will Hurd (@WillHurd), "I've taken a conservative message to places that don't often hear it. I'm going to say [sic] involved in politics to help make sure the Republican Party looks like America," Twitter, August 1, 2019, 7:00 p.m., https://twitter.com/willhurd/status/1157078759364841474.

35 Jacob Ogles, "Tea Party Express Gets on the Byron Donalds Train," Florida Politics, August 13, 2020, https://floridapolitics.com/archives/357642-tea-party-express-gets-on-the-byron-donalds-train/.

36 Eugene Scott, "Who Is Byron Donalds? The Latest Republican Nominee for House Speaker," *Washington Post*, January 4, 2023, https://www.washingtonpost.com/politics/2023/01/04/house-speaker-mccarthy-donalds-gop/; "Tea Party Star Answers to Charges of a Criminal Past," FOX 4 Now, April 28, 2014, YouTube video, 3:04, https://www.youtube.com/watch?v=wzPMeyw-urk.

37 Karen Yourish, Larry Buchanan, and Denise Lu, "The 147 Republicans Who Voted to Overturn Election Results," *New York Times*, January 7, 2021, https://www.nytimes

.com/interactive/2021/01/07/us/elections/electoral-college-biden-objectors
.html.

38 Dave Elias, "Byron Donalds Fighting to Overturn Election Results, FL Senators Re-
    mainTight-Lipped," WBBH-TV, Fort Myers, FL, January 6, 2021, https://nbc-2.com
    /news/politics/2021/01/05/byron-donalds-fighting-to-overturn-election-results
    -fl-senators-remain-tight-lipped/.

39 Jacob Ogles, "Was Byron Donalds Chillin' with Insurrectionists before the Capitol Ri-
    ots?," Florida Politics, February 10, 2021, https://floridapolitics.com/archives/402598
    -was-byron-donalds-chillin-with-insurrectionists-before-the-capitol-riots/.

40 "Byron Donalds' Voting Record," Vote Smart, accessed June 1, 2023, https://justfacts
    .votesmart.org/candidate/key-votes/137655/byron-donalds.

41 Frank Thorp V, Julie Tsirkin, and Dareh Gregorian, "Black Republican Lawmaker
    Says He's Being Snubbed by the Congressional Black Caucus," NBC News, June
    10, 2021, https://www.nbcnews.com/politics/congress/black-republican-lawmaker
    -says-he-s-being-snubbed-congressional-black-n1270376.

42 Jacob Ogles, "Donald Trump Gives Thumbs Up to Byron Donalds' Return
    to Congress," Florida Politics, December 14, 2021, https://floridapolitics.com
    /archives/480153-donald-trump-endorses-byron-donalds/.

43 Justine Coleman, "Rep-Elect on Trump's Electoral College Challenge: 'There's No
    Question in My Mind That I Think He Won,'" Hill, January 1, 2021, https://thehill
    .com/homenews/house/532308-rep-elect-on-trumps-electoral-college-challenge
    -theres-no-question-in-my-mind?rl=1.

44 Taylor Stevens, "Burgess Owens Touts Trump's Record on Race in Speech at the
    Republican National Convention," Salt Lake Tribune, August 26, 2020, https://
    www.sltrib.com/news/politics/2020/08/26/burgess-owens-touts/.

45 Ian Schwartz, "MSNBC's Joy Reid vs. Rep. Byron Donalds: Do You Not Believe
    It Was a 'Diversity Statement' to Nominate You for Speaker?," Real Clear Politics,
    January 10, 2023, https://www.realclearpolitics.com/video/2023/01/10/msnbcs_joy
    _reid_vs_rep_byron_donalds_do_you_not_believe_it_was_a_diversity_statement
    _to_nominate_you_for_speaker.html.

CHAPTER 11: TRUMPISM

1 Desire Thompson, "Omarosa Wanted Sheryl Lee Ralph to Join the 'Trump
   Train,'" Vibe, March 4, 2017, https://www.vibe.com/features/vixen/sheryl-lee-ralph
   -omarosa-trump-train-job-493454/.

2 Darren Sands, "Tara Wall, Top Black GOP Operative, Is Out at the RNC,"
   BuzzFeed News, November 3, 2015, https://www.buzzfeednews.com/article
   /darrensands/tara-wall-top-black-gop-operative-is-out-at-the-rnc.

3 Lauren Victoria Burke, "Yet Another Top African American Staffer Departs
   RNC," NBC News, March 31, 2016, https://www.nbcnews.com/news/nbcblk
   /yet-another-top-african-american-staffer-departs-rnc-n548506.

4   Anne Stein, "A Young Republican Spreads the Word," Haverford College, April 5, 2015, https://www.haverford.edu/college-communications/news/young-republican-spreads-word.

5   "RNC Launching Campaign Aimed at Black, Urban Voters in Ohio," *Akron Beacon Journal*, July 13, 2015, https://www.beaconjournal.com/story/news/politics/2015/07/13/rnc-launching-campaign-aimed-at/10455821007/.

6   "Chelsi P. Henry: I'm Young, African-American, Female and Republican," *Pioneer Press* (Saint Paul, MN), February 9, 2014, https://www.twincities.com/2014/02/09/chelsi-p-henry-im-young-african-american-female-and-republican/.

7   Wendy Wilson, "Meet 6 Black Women Voting for Mitt Romney," *Essence*, October 28, 2012, https://www.essence.com/celebrity/meet-6-black-women-voting-mitt-romney/#226504.

8   Nia-Malika Henderson. "Republicans Won 10 Percent of the Black Vote on Tuesday. That's Actually a Step in the Right Direction," *Washington Post*, November 6, 2014, https://www.washingtonpost.com/news/the-fix/wp/2014/11/06/the-gop-moved-the-ball-forward-with-black-voters-but-progress-is-slow/.

9   Burke, "Yet Another."

10   Tyler Tunes, "Top Black Staffers Leave the Republican National Committee," HuffPost, March 31, 2016, https://www.huffpost.com/entry/rnc-black-staffers_n_56fd4b3fe4b083f5c6070348.

11   Roland Martin, "Telly Lovelace Leaves the RNC," Facebook, August 3, 2017, video, 10:30, https://www.facebook.com/rolandsmartinfanpage/videos/10154947313802831/.

12   Jonathan Martin and Alexander Burns, "Hispanic Official to Leave R.N.C. in Sign of Disaffection with Donald Trump," *New York Times*, June 1, 2016, https://www.nytimes.com/2016/06/02/us/politics/rnc-trump-ruth-guerra.html.

13   Aila Slisco, "GOP Consultant Leaves Party Over 'Malignancy of Trumpism,'" *Newsweek*, November 15, 2020, https://www.newsweek.com/gop-consultant-leaves-party-over-malignancy-trumpism-1545319.

14   Shermichael Singleton, in discussion with the author, October 2022.

15   Maggie Haberman and Yamiche Alcindor, "A HUD Official Once Criticized Trump. Now He's an Ex-Official," *New York Times*, February 16, 2017, https://www.nytimes.com/2017/02/16/us/politics/shermichael-singleton-housing-urban-development.html.

16   Singleton, discussion.

17   Ewan Palmer, "Pastor Darrell Scott Claims Capitol Riot Was Congress 'Set Up' to Impeach Donald Trump," *Newsweek*, April 15, 2021, https://www.newsweek.com/darrell-scott-capitol-riot-congress-set-impeach-donald-trump-1583878.

18   "Diamond and Silk: 'My President Never Says Anything That's Stupid,'" BBC Newsnight, March 6, 2017, YouTube video, 4:58, https://www.youtube.com/watch?v=rZXOydtO5Ww&ab_channel=BBCNewsnight.

19   David Smith, "Candace Owens Woos the Right as Provocative Face of Trump

Youth," *Guardian*, March 2, 2019, https://www.theguardian.com/us-news/2019/mar/02/candace-owens-provocative-face-trump-youth.

20 Jamie Lovegrove, "Pastor Mark Burns: From Poverty to Trump Supporter and Now Candidate for Congress," *Post and Courier* (Charleston, SC), March 3, 2018, https://www.postandcourier.com/politics/pastor-mark-burns-from-poverty-to-trump-supporter-and-now-candidate-for-congress/article_feb3ea24-1bf2-11e8-a58f-9be4263d24dc.html.

21 "Judge Rules Cameron Is Eligible to Run as GOP Candidate for Kentucky Attorney General," WDRB-TV, Louisville, KY, October 10, 2019, https://www.wdrb.com/news/judge-rules-cameron-is-eligible-to-run-as-gop-candidate-for-kentucky-attorney-general/article_0855e702-eb73-11e9-99a1-3389b49549dc.html.

22 Reid Wilson, "McConnell Protégé Emerges as Kentucky's Next Rising Star," *Hill*, November 13, 2019, https://thehill.com/homenews/campaign/470181-mcconnell-protege-emerges-as-kentuckys-next-rising-star/.

23 "U of L Graduate Named McConnell's Legal Counsel," University of Louisville, March 11, 2015, https://louisville.edu/mcconnellcenter/news/archived/uofl-graduate-named-mcconnell2019s-legal-counsel.

24 Theresa Waldrop, "Breonna Taylor Killing: A Timeline of the Police Raid and Its Aftermath," CNN, March 3, 2022, https://www.cnn.com/2022/02/22/us/no-knock-raid-breonna-taylor-timeline/index.html; Tessa Duvall, "Charges Permanently Dropped against Breonna Taylor's Boyfriend for Shooting Officer the Night She Was Killed," *Louisville Courier Journal*, March 8, 2021, https://www.usatoday.com/story/news/nation/2021/03/08/kenneth-walker-charges-dropped-against-breonna-taylor-boyfriend/4629371001/.

25 Bruce Schreiner and Dylan Lovan, "Daniel Cameron Says Breonna Taylor Grand July 'Ultimately Decided' Charges in New Interview," Associated Press, August 5, 2021, https://apnews.com/article/breonna-taylor-54d7ec7293ebf8699c1d11745124abc7.

26 "Watch: Kentucky Attorney General Daniel Cameron's Full Speech at the Republican National Convention," *NewsHour*, PBS, August 26, 2020, YouTube video, 6:36, https://www.youtube.com/watch?v=FuBHecxGSl8.

27 Susannah Culliane, "Retired St. Louis Police Captain Killed after Responding to a Pawnshop Alarm during Shooting," CNN, August 27, 2020, https://www.cnn.com/2020/06/03/us/david-dorn-st-louis-police-shot-trnd/index.html.

28 "Man Charged in Slaying of Retired St. Louis Police Captain," Associated Press, June 8, 2020, https://apnews.com/article/91ae90ae49fc0e6851c19dd9dd77a04b.

29 "Joe Biden on Black Woman Running Mate."

30 Sonmez and Wagner, "Trump Says."

31 Quint Forgey and Myah Ward, "Biden Apologizes for Controversial 'You Ain't Black' Comment," Politico, May 22, 2020, https://www.politico.com/news/2020/05/22/joe-biden-breakfast-club-interview-274490.

32 Morgan Watkins, "What Breonna Taylor's Mother Thought of AG Daniel Cam-

eron's Republican Convention Speech," *Louisville Courier Journal*, August 26, 2020, https://www.courier-journal.com/story/news/2020/08/26/breonna-taylors -mother-reacts-daniel-cameron-rnc-speech/5635453002/.

33 "Look Back: Updates from Louisville on Long-Awaited Breonna Taylor Decision," WLKY, Louisville, KY, September 24, 2020, https://www.wlky.com/article /breonna-taylor-decision-charges-officers-lmpd-daniel-cameron-lmpd/34116457.

34 Erik Ortiz, "Kentucky AG Daniel Cameron Takes Heat after No Direct Charges Are Filed in Breonna Taylor's Death," NBC News, September 23, 2020, https:// www.nbcnews.com/news/us-news/kentucky-ag-daniel-cameron-takes-heat-after -no-direct-charges-n1240886.

35 Lisa J. Adams Wagner and Bruce Schreiner, "Black Attorney General Chokes Up during Taylor Announcement," Associated Press, September 23, 2020, https:// apnews.com/article/kentucky-frankfort-race-and-ethnicity-us-news-ky-state -wire-a2a2d2819d0c45b8f177ce3a94f18159.

36 Chris Sommerfeldt, "'Really Brilliant': Trump Praises Kentucky Prosecutor after No Charges in Breonna Taylor's Death," *New York Daily News*, September 23, 2020, https://www.nydailynews.com/news/politics/ny-trump-brilliant-kentucky -prosecutor-breonna-taylor-20200924-owpqzhxevbctdf4sda5tjn52ma-story.html.

37 Doha Madani, "Megan Thee Stallion Slams Kentucky AG Daniel Cameron over Breonna Taylor Case on 'SNL,'" NBC News, October 4, 2020, https:// www.nbcnews.com/news/nbcblk/megan-thee-stallion-slams-kentucky-ag-daniel -cameron-over-breonna-n1242048.

38 "BLM Activist Tamika Mallory Slams Kentucky AG Daniel Cameron," NowThis News, September 25, 2020, YouTube video, 3:26, https://youtu.be/islXphyHJNk.

39 "Interview with Daniel Cameron on *Fox & Friends*," Kentucky Attorney General's Office, October 6, 2020, YouTube video, 7:53, https://youtu.be/XzGfZfVFzhA.

40 Lucas Aulbach, "Daniel Cameron Rips 'Disgusting' Megan Thee Stallion 'SNL' Comments, 'Ben Crump Model,'" *Louisville Courier Journal*, October 6, 2020, https:// www.courier-journal.com/story/news/local/breonna-taylor/2020/10/06/daniel -cameron-responds-to-snl-performance-on-fox-and-friends/3635059001/.

41 "Commonwealth of Kentucky's Motion to Dismiss and Response to Plaintiff's Motion for Release of Grand Jury Transcripts/Recordings/Reports and for Declaration of Rights Pursuant to KRS 418.040," filed September 28, 2020, https:// interactive.whas11.com/pdfs/scannedmotiongjrelease.pdf.

42 Victoria Albert, "Kentucky Attorney General Files Motion to Keep Breonna Taylor Grand Juror from Speaking Publicly about Proceedings," CBS News, October 8, 2020, https://www.cbsnews.com/news/breonna-taylor-grand-juror-daniel-cameron -motion-silent/.

43 Andrew Wolfson, "AG Cameron's Office, Grand Juror's Lawyer Clash over Right to Speak on Breonna Taylor Case," *Louisville Courier Journal*, October 8, 2020, https:// www.courier-journal.com/story/news/local/breonna-taylor/2020/10/08/breonna- taylor-case-judge-decide-if-grand-juror-may-speak-freely/5921870002/.

44 "Breonna Taylor's Family Demand Kentucky Attorney General Daniel Cameron Recuse Himself from the Case," BET, October 6, 2020, https://www.bet.com/article/yf0ukr/breonna-taylor-s-family-wants-daniel-cameron-off-the-case.

45 Biba Adams, "Kentucky Governor Wants AG to Release 'Everything' in Breonna Taylor Case,"TheGrio, October 23, 2020, https://thegrio.com/2020/10/23/beshear-cameron-taylor/.

46 Roberto Aram Ferdman (@robferdman), "The anonymous juror's attorney just sent out a press release with a statement by the juror. It confirms what many have suspected," Twitter, October 20, 2020, 1:32 p.m., https://twitter.com/robferdman/status/1318605987738210305.

47 John P. Wise, "Breonna Taylor Case: 3 Grand Jurors Aim to Impeach Attorney General Daniel Cameron," WAVE-TV, Louisville, KY, January 22, 2021, https://www.wave3.com/2021/01/22/breonna-taylor-case-grand-jurors-aim-impeach-attorney-general-daniel-cameron/.

48 Nicholas Bogel-Burroughs, "Officer Acquitted of Endangering Breonna Taylor's Neighbors in Raid," *New York Times*, March 3, 2022, https://www.nytimes.com/2022/03/03/us/breonna-taylor-brett-hankison-acquitted.html.

49 Nadine El-Bawab et al., "DOJ Charges Current, Former Police Officers in Connection with Raid That Killed Breonna Taylor," ABC News, August 4, 2022, https://abcnews.go.com/US/doj-announces-charges-connection-raid-killed-breonna-taylor/story?id=87926113.

50 Daniel Cameron (@kyoag), "I won't participate in that sort of rancor. It's not productive. Instead, I'll continue to speak with the love and respect that is consistent with our values as Kentuckians,"Twitter, August 4, 2020, 5:59 p.m., https://twitter.com/kyoag/status/1555312468133552141.

51 Emma Austin and Joe Sonka,"Daniel Cameron Joins Republican AGs in Challenging Pennsylvania Mail-In Ballots," *Louisville Courier Journal*, November 8, 2020, https://www.courier-journal.com/story/news/politics/2020/11/08/pennsylvania-mail-ballots-daniel-cameron-joins-gop-ag-challenge/6217885002/.

52 Ben Mathis-Lilley, "The Republican Party Is the Reason It's Taking So Long to Count Votes in Pennsylvania," *Slate*, November 5, 2020, https://slate.com/news-and-politics/2020/11/the-pennsylvania-vote-count-is-taking-so-long-because-the-republican-party-slowed-it-down.html.

53 Quinn Scanlan, "Here's How States Have Changed the Rules around Voting amid the Coronavirus Pandemic," ABC News, September 22, 2020, https://abcnews.go.com/Politics/states-changed-rules-voting-amid-coronavirus-pandemic/story?id=72309089.

54 Wesley Muller, "Attorney General Jeff Landry Inserts Louisiana into Voter-Fraud Conspiracy Lawsuit," *Louisiana Illuminator*, December 9, 2020, https://lailluminator.com/2020/12/09/atty-general-jeff-landry-drags-louisiana-into-voter-fraud-conspiracy-lawsuit/.

55 Allie Morris and Todd J. Gillman, "Texas AG Ken Paxton Asks Supreme Court to

Overturn Trump's Defeat by Negating 10M Votes in Four States," *Dallas Morning News*, December 8, 2020, https://www.dallasnews.com/news/politics/2020/12/08/texas-ag-paxton-challenges-election-result-in-four-key-battleground-states/.

56   Jason Hancock, "Missouri AG Joins Lawsuit Challenging Presidential Election Results in Four States," *Missouri Independent*, December 9, 2020, https://missouriindependent.com/briefs/missouri-ag-supports-lawsuit-challenging-presidential-election-results-in-four-states/.

57   Austin and Sonka, "Daniel Cameron Joins Republican AGs."

58   "Exhaustive Fact Check Finds Little Evidence of Voter Fraud, but 2020's 'Big Lie' Lives On," PBS, December 17, 2021, https://www.pbs.org/newshour/show/exhaustive-fact-check-finds-little-evidence-of-voter-fraud-but-2020s-big-lie-lives-on; Nick Corasaniti, Reid J. Epstein, and Jim Rutenberg, "The Times Called Officials in Every State: No Evidence of Voter Fraud," *New York Times*, November 10, 2020, https://www.nytimes.com/2020/11/10/us/politics/voting-fraud.html; Christina A. Cassidy, "Far Too Little Vote Fraud to Tip Election to Trump, AP Finds," Associated Press, December 14, 2021, https://apnews.com/article/voter-fraud-election-2020-joe-biden-donald-trump-7fcb6f134e528fee8237c7601db3328f.

59   Ben Kamisar, "Carson Not Interested in Serving in Trump Administration," *Hill*, November 15, 2016, https://thehill.com/policy/healthcare/306045-carson-turned-down-offer-to-serve-in-trump-administration-report/.

60   "Who Lives in Federally Assisted Housing?," *Housing Spotlight* 2, no. 2 (November 2012), https://nlihc.org/sites/default/files/HousingSpotlight2-2.pdf.

61   Grace Guarnieri, "Ben Carson Announces $2 Billion for Homeless Programs Despite Trump's Proposed Cuts to Housing Programs," *Newsweek*, January 11, 2018, https://www.newsweek.com/ben-carson-billion-homeless-trump-housing-778976.

62   Teresa Wiltz, "Court OKs HUD Overhaul of Obama-Era Desegregation Rule," Stateline, August 23, 2018, https://stateline.org/2018/08/23/court-oks-hud-overhaul-of-obama-era-desegregation-rule/.

63   Yamiche Alcindor, "Don't Make Housing for the Poor Too Cozy, Carson Warns," *New York Times*, May 3, 2017, https://www.nytimes.com/2017/05/03/us/politics/ben-carson-hud-poverty-plans.html.

64   Tracy Jan March, "Ben Carson's Mission Statement for HUD May No Longer Include Anti-Discrimination," *Washington Post*, March 7, 2018, https://www.washingtonpost.com/news/wonk/wp/2018/03/07/ben-carsons-mission-statement-for-hud-may-no-longer-include-anti-discrimination-language/.

65   Glenn Thrush, "Ben Carson of HUD on His Vexing Reign: Brain Surgery Was Easier Than This," *New York Times*, March 5, 2018, https://www.nytimes.com/2018/03/05/us/ben-carson-hud.html.

66   Jeremy Diamond, "HUD Inspector General Looking into Role Ben Carson's Family Has Played," CNN, February 20, 2018, https://www.cnn.com/2018/02/20/politics/ben-carson-family-hud-investigation/index.html; Juliet Eilperin and Jack Gillum, "'Using His Position for Private Gain': Ben Carson Was Warned He Might Run Afoul

of Ethics Rules by Enlisting His Son," *Washington Post*, January 31, 2018, https://www.washingtonpost.com/politics/using-his-position-for-private-gain-hud-lawyers-warned-ben-carson-risked-running-afoul-of-ethics-rules-by-enlisting-son/2018/01/31/bb20c48e-0532-11e8-8777-2a059f168dd2_story.html.

67 Rene Marsh, "'$5,000 Will Not Even Buy a Decent Chair': HUD Staffer Files Complaint over Ben Carson Office Redecoration," CNN, February 27, 2018, https://www.cnn.com/2018/02/27/politics/ben-carson-office-furniture-whistleblower/index.html.

68 Jamiles Lartey and Jon Swaine, "Ben Carson Accused of 'Witch-Hunt' by Senior Member of His Department," *Guardian*, March 6, 2018, https://www.theguardian.com/us-news/2018/mar/06/ben-carson-hud-witch-hunt-accusation.

69 Glenn Thrush, "Ben Carson's HUD Spends $31,000 on Dining Set for His Office," *New York Times*, February 27, 2018, https://www.nytimes.com/2018/02/27/us/ben-carson-hud-furniture.html.

70 Josh Hafner, "OnPolitics Today: A $31,000 Table with Taxpayer Dollars? Ben Carson Blames His Wife," *USA Today*, March 21, 2018, https://www.usatoday.com/story/news/politics/onpolitics/2018/03/21/onpolitics-today-31-000-table-taxpayer-dollars-ben-carson-blames-his-wife/447566002/.

71 Jon Swaine, "Senior Housing Department Official Loses Job after Allegations of Corruption," *Guardian*, March 20, 2018, https://www.theguardian.com/us-news/2018/mar/20/ben-carson-hud-official-corruptions-claims.

72 "FFRF & CREW Sue over Ben Carson FOIA Violations," Freedom from Religion Foundation, January 18, 2018, https://ffrf.org/news/news-releases/item/31494-ffrf-crew-sue-over-ben-carson-foia-violations.

73 Christina Zhao, "Baltimore Church Kicks Ben Carson Out after He Attempts to Hold Press Conference to Promote Trump Administration," *Newsweek*, July 31, 2019, https://www.newsweek.com/baltimore-church-kicks-ben-carson-out-after-he-attempts-hold-press-conference-promote-trump-1452029.

74 Spencer Kimball, "Trump Calls Baltimore a 'Disgusting, Rat and Rodent Infested Mess' in Attack on Rep. Elijah Cummings," CNBC, July 27, 2019, https://www.cnbc.com/2019/07/27/trump-calls-baltimore-a-disgusting-rat-and-rodent-infested-mess-in-attack-on-rep-elijah-cummings.html.

75 *The Clay Cane Show*, aired July 24, 2019, on SiriusXM Urban View.

76 Rob Crilly, "Ben Carson: Trump Should Have Moderated Rally Speech but Was Not to Blame for Capitol Mob," *Washington Examiner*, January 14, 2021, https://www.washingtonexaminer.com/news/politics/ben-carson-trump-moderate-capitol-speech.

77 Brakkton Booker, "Ben Carson: 'Cancel Culture' Is the New Jim Crow," Politico, May 13, 2022, https://www.politico.com/newsletters/the-recast/2022/05/13/ben-carson-cancel-culture-is-the-new-jim-crow-00032418.

78 Katie Glueck, "Carson Likens Obamacare to Slavery," Politico, October 11, 2013, https://www.politico.com/story/2013/10/ben-carson-obamacare-slavery-098185.

79 Singleton, discussion.

80 David Smith, "Who Is Omarosa, the Former Trump Aide Turned Leading Detractor?," *Guardian*, August 10, 2018, https://www.theguardian.com/us-news/2018/aug/10/omarosa-who-is-the-former-trump-aide-turned-leading-detractor.

81 Sharon LaFraniere, Nicholas Confessore, and Jesse Drucker, "Prerequisite for Key White House Posts: Loyalty, Not Experience," *New York Times*, March 14, 2017, https://www.nytimes.com/2017/03/14/us/politics/trump-advisers-experience.html.

82 "Omarosa Reveals Audio of Trump Campaign Aides Allegedly Discussing Potential Fallout of N-Word," CBS News, August 14, 2018, https://www.cbsnews.com/news/new-audio-omarosa-trump-campaign-aides-apparently-discussing-fallout-of-n-word/.

83 Madeleine Aggeler, "This Isn't the First Time Omarosa's Been Fired from the White House," The Cut, December 15, 2017, https://www.thecut.com/2017/12/omarosas-been-fired-from-the-white-house-before.html.

84 Tina Nguyen, "Donald Trump Taps Omarosa for New Campaign Role," *Vanity Fair*, July 18, 2016, https://www.vanityfair.com/news/2016/07/donald-trump-omarosa-campaign.

85 "Omarosa on 'Bow Down to President Trump' Comment," ABC News, November 11, 2016, YouTube video, 1:35, https://www.youtube.com/watch?v=03cmSdHD4-k.

86 Hazel Trice Edney, "Omarosa's Final Days at White House Full of Controversy, Accusations," *Cincinnati Herald*, January 3, 2018, https://thecincinnatiherald.com/2018/01/omarosas-final-days-white-house-full-controversy-accusations/; Lola Fadulu, "The First Black Woman to Lead the Heritage Foundation," *Atlantic*, December 15, 2018, https://www.theatlantic.com/business/archive/2018/12/first-job-heritage-foundations-kay-coles-james/569449/.

87 Kwame Jackson, "Trump May Poll Zero Percent With Black Voters, But So Does Omarosa Manigault," *NewsOne*, July 19, 2016, https://newsone.com/3485579/former-apprentice-contestant-kwame-jackson-on-omarosa-trump/.

88 Paul Farhi, "Journalist Says Omarosa Manigault Bullied Her and Mentioned a 'Dossier' on Her," *Washington Post*, February 3, 2017, https://www.washingtonpost.com/lifestyle/style/journalist-says-omarosa-manigault-bullied-her-and-mentioned-a-dossier-on-her/2017/02/13/d852926e-f131-11e6-8d72-263470bf0401_story.html.

89 Carlos Greer, "Omarosa Causes Uproar at National Assoc. of Black Journalists Conference," Page Six, August 10, 2017, https://pagesix.com/2017/08/10/omarosa-causes-chaos-at-conference-for-black-journalists/.

90 Tanya Hart, "Omarosa Makes a Mess of the NABJ," American Urban Radio Networks, August 15, 2017, https://aurn.com/omarosa-makes-mess-nabj/.

91 "Ed Gordon Looks Back on Explosive Omarosa Debate at NABJ Convention," TheGrio, February 23, 2018, https://thegrio.com/2018/02/23/ed-gordon-omarosa-nabj/.

92 Suzette Hackney (@suzyscribe), "Attendees are standing and turning their backs to Omarosa Manigault's #NABJ17 panel participation. Others are walking out," Twitter, August 11, 2017, 4:39 p.m., https://twitter.com/suzyscribe/status /896108830299377664.

93 Ian Millhiser, "Trump's Justice Department Has a Powerful Tool to Fight Police Abuse. It Refuses to Use It," Vox, June 30, 2020, https://www.vox.com /2020/6/30/21281041/trump-justice-department-consent-decrees-jeff-sessions -police-violence-abuse.

94 "Omarosa vs Ed Gordon @ NABJ in New Orleans 2017 Silky Slims Chimes in #CultureCriticShow," JohnnieDominoProductions, August 13, 2017, YouTube video, 2:23, https://youtu.be/3yVVhlPPEyg.

95 Hart, "Omarosa Makes a Mess."

96 "Ed Gordon Looks Back."

97 Katie Rogers and Maggie Haberman, "Omarosa, Leaving the White House, Suggests the Show Will Go On," *New York Times*, December 15, 2017, https://www.ny-times.com/2017/12/15/us/politics/omarosa-manigault-newman-white-house.html.

98 Elex Michaelson, "Omarosa: Pres. Trump N-Word Tape Release Likely in October," KTTV, Los Angeles, September 25, 2018, https://www.foxla.com/news/omarosa -pres-trump-n-word-tape-release-likely-in-october.

99 *The Clay Cane Show*, aired September 12, 2018, on SiriusXM Urban View.

100 Bill Bostock, "Diamond and Silk Suggest Fox News Is Racist for Dumping Them over COVID-19 Conspiracies That Were Also Embraced by White Hosts Like Tucker Carlson and Sean Hannity," *Business Insider*, August 17, 2020, https://www.business insider.com/diamond-and-silk-suggest-fox-news-racist-coronavirus-conspiracy -theories-2020-8.

101 Brian Flood, "CNN's April Ryan Slams Omarosa: 'She Stabbed in the Back, the Neck, the Eyeballs,'" Fox News, August 15, 2018, https://www.foxnews.com/politics /cnns-april-ryan-slams-omarosa-she-stabbed-in-the-back-the-neck-the-eyeballs.

102 Tamara Keith, "Omarosa Tells NPR She Heard Trump 'N-Word Tape,' Contradicting Her Own Tell-All Book," *All Things Considered*, NPR, August 10, 2018, https://www.npr.org/2018/08/10/636955054/omarosa-tells-npr-she-heard -trump-n-word-tape-contradicting-her-own-tell-all-boo.

103 "Omarosa Reveals Audio."

104 Thompson, "Omarosa Wanted Sheryl Lee Ralph."

105 Nina Burleigh, "Omarosa Interview: 'Charlottesville Was My Breaking Point' with Donald Trump," *Newsweek*, August 22, 2018, https://www.newsweek.com /omarosa-trump-racism-tapes-white-house-nda-unhinged-1083769.

106 Tracy Jan, Caitlin Dewey, and Jeff Stein, "HUD Secretary Ben Carson to Propose Raising Rent for Low-Income Americans Receiving Federal Housing Subsidies," *Washington Post*, April 25, 2018, https://www.washingtonpost.com/news/wonk /wp/2018/04/25/hud-secretary-ben-carson-to-propose-raising-rent-for-low -income-americans-receiving-federal-housing-subsidies/.

107 Lauren Victoria Burke, "Exclusive: Omarosa Manigault on Trump's Executive Order on HBCUs," NBC News, March 1, 2017, https://www.nbc news.com/news/nbcblk/exclusive-omarosa-manigault-trump-s-executive-order -hbcus-n726521.

108 Joseph Bernstein, "The Newest Star of the Trump Movement Ran a Trump-Bashing Publication—Less Than Two Years Ago," BuzzFeed News, May 15, 2018, https://www.buzzfeednews.com/article/josephbernstein/the-newest-star-of-the -trump-movement-ran-a-trump-bashing.

109 Chauncey Alcorn, "NAACP Leader Who Defended Candace Owens from Racist Trolls Shocked to Learn She's Conservative Now," Mic, April 28, 2018, https://www .mic.com/articles/189097/naacp-leader-who-defended-candace-owens-from -racist-trolls-shocked-to-learn-shes-conservative-now.

110 FOX & friends (@foxandfriends), "The Democrats have been good at wiping away history and re-writing it' - @RealCandaceO talks about joining NRA which she says started as a civil rights organization," Twitter, March 4, 2018, 7:20 a.m., https:// twitter.com/foxandfriends/status/970287747062640641.

111 Jesse Singal, "The Strange Tale of Social Autopsy, the Anti-Harassment Start-up That Descended into Gamergate Trutherism," *New York Magazine*, April 18, 2016, https://nymag.com/intelligencer/2016/04/how-social-autopsy-fell-for-gamergate -trutherism.html.

112 Walker Bragman and Alex Kotch, "Candace Owens' 'Blexit' Operation Bankrolled by Wealthy White Conservatives," Exposed by Center for Media and Democracy, January 12, 2023, https://www.exposedbycmd.org/2023/01/12/candace-owens -blexit-operation-bankrolled-by-wealthy-white-conservatives/.

113 Gerren Keith Gaynor, "Candace Owens Argues Ahmaud Arbery Shooting Isn't about Race, Draws Outrage," TheGrio, May 10, 2020, https://thegrio.com/2020/05/10 /candace-owens-ahmaud-arbery-twitter/.

114 Gino Spocchia, "Candace Owens Condemned after Alleging 'Black Americans Are the Most Murderous Group in America,'" *Independent*, December 17, 2021, https://www.independent.co.uk/news/world/americas/us-politics/candace-owens -black-floyd-rittenhouse-b1967159.html.

115 Rachel Frazin, "Candace Owens: 'If Hitler Just Wanted to Make Germany Great and Have Things Run Well—OK, Fine,'" *Hill*, February 8, 2019, https://thehill.com /blogs/blog-briefing-room/news/429180-candace-owens-if-hitler-just-wanted -to-make-germany-great-and.

116 Joel Shannon, "After Backlash, Conservative Pundit Candace Owens Clarifies Viral Hitler Comment," *USA Today*, February 11, 2019, https://www.usatoday .com/story/news/politics/2019/02/08/candace-owens-clarifies-hitler-nationalism -remark-after-backlash/2818679002/.

117 Donie O'Sullivan, "Facebook and Google Will Face Congress over White Nationalism," CNN Business, April 8, 2019, https://www.cnn.com/2019/04/08/tech /facebook-youtube-white-nationalism/index.html; *Hate Crimes and the Rise of*

White Nationalism: Hearing before the Subcommittee on Crime, Terrorism, and Homeland Security, 106th Cong. (2019), https://www.govinfo.gov/content/pkg/CHRG-116hhrg36563/html/CHRG-116hhrg36563.htm.

118 Rosie Gray, "Herman Cain Wants You to Vote for 'Shucky-Ducky' Donald Trump," BuzzFeed News, June 15, 2016, https://www.buzzfeednews.com/article/rosiegray/herman-cain-wants-you-to-vote-for-shucky-ducky-donald-trump.

119 Reuteurs Staff, "Herman Cain, 2012 Republican Presidential Candidate, Hospitalized with Coronavirus," Reuters, July 2, 2020, https://www.reuters.com/article/us-health-coronavirus-usa-cain/herman-cain-2012-republican-presidential-candidate-hospitalized-with-coronavirus-idUSKBN2432Z2.

120 "Former GOP Presidential Hopeful Herman Cain Dies of Covid-19," Associated Press, July 30, 2020, https://apnews.com/article/virus-outbreak-election-2020-herman-cain-ap-top-news-ok-state-wire-8173fe14f7cf7095ced3b55fdc65581e.

121 Jonathan Karl, "Lawsuit Threats, Empty Seats, and a 'COVID Mobile': Trump's Disastrous Tulsa Rally Was Even More of a Train Wreck Than Originally Thought," *Vanity Fair,* November 11, 2021, https://www.vanityfair.com/news/2021/11/trumps-disastrous-tulsa-rally-was-even-more-of-a-train-wreck-than-originally-thought.

122 Alex Stovall, "My name is Alex Stovall and I'm running for Congress to take on AOC. Can you chip in $26 right now?" Facebook, May 25, 2021, https://facebook.com/AlexforArizona/videos/my-name-is-alex-stovall-and-im-running-for-congress-to-take-on-aoc-can-you-chip-/503579520788329.

123 "Alex Stovall Launches Historic Run for Congress to Be Youngest Black Republican Elected, Kicks Off Campaign with Ad Calling Him the 'Anti AOC,'" PR Newswire, June 10, 2021, https://www.prnewswire.com/news-releases/alex-stovall-launches-historic-run-for-congress-to-be-youngest-black-republican-elected-kicks-off-campaign-with-ad-calling-him-the-anti-aoc-301309853.html.

124 Ronald J. Hansen, "Led by Sen. Mark Kelly, Democrats Lead Most Congressional Fundraising Races in Arizona," *Arizona Republic,* July 16, 2021, https://www.azcentral.com/story/news/politics/arizona/2021/07/16/sen-mark-kelly-democrats-lead-congressional-campaign-cash/7988553002/.

125 Peter D'Abrosca, "Project Veritas Action Exposes Flip-Flopping Arizona Congressional Candidate," *Tennessee Star,* December 10, 2021, https://tennesseestar.com/2021/12/10/project-veritas-action-exposes-flip-flopping-arizona-congressional-candidate/.

126 Christian Hartsock, "Undercover Footage of AZ GOP Congressional Candidate: 'The Republican Party is DISGUSTING to Me,'" Project Veritas, December 8, 2021, https://www.projectveritasaction.com/news/undercover-footage-of-azgop-congressional-candidate-the-republican-party-is/.

127 Katie Campbell, "Walt Blackman: A Graduate of 'Real World U,'" *Arizona Capitol Times,* December 24, 2018, https://azcapitoltimes.com/news/2018/12/24/walt-blackman-a-graduate-of-real-world-u/.

128 Dillon Rosenblatt, "Black Lawmaker Calls BLM a Terrorist Organization," *Arizona Capitol Times*, June 4, 2020, https://azcapitoltimes.com/news/2020/06/04/black-lawmaker-calls-blm-a-terrorist-organization/.

129 Maria Polletta and Yvonne Wingett Sanchez, "African American GOP Legislator Draws Sharp Criticism after Calling Black Lives Matter 'Terrorist' Group," *Arizona Republic*, June 5, 2020, https://www.azcentral.com/story/news/politics/arizona/2020/06/05/black-gop-legislator-criticism-blm-terrorist/3149272001/.

130 Adam Waltz, "Seven Arizonan Republican Legislators Face Calls to Ban Them from the House and Senate," KNXV-TV, Phoenix, AZ, January 8, 2021, https://www.abc15.com/news/state/seven-arizonan-republican-legislators-face-calls-to-ban-them-from-the-house-and-senate.

131 Andrew Kaczynski and Em Steck, "NRCC-Supported Candidate Praised Proud Boys at September Rally for Capitol Rioters," CNN, October 13, 2021, https://www.cnn.com/2021/10/13/politics/kfile-arizona-republican-walt-blackman-praised-proud-boys/index.html.

132 Liz Skalka, "Arizona Republican Says His Daughter Got Text Calling Him 'N-Word,'" HuffPost, February 7, 2022, https://www.huffpost.com/entry/gop-arizona-walter-blackman_n_6201cb6be4b05004243174ee.

133 Jordan Conradson, "AUDIO: RINO Arizona State Rep. Walt Blackman Bashes Rep. Finchem, Claims Decertification Is Impossible: 'We Can't Do That,'" Gateway Pundit, January 27, 2022, https://www.thegatewaypundit.com/2022/01/audio-rino-arizona-state-rep-walt-blackman-bashes-rep-finchem-claims-decertification-impossible-cant/.

134 Skalka, "Arizona Republican."

135 Barnini Chakraborty, "Eli Crane Wins Arizona GOP House Primary to Face Democratic Rep. Tom O'Halleran," *Washington Examiner*, August 3, 2022, https://www.washingtonexaminer.com/news/campaigns/eli-crane-wins-arizona-gop-primary-to-face-tom-ohalleran.

136 Steve Benen, "Some Republicans Start Following Trump's Lead Following Defeats," *Maddow Blog*, MSNBC, November 23, 2020, https://www.msnbc.com/rachel-maddow-show/some-republicans-start-following-trump-s-lead-following-defeats-n1248646.

137 "Georgia Election Results: Fifth Congressional District," *New York Times*, November 3, 2020, https://www.nytimes.com/interactive/2020/11/03/us/elections/results-georgia-house-district-5.html.

138 Jeremy Stahl, "Weirdly, a Vaccine-Skeptical Radio Host Was Not Voted the Next Governor of California," *Slate*, September 15, 2021, https://slate.com/news-and-politics/2021/09/larry-elder-loses-gavin-newsom-wins-recall.html.

139 "2022 New York U.S. Senate Election Results," *New York Times*, November 8, 2022, https://www.nytimes.com/interactive/2022/11/08/us/elections/results-new-york-us-senate.html.

140 Samantha May, "Republican Candidate for Michigan Secretary of State Still

Hasn't Conceded," WWMT, Kalamazoo, MI, November 10, 2022, https://wwmt .com/news/state/republican-kristina-karamo-secretary-state-michigan-concede -jocelyn-benson-election-midterm-2022-vote.

141 Chris Ullery, "Photos of Senate Candidate Kathy Barnette Marching Near Proud Boys on January 6 Surface Online. Will It Matter?," *Bucks County Courier Times*, May 17, 2022, https://www.goerie.com/story/news/politics/2022/05/17/pennsylvania -gop-senate-candidate-kathy-barnette-pictured-near-proud-boys-jan-6/6535578 8007/; Charlotte Alter, "Kathy Barnette Is the Trumpiest Candidate Who Wasn't Endorsed by Trump," *Time*, May 16, 2022, https://time.com/6177232/kathy -barnette-pennsylvania-senate-republican-primary/.

142 "2022 Michigan 10th Congressional District Election Results," *New York Times*, November 8, 2022, https://www.nytimes.com/interactive/2022/11/08/us/elections /results-michigan-us-house-district-10.html.

143 "Wesley Hunt Wins Election for US House Representative for Texas's New 38th District," FOX 26 Houston, November 8, 2022, https://www.fox26houston.com /news/wesley-hunt-has-won-election-for-u-s-house-rep-for-texas-new-district-38.

144 Shannon Bugos, "Biden Approves $29 Billion Increase in Defense Budget," Arms Control Association, April 2022, https://www.armscontrol.org/act/2022-04/news /biden-approves-29-billion-increase-defense-budget; "Wesley Talks to Newsmax about CTR in Military," Wesley Hunt, July 8, 2021, YouTube video, 5:55, https:// www.youtube.com/watch?v=Vd3BSuUMATs.

145 "Georgia Midterm Election 2022," NBC News, November 8, 2022, https://www .nbcnews.com/politics/2022-elections/georgia-results?icid=election_nav.

146 "North Carolina Midterm Election 2022," NBC News, November 8, 2022, https://www.nbcnews.com/politics/2022-elections/north-carolina-senate-results ?icid=election_usmap.

147 George Santos (@Santos4Congress), "Caucasian and black," Twitter, July 6, 2020, 12:41 p.m., https://twitter.com/Santos4Congress/status/1280180135510056960.

148 Victor Nava and Carl Campanile, "Liar Rep.-Elect George Santos Admits Fabri-cating Key Details of His Bio," *New York Post*, December 26, 2022, https://nypost .com/2022/12/26/rep-elect-george-santos-admits-fabricating-key-details-of-his-bio/.

149 *The Karen Hunter Show*, "Karen Hunter-Pam Keith," aired October 18, 2022, on SiriusXM Urban View.

150 Reginald Grant, in discussion with the author, January 2023.

151 Rishika Dugyala, "Rep. Dan Huberty's Primary Challenger Declared Ineligible to Run," *Texas Tribune*, January 19, 2018, https://www.texastribune.org/2018/01/19 /texas-rep-dan-hubertys-primary-challenger-declared-ineligible-run/.

152 Grant, discussion.

153 GOP (@GOP), "We currently have a record number of Black Republicans running for office and winning at all levels. Over 40 Black Republicans are running in GOP primaries for both local and federal office," Twitter, February 6, 2022, 9:34 a.m., https://twitter.com/GOP/status/1490332956703043590.

154 Peter Weber, "GOP Mocked for Celebrating 'Record Number' of Black Republican Candidates," *Week*, February 7, 2022, https://theweek.com/republicans/1009847/gop-mocked-for-celebrating-record-number-of-black-republican-candidates.

155 Singleton, disccusion.

156 Steele, discussion.

157 Lateshia Beachum, "Maxine Waters Says She Will 'Never Ever Forgive' Black Men Who Vote for Trump," *Washington Post*, November 2, 2020, https://www.washingtonpost.com/politics/2020/11/02/maxine-waters-clyburn-black-voters/.

158 Jennifer De Pinto and Fred Backus, "How Biden Won the 2020 Election," CBS News, November 7, 2020, https://www.cbsnews.com/news/election-2020-exit-poll-analysis-how-biden-became-the-projected-winner/.

159 Ruth Igielnik, Scott Keeter, and Hannah Hartig, "Behind Biden's 2020 Victory An Examination of the 2020 Electorate, Based on Validated Voters," Pew Research Center, June 30, 2021, https://www.pewresearch.org/politics/2021/06/30/behind-bidens-2020-victory/.

160 Mara Ostfeld and Michelle Garcia, "Black Men Shift Slightly toward Trump in Record Numbers, Polls Show," NBC News, November 4, 2020, https://www.nbcnews.com/news/nbcblk/black-men-drifted-democrats-toward-trump-record-numbers-polls-show-n1246447.

161 "2020 Presidential Election Exit Polls," CNN, accessed June 2, 2023, https://www.cnn.com/election/2020/exit-polls/president/national-results/20.

162 Marina Watts, "Everything Candace Owens Has Said about George Floyd So Far," *Newsweek*, June 5, 2020, https://www.newsweek.com/everything-candace-owens-has-said-about-george-floyd-so-far-1508959.

163 Tanasia Kenney, "Candace Owens Immediately Slammed after Claiming It's a 'Fact' That Rep. Maxine Waters Has 'a Low IQ,'" *Atlanta Black Star*, May 24, 2019, https://atlantablackstar.com/2019/05/24/candace-owens-immediately-slammed-after-claiming-its-a-fact-that-rep-maxine-waters-has-a-low-iq/.

164 John Bowden, "Candace Owens Tells Congress White Nationalism Not a Problem for Minorities in US," *Hill*, September 20, 2019, https://thehill.com/homenews/house/462395-candace-owens-tells-congress-white-nationalism-not-a-problem-for-minorities-in.

165 Mark Hosenball, "Acting U.S. DHS Security Intelligence Chief Says He Agrees with FBI on White Supremacist Threat," Reuters, October 2, 2022, https://www.reuters.com/article/us-usa-intelligence-homeland/acting-u-s-dhs-security-intelligence-chief-says-he-agrees-with-fbi-on-white-supremacist-threat-idUSKBN26N35E.

166 Alex Isenstadt, "The Inside Story of How Ice Cube Joined Forces with Donald Trump," Politico, October 15, 2020, https://www.politico.com/news/2020/10/15/ice-cube-trump-partnership-429713.

167 Allyson Chiu, "'Woefully Uninformed': Kanye West Slammed for Saying Harriet Tubman 'Never Actually Freed the Slaves,'" *Washington Post*, July 20, 2020, https://

www.washingtonpost.com/nation/2020/07/20/kanye-harriet-tubman/; Jason Szep and Linda So, "Kanye West Publicist Pressed Georgia Election Worker to Confess to Bogus Fraud Charges," Reuters, December 10, 2021, https://www.reuters.com /business/media-telecom/kanye-west-publicist-pressed-georgia-election-worker -confess-bogus-fraud-charges-2021-12-10/.

WHAT'S NEXT?

1   Kenya Vaughn, "Kinloch's Star Jenifer Lewis Enshrined on Hollywood Walk of Fame," *St. Louis American*, July 21, 2022, http://www.stlamerican.com/arts _and_entertainment/living_it/kinloch-s-star/article_bc2600c0-08f1-11ed-8f17 -73da0898b67c.html.

2   Brittany Bernstein, "Kevin McCarthy Thanks Trump after Speakership Win: 'I Don't Think Anybody Should Doubt His Influence,'" *National Review*, January 7, 2023, https://www.nationalreview.com/news/kevin-mccarthy-thanks-trump-after -speakership-win-i-dont-think-anybody-should-doubt-his-influence/.

3   Steele, discussion.

4   Domenico Montanaro, "Poll: Despite Record Turnout, 80 Million Americans Didn't Vote. Here's Why," *Morning Edition*, NPR, December 15, 2020, https:// www.npr.org/2020/12/15/945031391/poll-despite-record-turnout-80-million -americans-didnt-vote-heres-why; Haili Blassingame, "Nearly 100 Million Eligible Americans Didn't Vote in 2016. Why Not?," 1A, NPR, September 16, 2020, https://the1a.org/segments/why-americans-dont-vote/.

5   Franklin, "King in 1967."

6   Kristen Gwynne, "4 Biggest Myths about Crack; For U.S. Politicians, Targeting Drug Users in Black Communities Is Easier Than Addressing Poverty and Unemployment," Salon, August 10, 2013, https://www.salon.com/2013/08/10/busting_the_crack _propaganda_myths_partner/.

7   Jan, "Biggest Beneficiaries."

8   "Remains of 2 Children Killed in Controversial 1985 Philadelphia Bombing by Police Returned to Family, Brother Says," CBS News, August 4, 2022, https://www.cbsnews .com/news/move-bombing-1985-philadelphia-remains-2-children-returned-to -brother/.

9   "Mumia Abu-Jamal's 1982 Death Sentence Is Again Declared Unconstitutional," NAACP Legal Defense Fund, April 26, 2011, https://www.naacpldf .org/press-release/mumia-abu-jamals-1982-death-sentence-is-again-declared -unconstitutional/.

10 "'Fahrenheit 9/11': Not a Single Democratic Senator Joins with House Objections to Bush/Gore," Michael Moore, January 3, 2011, YouTube video, 2:47, https:// www.youtube.com/watch?v=TnNMlBTkF_s&ab_channel=MichaelMoore.

11 "Al Smith Memorial Dinner," C-SPAN, October 19, 2000, https://www.c-span .org/video/?c4500665/user-clip-people-call-elites-call-base.

12 *Fahrenheit 9/11*, directed by Michael Moore (Culver City: Columbia TriStar Home Entertainment, 2004).

13 *Fahrenheit 9/11*.

14 Jared Gans, "Half of Americans Expect a Civil War 'in the Next Few Years,'" *Hill*, July 21, 2022, https://thehill.com/blogs/blog-briefing-room/3569350-half-of -americans-expect-a-civil-war-in-the-next-few-years/.

15 *Reconstruction: America after the Civil War*.

16 Jens Manuel Krogstad and Mark Hugo Lopez, "Black Voter Turnout Fell in 2016, Even as a Record Number of Americans Cast Ballots," Pew Research Center, May 12, 2017, https://www.pewresearch.org/fact-tank/2017/05/12/black-voter-turnout -fell-in-2016-even-as-a-record-number-of-americans-cast-ballots/.

17 Aaron O'Neill, "Voter Turnout Rates among Select Ethnicities in U.S. Midterm Elections from 1966 to 2018," Statista, October 2019, https://www.statista.com /statistics/1096123/voter-turnout-midterms-by-ethnicity-historical/.

18 Kevin Morris and Coryn Grange, "Large Racial Turnout Gap Persisted in 2020," Brennan Center for Justice, August 6, 2021, https://www.brennancenter.org /our-work/analysis-opinion/large-racial-turnout-gap-persisted-2020-election.

19 Roy, "No, Trump Didn't Win."

20 Perry Bacon Jr., "How Georgia Turned Blue: And Why It Might Not Stay That Way," FiveThirtyEight, November 18, 2020, https://fivethirtyeight.com/features /how-georgia-turned-blue/.

21 Jeff Amy, "Georgia Official: Trump Call to 'Find' Votes Was a Threat," Associated Press, November 1, 2021, https://apnews.com/article/donald-trump-joe-biden-arts-and -entertainment-elections-georgia-2b27f4c92919556bf6548117648693b7.

22 "Voting Laws Roundup: December 2021," Brennan Center for Justice, December 2021, https://www.brennancenter.org/our-work/research-reports/voting-laws -roundup-december-2021.

23 Alex Ashlock and Jeremy Hobson, "How Ross Perot's Third Party Presidential Bids Shook Up American Politics," *Here and Now*, WBUR Radio, Boston, July 10, 2019, https://www.wbur.org/hereandnow/2019/07/10/perot-third-party-presidential-bids.

24 David Paul Kuhn and Joel Roberts, "The Nader Effect," CBS News, February 23, 2004, https://www.cbsnews.com/news/the-nader-effect/.

25 "Österreichischer Demokratie Monitor" [Austrian Democracy Monitor]," SORA Institute for Social Research and Consulting, December 14, 2021, https://www .sora.at/fileadmin/downloads/projekte/2021_SORA_Praesentation-Demokratie -Monitor-2021.pdf.

26 "Charles Blow: Why Black Americans Should Migrate Back South," *Amanpour & Co.*, PBS, February 4, 2021, https://www.pbs.org/wnet/amanpour-and-company /video/charles-blow-why-black-americans-should-migrate-back-south/.

27 Paul Prescod, "The Fight for Racial Justice Must Include Defending Public-Sector Jobs," *Jacobin*, August 10, 2020, https://www.jacobinmag.com/2020/08 /racial-justice-public-jobs; "Black Capitalism Won't Help Black Workers," Jacobin, February 10, 2021, YouTube video, 19:32, https://www.youtube.com/watch?v=IyB80rG6EJc.

28 Leah Donnella, "Research Shows Black Boys Are Most Likely to Be Stuck in Cycle of Poverty," *All Things Considered*, NPR, March 19, 2018, https://www.npr.org/2018/03/19/595018784/research-shows-black-boys-are-most-likely-to-be-stuck-in-cycle-of-poverty.

29 Interview with Bayard Rustin, Washington University in St. Louis, 1979, video, 54:21, http://repository.wustl.edu/concern/videos/vm40xt471.

30 A. Philip Randolph and Bayard Rustin, "How the Civil Rights Movement Aimed to End Poverty," King Issue, *Atlantic*, February 2018, https://www.theatlantic.com/magazine/archive/2018/02/a-freedom-budget-for-all-americans-annotated/557024/.

31 "History of Federal Minimum Wage Rates Under the Fair Labor Standards Act, 1938–2009," Department of Labor, accessed June 2, 2023, https://www.dol.gov/agencies/whd/minimum-wage/history/chart.

32 "Drug Companies Reaped Billions from New US Tax Law," Oxfam, April 9, 2019, https://www.oxfamamerica.org/press/drug-companies-reaped-billions-new-us-tax-law/; Michael Hiltzik, "Boeing Got a Record Tax Break from Washington State and Cut Jobs Anyway. Now the State Wants to Strike Back," *Los Angeles Times*, May 3, 2017, https://www.latimes.com/business/hiltzik/la-fi-hiltzik-boeing-washington-20170503-story.html.

33 "From 1968 to 2018—An Economic Bill of Rights for 21st Century," MLK Global, November 23, 2017, https://mlkglobal.org/2017/11/23/dr-kings-econ-bill-of-rights-revived/.

34 Liz Covart, "Episode 042: Heather Cox Richardson, A History of the Republican Party," August 22, 2015, in *Ben Franklin's World*, produced by Leslie Clark, podcast, 1:07:50, https://benfranklinsworld.com/episode-042-heather-cox-richardson-a-history-of-the-republican-party/.

35 Prescod, "Fight for Racial Justice"; "Black Capitalism Won't Help."

36 Mairead McArdle, "Gillibrand Says She Can Explain White Privilege to 'White Women in the Suburbs' Who Voted for Trump," *National Review*, July 31, 2019, https://www.nationalreview.com/news/kirsten-gillibrand-says-she-can-explain-white-privilege-to-white-women-in-suburbs/.

37 Paul Meara, "Bernie Sanders: Obama Getting 10 Percent of the White Vote in Mississippi Speaks to the 'Bad Work' by Democrats," BET, January 18, 2020, https://www.bet.com/article/uyzibn/bernie-sanders-rips-dems-over-obama-s-low-numbers-in-miss.

38 Ben Waldron, "Mississippi Officially Abolishes Slavery, Ratifies 13th Amendment," ABC News, February 19, 2013, https://abcnews.go.com/blogs/headlines/2013/02/mississippi-officially-abolishes-slavery-ratifies-13th-amendment.

39 Steve Phillips, "What About White Voters?" Center for American Progress, February 5, 2016, https://www.americanprogress.org/issues/race/news/2016/02/05/130647/what-about-white-voters/.

40 Glenn Thrush, "Keith Ellison's One-man March," Politico, December 20, 2016, https://www.politico.com/story/2016/12/keith-ellison-democrats-dnc-232838.

41 Vaughn, "Kinloch's Star Jenifer Lewis."

42 Doug Jones on *The Clay Cane Show*, aired August 11, 2022, on SiriusXM Urban View.

Index

About the Author

Photo Credit: Antar Bush

Clay Cane is an award-winning journalist, writer, radio host, and political commentator. A graduate of Rutgers University with a degree in African American studies, his work on race, culture, and politics has appeared in national publications, including the *Washington Post*, CNN, and TheGrio. He is the director of the original BET documentary *Holler If You Hear Me: Black and Gay in the Church*, which was screened at the Obama White House. In 2017, *The Clay Cane Show* launched on SiriusXM Urban View channel 126. Clay is a regular political commentator on MSNBC. *The Grift* is his second book, his first being *Live Through This: Surviving the Intersections of Sexuality, God, and Race.*

Connect with him on his website, ClayCane.net, or on Twitter @claycane.